Property and Equality

Property and Equality
Volume 2

Encapsulation, Commercialisation, Discrimination

Edited by

Thomas Widlok

and

Wolde Gossa Tadesse

Berghahn Books
New York • Oxford

First published in 2005 by

Berghahn Books

www.berghahnbooks.com

First paperback edition published in 2007.

Library of Congress Cataloging-in-Publication Data

Property and equality: ritualisation, sharing, egalitarianism / edited by Thomas Widlok and Wolde Gossa Tadesse.
p. cm.
Includes index.
ISBN 1–57181–616–X (v. 1 : hbk) -- ISBN 1-57181-617-8 (v. 2 : hbk)
ISBN 1–84545–213–5 (v. 1 : pbk) -- ISBN 1-84545-214-3 (v. 2 : pbk.)
1. Equality--Cross-cultural studies. 2. Property--Cross-cultural studies. I. Title: Ritualisation, sharing, egalitarianism. II. Widlok, Thomas. III. Tadesse, Wolde Gossa.

HM821.P67 2004
306.3'2--dc22 2004049096

British Library Cataloguing in Publication Data

A catalogue record for this book is available from the British Library.

ISBN 1-57181-617-8 (vol. 2, hardback)
ISBN 1-84545-214-3 (vol. 2, paperback)

Contents

List of Figures and Tables

Figures

Tables

Preface

Property relations have long been considered the key to our understanding of equality and inequality, not only through the work of thinkers such as Rousseau, Marx, Engels and others, but also through common everyday experience. Social anthropologists continue to collect data that are relevant to the fundamental issue of property and equality, but so far this work has rarely been a concerted effort. For this two-volume book we have brought together a wide range of well-known international specialists who have worked on issues of property and equality. They are the core group of more than fifty participants who came together at a conference held at Halle/Saale in June 2001. The conference, entitled 'Property and Equality', was the basis on which the present volumes have been compiled. Despite their different backgrounds the contributors share considerable common ground: all are anthropologists, all had read James Woodburn's seminal article on 'Egalitarian Societies' and have been inspired or challenged by his thoughts on the matter. Many of the participants had done field research with hunter-gatherers in the Arctic, in Africa, Australia or Asia. However, the present volumes do not deal exclusively with these groups. Some contributors have worked with pastoralists, with horticulturalists, agriculturalists, in industrial societies, and with nonhuman primates, comparing their results with the theoretical ideas that have been developed in hunter-gatherer studies.

The ethnography on egalitarian hunter-gatherer societies sent shock waves through anthropology in the 1960s' when ethnographers came forward and suggested that forager societies worked well without structures of dominance, without rigid hierarchies, without binding property relations, and without inherent inequality with regard to gender, age and status. This book brings together the current work of prominent members of this original group of researchers and the very recent ethnography of a new generation of researchers who are dealing with problems of property and equality. In preparing their contributions to the book the authors have revisited key debates of the field; they have taken stock, and have tackled issues that remained unresolved. They have reassessed how the existence of egalitarian societies still challenges established assumptions about the conditions of human political and economic life, how it continues to stand much of anthropological theory on its head and how it relates to research done in other fields. In the past the ethnography of egalitarian social systems was first met with sheer disbelief. Today it is still hotly debated in a number of ways but has gained sophistication as well as momentum. As the editors of this book, we have tried to account for this diversification by presenting two complementary volumes. Volume 1 focuses on the embeddedness of egalitarian property relations in dynamic processes of human sociality over time. Contributions highlight the role of ritual, of sharing in its various articulations, and of discourses of egalitarianism. Volume 2 focuses on the embeddedness of egalitarian property relations in the dynamics of larger social systems. It highlights the issues of encapsulation, commercialisation and discrimination. Despite their distinct foci there are many connecting lines between the two volumes, both in terms of the groups and regions that are being discussed and also with regard to systematic links that exist between the terms of the debates and the questions under consideration. Several contributions explicitly underline that 'internal' institutional dynamics and 'external' historical developments are really two sides of the same coin.

The Halle conference was fully funded by the then newly founded Max Planck Institute for Social Anthropology and, as conveners, we are indebted to the staff of the Institute who helped in organising the conference and who also assisted in preparing these two volumes. We are thankful to the Department of Anthropology at the University of Heidelberg for its institutional support in preparing the manuscript. We also gratefully acknowledge the intellectual input that we have received from Olga Artemova, the late Susan Kent, Nicolas Peterson, and Aiden Southall who do not appear in these volumes as authors but who have actively participated in our discussions at Halle and therefore shaped the course of the conversations. Thanks also go to Berghahn Books, who shared our conviction that, despite the size of the project, it was important not to let the contributions diffuse into isolated voices but to keep them together in these two volumes, reflecting the current state of anthropological research concerning the relation between 'property' and 'equality'.

Thomas Widlok
Heidelberg and Nijmegen

Wolde Gossa Tadesse
Palo Alto and Halle/Saale

Introduction

Wolde Gossa Tadesse

Property Relations and Relations of Equality

Intellectual concerns surrounding property date back to ancient times. Philosophers such as Plato and his student Aristotle debated the merits of public versus private land holdings. This has been echoed in European and American traditions. John Locke, Adam Smith and Herbert Spencer are still widely cited by 'advocates' of private property while Jean-Jacques Rousseau, Karl Marx, Pierre Proudhon and Henry George are champions of its critics (Shipton 2001, 2003). In our two volumes we continue the debate along different lines by focusing on a number of related themes. In particular we want to illustrate what forms of property relations are engendered in situations where local groups are experiencing processes of encapsulation.

Property and equality as used in our volumes are concepts referring to the relation between a people's identity and its social reproduction with regard to the resources of the environment. The degree of access such groups have to property and their entitlement to use, share or to dispose of such property, defines their relation to other groups. It is these arenas of property relations in which powerful external forces such as the state attempt to redefine existing relationships. The contributors to this volume document and analyse the impacts of such redefinitions of relations and the responses of indigenous and ethnic minorities in these contexts. Although property is not the only area where equality or inequality are manifested, it would be misleading and naive to think that property is not crucial in shaping relations of equality and inequality between persons and between groups. Anthropological discussions concerning these issues were invigorated when James Woodburn gave his Malinowski Memorial Lecture at the London School of Economics in 1981. In this lecture, entitled 'Egalitarian Societies', he stated that:

> Greater equality of wealth and of prestige has been achieved in certain hunting societies than in any other human societies. These societies are assertively egalitarian. Equality is achieved through direct, individual access to resources;

> through direct, individual access to means of coercion and means of mobility which limit the imposition of control; through procedures which prevent saving and accumulation and impose sharing; through mechanisms which allow goods to circulate without making people dependent upon one another. People are systematically disengaged from property and therefore from the potentiality in property for creating dependency. (Woodburn 1982: 431)

His findings gave rise to a new focus of enquiry into the property situation of encapsulated indigenous and ethnic minority peoples in those parts of the world conventionally labelled as 'the marginal peripheries of the West'. Two decades after Woodburn's landmark lecture, Thomas Widlok and I organised a conference at the Max Planck Institute for Social Anthropology in Halle on the theme of 'Property and Equality', to honour James Woodburn's contribution to anthropology and to take stock with the aim of seeing what progress had been made on the key issues that he had raised. The participants to the conference approached the subject from different thematic perspectives and thereby covered considerable ground with regard to the complexity of the issues of property and equality. James Woodburn himself revisited his 'Egalitarian Societies' material in the light of developments since the 1980s, and he suggests that the transformation of immediate-return systems cannot be explained with reference to external political and economic factors. Taking into account data from many hunter-gatherer communities and his own Hadza material, Woodburn argues that the domain of ritual and religion are the likely spheres in which a degree of inequality and ideas of property are generated. He concludes: 'My opinion now is that the religious route is likely to have been a major route, perhaps even the major route in the repeated historical transitions from immediate to delayed return' (Woodburn, Volume 1).

The contributions to this second volume resulting from the Halle conference view issues of property and equality from the thematic vantage points of encapsulation, commercialisation and discrimination. The three concepts are elaborated by Richard Lee (this volume) in a separate chapter, providing the reader with a general framework for thinking about the issues at hand. It should be noted, however, that the contributors were not restricted and have not restricted themselves to dealing with only one of these themes. Instead they emphasised the links between themes and have also included themes developed in the first volume. Hence this second volume not only broadens the range of cases and the empirical basis of our debates, it also extends and elaborates the discussions that feature in Volume 1.

Encapsulation

Lee (this volume) argues that encapsulation, the first of the central themes of this volume, represents the economic aspect of a larger process: the loss of autonomy. However, he warns that economic autonomy must not be equated with isolation, and exchange should not simply be equated with domination and loss of autonomy. Encapsulation, a concept that is covered in various ways in many of the contributions, is the general incorporation of groups into structures of larger and more powerful entities such as the nation state and international institutions. The actions of these power holders have considerable impact on the lives of societies which are usually referred to as indigenous or marginalised ethnic groups at the peripheries of power centres. Such people are, in the words of Jerome M. Levi and Bartholomew Dean (Dean and Levi 2003), people who are 'all too often caught in the crossfire between competing political and commercial interests seeking a foothold in their territories. Squeezed by global avarice for their natural resources, fearful of military might, and threatened by dominant groups' intolerance for their distinctive ways of life'.

All of the people under consideration in this volume have for much of their current history been engaged in fierce struggle in their encounters with colonial and postcolonial nation states. They were often objects of both homogenising as well as heterogenising policies of nation states in exercises of nation building. Larger ethnic groups wielding political and economic power in these nation states often consider the lifestyle of marginal people as backward and as an obstacle to progress. Today nation states often continue the practices of old colonial times and in some cases they conduct the very same practices, in particular that of marginalising smaller groups of peoples such as pastoralists, hunter-gatherers and horticulturalists having ways of life different to theirs. In cases I observed in Ethiopia both bigger and smaller ethnic groups subsisting on agriculture, cattle pastoralism as well as on hunting and gathering are marginalised politically and economically both by bigger ethnic groups and by the nation state, which also plays a mediatory role between its people and global economic institutions.

In the past the response of the weak to conquest and ultimate encapsulation varied from place to place and from people to people. In the 1890s in Ethiopia peoples of the south and the southwest were conquered and enslaved by Abyssinians, who were using firearms they had received from Europe. The Abyssinians prevailed in spite of the commendable courage and fierce resistance of the weaker groups (see Vanderheym 1896; Dilebo 1974). During the conquest some ethnic groups abandoned their territories and sought refuge elsewhere among friendly neighbours (Tadesse 1999), while others were wiped out in such great numbers that in one area only a chief and a handful of his people were left. Some chilling accounts of the period indicate that even sovereigns had taken part in hunting expeditions and returned home with a great number of slaves they raided from among their subject peoples (Hodson n. d.). These atrocities of the conquest army perpetrated in the late 1890s in Ethiopia's southwest have also been engraved in the oral traditions of the peoples concerned that are passed down from generation to generation as heritable property linking different generations. More recent responses to increasing domination and appropriation of group property (especially landed property) were equally varied. Some indigenous peoples rebelled or joined rebellious ethnic political movements which fought against the state or threatened to do so, thereby triggering a massive blow from the nation state and becoming perpetual suspects. Some have legitimately used their constitutional rights, using the political structures of the nation state to fight against land appropriation which provincial and central authorities had initiated and which had in the past reached the imperial court (Tadesse 2003). Others evaded the nation state, NGOs (nongovernmental organisations) and religious organisations by insulating themselves in ancient traditions to protect their ways of life and their resources (Tadesse 2002). By mere evasion, avoiding any significant contact with a patronising nation state and with other outsiders, and by refusing entry to members of bigger discriminating groups, some ethnic groups have maintained a degree of autonomy. Although these measures have helped the people in maintaining autonomy and keeping their lifestyle, they have also prevented them from taking an active role in influencing the policies of the nation state regarding ethnic minorities. The resilience of such groups, despite the devastation caused by conquerors, and their determination in ensuring their own social and cultural reproduction is an indicator and proof that, given the political and economic space and the right to practise their customs, they would stand on their own feet and flourish. Such groups want to be taken seriously on their own terms and conditions. The pastoral Hor, with whom I have worked since 1994, and their western neighbours, the Hamar, whom Jean Lydall (this volume) and Ivo Strecker (Volume 1) deal with at length, are examples of such cases of extraordinary resilience and the ability to keep outside forces at bay. The cases discussed by contributions to this volume should be read also with such responses in mind; taken together they indicate the large spectrum of historical developments.

The indigenous peoples who provide the case studies of this volume live in insecurity and uncertainty about their future, and they want to be heard. To be recognised, to claim entitlements as citizens of their respective countries and to secure rights as groups that have lost their political, economic and cultural autonomy, they make efforts to win friends and guarantees for a secure future. Being vocal involves a variety of risks for indigenous people (Dean and Levi 2003). By being silent, on the other hand, indigenous peoples and ethnic minorities risk remaining invisible and without a voice. In most cases these groups are not in a position to embark on the trail of visibility on their own. They need the support of global forces to aid them in this endeavour to be heard and to be visible, including allies who in the past may have been indifferent to atrocities perpetrated and unleashed on indigenous groups and ethnic minorities.

Commercialisation

Commercialisation, the second theme of this volume, is a key aspect of the economic dimension to encapsulation. It is often an important part of a conscious effort made by indigenous peoples to cope with the loss of economic autonomy. Contributions by Köhler, Endicott, Guenther and Lewis deal with varying degrees of commercialisation as it is experienced today among groups which used to produce for subsistence consumption and for sharing their produce internally. The studies in this volume indicate that the process of commercialisation has brought about a change in the practices of sharing as outlined by James Woodburn (Woodburn 1982: 431–51). They show that sharing and commoditisation often coexist. As Endicott (this volume) indicates, Batek involvement in trade has not brought an end to their immediate-return practices or sharing. Mathias Guenther illustrates how the trance dance has evolved from being a shared consumable of an immediate-return system for the treatment of patients into a professionalised and marketable commodity. At the same time, however, the dance has maintained its traditional purpose of healing (see Boyd 1985 for parallels in New Guinea). What the situation of encapsulated indigenous peoples around the globe indicates is that the degree of encapsulation and the responses to it vary and do not follow exactly the same pattern across the board. My own study of the Hor and the Gamo (Tadesse 1999, 2002, 2003) of Ethiopia shows that many indigenous groups in this area are also part of an extensive trade network. However, their practices are clearly different from most of the cases dealt with in this volume. Agricultural groups such as Konso or Gamo people of southwest Ethiopia, to mention only two, engage in the laborious enterprise of cultivation and pastoralism, in weaving clothes and blankets of cotton, and engage in a wide network of regional trade. The latter are principal manufacturers and traders of woven products at the nation's central markets. Pastoralist groups further south are also integrated into a regional trade network and take part in a system controlling the secure exchange and safe passage of marketable commodities, livestock and property in the network area. This is notwithstanding their chilling experience during the conquest period little over a century ago and the consequent discrimination and appropriation of their land and labour. Within these regional networks most local knowledge, ritual knowledge and skills such as animal entrails reading are shared. Leading prayers amid the serving of sacrificial honey mead follows seniority and whoever is senior at a given moment in time says the prayers. Honey mead, sacrificial coffee and tobacco are distributed on the occasion equally among a class of initiated fathers of the land. Divinatory skills of qualified practitioners are exchanged for a nominal gift of butter (among the agricultural Gamo) and for a bowl of honey mead (among pastoral Hor/Arbore and Hamar) during wedding feasts or other events. Every member of a group, however, is entitled to consult persons attributed with such knowledge. In this situation certain aspects of ritual knowledge and power are hereditary while other parts of the politico-religious powers are transferred from incumbents of political office to their successors in the assembly of fathers who have been initiated to positions of power. In some of these areas a notion that labour is a form of property which should be developed by working and growing together in a team under a leadership that mimics the structures of local politics is widespread. Work group leaders are nominated for the purpose of agricultural labour and are organised along gender lines. These named labour groups grow together until late in life sharing and exchanging labour and at times working for payment which is saved and used by members during an annual feast. These specific practices observable in the region are a result of the fact that neither global impacts nor a state presence are strong, which contrasts with the commercialisation processes in many other contexts presented in this volume. As elsewhere, political developments of the last hundred years have brought about wider commercialisation, for instance in the area of weaving which was previously practised for private use and was subject only to limited exchange. Indigenous land tenure involving individually owned fields, common pastures, and common sacred spaces for religious and ritual purposes and grave yards are still in collective use. However, a threat by some religious groups claiming exclusive rights to some of these common property regimes and a state policy that does not recognise indigenous tenure are contributing to rising tensions.

In many case studies commercialisation indicates the increasing inclusion of indigenous and minority ethnic groups in the wider economic sphere of the globalised world. By commoditising their produce indigenous people and ethnic minorities are able to take part in the exchange process and to obtain essential items for consumption. Their produce – be it bush meat, forest products or trance dances – and their labour are the readily available commodities that they can exchange for cash (see the contributions by Köhler, Lewis, Guenther, Endicott, and Lye in this volume). However, in contrast to these relatively peaceful processes of intensifying interactions there is evidence of groups holding fresh memories of terrible atrocities which were perpetrated unto their forefathers during times of conquest. Many groups did successfully avoid contact with conquest forces after an initial encounter or even before encountering any disaster. Others have intentionally been evasive of any contact hence minimising the risk of being annihilated. In these ways groups have maintained their autonomy and have been able to maintain their way of life. Some have succeeded in maintaining autonomy (as explained earlier) while also being connected to their neighbours in a regional trade and friendship network. Through this network they supply livestock and receive firearms, ammunition and tools of production and ritual items in exchange. Today they are visited by international tourists who camp in their midst and watch their dances for limited fees while dining on small stock roasted in the style of pastoralists of the region. With the further development of infrastructure, the state and a global audience will be drawn closer to these marginal groups. Furthermore, the development of infrastructure is likely to create possibilities for people to come into contact with allies who may air the concerns of these indigenous people and of ethnic minorities to a global audience.

Discrimination

Discrimination refers to the situation experienced by encapsulated groups when they join the margins of larger societies. Being discriminated against involves mainly economic alienation and political marginalisation but it also takes other forms (Woodburn 1997; Lewis 2000; see also Kenrick, Köhler, and Lewis in this volume). By way of illustration I will draw on more examples from Ethiopia's southwest, my own area of field research. Members of larger ethnic groups that have wielded political and economic power since the time of conquest discriminate against ethnic minorities from the newly conquered areas in terms of their skin colour, the part of the country they come from, the language they use and their ethnicity and religious beliefs. The abuses directed against indigenous groups and ethnic minorities are mainly verbal. The food they eat, the clothes they wear and their customs are subjects of derision and it is not uncommon to see members of such groups being teased, bullied and even attacked in the streets of the capital Addis Ababa. Even in their own territories in government outposts where police and a few other civil servants dwell, members of indigenous groups are bullied, verbally assaulted and even beaten. Their customs and religious practices are despised. Their hair styles are condemned. The food they eat is considered to stink. Farmers who till the land are likewise insulted as a stinking lot, and nomads are considered to be idle wanderers. Often schools, missionary organisations and officials of government lead campaigns against the 'backward' way of life of these groups. They often accuse indigenous groups of 'devil worship' because of their dreadlock hair. Members of more powerful ethnic groups do not consume food with indigenous groups because they accuse them of eating 'impure' slaughtered animals. Christian organisations attack the religious practices of indigenous groups and ethnic minorities and humiliate the practitioners, notwithstanding the constitution which promotes secularism and the right to freedom of belief. Schools rename children who have local names; teachers bully children who come to school wearing local clothing and encourage salvaged urban-style clothes which are often too expensive for parents to afford. This is discrimination as experienced locally and collectively. Political and economic discrimination takes different forms. State-run social services are poorly organised and often the people who are entrusted to provide these services to indigenous peoples and minority ethnic groups are themselves brought up under circumstances of discrimination and perpetuate discrimination in various ways. State policies are patronising; they view weaker groups as incapable and maintain that their lifestyles ought to be changed by establishing projects which increase the state's power of control. This is achieved by introducing plantation and forestry projects which do not benefit local people but legitimise state appropriation of land. In addition the state has hierarchised ethnic groups as 'nations', 'nationalities' and 'peoples', placing indigenous peoples on the lowest rung of its hierarchy and establishing justifications to make the state's patronising role appear sensible and philanthropic. In actual fact, however, the state paves the way to appropriate resources of such groups be they big or small. The forms of discrimination as perpetrated against indigenous peoples and ethnic minorities are varied. Some are subtle, others obvious, but it always takes courage and determination to resist. The international climate of the last twenty-five years, however, has been more open to appeals for help made by such minority groups. On the other hand, the political and economic pressures that they currently face in many parts of the world cannot be underestimated.

A number of contributions in this volume show the degree of external discrimination that is perpetrated on nonliterate groups. In one particular case, Justin Kenrick describes a situation where land which Bagyeli of southwest Cameroon have been cultivating for years, and where they used to live, was claimed by literate villagers so that these villagers could obtain compensation due for damages caused by the World Bank-funded Chad–Cameroon oil pipeline. In a similar way, Lewis, Köhler and Hitchcock in this volume discuss the varying degrees of discrimination to which the Yaka and Baka of Central Africa and the Ju/'hoansi of Southern Africa are exposed and the ways in which these groups have reacted to these external pressures.

Property and Equality Revisited

The links between the three themes of this volume become particularly clear in a collection of contributions as presented here. Moreover, in some cases contributions to this volume also touch upon the themes of Volume 1 (Ritualisation, Sharing and Egalitarianism) and give a variety of perspectives for looking at property and equality in societies which are affected by global and national political and economic developments. Parallels emerge across the diverse regions that are covered. For instance, the contributions by Weiner, Lydall and Keen show parallels although they are dealing with such far-apart cases as Papua New Guinea, Ethiopia and Aboriginal Australia respectively. All of these peoples have been incorporated by forces of the state or outside forces. In all these cases the groups are delayed-return societies who practise cultivation, cattle pastoralism or hunting and gathering. In some areas state law mediates the commercialisation of resources between subject indigenous peoples and global big business, as is shown in Weiner's contribution. His study focuses on a deal between the Chevron Company and the local landowner corporation. He investigates the commercial encounter between Chevron and the ILG (Incorporated Land Groups) and indicates the benefits the latter reap from these contracts. Weiner's contribution indicates the inherent contradiction in the designs of fixed royalty payment by a global oil firm and the culturally continuous instability and reconfiguration inherent in the structure of clan membership. The problem they face is the fragmentation of clan groups in order to register for incorporated land group status so that they can claim benefits. However, his study indicates the egalitarian aspect of distribution of royalty money and equity benefit in the terms of the deal between Chevron and the state. Jean Lydall's study focuses on pastoralist Hamar of southern Ethiopia. The Hamar have been subjects of the Ethiopian state for over a century, but they occupy a dry and infertile terrain. At the moment, neither the state nor other multinational groups show great interest in their resources. Some missionary activity has been going on for over two decades and Norwegian NGOs are actively involved in education, health, emergency relief and in drilling water wells. In their day-to-day life Hamar do not suffer from discrimination by larger groups, but like most of their neighbours in southern Ethiopia they do not benefit from education on their terms and do not get sufficient protection from the nation state either. Lydall's study focuses on the process of internal power differentiation and its replication. Her contribution on the internal dynamics of Hamar pastoralist society reveals hierarchy and the distribution of power along gender lines in the domestic sphere quite independently of externally generated encapsulation processes. Similarly, Ian Keen looks at Aboriginal relations of marriage and compares the marriage systems of six Aboriginal communities in Australia. He addresses issues of power and inequalities in ritual, exchange of women and the differential return earned by the powerful. Here again we see the internal reproduction of inequality independent of the processes of encapsulation.

As mentioned at the beginning, this volume does not claim that the same dynamics apply to all cases. For instance there are cases where, after a century of incorporation, small groups have managed to keep their autonomy by controlling their members, by keeping outsiders in separate villages, and by refusing to send their children to schools outside their country out of fear that these places would transform their children into different persons (Tadesse 1999, 2002). What the diverse examples show us is that although nearly all the groups that we deal with in this volume are incorporated into the nation state, their lives are not all affected in the same way by the processes of encapsulation. Their responses to this situation also vary.

The spectrum of cases shows how changes that are brought about by global, national and local actors affect the economic, political and social arrangements of former hunter-gatherer and other small-scale societies. The anthropological observers aim to understand the lived experiences of these societies and to compare their lives today with earlier periods of relative autonomy. In particular, the contributors to this volume clarify the implications of the powerful external forces for the egalitarian principles on which these societies have been based.

The idea of property and its relation to equality/inequality has interested and continues to interest the academic world within the framework indicated above. Property has been the subject of debate in many disciplines but the papers assembled here take a specific anthropological perspective on the issue. Relying on comparative ethnographic data, anthropology is able to investigate and compare a range of cases in which people have varying understandings of property and to show how various groups of people relate to it. Comparative ethnography has provided various ways of looking at issues of property and at how people conceive of it in different parts of the world. This comparative approach has broadened the scope of the investigation of property and claims to rights in various forms of property (material property, intellectual property, incorporeal, virtual property etc.) which have developed to include, for example, patent rights in animal and human genetic information. The debate on property and (in)equality is also advancing as a consequence of the great interest devoted to the current situation of postsocialist rural property relations (Verdery 1999; Swaine 2000; Hann 2002; Hann et al. 2003), a property situation in which political and economic disruptions and rearrangements have occurred following the collapse of the Soviet system. This volume demonstrates how groups which are faced with equally extraordinary circumstances respond to new economic and political situations and how this affects their own practices. It is one of the main concerns of the contributors to portray the actual range of agents with their differing power relations, the effect of power on the behaviour of weaker groups and the impact of such power on access to crucial resources.

In his 'Egalitarian Societies' James Woodburn (1982) described egalitarian practices as being central to the life of hunter-gatherers in terms of individuals having direct access to ungarnered resources of their country, only limited by the division of labour between the sexes (Woodburn 1982: 437). 'In these societies', he wrote, 'equalities of power, equalities of wealth and equalities of prestige or rank are not merely sought but are, with certain limited exceptions, genuinely realised.' Equality is repeatedly acted out, publicly demonstrated, in opposition to possible inequality. He also emphasised that 'only the hunting gathering way of life permits so great an emphasis on equality' (Woodburn 1982: 432). Whilst early work on small-scale societies made scant reference to relations with larger-scale economic and political forces, such as the nation state and global economic power relations, all the papers assembled here address these issues in one way or another. In general terms they do so in the light of the three general themes of this volume. This has led us to take a thematic rather than geographic approach to organising the contents of the two volumes, in order to highlight parallel debates across regions.

The contributors to this volume, therefore, do not simply indicate developments in the scholarly debate since 1982 but they also shift the emphasis by trying to give general answers to the question, 'What did encapsulation engender in the social, political and economic life of small scale societies?'

Richard Lee explores the large-scale social processes affecting foragers and post-foragers today and gives a survey of the foragers' past and current situations. The future of post-foragers he suggests, is intimately linked to their ability to identify themselves as Indigenous Peoples. 'After centuries of negative stereotyping, images of denigration that still persist in pockets, being recognised as indigenous has become an avenue for entitlement, enfranchisement and empowerment.' Among other things, Lee's contribution also highlights the necessity for a historical perspective on the current situation.

Axel Köhler looks at commodity sharing, gifting and exchange in the Congo. He puts the Baka, their precolonial trade networks, their Bantu neighbours, the colonial and postcolonial states in perspective and illustrates how the economic life of the Baka has been affected by regional trade networks and by the Atlantic trade long before the advent of colonialism. He shows how alternating periods of accelerated trade relations and relative calm characterised their economic life in the past and how the 'rationality of money, its potential as a repository of wealth and as measure of value, and the idea of investment with incremental interest (through gifting), were not intrinsically alien concepts that had to be implanted from outside, but had rather developed in step with ever widening exchange relations'. He argues that the Baka have ingeniously appropriated and adapted money and commodities to their own cultural understanding and social purposes. Only in moments of financial crisis such as the 1990s in the Congo did barter constitute an appropriate response. A major theoretical point of this paper is that it connects the two questions – discrimination on the one hand, and the internal dynamics of immediate-return systems, on the other hand – which up to now are usually considered to be separate issues.

Jerome Lewis focuses on the notion of property as held by the Mbendjele and their Bilo neighbours, the state and multinational organisations, discussing the role of the colonial and postcolonial governments in relation to their land policies. He also illustrates how these intruding groups today claim forest territory that was once held exclusively by the Mbendjele. Lewis indicates that rights to land are sold and traded to multinational companies as rights to specific resources: trees for loggers, minerals for miners, game for conservationists and safari hunters, thus discriminating against the Mbendjele. The national laws work against the Mbendjele, not only by denying them entitlement to their territory but also by not allowing them access to parts of their territory acquired by new conservationists. The original holders of these rights only gain incidental benefits (as workers/employees or through infrastructure). Benefits are hierarchically distributed so that those most recently involved in colonisation get most of the benefits. Thus the Europeans earn most from logging and mining, the Bilo come second and lastly, if at all, the Mbendjele.

Kirk Endicott examines the nature of the external trade among the Batek of Malaya in an effort to see how it is accommodated within their egalitarian social system and to determine why trade does not lead to predicted social inequalities. His point of departure is Woodburn's assumption that the absence of delay between the point when people acquire food and other resources and when they distribute and consume them engenders egalitarian relations in immediate-return hunting and gathering societies. His study suggests that values and social obligations can, in some circumstances, exert control over economic processes and their consequences and that food-sharing obligations and other levelling mechanisms can prevent the rise of economic and social differences in foraging societies that engage in trade.

Lye Tuck-Po starts with an extensive examination of the implications of roads and road building through indigenous territory, and what pathways mean to the Batek. In particular she investigates how roads enter the Batek idiom of property. She expands her argument by stating that roads function as markers of socioecological change and can lead us to an examination of how they are assimilated into the cognition and practice of immediate return hunter-gatherers, providing insights into the emergence of inequalities. She concludes that 'roads are a delayed-return phenomenon but, as used by the Batek, they become a bridge between immediate and delayed returns, and therein lies the tension', a tension that could be a fruitful source of insight.

Justin Kenrick questions the established academic interpretation of the dominant colonial and postcolonial discrimination against Central African hunter-gatherers by their farming neighbours, and suggests that it intensifies rather than alleviates the experience of discrimination. He also questions the hitherto dominant anthropological ways of understanding the relationship between hunter-gatherers and their neighbouring farmers, suggesting that it ultimately impedes rather than enables these hunter-gatherers to claim equality with their neighbours. He suggests that 'the need is not only to identify the processes of discrimination and domination present within and between both peoples, but also to identify and support equalising processes of inclusion'. Thereby, Kenrick's argument opens up a new dimension for combating discrimination.

Drawing on a wider study of variation in Aboriginal economy and society, Ian Keen's study considers variations in Aboriginal kinship and marriage, and the association of this variation with difference in power. To make his points he outlines the classification of kin and affines in the communities under consideration, showing the boundaries of marriage, the returns and the kin who are entitled to these returns. Some of the arrangements demand an investment in time, as in the bestowal of a young spouse on an aging husband and the bestowal of a yet unconceived child. Using detailed data comparatively, Keen argues that 'there is an association between the length of the "delay" in marriage bestowal and the size of return for males as measured by the level of polygyny'. He shows that the level of polygyny bears a strong relationship to the degree and kind of power differences in Aboriginal societies. This contribution provides a case of internal inequalities and their reproduction in the sphere of marriage arrangements.

Jean Lydall looks at the domestic sphere to analyse the power women exercise over members of their families, over property and even over the fertility of animals and fields and over certain rituals, in what is usually alleged to be the male-dominated world of Hamar pastoralists of southwest Ethiopia. Her description relates to what Woodburn (Volume 1) suggests with regards to ritual: that it may be the weak spot in the immediate-return system. Her material reveals, however, that women, too, have access to and power in ritual and in mundane matters.

James Weiner focuses on the distribution of royalty money and equity benefits by Chevron Niugini to Foi and Fasu clans in the Kutubu Oil Project Area in Papua New Guinea. He investigates the relation between the Incorporated Land Groups established according to the 1974 Incorporated Land Groups Act, Chevron Niugini and clans, which are the corporate owners of land in oil resource areas and consequent receivers of royalty and other benefits. He explains multiplicity in the number of new applications for the status of Incorporated Land Groups from subgroups that were incorporated in the early 1990s. He indicates predictable faults for fission in clan organisation and the reasons for why such fissioning takes place (see also Weiner 2002). While the oil company views this trend as resulting from dishonesty of leaders of Incorporated Land Groups, Weiner explains it in cultural terms. Weiner's contribution is an example of a case where a nation state legislates a favourable land policy to benefit its subjects based on the terms of agreement between the state and the oil company.

Robert Hitchcock questions the general assumption regarding property rights among hunter-gatherers that access to land was relatively equitable and that hunter-gatherers shared the land with one another. He argues that in fact individuals and groups always had differential access to land and resources, depending on a whole range of variables, including kinship, age, social and marital status, language-group affiliation, and personal and group identity. He takes cases from the San and Ju/'hoansi groups of Southern Africa to illustrate his argument and indicates that currently there is a struggle between these groups and their powerful opponents (governments, wealthy individuals, multinational corporations and other groups) for control over land. He expresses the necessity for an understanding of the complexity of San territoriality and an appreciation of the complex history of land tenure, land use and resource management in order to be able to make a cogent case for the recognition and the institutionalisation of their land, and for resource claims, and to secure various rights: residential rights, hunting rights, gathering rights including commercial rights to wild plants, water rights, grazing rights, arable land rights, rights to do business, etc. Hitchcock's paper shows that these groups are in a much better position, both in terms of getting international support and in terms of organising themselves to secure a better future legally, compared to other encapsulated Pygmy groups and other groups, for example in southern and southwestern Ethiopia.

Mathias Guenther discusses how the Bushman trance dance, which was originally performed by experts as part of the wider sharing practice and as part of a healing process, has been transformed. It is now performed both to local and international audiences with the goal of making money. This has involved professionalisation and commoditisation. The traditional expectations of healers by those who expect to be cured from ailments, and the expectations of international visitors intending to consume the performances as marketable substances, coexist. The trance dance, Guenther concludes, will endure both in its traditional form and its commoditised shape, thus contributing to social integration and political change.

Thomas Gibson casts some light on Woodburn's argument that the origin of social inequality in immediate-return hunter-gatherer societies lies in the appropriation of the religious domain by senior men. Comparing egalitarian religious images in one of the most hierarchical societies, the Makassar of South Sulawesi, with the hierarchical religious images that exist in one of the most egalitarian societies, the Buid of highland Mindoro, Gibson argues that the major threat to society comes from individuals who place their autonomy above the needs of the group. The seeds of hierarchy lie in those aspects of social life in which the desires of the individual are subordinated to the needs of the group, combined with the ability of one part of the social whole to claim the right to interpret and represent those needs. Gibson thus argues that an egalitarian ethos exists as an oppositional response to either factional attempts or continued efforts to encapsulate.

Processes of encapsulation may often appear to have predictable responses but the range and degree of responses to encapsulation vary widely from group to group, as evidenced in the various examples in this volume. For some former hunter-gatherers and other small groups presented in this volume maintenance of their original lifeworld after the loss of autonomy becomes increasingly difficult. In many cases these groups occupy the margins of larger social systems and their acquired status is characterised by discrimination. Torture, insults and humiliating experiences become part of their daily experiences. The discrimination these groups experience involves the denial of equality and of a recognition of political or social rights. At the heart of this process is the denial of political autonomy by dominating groups and the nation state and, in particular, as the contributors to this volume show, the denial of property rights.

References

Boyd, D.J. 1985. 'The commercialisation of Ritual in the Eastern Highlands of Papua New Guinea.' *Man*, N.S. 20(2).

Dean, B. and J.M. Levi. 2003. 'Introduction'. In: B. Dean and J.M. Levi (eds), *At the Risk of Being Heard: Identity, Indigenous Rights and Poastcolonial States*, pp.1–44. Ann Arbor, University of Michigan Press.

Dilebo, G.L. 1974. 'Emperor Menelik's Ethiopia, 1865–1916: National Unification or Amhara Communal Domination?' Ph.D., Howard University.

Hann, C. and the 'Property Relations Group', (eds). 2003. *The Postsocialist Agrarian Question : Property Relations and the Rural Condition.* Halle Studies in the Anthropology of Eurasia. Münster: Lit.

Hann, C.M. (ed). 2002. *Post Socialism: Ideals, Ideologies and Practices in Eurasia.* London: Routledge.

Hodson, A.W. n.d. *Where Lion Reign: an Account of Lion Hunting and Exploration in South West Abyssinia.* London: Skeffington and Son Ltd.

Lewis, J. 2000. *The Batwa Pygmies of the Great Lakes Region.* London: Minority Rights Group International.

Marru, I. 2002. *Customary Corporations as Mechanisms for Landowner Representation and Benefits Distribution: A Review of Incorporated Land Groups in Petroleum Development Projects in Papua New Guinea*, http://www.fdc.org.au/files/marru.pdf.

Shipton, P. 2001. 'Land Tenure'. In: N.J. Smelser and P.B. Baltes (eds), *International Encyclopedia of the Social and Behaviorial Sciences*,. 12: 8256-61. Amsterdam: Elsevier.

Shipton, P. 2003. 'Legalism and Loyalism: European, African and Human "Rights"' In: B. Dean and J.M. Levi (eds), *At the Risk of Being Heard: Identity, Indigenous Rights and Postcolonial States*, pp. 45–79. Ann Arbor: University of Michigan Press.

Strecker, I. 2002. *Berimba's resistance: The Life and Times of a great Hamar Spokesman as told by his son Aike (Baldambe)* http://www.uni mainz.de/~ifeas/ethno/kulturanthro_afrika/berimba2.htm

Swaine, N. 2000. *The Rural Transition in Post-Socialist Central Europe and the Balkans.*Working Paper no. 9, Halle/Saale: Max Planck Institute for Social Anthropology.

Tadesse, W.G. 1999. *Warfare and Fertility: A Study of the Hor (Arbore) of Southern Ethiopia.* Department of Anthropology, London School of Economics. London: University of London.

—— 2002. 'Evading the Revolutionary State'. In: W. James, D.L. Donham, E. Kurimoto and A. Triulzi (eds), *Remapping Ethiopia: Socialism and After.* Oxford: James Currey.

—— 2003. 'The Postsocialist Agrarian Situation in Southern Ethiopia'. In: C. Hann and the 'Property Relations Group' (eds), *The Postsocialist Agrarian Question: Property Relations and the Rural Condition.* Münster: Lit.

Turton, D. 1979. 'War, Peace and Mursi Identity'. In: K.Fukui and D. Turton (eds), *Warfare among East African Herders.* pp. 179–209. Osaka:National Museum of Ethnology.

Vanderheym, G. 1897. *Une Expedition avec le Négus Ménélik.* Paris: Librairie Hachette.

Verdery, K. 1999. 'Fuzzy Property: Rights, Power and Identity in Transylvania's Decollectivisation'. In: M. Burawoy and K. Verdery (eds), *Uncertain Transitions: Ethnographies of Change in the Postsocialist World.* Lanham: Rowman and Littlefield.

Weiner, J.F. 2002. *The Foi Incorporated Land Group: Law and Custom in Group definition and collective action in Kutubu Oil Project Area, PNG.* Research School of Pacific and Asian Studies, Australian National University.

Woodburn, J. 1982. 'Egalitarian Societies'. *Man,* N.S. 17(3): 431–51.

—— 1997. 'Indigenous Discrimination: the Ideological Basis for Local Discrimination against Hunter-Gatherer Minorities in Sub-Saharan Africa'. *Ethnic and Racial Studies,* 20(2).

1

Power and Property in Twenty-First Century Foragers A Critical Examination

Richard Borshay Lee

Hunting and gathering peoples in the Twenty-first century live in a vastly different world than that of their parent's and grandparent's generation of the 1960s. It was in that decade that the study of hunting and gathering peoples experienced a renaissance of scholarly interest. Researchers such as James Woodburn, Mervyn Meggitt, Eleanor Leacock, Les Hiatt, June Helm, Nic Peterson, and others found that, even in the 1960s, it was still possible to work with foragers who lived with a degree of autonomy and self-sufficiency. Collectively researchers were able to build up a detailed and nuanced picture of hunter-gatherer life-ways and world-views, a picture that became part of the anthropological canon (Lee and DeVore 1968; Bicchieri 1972; Ingold, Riches and Woodburn 1988a, 1988b; Kelly 1995).

Four decades later even that degree of autonomy has disappeared, as the world's indigenous peoples have merged rapidly into the underclass of First World, Third World, and post-Socialist social formations. Most of the peoples whose lives were highlighted in 'Man the Hunter' (Lee and DeVore 1968) now find themselves in settled communities, on reserves, or in peri-urban slums. Even those who continue to occupy ancestral land and preserve access to resources, do so as encapsulated minorities within a larger system (Woodburn 1988). The condition of 'encapsulation', whether partial or full, is accompanied by the penetration of market forces into their subsistence and small-scale exchange-based economies. Today all former foragers find their economic order partially to fully enmeshed with the commerce of their surrounding region and beyond.

How have these altered circumstances, shaped by the tidal forces of globalization, affected the foraging peoples? Have they entirely lost the social, political, and spiritual characteristics that made them unique? Or despite the shrinking world they inhabit, of bureaucratic states dominated by market forces, have they managed to maintain some of the characteristics that set them apart?

The papers in this volume attempt to offer answers to these questions, against the baseline of understandings about prior hunting and gathering autonomy, egalitarianism, and sharing. Authors have tried to come to grips with the diversity of current living situations, the spectrum of economic and governance arrangements, and the muliplex ways in which the former foragers have been incorporated into the class structures of surrounding societies. In comprehending this diversity, observers have pinpointed certain large scale social processes that appear at work in case after case, indicating that parallel processes are shaping the lives and futures of foragers and similar peoples in such diverse settings as the Congo, Australia, New Guinea, Malaysia, and Botswana.

'Encapsulation' refers to the processes by which formerly autonomous groups are drawn into the orbit of regional social formations and eventually undergo incorporation into state-level entities. The term refers to processes which are primarily political in nature. Understanding encapsulation requires a prior familiarity with what is meant by the concept of 'autonomy'.

In the realm of the economic, 'commercialization' refers to the replacement in a classic Marxist sense, of 'use value' by 'exchange value', of production for consumption by production for export. For foraging peoples long immersed in an economy based on reciprocity and small-scale exchange, the transition to a monetized economy engenders profound changes, not just in economic, but in many other areas of social life, for example in the transition from bride service to bride price (J. Collier 1988) and in the conduct of ritual and healing (Guenther, this volume and Tonkinson, volume 1). Commoditisation is another way of characterising the conversion of use values to exchange values. The introduction of buying and selling is not the only major innovation. The complexities of their economic situation are compounded by the addition of such diverse activities and income sources as migrant labour, government welfare payments, royalty payments for mineral rights, the professionalisation of traditional healers, as well as receipts from tourism and craft production (Peterson and Matsuyama 1991; Guenther, Weiner this volume).

In the social sphere, the foraging peoples were formerly – to a degree – masters in their own houses, living in the centre of their world. Some groups like the Pygmies, Nayaka, and Palayan, maintained long-standing trade and other relations with non-foraging peoples. But periodically they would retreat into the forest and there live on their own turf by their own codes of conduct (Turnbull 1965; Bird-David 1994; Gardner 2000). Encapsulation brings about not just political changes but social ones as well. As foraging peoples become incorporated into surrounding social formations their daily interactions intensify and opportunities for escape to the forest decline. Entering usually at the lowest rungs of the social ladder, they experience heightened levels of stigmatization and discrimination, and intensified feelings of 'otherness' and marginality.

Underlying all these processes is a common thread, the process of becoming subaltern; the loss of autonomy and the articulation of formerly independent people with the political, economic and social structures of the dominant. In this new world of alien property relations and power structures an important question raised by the authors is how to rebuild their base of power? How can they be actors on new regional, national and international stages? How can they overcome discrimination to reassert their humanity in a world of powerholders who may regard their plight with condescension, indifference, or hostility?

In this paper I will explore the large-scale social processes affecting foragers and post-foragers today, against the background of the original paradigm. In setting the stage for our inquiry it is essential to trace the prior phase of the study of hunters and gatherers as its emerged in the 1960s and 70s, when pioneering social anthropologists delineated the nature, contours, and internal dynamics of autonomous egalitarian societies.

Egalitarian Societies: Myth or Reality?

The study of egalitarian societies has had a long and distinguished history in anthropology, dating back at least to the publication in 1883 of Lewis Henry Morgan's *Houses and house life of the American aborigines.* However by the 1980s the study of egalitarian societies had declined and even their very existence was in some circles moot. A turning point came in 1982, when in his Malinowski lecture James Woodburn argued for the empirical validity of egalitarian society and restored their study to a place on the anthropological agenda. Bringing to bear the analytical apparatus of classic British social anthropology, Woodburn critically re-examined the principles of egalitarianism, assessed their centrality to hunter-gatherer life, and documented their considerable range of variation.

The empirical basis of the egalitarianism and the sharing ethos of small-scale indigenous societies had been a fixture in the theoretical apparatus of earlier generations of scholars from Morgan to Radcliffe-Brown, Kroeber, Lowie, and Karl Polanyi. But under the impact of global capitalism the very reality of societies based on such alternate principles had been called into question. It was James Woodburn's examination of the phenomenon that reaffirmed the existence of egalitarian societies and also legitimized it as subject worthy of study.

Twenty years after the Malinowski lecture, the study of egalitarianism and its accompanying property relations are well established in the writings of Pierre Clastres, Fred Myers, Basil Sansom, Laura Rival, Grete Hovelsrud-Broda, Nobuhiro Kishigami and many of the authors represented in the two volumes of 'Property and Equality.' At the same time the understanding of egalitarian societies based on regimes of common property has undergone, since the 1980s, significant development. And this development is linked closely (though not exclusively) with the study of hunting and gathering societies and their transformations under the impact of modernity.

The image of hunter-gatherers has changed significantly since James Woodburn and I started our work 40 or more years ago. Foraging peoples used to be defined primarily in terms of their subsistence, based on hunting of wild animals, gathering of wild plant foods, and fishing. In contemporary theory, this minimal definition is only the starting point. In defining foragers we recognise that contemporary foragers practise a mixed subsistence: gardening in tropical South America, reindeer herding in northeast Asia, trading in south and southeast Asia and parts of Africa and articulation with the world economy in all contemporary cases. A multi-faceted definition of hunter-gatherers has gone well beyond subsistence to encompass a more nuanced understanding including social organization and world view (Lee and Daly 1999).

Crucial to contemporary understandings is Woodburn's key distinction between immediate-return vs. delayed-return societies. Although both were subsumed under the heading of 'band society', a staple of anthropological theory since the 1930s, there were important differences. In immediate-return societies food was consumed on the spot or soon after, while in delayed-return societies food and other resources might be stored for months or years, with marked effects on social organization and cultural notions of property (Woodburn 1978, 1982).

With this distinction in mind, and despite the epochal changes of the last century, features applicable primarily to immediate-return societies, identified in the decades before and since the 1960s, have held up remarkably well. Most observers represented in these volumes would subscribe to the view that the social and economic life of small-scale hunter-gatherers shared certain core features:

First the band was the basic unit of social organization, small in numbers with 20–50 persons, fairly mobile, flexible in membership, and constituted on a variety of pragmatic and formal principles of post-marital residence, consanguinity, affinity and compatibility.

Second, the egalitarian nature of these societies has withstood the scrutiny of critics determined to prove otherwise. As eloquently summarized by Southall at the Halle conference, leadership was less formal and more subject to constraints of popular opinion than was the case in neighbouring village societies governed by headmen and chiefs. The leader of a band could persuade but not command. This important aspect of their way of life allowed for a degree of freedom unheard of in more hierarchical societies, but at the same time, put them at a distinct disadvantage in their encounters with centrally organised 'tribal societies' and colonial authorities, a theme addressed in several of the papers in these volumes, including those by Thomas Gibson, Justin Kenrick, and Jerome Lewis.

Mobility is another characteristic of band societies. People tended to move their settlements frequently, several times a year or more in search of food, and this mobility was an important element of their politics. People in band societies tended to 'vote with their feet,' moving away rather than submitting to the will of an unpopular leader. Mobility was also a means of resolving conflicts that would be more difficult for settled peoples.

A fourth characteristic is the remarkable fact that all band-organized peoples exhibited a pattern of concentration and dispersion. As Marcel Mauss and Henri Beuchat demonstrated for the Eskimo a century ago (1907 [1979]), rather than live in uniformly sized groupings throughout the year, band societies tended to spend part of the year dispersed into small foraging units and another part aggregated into much larger units. The Cree of northern Quebec studied by Harvey Feit and the Innu of Labrador are typical, spending the winter dispersed in small foraging groups of 10-30, while in summer aggregating into groups of up to 200–300 at lake or river fishing sites. Despite Mauss's original assertion that these annual movements obeyed social not ecological imperatives, it seems clear that the concentration-dispersion patterns of hunter-gatherers represents a dialectical interplay of social *and* ecological factors (Lee 1979: 443–47).

A fifth characteristic common to almost all immediate-return foraging societies (as well as most delayed-return societies; including simple farming and pastoral societies) is a land tenure system based on a common property regime (CPR). These regimes were, until recently, far more common worldwide than regimes based on private property. In traditional CP regimes, while movable property is held by individuals, land is held by a kinship-based collective. As set out in papers in these volumes by Barbara Bodenhorn on the Inupiat, by Mitsuo Ichikawa on the Pygmies and by Strecker and Lydall on the pastoral Hamar, and by others, ownership of resources obey complex rules of access, the details of which will vary from people to people. One common theme though, is that in almost all cases on record, attachment to land and the obligation to share the fruits of the land (and sea) play absolutely central roles in the spiritual and ethical life of the people.

This pinpoints the sixth broad area of commonality. Sharing was the central rule of social interaction among hunters and gatherers (Ingold 1999), what Endicott has termed a 'strict' and 'absolute' obligation (1988: 117). Generalized reciprocity as the dominant form of reciprocity within face-to-face groups is almost universal (Sahlins 1965). Between groups, rules of reciprocal access made it possible for each individual to draw on the resources of several territories. These, combined with an absence of private ownership of land, led many observers from L.H. Morgan forward, to attribute to hunter-gatherers a way of life based on 'primitive communism.' (Morgan 1881; Testart 1985; Lee 1988).

The central themes of the moral economy of hunters and gatherers are summed up by Les Hiatt (as quoted in Peterson and Taylor 2001).

Probably everywhere in Aboriginal Australia the highest secular value is generosity. Readiness to share with others is the main measure of a man's goodness, and hospitality an essential source of his self-esteem. It is likely that this pervasive and highly-developed ethic of generosity emerged as a cultural adaptation to the exigencies of hunting and gathering, and conceivably conferred improved fitness on those who adopted it (Hiatt 1982: 14–15).

These ethical and organisational principles constituted the bedrock of hunter-gatherer lifeways. Laura Rival makes the point that two South American tropical forest peoples might well have a rather similar subsistence mix, but one would have a clearly agricultural orientation while the other a foraging one, based on a study of their social organisation and mobility patterns, as well as their mythology, rituals and interpersonal relations (Rival 1999).

What is remarkable is that despite marked differences in their historical circumstances, foragers seemed to arrive at similar organisational and ideational solutions to the problems of living in groups, a convergence that Tim Ingold, has labelled 'a distinct mode of sociality'.

The nature of this egalitarianism needs further comment. It was not a passive absence of hierarchy, rather the people were observed to hold a fierce adherence to the principles; a conscious limiting of aggressive self-aggrandising tendencies through gossip, ridicule, and the famous levelling devices. One vivid example of this pattern appears in my account 'Eating Christmas in the Kalahari' in which the Ju/'hoansi subjected a visiting anthropologist to relentless criticism when he sought to gain their favour through the slaughtering of a Christmas Ox (Lee 1969; theorized in Lee 1988, 1990). The changing nature of forager egalitarianism is addressed *inter alia*, in the papers by Ichikawa and Ingold (volume 1), and by Gibson and Kenrick (this volume).

It is necessary to note that not all foraging peoples fit into the model presented above. Two areas of divergence need to be noted. First is the important distinction between simple vs. complex hunter-gatherers, drawn in part on Woodburn's immediate-delayed return distinction, but expanded to include an even broader range of cases. Not all hunting and gathering peoples – prehistoric and contemporary – lived in small mobile bands (Price and Brown 1985). Some, like the Indians of the Northwest Coast (Donald 1984, 1997; Mitchell and Donald 1985) and the Calusa of Florida (Marquardt 1988), as well as many prehistoric peoples, lived in large semi-sedentary settlements with chiefs, commoners, and slaves, yet were entirely dependent on wild foods. In social organisation and ethos these societies showed significant divergence from the patterns outlined above, yet in other ways a basic foraging pattern is discernible. For example even the Northwest Coast peoples maintained a concentration-dispersion pattern, breaking down their large permanent plank houses in the summer and re-erecting them in temporary structures at seasonal fishing sites (Boas 1966; Daly 1999). With their simple technology but complex kinship organization and cosmology, the Australian Aborigines are seen by some analysts as exhibiting characteristics that do not fit easily into the immediate or the delayed-return category (see Layton). Other delayed-return systems represented in this volume include the pastoral Hamar or Ethiopia (Lydall, Strecker) and the agricultural Kutubu of New Guinea (Weiner).

Gender is another dimension along which hunting and gathering societies show considerable variation. Women of hunter-gatherer societies do have higher status than women in most of the world's societies, including industrial and post-industrial modernity. This status is expressed in greater freedom of movement and involvement in decision-making and a lower incidence of domestic violence when compared to women in farming, herding, and agrarian societies (Leacock 1978, 1982; Lee 1982). Nevertheless variation exists: Wife-beating and rape are recorded for societies as disparate as the Eskimo of North Alaska and Aboriginal northern Australia (Friedl 1975; Abler 1992) and are not unknown elsewhere; nowhere can it be said that women and men live in a state of perfect equality. In these volumes gender issues are addressed in the papers by Bodenhorn, Biesele and Sugawara (volume 1) and Keen, Lydall, and Weiner (this volume).

The Great Transformation: When Foragers Meet States and Markets

It is a remarkable accomplishment of the discipline of anthropology that these principles and commonalities along with their variations, have been gleaned from diverse ethnographic case studies of societies on five continents, even as these societies were undergoing rapid change brought about by the imposition of states and markets. Yet since 1982, anthropological attention has turned specifically to what happens when these deeply entrenched and now well-documented principles are impacted by state bureaucracy and the market economy. Do they transform themselves into something entirely different, or do they bend but not break, preserving and adapting, and displaying resilience in the face of seemingly unstoppable pressure? With their focus on encapsulation, commercialization and discrimination the analysts represented in this volume place these questions at the centre of their concerns.

What happens to egalitarian relations of production when foraging subsistence is replaced (in part) by regular food handouts? How does the building of schools, clinics, and other state institutions affect mobility, anchoring the population in space and altering the pattern of concentration and dispersion? How are the ubiquitous Common Property Regimes and patterns of sharing impacted as the communities move from a subsistence based primarily on foraging to one based on a mixed economy of petty-commodity production, government welfare, and small-scale farming and herding? And finally what possibilities exist for linking to the market economy and the bureaucratic state that allow former foragers to avoid total transformation and dissolution of their common property- and sharing-based way of life?

Autonomy and Articulation Problematized

To begin, encapsulation and commercialisation cannot be treated as distinct entities. Each represents aspects of the larger process of *articulation.* Thus in unravelling these issues, drawing upon Articulation of Modes of Production theory could be useful (Foster-Carter 1978). Where capitalist relations of production and their accompanying bureaucratic powers penetrate deeply into the daily lives of foraging people, change is more profound and the ability to preserve alternate lifeways severely diminished.

For our purposes I will argue that encapsulation represents the political, and commercialization the economic aspects of a single larger process: the loss of autonomy. The first signals the loss of political autonomy, the second the loss of autonomy on the economic front. But what do we mean by autonomy? If it represents the baseline from which these processes unfold, there has been a remarkable lack of attention paid to the question of what constitutes autonomy (or dependency) of local cultures in an era of global systems.

The dictionary defines autonomy as 'the fact or condition of being autonomous; self government; independence.' Autonomous refers to 'functioning independently without control by others.' (Webster's 1976: 95) 'Autonomy' has a wide range of usages and nuances at the group and individual levels in the human sciences in a variety of fields including anthropology, politics, economics, feminism, and psychotherapy.

It is necessary to clear the ground of some misconceptions which have clouded debates about the status of hunter-gatherers. First of all, economic autonomy must not be equated with isolation. It is a given that all societies through history have been involved in economic exchanges and political relations with their neighbours. The first general point to be made then is that trade and exchange should not simply be equated with domination and loss of autonomy. Exchange is a fundamental part of human life and appears in all cultural settings (Mauss 1954; Lévi-Strauss 1949). Further, many gatherer-hunter peoples have successfully carried on exchange relations with farming and market societies for hundreds of years in India, Southeast Asia, East Africa) while still maintaining a foraging mode of production.

What then constitutes autonomy? As an *economic* concept it refers to ideas of economic self-sufficiency, and self-sufficiency in turn hinges, not on the *existence* of trade – since all societies trade – but whether that trade is indispensable for the society's reproduction and survival. To demonstrate autonomy one must be able to demonstrate self-reproduction. Dependency therefore may be defined as the inability of a society to reproduce itself without the agency of another society. At any given moment a society may exhibit greater or lesser 'autonomy' in its productive relationships, and it should be possible to make assessments of this degree through empirical investigation.

Commercialisation denotes, not just a loss of economic autonomy, but the subordination of a local economy to a particular form of outside control, to use Sahlins' framework, the replacement of a regime of *generalized* and *balanced* reciprocity by one of market-driven *negative* reciprocity (Sahlins 1965)

Political Autonomy

Political autonomy and its opposite, political subordination, raise interesting problems of their own, hinging, not on a society's capacity to reproduce itself – it may do that very well – but on the willingness of other (dominating) societies to *let* it remain autonomous. To put it another way political autonomy is about another society's ability and desire to impose its will, and the core society's ability to *resist* that imposition. Encapsulation thus becomes a process by which a formerly free-standing unit becomes incorporated into the political structures of a larger entity.

In this perspective encapsulation is not an endpoint, but rather a stage in the process of integration, during which the contours of a subordinated entity's former independence remains visible. Eventually even that hazy outline will disappear as the process of integration continues towards its logical conclusion. Surely almost every region, district and municipality in a modern state must have passed, at some point in its history, through a stage of encapsulation. And each unit must retain however distant, some collective memory of its autonomy as a basis for forging identity.

Another interesting aspect of the problem is the question of whether political autonomy is *imposed* or *asserted*. In the former case the economic autonomy of a subject group may serve the interests of a dominant group. Therefore the subordinates are encouraged to pursue their habitual round of activities at their own pace while providing goods or services – often at equitable terms – to the dominant group. In the latter case the autonomous group asserts its claims to autonomy through its own strength and political will and these claims are not contested by their neighbours. In practice these two forms may be difficult to distinguish, and the interpretation of which form is present will rely heavily on subjective judgements both by the peoples involved and particularly by the observers. Thus the Ituri Forest Mbuti Pygmies observed by Turnbull (1965) appeared to be entirely subservient to their black neighbours while they were in their villages, but quite autonomous when they were on their own in the forest (see paper by Justin Kenrick for a critique of Turnbull's views).

Crossing the Permeable Barrier: Transformations of Property

During the Kalahari debate of the 1990s it was commonplace to attribute dependent status to any and all hunter-gatherers throughout their history. But the burden of evidence from studies of Kalahari foragers and elsewhere indicate that such a fate is not inevitable. Foraging peoples as disparate as Michael Asch's Dene trappers in subarctic Canada and Basil Sansom's Aboriginal fringe-dwellers near Darwin, Australia appear to be able to erect barriers to the penetration of capitalist relations of production. Here and elsewhere values in the capitalist world of cash and commodities cross a permeable barrier to become converted into values congruent with the 'traditional economy' of sharing.

Several of the papers in these volumes make outstanding contributions to the understanding of this process. Two examples: Barbara Bodenhorn (volume 1) has done a masterful analysis of Alaskan Inupiat whaling captains who contribute much of their own capital to the mounting of a bowhead whaling expedition but who, through the strict rules of sharing, must give away most of the proceeds, consisting of many tons of whale meat. And Axel Koehler's study (this volume) of the Baka Pygmies of the Congo (Brazzaville) documents that the Baka did not have the market thrust upon them; they entered voluntarily and some Baka became wealthy through the ivory trade. The Baka proved to be skilled traders and in their dealings with their Bantu neighbours, debits and credits flow in *both* directions. But they did not abandon the moral economy of sharing. Baka now sell part of the hunted meat from kills in the local market, but only on the strict condition that at least half of each kill be shared out through Baka traditional kin networks.

Among the Ju/'hoansi, men returning from the Witwatersrand Gold Mines would come home dressed head-to-toe in western clothing purchased with mine wages. After a few days back home their entire wardrobe would have been dispersed item-by-item to family and friends through the 'cashless' hxaro exchange network. Women participating in the new home-brew economy would charge even close relatives the going rate in cash for a cup of home brew made from store bought sugar and yeast, but at the end of the day they would share their gathered nuts and berries with their former 'customers' (Lee 1979).

In Michael Asch's northern Dene and across the Canadian subarctic, the acquisition of electric freezers has made it possible not only to preserve and store moose, deer, rabbit, and other country-food more effectively, but also to participate in feasting and food distribution on a greatly expanded scale. And Basil Sansom has shown how the Wallaby Cross fringe-dwellers made sharp distinctions between whitefella economics and blackfella practices, preserving deeply meaningful patterns of sharing at least to a degree in a situation of poverty and deprivation (Sansom 1980; see also David Trigger 1996).

Obviously there are more desirable fates than that of being a fringe-dweller on the outskirts of Darwin or a Ju/'hoan shebeen patron spending hard-earned pennies on home-brew. These examples nevertheless show the strength and persistence of sharing practices even with the incorporation into the cash and welfare economy.

Summing up the findings of a generation of observers of Australian Aborigines Nicolas Peterson and John Taylor (2001) note that the moral economy of sharing persists even in areas that have experienced centuries of colonial rule:

Some indigenous Australians in the settled part of the country have, collectively, been in contact with a capitalist economy for as long as 200 years, yet it is evident that even in these areas a distinctive egalitarian moral economy still exists. Sharing is still prevalent and it is widely understood to be an important factor in the reproduction of the poor material circumstances of the Aboriginal population which are substantially below that of the population at large. The observation made by Diane Barwick thirty-six years ago, writing of Aboriginal people in Victoria, that, 'Families accumulating property will be called flash [mimetically ostentatious], and will be placed in a humiliating position if they ever find themselves in need' (1965: 18), and the comment of Jeremy Beckett that 'Aboriginal people in western NSW find it very difficult to contract out of the system [of sharing]' (1958: 187) remain true today. Writing of contemporary practice in western NSW, Gaynor MacDonald (pers. com.) comments that people there have maintained a distinctive system of sharing despite not having lived independently by hunting and gathering for at least a century.

What accounts for the extraordinary persistence of sharing among former hunter-gatherers? An interesting divergence of views has sprung up. While some see this as a survival of a strongly-held and still meaningful ethos from the hunting and gathering past, another school of thought, represented in this volume by Thomas Gibson, sees the presence of the moral economy as itself a product of encapsulation, a set of values erected specifically in dialectical opposition to a surrounding milieu of hard-edged, competitive, dog-eat-dog ethics. A similar argument has been put-forward by Carmel Schire (1984). Against this position is Hiatt's argument that such sharing confers long-term evolutionary advantage, long antedating the present conjuncture. Also relevant is the question of how to explain the presence of the moral economy of sharing equally in encapsulated and non-encapsulated environments. Given the enormous emotional and spiritual power of its presence, it is hard to believe that the moral economy of sharing is a recent invention, existing solely as a defence mechanism against an encroaching dog-eat-dog world.

Discrimination and Marginality

It is fortunate that former hunter-gatherers bring with them such a strong ethic into their encounters with more powerful societies. They need all the strength they can muster in countering the attitudes of superiority held by the large majority of their neighbours. Richard Grinker summed up these attitudes in his important paper 'Images of denigration' (1990), documenting the attitudes of Lese farmers towards the Efe Pygmies whose lives they have come to dominate. In Botswana the San, or as they are known locally, the Basarwa, occupy the lowest rungs of the social ladder, whether they live on rural cattle-posts or in peri-urban slums. Observers have been shocked by the depth of the racism expressed by the dominant Tswana towards their Basarwa servants, an attitude tempered, however, by paternalism and occasionally benevolence. Hitchcock has documented the harsh treatment, including beatings and torture, of Basarwa hunters suspected of game law infractions (2002). Similar patterns are reported for the Twa of Rwanda who suffered grievously at the hands of the Hutu militias during the massacres of 1994 (Lewis, this volume).

As Justin Kenrick notes, farming people look down on the Pygmies, who for their part are willing to 'put on poverty', that is to conform to the image expected of them, in order to get favours from their more powerful neighbours. They liken this behaviour to the dissimulation required in hunting. In the forest however they can reassert their autonomy and humanity. This attitude is reflected as well among the Namibian Ju/'hoansi, where peoples of the interior carried on a mutually lucrative trade with riverine Bantu-speaking farmers, exchanging desert products like furs and ostrich eggshell beadwork for ironware, ceramics, and tobacco. When asked whether they addressed their trading partners as equals or as 'Masters' one experienced Ju/'hoan trader replied, 'I would call him anything he wants, as long as he gave me good value for my furs!'

Kenrick, citing Woodburn (1997), sums up the forms of discrimination experienced by Central African hunter-gatherers as involving negative stereotyping, a denial of their rights, and segregation. Despite the flexibility of ethnicity in many parts of Africa, hunter-gatherers seem to be particularly stigmatised by farmers and herders, epitomised in the extreme by the example of the BaTwa of Rwanda. Despite being numerically small and politically unthreatening, the BaTwa, in the 1994 Rwandan genocide, suffered a disproportionately high rate of loss at the hands of ethnic cleansers (Lewis and Knight 1995: 93).

Their stigmatised status is often used as a justification for the denial of rights. Although this denial of rights is widely contested by Forest Peoples themselves and their allies, their subordinate status makes them squatters in their own territories. Denied rights to the land they hunt and gather over and 'are freely, even casually, dispossessed of the land by agricultural and pastoral people' (Woodburn 1997: 350). It must be added however that these acts of discrimination mirror precisely the acts of dispossession and even genocide, so freely practiced by Europeans colonialists on five continents in the eighteenth and nineteenth centuries. And elsewhere in the current post-foraging world there are many examples of indigenous peoples and their allies challenging discrimination successfully in the courts, the media, and in political arenas (Dean and Levi 2003; Lee 2003).

Post-Foragers and the Future

The foregoing has revealed a complex picture of alternate pathways and outcomes as hunter-gatherers travel the road from being, even to a degree, masters in their own houses, to the contemporary conditions of encapsulation. We have seen how encapsulation is a process not an end point, and how – in spite of pressures from the outside – former foragers and peoples like them do manage to adhere to a set of values that emphasizes sharing and egalitarianism.

These values do not prevent outsiders from taking advantage of them or engaging in sharp dealing. Perhaps even more serious than the reported cases of outright aggression against foragers, are the longer-term and more insidious injuries of class. Although not addressed directly by the papers in these volumes, the social and physical harm done by alcohol abuse is probably a greater threat to the well-being of twenty-first-century foragers than the beatings of game wardens. Unfortunately, the successful Baka pygmy entrepreneurs described by Koehler (this volume) are the exception rather than the rule for African post-foragers. And the over-consumption of alcohol and other substances is well-documented for aboriginal peoples in Canada, Australia, Siberia, and elsewhere.

Despite incorporation at the lowest rung of the social ladder, foraging people do bring certain strengths to their encounters with the wider world. Against this ongoing discrimination there are some powerful countervailing forces. In his contribution to this volume Justin Kenrick enjoins his fellow anthropologists to follow the example of James Woodburn and combine their anthropology with political work on behalf of indigenous peoples. It is clear that many if not most of the authors have already made this commitment. The politics of engagement are part of a larger trend. As foraging peoples enter wider arenas they are the beneficiaries of a rising tide of positive awareness in the global public consciousness of the concept of the 'Indigenous'. It is under the banner of 'Indigenous Peoples' that the diverse peoples represented in these volumes will make their futures and find their niches. Whatever uneasiness anthropologists may have about the term, what it implies and who it applies to, the fact remains that politically and socially, nationally and internationally, the concept of indigenous has become a powerful tool. After centuries of negative stereotyping, images of denigration that still persist in pockets, being recognised as indigenous has become an avenue for entitlement, enfranchisement, and empowerment. I would argue that the very existence of these two volumes on 'Property and Equality' attests to the power that the significance of these peoples exerts on at least one segment of the global intelligentsia.

If indeed a breakthrough has occurred, it has been achieved by the dint of efforts by countless individuals and collectivities of indigenous peoples around the world, providing for formerly oppressed peoples, a 'seat at the table' in negotiations with governments over land rights, compensation packages, and acknowledgement of past wrongs. Increasingly indigenous groups are setting their own agendas in ways that discomfit elites and make them squirm in the glare of unfavourable publicity, what Niezen has labelled 'the politics of embarrassment.' Land invasions, roadblocks, and guerrilla theatre send messages that official spin-doctors find difficult to counter. Continuing media and human rights scrutiny makes the costs of state suppression unacceptably high. In this process sympathetic outsiders have an ongoing role to play. Media workers, human rights activists, and like-minded anthropologists thus play the important role of bearing witness.

This volume offers a rich harvest of ideas about the how former foragers have maintained some of their social integrity and have adhered to their deeply-held codes of sharing and egalitarianism. It is still an open question whether the diverse peoples covered here will find ways to recover from the wounds suffered by the process of encapsulation and domination. Yet in paper after paper there were signs for some optimism. The papers also suggest that anthropologists have something to offer to indigenous groups, not just as observers, but as allies and advocates in finding ways of finding their futures in a commodified world.

If governments claiming legitimacy are going to pay more than lipservice to democracy and human rights, they will have to acknowledge indigenous claims. Right of prior occupation is a powerful judicial principle that lies at the heart of capitalist land tenure. The primary story presented here is how indigenous people are connected to the land; how indigenous people are living in cultures that are profoundly non-capitalist, and how their on-going existence bears witness that even in this hard-bitten age of real-politik and globalisation, other ways of being, other ways of living in the world are possible.

Acknowledgements

I wish to thank Robert Hitchcock and Megan Biesele for their insightful discussions of the issues raised here. Thanks are due as well to Axel Thoma, Maitseo Bolaane, Tom Patterson, Hilary Cunningham, Nicolas Peterson, Renee Sylvain and Thomas Widlok for their insights into the changing worlds of indigenous people in southern Africa and elsewhere.

References

Abler, T. 1992. 'Scalping, Torture, Cannibalism and Rape: an Ethnohistoric Analysis of Conflicting Cultural Values'. *Anthropologica*, 34: 3–20.

Barwick, D. 1980. 'The Aboriginal Family in South-eastern Australia'. In: J. Krupinski and A. Stoller (eds), *The family in Australia*. Sydney: Pergamon Press.

Bicchieri, M. 1972. *Hunters and Gatherers Today*. New York: Holt, Rinehart and Winston.

Boas, F. 1966. *Kwakitl Ethnography*. Ed. By Helen Codere. Chicago: University of Chicago Press.

Bird David, N. 1990. 'The Giving Environment: Another Perspective on the Economic System of Gatherer-hunters'. *Current Anthropology*, 31: 183-96.

Collier, J. 1988. *Marriage and Inequality in Classless Societies*. Stanford: Stanford University Press.

Daly, Richard H. 1999. 'Witsuwit'en and Gitxsan'. In: Richard B. Lee and Richard H. Daly (eds), *The Cambridge Encyclopedia of Hunters and Gatherers*, pp. 71–75. Cambridge and New York: Cambridge University Press.

Dean, B. and L. Jerome (eds) 2003. *At the Risk of being Heard: Identity, Indigenous Rights and Post-Colonial States*. Ann Arbor: University of Michigan Press.

Donald, L. 1984. 'The Slave Trade on the Northwest Coast of North America'. *Researches in Economic Anthropology*, 6: 121–58.

—— 1997. *Aboriginal Slavery on the Northwest Coast of North America*. Berkeley: University of California Press.

Endicott, K. 1988. 'Property, Power and Conflict among the Batek of Malaysia'. In: T. Ingold et. al. (eds), *Hunters and Gatherers: Volume 1: History. Evolution and Social Change*, pp. 110–27. Oxford: Berg Publishers.

Foster-Carter, A. 1978. 'The Modes of Production Controversy'. *New Left Review*, 107: 44–77.
Friedl, E. 1975. *Women and Men: An Anthropologist's View.* New York: Holt, Rinehart and Winston.
Gardner, P. 2000. *The Paliyan: Persistent Hunter-gatherers of South India.* Lewiston and Toronto: Edwin Mellen Press.
Grinker, R.R. 1990. 'Images of Denigration: Structuring Inequality between Foragers and Farmers in the Ituri Forest, Zaire'. *American Ethnologist*, 17: 111–30.
Hiatt, L. 1982. *Traditional Attitudes to Land Resources. In Aboriginal Sites, Rights and Resource Development.* In: R.M. Berndt (ed.), pp. 13–26. Perth: University of Western Australia Press.
Hitchcock, R. and M. Biesele. 2002. 'Central Kalahari Game Reserve. I. Political and Human Rights'. In: R.B. Lee, R. Hitchcock and M. Biesele (eds), 'The Kalahari San: Self-determination in the desert'. Special Issue of *Cultural Survival Quarterly*, 25: 19–22.
Ingold, T. 1999. 'On the Social Relations of the Hunter-gatherer Band'. In: R.B. Lee and R.H. Daly (eds), *The Cambridge Encyclopedia of Hunters and Gatherers*, pp. 399–410. Cambridge and New York: Cambridge University Press.
Ingold, T., D. Riches and J. Woodburn. 1988a. *Hunters and Gatherers: Volume 1: History. Evolution and Social Change.* Oxford: Berg Publishers.
Ingold, T., D. Riches and J. Woodburn. 1988b. *Hunters and Gatherers: Volume 2: Property Power and Ideology.* Oxford: Berg Publishers.
Kelly, R.L. 1995. *The Foraging Spectrum: Diversity in Hunter-gatherer Lifeways.* Washington: Smithsonian Institution Press.
Leacock, E. 1978. 'The Status of Women in Social Evolutionary Perspective'. *Current Anthropology*, 19(2): 247–75.
—— 1982. *Myths of Male Dominance.* New York: Monthly Review of Books.
Lee, R.B. and I. Devore (eds). 1968. *Man the Hunter.* Chicago: Aldine Publishing.
—— 1969. 'Eating Christmas in the Kalahari'. *Natural History*, 14–22: 60–63.
—— 1979. *The !Kung San: Men Women and Work in a Foraging Society.* Cambridge and New York: Cambridge University Press.
—— 1982. 'Politics Sexual and Non-sexual in an Egalitarian Society'. In: E. Leacock and R. Lee (eds) *Politics and History in Band Societies.* Cambridge: Cambridge University Press.
—— 1988. 'Reflections on Primitive Communism'. In: T. Ingold et al. (eds), *Hunters and Gatherers: Volume 1: History. Evolution and Social Change*, pp. 200–216. London: Berg Publishers,.
—— 1990. 'Primitive Communism and the Origin of Social Inequality'. In: S. Upham (ed.), *The Evolution of Political Systems: Sociopolitics in Small-scale Sedentary Societie*, pp. 225–46. Cambridge: Cambridge University Press.
—— and R.H. Daly (eds). 1999. *The Cambridge Encyclopedia of Hunters and Gatherers.* Cambridge and New York: Cambridge University Press.
—— 2002. 'Solitude or Servitude? Ju/'hoan Images of the Colonial Encounter'. In: S. Kent (ed.), *Ethnicity and Hunter-Gatherers: Association or Assimilation*, pp. 178-96. Washington: Smithsonian Institution Press,.
—— 2003. 'Human Rights and Indigenous People in Post Apartheid South Africa'. In: B. Dean and J. Levi (eds), *At the Risk of Being Heard: Identity, Indigenous Rights and Post-Colonial States.* Ann Arbor: University of Michigan Press.
Lévi-Strauss, C. 1949. *Les Structures Elémentaires de la Parenté.* Paris: Presses Universitaires de France.
Lewis, J. 2000. *The Batwa Pygmies of the Great Lakes Region: The Problem of Discrimination.* London: Minority Rights Group Report.
Lewis, J. and J. Knight. 1995. *The Twa of Rwanda: Assessment of the Situation of the Twa and Promotion of Twa Rights in Post-War Rwanda.* Copenhagen, World. Rainforest Movement and IWGIA.
MacDonald, G. 2000. 'Economies and Personhood: Demand Sharing among the Wiradjuri of New South Wales'. In: G. Wenzel, G. Hovelsrud-Broda and N. Kishigami (eds), *The Social Economy of Sharing: Resource Allocation and Modern Hunter-gatherers*, pp. 87–112. Osaka: Senri Ethnological Studies No. 53.

Marquardt, W. 1988. 'Politics and Production among the Calusa of South Florida'. In: T. Ingold, D. Riches and J. Woodburn (eds), *Hunters and Gatherers, Volume 1: History, Evolution and Social Change,* pp. 161–88. Oxford: Berg Publishers.
Mauss, M. 1954. *The Gift.* London: Cohen and West.
Mauss, M. and H. Beuchat. 1979. *Seasonal variations of the Eskimo: a study in social morphology.* Trans. J. Fox. London: Routledge [French original: Essais sur les variations saisonieres des societes Eskimos: etude de morphologie sociale. *L'Annee Sociologique* 9: 39–132].
Mitchell, D. and Leland D. 1985. 'Some economic aspects of Tlingit, Haida, and Tsimshian slavery'. *Research in Economic Anthropology,* 7: 19–35.
Morgan, L.H. 1881. *Houses and house-life of the American aborigines. Contributions to North American Ethnology,* Vol. IV. Washington, DC: Government Printing Office.
Peterson, N. and T. Matsuyama (eds). 1991. *Cash, Commoditisation and Changing Foragers.* Osaka (National Museum of Ethnology): Senri Ethnological Studies 30.
Peterson, N. and J. Taylor. 2001. 'The modernising of the indigenous Australian moral economy: sharing, accumulation and household composition'. Paper presented at the Workshop on Power and Property Max Planck Institute, Halle Germany, June 2001.
Price, T. and J. Brown. 1985. *Prehistoric Hunter-gatherers: The Emergence of Social Complexity.* Orlando: Academic Press.
Rival, L. 1999. 'Introduction: South America'. In: R.B. Lee and R.H. Daly (eds), *The Cambridge Encyclopedia of Hunters and Gatherers,* pp. 77–85. Cambridge and New York: Cambridge University Press.
Sahlins, M. 1965. 'On the Sociology of Primitive Exchange'. In: Michael Banton (ed.), *The Relevance of Models in Social Anthropology.* London: Tavistock.
Sansom, B. 1980. *The Camp at Wallaby Cross: Aboriginal Fringe Dwellers in Darwin.* Canberra: Australian Institute of Aboriginal Studies.
Schrire, C. (ed.). 1984. *Past and Present in Hunter-gatherer Studies.* Orlando: Academic Press.
Testart, A. 1985. *Le Communisme Primitif.* Paris: Presses Universitaires de France.
Trigger, D. 1992. *Whitefella Comin': Aboriginal Responses to Colonialism in Northern Australia.* Cambridge: Cambridge University Press.
Turnbull, C. 1965. *Wayward Servants: The Two Worlds of the African Pygmies.* Garden City: Natural History Press.
Webster's. 1976. *Dictionary of the American Language.* Cleveland: Wm. Collins and World Publishing.
Widlok, T. 1999. *Living on Mangetti: 'Bushman' Autonomy and Namibian Independence.* Oxford and New York: Oxford University Press.
Wenzel, G., G. Hovelsrud-Broda and N. Kishigami (eds). 2000. *The Social Economy of Sharing: Resource Allocation and Modern Hunter-gatherers.* Osaka: Senri Ethnological Studies No. 53. pp 87–112.
Woodburn, J. 1980. 'Hunters and Gatherers Today and Reconstruction of the Past'. In: E. Gellner (ed.), *Soviet and Western Anthropology,* pp. 95–117. London: Duckworth.
—— 1982. 'Egalitarian Societies'. *Man,* 17: 431–51.
—— 1988. 'African Hunter-gatherer Social Organization: is it Best Understood as a Product of Encapsulation?'. In: T. Ingold, D. Riches and J. Woodburn (eds), *Hunters and Gatherers Volume 1: History, Evolution and Social Change.* Oxford: Berg Publishers.

2

Money Makes the World Go Round? Commodity Sharing, Gifting and Exchange in the Baka (Pygmy) Economy

Axel Köhler

Introduction

Sociological and historical research on money has often suggested that an all-purpose medium of payment and exchange works as a catalyst for modernisation and that its introduction into premodern societies engenders particularly radical social and cultural transformations. The spread of Western capitalism together with colonisation has been blamed, in particular for the devaluation and destruction of precolonial, indigenous orders. Moving beyond a polarised and simplified moralising of commoditisation as either destructive or, at the other extreme, as rationalising and liberating, this chapter argues for a culturally and historically specific dynamic from an actor-centred perspective.

My ethnographic focus here is on Baka people, a Li-Baka-speaking ethnic minority better known in the literature and locally by the derogatory term 'Pygmies'. I conducted fieldwork in the northwest of the Republic of Congo in a region bordering Cameroon, where 3,000–4,000 Baka live in neighbourly relations with approximately 20,000 members of different Bantu-speaking groups. In this chapter I want to show that in Baka thought and practice neither money nor commodities appear to carry intrinsically alien ideas. Looking at the way Baka handle both, I will argue that they have indeed ingeniously appropriated and adapted them to their own cultural understandings and social purposes.

Baka, like other Pygmy groups, have a long history of participation in Central African trading networks, usually as specialised providers of ivory and other forest produce in return for cultivated food, salt and iron tools. Their integration into modern markets began with the Atlantic trade which ushered into an era of unprecedented economic transformations and social upheaval as its influence gradually spread into the African interior (Klieman 1999). Until a few decades ago, Baka involvement in markets had been mediated by Bantu' or other non-Pygmy neighbours and was not characterised by a linear and progressive history of commoditisation; rather, it went through phases of varying intensity. Contrary to still popular stereotypes of isolated, conservative and shy forest populations, one can assert that Baka market behaviour has often been voluntary and proactive.

European currencies were introduced into the Baka area of southern Cameroon and northwestern Congo during the colonial period, that is, from the late nineteenth century onwards. Baka assimilation of these currencies was preceded, however, by their assimilation of regionally used precolonial African iron currencies. These appear once to have been limited to the sphere of bridewealth exchanges, but entered into increasingly less specialised circulation with the gradual expansion of the Atlantic trade, before they finally became obsolete in the twentieth century (see Vincent 1963; Guyer 1986, 1993).

At the beginning of the twentieth century, when colonial demand for ivory reached its peak, the Baka, too, were exchanging bridewealth among themselves transacting mainly tusks and heavy metal objects in addition to performing brideservice. The importance of ivory as an item of exchange also encouraged polygyny among Baka master hunters, and some of them even married a number of Bantu wives. Today this kind of interethnic union is almost unheard of. Due to overhunting, forest elephant populations declined rapidly after 1905 and with them ivory production for export (Stoecker 1986: 72). By the 1920s and 1930s, the French government finally decided to take over its possessions in equatorial Africa from the previous concessionary regime of private trading companies, and to establish the infrastructure for a far-reaching colonial transformation of local economies (Coquery-Vidrovitch 1972; Austen and Headrick 1983). In 1933, the colonial administration launched the so-called 'taming policy' for Pygmies, which was designed as a watered-down version of the measures enforced upon the Bantu population. Its main socioeconomic objectives were to concentrate the scarce forest population in villages along newly constructed roads, to introduce cash-cropping and to create a readily available labour force. Initially these policies had little direct influence on the Pygmy population, whose Bantu neighbours were bearing the brunt (Delobeau 1984).

From the 1950s and 1960s onwards, however, Baka integration into an expanding postcolonial cash and commodity economy accelerated with their proactive sedentarisation in roadside villages and their participation in a then booming cocoa cash-crop production. The 1970s and 1980s saw the emergence of some independent Baka cocoa planters, first in the Sembé District

(Guillot 1977: 161) and later also in Souanké. The majority of Baka, however, still worked in a variety of labour arrangements with Bantu patrons or procured a semi-autonomous subsistence. Until the Congolese state cocoa marketing board went into liquidation in the mid-1980s, there was an increasing influx of cash into the region that also benefited the Baka. Since then local populations at large have reverted more or less to a subsistence economy, and the limited opportunities to earn cash money are found in gold digging, ivory hunting, and a local market for agricultural products and bushmeat. Baka participate in these activities both independently and in the services of Muslim traders and Bantu farmers.

In order to elucidate previous and current Baka forms of engagement with money and commodities, it is useful to draw on the analytical distinctions that have been elaborated for different 'local economic models' as Gudeman (1986: vii) calls them. What Woodburn (1982) conceptualised as the 'competitive egalitarianism' of tribal societies versus a 'noncompetitive egalitarianism' of band societies, and Bird-David (1990, 1992) distinguished as 'gifting' versus 'giving', are socioeconomic categories that can roughly be mapped onto the differences between Bantu and Baka. Bird-David (1990), in particular, suggested a third type of economy, found in hunting-and-gathering societies and distinct from both commodity and gift economies. What she calls a 'cosmic economy of sharing' refers to an unbounded extension of egalitarian exchange and encompasses the totality of economic and social involvement with the world including, in particular, nonhuman agents such as plants and animals. As Ingold (1986) points out, sharing is an 'experience' rather than a behavioural code or a rule of prescriptive altruism and covers both the distributive aspect of 'sharing out' and 'the principle of unbounded inclusion' in productive and consumptive 'sharing in' (1986: 113–17, 239).

How do these three models articulate in Baka economics and how does sharing fit with both the gifting practices of their Bantu neighbours and the commodity exchanges favoured by Muslim traders? Let me elucidate the interweaving of these models and a context-dependent and flexible Baka adaptation of them by giving a number of ethnographic examples.

Commoditisation and the Impact of Money

Money often serves as an instrument for an expanding market or is an index of it rather than constituting its cause. However, it has time and again been credited with an intrinsic revolutionary force and the power to effect profound social and cultural transformations by itself (Bloch and Parry 1989: 3). Simmel (1978 [1907]), for instance, saw money as instrumental in objectifying and depersonalising social relations by bringing about a decrease in interpersonal dependency and an increase in the differentiation of people. He further argued that it expands the circle of trust and acts as a medium of liberation from the constraints of time and space. On the other hand, it carries the seeds of alienation and has the potential to threaten the moral order (Bloch and

Parry 1989: 3–6; Peterson 1991a: 3). Although Simmel's latter-day critics have pointed out that his analysis reproduced a specific set of social constructions, his view of money as a vehicle of modern, 'rational' society certainly strikes a chord with how Baka view and handle money and, particularly, with the symbolic value and ideological role with which they have endowed it. The presence of European money and its quality as an all-purpose medium of payment and exchange, and as a standard and store of value, have undeniably influenced Baka perceptions and practices of exchange. The Baka encounter with European currency was, however, not by way of a one-sided penetration and subversion of local economy and consciousness, nor did it effect a radical and abrupt transformation of social relations. There was, rather, a process of assimilation that occurred over a long period of time spanning the late precolonial, colonial and early postcolonial eras. Significant events and developments can be identified with each of these historical phases.

Although relatively inaccessible even in the heyday of the Atlantic trade, the peoples in this area of the Congolese panhandle were not living as self-sufficient communities in splendid isolation. Interethnic networks established connections to the Atlantic trade and the inner Congo Basin trade and were the agents of a progressive expansion of modern markets that gathered momentum during the nineteenth century. A growing deployment of indigenous iron currencies and an increasing commoditisation of local products and services fall precisely into that historical period. A corollary of these interlocking processes is that the rationality of money, its potential as a repository of wealth and as a measure of value, and the idea of investment with incremental interest (through gifting), were not intrinsically alien concepts that had to be implanted from outside, but had rather developed in step with ever-widening exchange relations.

The problems with the introduction of European money in colonial times lay not in a 'primitive', irrational mentality, nor in a 'tribal', kin-based society or a 'traditional', subsistence-based economy. What local people understandably opposed were the violent conditions under which European money was initially enforced upon them, and with which this type of new money came to be associated: taxation, administration, a foreign work and exchange ethic, and the ruthless exploitation of their labour.

The third phase, which is marked by the assimilation of European money and its active insertion into 'traditional' forms of exchange, coincided with a boom in the cocoa market. Outside of the commercial sphere indigenous iron currencies were rapidly replaced with European money in bridewealth exchanges, once cocoa planting provided an acceptable and respectable form of cash income. Cocoa planting itself had been actively embraced and had expanded mainly through local initiative, although its role and success as a major cash-earner developed in response to state-sponsored marketing opportunities. There was thus an expanding commoditisation of the economy accompanied by a gradual move towards standardisation and monetisation, a process that culminated in the assimilation of European currency.

For a long time Bantu played a buffer role in absorbing and mediating European encroachment. In precolonial times they were the main agents for the exchange of local produce for European commodities, and in colonial times they bore the brunt of the direct exercise of European power and the enforced reordering of local geography, society and economy. Until the early postcolonial phase, Bantu also successfully interceded in affording Baka access to European money once they had begun to value it more positively themselves. It seems that Baka involvement with money proper was connected with the general advance of cocoa cash-cropping and the Baka sedentarisation process. Elsewhere, I have interpreted Baka participation in cocoa production and their move towards settlement as a joint strategy to obtain greater recognition of human equivalence and to actively share in a world concentrated in settlements along roads, including the lifestyle and wealth created there (Köhler 1999). A more widespread circulation of European currency among Baka certainly coincided with this phase that ushered in after Congolese independence. Probably, and seemingly paradoxically, it was also a less controversial process than among local Bantu. Baka earnings in the form of cash money, their independent, first-hand purchase of imported things, and unmediated contacts with foreign traders and the realm of shops are interrelated events that occurred in the less conflictual circumstances of a postcolonial boom time. No wonder that money was rather unambiguously embraced by Baka as one of the features of a desired roadside village life. It was perceived as part of the exchanges taking place in that sphere and particularly associated with the market-places of district centres.

The Credit ('pour bon') System

Early on during fieldwork, I was struck by the existence of a credit system that was in operation within both Bantu and Baka communities, and in exchanges between them. What amazed me most of all was the fluency with which everyone engaged discursively in monetary calculations. This stood in sharp contrast to the apparent absence of money outside of commercial centres. In the beginning, I had the impression that no Baka in an outlying village seemed to carry any cash, nor did I ever see money changing hands there. But sitting in front of the house, my Baka host would comment quietly on those Bantu passing in front of us along the road without greeting us: 'He doesn't greet us, because he knows that he owes me Francs CFA 3,000 for over two years without ever paying anything back!' Others, I was reminded with slight irritation, had 'taken their debt into the grave'. Some Bantu approached, greeted, chatted and then reminded him of a debt, which was also usually calculated in Francs CFA.[2]

Abandoned by his last wife, a Njem man in his fifties lived all by himself in a big house next to the Baka part of the village. He was a good-natured and hard-working man who maintained good relations with a number of Baka villagers. Although his literacy was very limited, he kept a diagram of debtors and their debts upon a wooden window shutter in his kitchen-cum-living-room. With a piece of crayon he marked the names of all the Baka to whom he had extended credit, and the amount of money they owed him.[3] Some debts went into thousands of francs and originated in transactions of tobacco, salt, food, alcohol, cartridges, matches, or whatever he had given in credit for an agreed-upon sum of money which remained fictional because in almost all cases he never got any cash money back. The numerals served mainly as an instrument to evaluate what he had given, and what he would eventually receive or demand in return (labour, meat and honey) was again calculated in Francs CFA and entered into the credit chart on the shutter. Once a group of three Baka men brought him, for instance, a large aluminium basin full of honeycombs that he evaluated at Francs CFA 5,000 after a lengthy discussion. They then told him how much to take off each man's credit balance. He ate some of the honey himself, gave me a little present, and then took the major part to Souanké Town for sale.

Baka also extend credit to Bantu, when they deliver honey, meat, forest medicine, raphia shingles for roofing, or labour without immediate recompense. They hand their products over in mutual agreement to receive money or commodities in return for them later. However, when Baka perform labour with the explicit aim to gain money, or when they deliver a product charging a price for it, they usually have a particular purchase in mind. When they want to obtain a necessity such as salt, batteries, matches, razor blades, clothing, etc., Baka tend to insist on cash or else ask to be paid with the item they are looking for. In general, Baka are therefore not happy as creditors because their credits are often bound up with the satisfaction of immediate or short-term needs, and they talk about uncooperative Bantu debtors as cheaters and liars. Bantu, on the other hand, are quite happy to keep Baka indebted to them, because it gives them a lever to demand labour or some service in return.

Mostly in the village context a common and highly acceptable practice among Baka was that a hunter brought game or honey back from the forest and set aside a portion 'to be sold', before handing over half to three-quarters of the catch to be shared out. This was considered a correct practice, as long as at least half of the produce was shared in an acceptable manner. The hunter could then still receive a portion of the share-out for his own consumption, since he had set aside only a small part of the game for sale. Sometimes those receiving a share would then increase their portion by 'buying' on credit – i.e., without paying – part of what had been singled out for sale. In order to cancel such a debt they would have to act in the same way on another occasion, that is, share out at least half of a game animal, put the other half aside for sale, and then repay from that part a debt previously incurred. In forest camps, I never witnessed this practice in regard to meat, of which particularly the intestines and organs were always shared out and eaten together. The meat that was smoked was usually set aside for absent 'comrades in the village', but not for sale. With honey, however, the parallel practice of part sharing and part commoditisation was common in camps, too.

The market-type sale of products is, however, far more common in Bantu than in Baka villages. An item on sale is usually indicated with a sign hung from a beam of the roof near the main door of a house. Thus an empty litre-bottle stands for strong liquor, pieces of cardboard from the packaging of articles such as cigarettes, batteries, cartridges and matchboxes indicate the brand and the specification of the imports on sale. Other local products, such as smoked meat, manioc sticks or raw plantain bananas, are indicated by displaying a sample on a piece of liana string. Some villagers are also known to regularly sell, for instance, salt or cartridges like in a shop. The sale of most imported commodities on credit is, however, limited by the purchasing power of the seller who needs to recuperate at least the invested capital in order to be able to stock up again.

Pawning of commodities was also common practice among both Bantu and Baka. Notorious alcoholics, in particular, were known to pawn out precious articles such as petroleum lamps, torches, cartridges, or someone else's radio, in order to obtain a few glasses of strong liquor. Like elsewhere the idea of pawning is precisely that the transaction is provisional and constitutes a conditional debt rather than an irrevocable sale, but a problem for Baka is that they may find it difficult to repay the debt in time. It also happens that a Bantu pawnbroker likes to keep the article or wants to cheat and will then simply try to interpret the original deal as a purchase. The problem with pawning among Baka themselves is that most items have a use value that may well decrease over time. One man, for instance, pawned out a pair of second-hand trousers for the hind-leg of a small duiker worth around Francs CFA 500. First, the trousers were worn by the Baka pawnbroker and then one day he threw a pile of his clothing including the pawned item into the fire in the middle of a heated argument with his wife. The trousers were burnt, and that was the end of the affair.

Money and Gender

Muslim traders recounted how Baka only approached their shops in groups. According to their accounts, Baka would slowly advance in line and then stand in the middle of the road at a safe distance from the building, observing carefully the commercial activities going on inside, before the most courageous individual, probably an elder at the top of the queue, would eventually venture into the shop to buy something. From the mid-1970s onwards this attitude gave way to a more relaxed and individual approach, and nowadays Baka men stroll into a shop almost as casually as any Bantu, to buy cigarettes, matches, sweets, wire for snares, etc.

By contrast, Baka women remain fairly shy and prefer to get a man to purchase things for them, so that the shops and the market-place are almost exclusively visited by Baka men. This reticent female attitude to shopping reflects a number of connected factors: Baka women have no work experience with Muslim shop-owners; exceptionally they may work as long-distance porters accompanying a male Baka friend or companion, but this kind of job arrangement, as well as the pay, are usually mediated by the Baka man. Female Baka work and exchange relations are predominantly with Bantu partners and patrons, and for two reasons the emphasis is on kind rather than on money in these exchanges. First, money is an important commodity for Bantu, and its supply has been perceived to be more and more limited in recent times. This makes them reluctant to part with it. Second, Baka women get a better deal when they exchange their labour for raw agricultural food, compared to what they could ask for in money. And their primary exchange goal is to be able to feed their children and their husband. A lot of the Baka planting and seeding stock, especially for new fields, also derives from the Bantu, i.e., new banana shoots, stems from manioc plants and groundnuts.[4] Payment or remuneration in kind rather than in money is thus due to a convergence of both exchange partners' interests. At the same time that Baka can thus ensure sufficient supply of agricultural foods and even engage in their own independent production, it helps Bantu to maintain relations of dependence. For these reasons access of female Baka both to imported items and to money is limited and mediated either by Bantu exchange partners/patrons of both sexes or by Baka men.

Ideally, it is up to a Baka husband to supply meat and honey from the forest and to provide imported consumer items (household wares such as aluminium basins, bowls, plates, dishes, cups and spoons; as well as clothing, salt, soap, canned sardines, etc.) and metal tools such as hoes and machetes for his wife, children and other dependants of his household. Above all, he is in charge of building a house for his own family, and may be asked to build one for his parents-in-law. As brideservice is decreasing in favour of bridewealth, imported consumer items and money are gaining in gifting appeal for bridewealth exchanges over local forest produce such as meat and honey.[5] Indeed, the Li-Baka word for 'bridewealth' also designates 'wealth' and 'goods' in general, 'money' as an abstract concept, 'iron' and other 'metals'.[6] Standard items for the return gifts ('*contre-dot*') presented by the father of the bride are chicken and woven mats. Baka bridewealth transactions are currently reduced in quantity compared to what men claim to have given during the years of the cocoa boom and before the international ban on trade with ivory came into effect. In composition, though not in scale and ostentatiousness, Baka bridewealth transactions resemble Bantu bridewealth transactions before these were largely monetised. And they strangely echo *bilaba* exchanges with their polarity and associated male-female symbolism.[7] In *bilaba* transactions, local produce had a female valence; imported trade items were male (Fernandez 1982: 138).

A Baka wife is expected to provide agricultural staples in addition to gathered produce and, basically, to run the kitchen and to look after her offspring in the village. In contrast to the forest camp she only assists with house-building in the last stages, although these include the very important finishing process of filling in the wall structure with clay. In practice, the ideal complementarity of daily tasks, provisioning and the care of children depends a lot on individual marital arrangements. Nevertheless there is a certain consensus concerning the expectations *vis-à-vis* a marriage partner, and such expectations influence an already gendered pattern of internal Baka exchanges and external Baka exchange negotiations. All these factors play into and reproduce a familiarity with money that is greater among Baka men than women.[8]

Commoditisation, Money and Sharing

Interpreting Aka economy in the early 1980s Bahuchet and Guillaume envisage two separate spheres of production and consumption that exist in the village and the forest respectively. By and large, their distinction corresponds to the polarity drawn up by Turnbull for the Mbuti (1965). In the village sphere, production is dependent and involves personally binding arrangements with village patrons and individually contracted, temporary wage labour employment on plantations, for logging and mining companies, and in saw-mills. With the exception of traded food – still the most likely commodity to be shared to a large extent – the distribution and consumption of what Aka receive in return in manufactured items, alcohol, tobacco and money, tends to be equally atomised in this sphere.

In the forest sphere, on the other hand, the production of meat and other food, both for subsistence and exchange, is independent and often organised in groups, and as long as meat stays in camp for consumption, egalitarian values of sharing are still dominant. Ownership of meat tends to be rather exclusive, however, when it is designated for exchange, and the distribution and consumption of the items traded in for the meat depends on the status of these items. Again, cultivated food is the commodity most likely to be shared beyond the nuclear family (Bahuchet and Guillaume 1982: 208–9).

Among Baka, the forest is likewise the sphere where egalitarian values and sharing reign supreme. Here companionship, friendship and a spirit of *communitas* transcend the neighbourhood feeling and nuclear family householding that impose themselves to some extent in the domestic circumstances of roadside villages. However, I do not want to exaggerate the contrast between forest and village. Production in small task groups, formed beyond household boundaries and according to personal networks, is as common in village agriculture as in forest-related activities. The experience of sharing is of unequivocal value in the forest, but 'for sale' partitioning for target saving is openly and undisputedly practised.[9] Sharing out may be under strain in certain village situations, but it is still accorded a high priority and practised despite domestic conditions that do not in themselves promote a sharing experience. And as much as sharing is under pressure in the village, so is commoditisation in the forest sphere. Both nevertheless coexist in either sphere.

Sharing of unprepared as well as prepared food tends to be more inclusive and open in temporary forest camps than in Baka villages. In villages, demand-sharing and the awareness of a much higher potential number of sharers has made it common practice for people to eat in small groups of core household members inside houses, and primary sharing is rather more specific than in camps. However, secondary sharing out by those who benefited in the first round makes in the end for wider distribution, and there is no question about including anyone staying as a visitor. Women cook in their respective kitchens inside the house – rather than on open, shared fires as is common practice in forest camps – and it is very unusual to send plates of prepared food across households in the village. I shall sketch sharing practices for the most common commodities to make the point.

Money is not shared out as such, but the things it buys generally are. The prevalent Baka ethic is to use money for consumption, and demand-sharing as well as a preference for direct need satisfaction prevent accumulation beyond target saving for particular consumer items. Highly valued articles such as clothing, battery-operated torches, batteries, kerosene lamps, radio-cassette machines, cassettes, etc. are clearly identified as belonging to someone. With the exception of clothing, a man usually owns these things, but individual ownership does not prevent their use and possession from being widely shared on demand. Clothing is often shared between a man and his wife, but also between close friends, especially those sharing what is called *kendi* or 'special friendship'. Clothes are often passed down to younger ones and spend the last stages of their lives on children.

The iron parts (that is, the blades) of basic tools such as hoes, knives and axes, and spearheads are essential means of production that are forged by local Bantu smiths from scrap metal. The shafts and handles are produced by Baka themselves. These iron utensils are widely available, and the tools made with them are usually personal property. They are, however, often left lying around in the house and its surroundings, and their use is unproblematically shared.

A prevailing sharing ethos concerning tools and consumer items is even more pronounced when it comes to guns, one of the most important and most expensive means of production. A Baka-owned gun is lent out or 'shared in' by virtually all Baka hunters in the village and beyond. Cartridges are rarely shared, but the meat produced with them usually comes again within the sharing sphere, unless it is too small.[10] A cartridge can, for instance, be handed over to a hunter going into the forest, but it is the 'owner' of the cartridge who can set aside a part 'for sale' by himself and who has the right to designate a person to partition the rest of the game being brought back. The one who shot the game and the owner of the gun – should he be present – both have a share in the spoils. Indeed, a Bantu rule of reserving a leg of any game shot with a borrowed gun for its owner is mostly respected with Bantu gun owners, but is not taken as a template for inter-Baka lending operations.[11]

Wire for snaring is available in shops in Souanké Town, but is also sold by ambulant traders and passed on in other ways.[12] Friends, brothers and brothers-in-law can set up snare-lines together, but wire can also be borrowed, since it is reuseable. In any case, the person who sets the snare counts as the hunter of the game irrespective of who lent him the wire and who went to check the snare and collect the trapped animal. Unlike cartridges, which con-fer rights over the game unless they have been gifted or given away unconditionally, wire is conceptually and practically situated in between guns and iron tools. The borrower of snare-wire will negotiate the conditions with the lender, who will most likely be promised and receive something in return. A share in the produce depends, however, on the wire lender's presence, and even then he is more likely to receive in accordance with general sharing rules rather than be prioritised. In a similar way, the lender of an axe has no more claim on the honey achieved with it than others, despite the fact that it was with his axe that the companion cut down the tree and got to the bees' hive.

Baka do not gamble, neither with money – as has been reported for Australian Aborigines – nor with scarce local objects, as is common among the Hadza of Tanzania.[13] Among Baka relatively large sums of money do come in irregularly as a result of big-game hunting. They are usually redistributed or shared out in unceremonious but conspicuous consumption, which takes the form of either gifting or sharing. Part of the money serves to purchase imported items, which are either stored and channelled into bridewealth transactions or shared out among relatives and friends. Distribution among affinal relatives is, however, likely to be perceived as a form of gifting rather than sharing, i.e., as part of a life-long mutual involvement in continuous bridewealth transactions. Once distributed, consumer items can then enter into wider circulation and use within the village community.

Among Baka, big money earners are exclusively men, and nowadays particularly great hunters. When money for an ivory transaction with a patron finally comes in, they have a penchant for going on extravagant, alcohol-fuelled spending sprees that last until all the money is gone – usually to the dismay of their wives and other interested women. These drinking bouts also involve predominantly men. The alcohol is bought by the hunter who earned the money or by members of his team, when the head of the team has distributed the earnings among them. Drinks are then mostly shared out indiscriminately to everyone present or to those demanding a share. The alcohol-selling Bantu will most likely benefit in addition to the commercial profit he or she is making by starting to cheat, once the party is sufficiently drunk and the principal spenders have lost touch with the purchasing power of their money.

To give an idea of the ways in which great hunters spend big money I shall present four cases. The first is based on a shortened account given by the hunter himself, the second is a story recounted by a couple of the hunter's village neighbours and companions, and the last two are based on my own observations.

1. In the late 1980s, a Baka hunter in his early twenties inherited a gun from his successful elephant-hunting elder brother, when the latter died in a violent hunting accident. In a subsequent ivory sale in Cameroon, the young Baka hunter claimed to have received a sum of Francs CFA 50,000. Having not only inherited the gun, but also taking care of the deceased brother's wife and their infant child, he gave the widow half of

the money. With the remaining Francs CFA 25,000 he went to town, bought himself a set of new clothes and then spent the rest in a bar where he 'had a good time' (*faire la fête* was the French expression he used).

2. In the early 1990s, a successful elephant hunter in his late forties nicknamed Renault (after the French carmaker and for being as steady and solid as one of their trucks) had reportedly received Francs CFA 70,000 plus a gift of ten litres of local liquor, a goat and some chickens from an exceptionally 'good' Bantu patron.[14] He was thus remunerated for a solid 'head' – a matching set of ivory tusks – weighing 18 kg and 19 kg respectively, for which the patron himself must have received between Francs CFA 148,000 and 185,000. Without distributing any of the money to his wife or hunting companions, Renault said that he wanted to go and see his sister in another village. With all the money in his pocket[15] he stopped in '*L'Escale du Marché*', the only bar then operating in Souanké Town, and started to drink. Renault generously began to pay rounds and was later presented with a totally overpriced bill by the notoriously shrewd Fang owner of the bar. When he came home later that night, he had only Francs CFA 20,000 left. He gave a few thousand Francs CFA each to his hunting companions and the rest to his wife.
3. An old *tuma* ('great hunter' or 'master hunter') and his son, both from the Lomié area in neighbouring Cameroon, had followed a Njem patron across the border to Djampouo, the latter's home village north of Souanké Town. There they had teamed up with a local Baka man, and the newly formed trio then continued elephant hunting for the same patron. Out on one of their missions they found the skeleton of an elephant. The animal had been wounded, but had got away and then died on its own. Thus the hunter had not managed to recover the ivory. The lucky trio decided against handing the two tusks over to their patron, because they were not satisfied with previous remunerations. Instead they took the two tusks – weighing around 12 kg each – to a Muslim trader in order to sell them on their own account. They asked for Francs CFA 55,000, but the trader got them down to 40,000, of which they were to receive 10,000 in cash and 30,000 in merchandise. According to the trader's experience, Baka 'prefer merchandise to money'. He gave them an advance payment of CFA 2,000, because they wanted to buy some food. The arrangement was that they would come back discreetly at night to make their choice of goods and to receive the rest of the money. They got completely drunk on local liquor, and further transactions had to be postponed. The day after, they selected a battery-operated torch, five batteries, a big and a small aluminium basin, one small rucksack, two purses, two hats, three pairs of plastic sandals, two bottles of skin cream, three bottles of perfume and five standard cartridges. The trader gave them the remaining value of Francs CFA 12,000 in cash and another five standard cartridges as a present. The sandals and hats the trio put on themselves. The torch and the cartridges they used for their next hunt; the cosmetics, the basins and some of the money they gave to their wives.

4. Djokàmba Jeannot, also known as Metoul, the headman of the Baka village Bethel, is my last, most sober example. In Souanké District he was one the most, if not *the* most respected *tuma* of the younger generation, men in their thirties and early forties. In early 1994, Metoul received a few provisions and two bullets from a young Bakwele man, to go hunting with a Yugoslavian-made 458 rifle that a former patron had left in Metoul's possession. By then, such bullets were rare to come by and rather expensive (around Francs CFA 5,000 a piece for 'originals' made in the USA), but this kind of rifle had the reputation of being the supreme weapon for big game. The hunt was successful in a very short time, and the two men simply divided the result, a small 'head' of around 20 kg. The Bantu managed to get Francs CFA 15,000 and goods worth another Francs CFA 15,000 (trousers, batteries and cloth) from a well-disposed Muslim trader. Metoul went to see another Muslim trader stationed at a nearby outlet for the local gold mine and known among the Muslim community and the local Bantu alike for cheating with the gold scales. After some discussion, Metoul converted his tusk into basic consumer items worth precisely Francs CFA 18,900. He got a box of standard cartridges that he kept in his house and handed out from whenever a hunter from his village was in need of ammunition and went out to shoot something 'for the village'. He also obtained two pieces of cloth that he gave to his wife and a widowed sister of his brother-in-law's wife. Of two pairs of plastic sandals Metoul kept one for himself and the other he gave to a divorced 'clan-sister' whom he had taken under his protection. She was the illegitimate child of a man belonging to the same clan as Metoul's mother. Being the child of a classificatory maternal uncle Metoul also referred to her as his 'mother'. Last but not least, he gave three glasses of salt to his wife and arranged a treatment of penicillin worth Francs CFA 2,000 for the wife of a half-brother who suffered from a skin disease.

What comes out in the first two stories is the primacy accorded to the money and the spontaneous tendency to have a good time and to get drunk. At the same time, there is a desire to be recognised among the Bantu as a big spender and someone of value. Supported by other experience, the last two stories bring home a prevailing emphasis on social values, careful provisioning and redistribution in Baka handling of sudden concentrations of wealth.

Money and the Mental Economy

Since the decline of the cocoa market in the mid-1980s and, subsequently, of the means of transport and communications, the local economy has reverted largely to subsistence and simple commodity exchanges. Money is perceived to be in short supply, and people used to say that it had gone 'back to its producers'.[16] The potential of money as a motor or catalyst of economic and social change became therefore increasingly limited. However, the money-based credit calculations that continued in the absence of actually monetised exchange betray the considerable cognitive impact of money and its morally and emotionally ambivalent ramifications, much as Simmel (1978 [1907]) has suggested.[17]

Recently, however, monetisation of exchanges has been judged by some anthropologists as unambiguously positive both for the mental and the material economy. The claim is that money promotes rationality and provides the key to the realisation of latent economic potential. Bourdieu describes it as the demystifying transformer of the 'good-faith economy':

> The generalization of monetary exchange, which exposes the objective workings of the economy, also brings to light the institutional mechanisms, proper to the archaic economy, which have the function of limiting and disguising the play of economic interest and calculation. (1977: 172)

According to Kopytoff (1986), commodity exchange exists in all societies to a variable extent and depending on the development of the exchange technology. He stresses:

> a drive inherent in every exchange system toward optimum commoditization – the drive to extend the fundamentally seductive idea of exchange [...] Hence the universal acceptance of money whenever it has been introduced into non-monetized societies and its inexorable conquest of the internal economy of these societies, regardless of initial rejection and of individual unhappiness about it [...] Hence also the uniform results of the introduction of money in a wide range of otherwise different societies: more extensive commoditization and the merger of the separate spheres of exchange. It is as if the internal logic of exchange itself pre-adapts all economies to seize upon the new opportunities that wide commoditization so obviously brings with it. (1986: 72)

The Baka habit of making monetary calculations of credit and debt in the physical absence of money, or simply without actually making use of it, seems to confirm these statements. By contrast, the Baka practice of simultaneous and complementary pricing and sharing of one and the same product is rather curious, contradictory and open to conflicting interpretations. It could well be the sign of an advance of economic rationality and of a revelation of economic interest and calculation. Interpreted in this way, this practice would conform to the presently achieved stage in a development described by a Kopytoff as a drive 'toward optimum commoditization' and a merging of 'separate spheres of exchange'. In other words, it would indicate the incipient fusion of an internal Baka sharing 'experience' and an external rationality of market exchange or, at least, their mutual accommodation. There may be a certain truth in this interpretation, but a more actor-centred perspective focuses rather on the form of concrete practices than on the logic of abstract economics.[18]

From such a perspective, the complementarity of Baka economic practices clearly points to an active maintenance of the heterogeneous value of objects.

Despite a physical and spiritual encroachment of markets and money, and a concomitant incentive to homogenise the value of things, the distinct internal value of Baka forest products continues to be appreciated according to their own cultural and social motivations. The point is not that Baka sharing practices remain uninfluenced and unmodified in a changing world. This would indeed be rather improbable given their currently more sedentary circumstances and their consumer and producer interests developing in response to market opportunities and the wider socioeconomic milieu of which they form a part. The point is that in the mid-1990s, Baka were in a position to control the destination of their products according to their own designs and were not coerced either by external conditions or by the compelling rationality of money and markets onto the highway to commoditisation, as predicted by neoclassical economic theory. Baka were accommodating the logic of a market economy just as they did the logic of reciprocity and gifting underlying the economic practices of their Bantu neighbours. A Baka concept of essential humanity emphasises exchange as an intrinsic, constitutive feature of society. This qualitative 'local economic model' of society, to use Gudeman's expression (1986: vii), predicates social engagement upon mutual 'help' and 'assistance', but does not rule out the quantification of such mutuality in some contexts of exchange.

Baka forest produce of meat and honey are 'priceless' consumer goods as well as prized and priced commodities. The treatment of meat and honey as objects for marketing, gifting and sharing therefore seems to attest to the persistence of a Baka logic of complementary integration. The same is true for forest products gathered by women and children, such as snails, caterpillars, mushrooms, *jekè* fruits (*Irvingia gabonensis*) and certain leaves, for instance *kɵ̀kɵ̀* (*Gnetum africanum* and *Gnetum buchholzianum*), appreciated by both Baka and Bantu, but purveyed largely by Baka women and their children. Underlying this continued appreciation of the complexity of value is, in my view, a good understanding of the 'guises' of their own 'archaic' economy of giving/sharing and that of their reciprocating neighbours,[19] as well as a good grip on the workings of Bourdieu's 'undisguised self-interest' economy (1977: 172). This is evident in the active application of their respective rationalities according to merit and situational context. Although money enters into internal Baka distribution, the unchecked penetration of its rationality is curbed by a continuing respect for the experience of sharing.

I believe that current Baka economic practices demonstrate an understanding and appreciation of the different kinds of economic rationality, which comes out most clearly in internal spheres of production, distribution and consumption and when not under pressure from external power configurations. In the prevailing circumstances of a wider regional economic recession, continuously lamented by the Bantu but apparently propitious for Baka integration, this intuitive and practical rather than analytical understanding of different economic modes also results in a certain amount of external control over their application. I believe that for the moment Baka have struck a relatively good balance in articulating their own 'giving' economy with that of their 'reciprocating' neighbours. Furthermore, they seem increasingly to be coming to grips with the requirements and opportunities of market exchange and money.

Money as Capital and the Commoditisation of Land and Labour

The appropriation of European currency by Bantu and Baka alike has mainly been limited to its capacity as a general-purpose medium of payment and exchange. The employment of money as capital, which has often been cited as a major cause for the disruption of communal social relations and one of the driving forces for the transformation of 'traditional', kinship-based societies into 'modern', class-based societies, has not taken place. An exception is the limited Bantu investment in the acquisition of houses and shops that were built by European colonisers in the district centres and that are now being rented out by their new proprietors to immigrant Muslim traders from countries to the north such as Cameroon, Central African Republic, Niger and Chad. The geographical, economic and infrastructural enclavation of the area, its demography and diminishing transport capacities, have also been a deterrent to an influx of foreign capital.

Land has not been commoditised at all, and this is due to a combination of factors, of which the following need to be emphasised: there is a very low population density (less than one person per square km) and no shortage of uncultivated land; following the collapse of the cocoa market and the country's political instability in the late 1990s, there are presently no cash-cropping alternatives, no logging enterprises, and neither government nor private investment in the development of an agro-industry or industrial mineral exploitation, other than a few government-sponsored farming experiments (in Elendjo, Bellevue and Elogo), which had run out of funding by the 1980s. There has thus been little incentive to discontinue existing communal systems of land tenure.

Baka labour, of course, is commoditised to a certain extent, but only in some exceptional cases has dependent labour become the only means of gaining a livelihood. Even in these extreme cases, such a decision is not irrevocable and reflects rather a personal choice than external constraints. The overwhelming majority of dependent Baka labour is additional or part-time, and income in cash money or in kind has nowhere replaced an independent resource base or deprived the concerned individual of the possibility to decide anew upon an independent agriculture and forest-related subsistence, or to try to go back to one.

The absence of any organised meat trade other than for local subsistence has not forced Baka men into a market niche of professional hunting, as has happened elsewhere with dramatic consequences. The effects of an intensification and specialisation of hunting for the market have been documented for the Mbuti living in the central and southern Ituri (Hart 1978; Ichikawa

1991) and the Aka in the Lobaye region of the Central African Republic (Bahuchet and Guillaume 1982). The Baka resource domain has remained diverse, there has not been a significant degradation of forest resources and the options to create a suitable livelihood according to personal design have largely remained open.

The creation of new needs, another symptom of increasing commoditisation, has always been limited by the moderate range of available import supplies, and in the current economic and transport situation imports are down to the most basic consumer items. Commoditised labour has resulted in a certain individualisation in the spheres of production and consumption. These individualising effects have largely been balanced, however, by a Baka inclination to work in groups, even when only a single individual has been employed. An individually contracted labourer is often assisted by unpaid family members or friends who may share in the work and at least the food being handed out, and an employer or patron not uncommonly takes the Baka work ethic into account and allocates work that can be done in small groups. Unless when target-saving it is also rather the rule than the exception that consumption of what is being bought with the pay is shared with accompanying friends and dependants of the close family. Being paid in kind or asking for things rather than for money, makes it, of course, more difficult *not* to share, and is an implicit recognition of its value. An ethic of sharing is thus upheld even if it is at a more muted level. Furthermore, the spending pattern of relatively large sums of cash money, channelled either into (durable) consumer goods or in rather short-lived alcohol excesses, highlights the quality of an economy that can work to a great extent without direct access to money. There is a tendency for spending money quickly when it is available. This can be linked to a high level of poverty – as Caroline Humphrey reminds us, 'very poor people literally cannot afford to keep wealth in money' (1985: 66) – but poverty must always be defined in relation to the surrounding society and its level of economic capacity and performance. It can also point to the status of an economy in which money is not very important. When there is no perceived vital or essential need for money, it can be spent quickly and without a second thought.[20]

In sum, Baka involvement with markets and money has not led to large-scale commoditisation of productive relations, land or labour, nor to a marked external dependency or an intensification of exploitative patron–client ties, nor has it produced any considerable transformation of social relations on its own. Money has certainly affected egalitarian morals and may to a certain extent have had a 'rationalising' effect on exchanges, but it has not caused an irreversible disruption of relations of sharing, nor led to an internal Baka stratification according to monetary wealth. Although money is diffusely associated with wealth, it is not accumulated as a goal of wealth. Focus on consumption, demand-sharing and the almost exclusive use of money as a medium of payment and exchange have so far prevented its accumulation and/or use as capital. In these circumstances, Peterson's conclusion that for Australian Aborigines 'capital still inheres in social relationships' (1991b: 84), is largely applicable to Baka, too.

Conclusion

On the one hand, the potential of European money to act as 'the radical leveller, that [...] does away with all distinctions' (Marx 1961: 132, quoted in Bloch and Parry 1989: 6) by reducing differences of quality to those of mere quantity has certainly been kept in check by external conditions of limited money supplies and commoditisation, and a balance of internal social organisation and economic practices. So far, money has also not become an end in itself. On the other hand, it would be an exaggeration to claim that Baka handling of money demonstrates perfect control and management, and that it exclusively serves as a means to cultural ends. Bahuchet and Guillaume's statement that among Aka 'money from cash wages immediately returns to its original source' (1982: 208) rings familiar in the Baka context, too. A great Baka hunter's puzzled comment concerning his continuing poverty comes to mind. Looking back on the dozens of elephants he had killed and contemplating all the ivory he had thus produced, Metoul mused on the patent enrichment of his patrons and then asked: 'Tell me: why is it that I am not rich, too?' Certainly he was not one to be accused of indulging in alcoholic excesses and, indeed, he was a very considerate and caring village chief, but his gains had been divided between shrewd and advantage-seeking patrons and a Baka village crowd demanding their share.

Baka have nevertheless assimilated cash and commoditisation to a considerable extent to their own cultural understandings and social purposes. The egalitarian ethos concerning the shared consumption of money-bought durables and consumer items is a good example. The continuation and recurrence of barter-type exchanges of labour for kind in lieu of monetised ones, or as an alternative to them, equally attests more to an apt crisis management, flexibility of approach, and an emphasis on autonomy than to a growing Baka dependence and lack of defence against the penetration of money.[21] In the Baka case an insistence on one-to-one barter exchanges is linked to the continuation of relationships of gifting and giving. Apart from being conceptually and practically closer to these forms of exchange from which it can often not be clearly separated out, barter also reflects an active choice of the terms of trade and an adequate response to insufficient currency circulation, and particularly the negative effects of the devaluation of the Franc CFA. In view of the high symbolic value of money, barter thus constitutes an appropriate response in times of financial crisis and attests to an emphasis on autonomy. One would certainly be mistaken, however, in interpreting it as a form of active 'resistance' to money.

The oral history concerning major Baka settlements in and around Souanké Town also testifies to a remarkable residential continuity in time and space, centred around a nucleus of village founders and co-founders and their descendants but incorporating members of far-flung personal networks. Baka friends, visitors and newcomers cluster exclusively in Baka settlements, where they get drafted into existing residential, labour and exchange networks. Residential, social and ethnic cohesion are thus equally putting a curb on an atomisation of Baka society. Almost three decades of involvement in the modern sector and the cash economy, predominantly in the form of cocoa farming and ivory hunting, have temporarily produced an inflationary development of bridewealth among the Bantu and have most likely ushered in an incipient monetarisation of Baka bridewealth, but since the collapse of the cocoa market, and the CITES[22] ban on ivory in October 1989, this process has been in reverse.

All these factors have favoured a situation in which Baka can legitimately aspire to greater ethnic equivalence, more material equality, and a higher socioeconomic and political integration despite an emphasis on personal autonomy.[23] Most Baka participation in current local exchanges and the cash economy certainly places them in a subordinate position compared to that of other, more privileged actors, but it is not divorced from their own terms of trade, and the kind of rural proletarisation reported by Bahuchet and Guillaume (1982) for the Aka of the Lobaye region in C.A.R., and by Mukito and Mbaya (1990) for a Mbuti community in the forest fringe zone of eastern Zaïre (now the Democratic Republic of Congo), has not taken place among the Baka of Souanké and Sembé Districts in the Congolese panhandle. Considering the current economic and political enclave situation of these districts, it is also highly unlikely to occur in this area in the near future.

As a final comment I would like to pick up a comparison made by James Carrier between the market model and a lingua franca (1997: 47–9). The suggestion I draw from this comparison is that both a Baka competence in different regional and national languages and their practical versatility in different modes of exchange serve them as appropriate tools for communication and for establishing and maintaining social relations. Amongst themselves Baka speak Li-Baka, with Bantu neighbours the Bantu language, and with Muslim traders and nonlocal Congolese either Lingala or French. A corollary of this comparison is that economic activities are about social relations and not only embedded in them. Baka economics, then, in their emphasis on relations between people rather than between things, are also a good reminder that whatever purely economic models may tell us about the universal logic supposedly underlying human exchange; fundamentally it has social ends and is conditioned by culturally specific means and moralities.

Notes

* Field research was carried out in the Souanké District, Sangha Region, northwestern Republic of Congo, from mid-1992 to mid-1994, and was supported by a grant from the DAAD (Deutscher Akademischer Austauschdienst).

1. The term 'Bantu' was originally coined in the 19th century for the purpose of linguistic classification. Conscious of the debate surrounding this somewhat outdated term I am using it as a shorthand for the Bantu-speaking neighbours of the Baka, i.e. Bakwele, Njem and Fang, in order to distinguish members of this ethnic cluster both from the Baka and the mainly Hansa-, Fulbi-, and Sango-speaking Muslim immigrants from countries further north.
2. Long gone are the days when Baka villages had a 'money specialist' who was capable of recognising the numerical value of banknotes and coins (cf. Althabe 1965: 570). The act of selling and buying are both expressed with the same word, *na bɵmɵ̀*, *bɵmɵ̀* being originally a

Njem (A 84) word. *Wà-bɵ́mɵ̀* is the 'merchant', the 'trader'; *ndánda na bɵmɵ̀* is the 'market' (i.e., the 'place to buy/sell'), and *nda na bɵmɵ̀* is the 'shop' (i.e., the 'house to buy/sell'). Before the devaluation of the Francs CFA in early 1994, the exchange rate of Francs CFA to French Francs was fixed at 50/1, thereafter at 100/1.

3. Particularly bridewealth gifts are marked among Bantu in notebooks, so-called '*cahiers*', into which every item enters. Marriage carries a life-long obligation for gifts and counter-gifts within the affinal community at the occasion of the ceremonies organised around major events and stages of anyone's life. To keep track most people keep such a book, for it is important to know how much to add to a gift for a countergift and, in the case of divorce, to reclaim what one has given. Some Baka also keep records of bridewealth gifts, but these are mostly scribbled on a piece of paper, which is kept somewhere among the valuables in a metal box at the back of the house.
4. Keeping part of the groundnut harvest for next season's planting is common Bantu practice, but a difficult task for Baka women. The comparatively much smaller Baka groundnut production is usually consumed entirely, and at the start of the new season Baka women do work for bowls of groundnuts in order to do their planting. A day's labour can procure them an equivalent market value of Francs CFA 400 to 700, that is, they get between four and seven glasses full of groundnuts which are sold at a price of Francs CFA 100 each at the height of the season and go up to 150 at the start of the new season, when supplies are getting low. This compares with remuneration in cash of between Francs CFA 200 and 500 for a day's labour, on average a three- to six-hour shift.
5. Althabe (1965: 574–75) claims that among Baka in southeastern Cameroon brideservice or exchange of women, '*système par échange*', had been completely eliminated in favour of '*mariage par prestation*' based on bridewealth. Althabe gives four examples of such bridewealth prestations. In one of them, meat and honey figure prominently alongside a small additional sum of money and two pieces of cloth. The other three consisted of money, iron tools and imported consumer items (cloth, a hat and a bucket). Peacock (1984) has called meat and honey 'prestige food' because both are characterised by a high value in a cultural and/or a nutritional sense, and are subject to uncertainty in supply (cited in Terashima 1987: 78).
6. The term for 'bridewealth' is *(?è)lùwà*. The full expression is *(?è)lùwà na njò wóse* (bridewealth on/of/for the head of a woman). The job a man does in order to accumulate bridewealth is referred to as *bèlà na je-wóse*, which translates as 'work on the back of a woman', and 'brideservice' is *bèlà na gí-lè-o* or 'work for my in-laws'.
7. *Bilaba*, which means 'exchanging words' in Ngumba (Guilbot 1951: 163–64), was a complex socio-economic institution preceding colonial intervention but continuing into the early colonial phase. Based on incremental gift exchanges, *bilaba* promoted trade, the creation of wealth and prestige, and a widespread intraethnic redistribution of goods. Such potlatch-type exchanges also took place across ethnic boundaries among all the Pahouin peoples (Fang, Bulu, Ngumba, Ntumu, Beti, Eton and Ewondo) as well as the Njem (Guilbot 1951; Horner 1962: 174–75; Robineau 1966; Vincent 1963: 278; Fernandez 1982: 138). Some of these Bantu-speaking groups are direct neighbours of the Baka.
8. In the Ituri, Efe and Mbuti women appear to be much more familiar with the village world than the men and often mediate exchanges of agricultural produce for forest produce. Terashima (1987) has pointed out the crucial role of Efe women for the exchanges between Lese and Efe in general, and has linked it to the circulation of Efe women for agricultural food via the *efe-maia muto-maia* (my Efe-my villager) relationship. Among Mbuti groups in the central and southern Ituri, the situation appears to be similar because of a male specialisation in professional hunting and a trend among women to work for villagers. The volatile currency of former Zaïre (now Democratic Republic of Congo), however, has pushed people in general, not only the Mbuti, to rely predominantly on barter and imported foreign currencies. Overall the familiarity of men with the meat trade is probably balanced out by the greater familiarity of women with exchanges in the village sphere.
9. For instance in a fishing camp, the 'secretary' and brother-in-law to the headman of a Baka village took me to a spot where he and his companions had earlier felled an oil palm tree

(*Elaeis guineensis*). The women were making palm oil for cooking out of the nuts, while he was cutting the trunk for the production of palm wine. His reference, in French, was to 'my little market (bargain, deal) ('*mon petit marché*'), presumably, because palm-wine is often sold in the village. We shared, however, the result of his efforts on the spot.

10. In 1994, after the devaluation of the Franc CFA, the price of a '*passe partout*', that is, the most popular lead-pellet cartridge for a 12-gauge shotgun, varied according to availability and individual trade policy from Francs CFA 250 to 450. If a hunter did not miss a shot and killed, say, a small-sized animal such as a blue duiker (*Cephalophus monticola* or *Cephalophus Baxwell*), he could recover the price paid for one such cartridge by selling a quarter of the game shot, i.e., the hind leg for Francs CFA 300 to 400. In practice, however, the sale of meat in villages is rather difficult compared to a market-place such as Souanké Town.
11. Once, in the forest, Metoul, a Baka village headman, went hunting with the gun of a Bantu man and a cartridge provided by his own half-brother. The result, a *ngendì* (*Cephalophus dorsalis*), was jointed by his half-brother, who kept a hind leg, gave the other to the Bantu owner of the gun, and the rest of the animal to Metoul, who divided it among the women of the camp for cooking.
    When Àngama once set off from the village to hunt with the gun and a cartridge provided by a Bantu 'friend', the latter divided the game in two equally sized parts, one for himself, one for the hunter. According to Àngama and Metoul, this was the proper way to divide game and showed a fair assessment of the investment by the Bantu himself as well as an acknowledgement of the hunter's work effort.
12. Metal wire used for snaring is relatively cheap. The village retail price for wire to make a snare strong enough to hold medium-sized game was around Francs CFA 300, less than the price for a cartridge needed to shoot the same kind of game. In addition, snares can of course be used many times, until the wire breaks or gets too rusty.
13. Among Aborigines gambling, which effects the circulation and redistribution of money within the community, follows on from the input of large sums of money as a result of social service back-pay and because there is no outlet for the cash (Peterson 1991b: 73–4). Among Hadza, gambling has been interpreted as a 'powerful levelling mechanism' underpinning egalitarian values and the ethic of sharing, and as a means to make these items circulate throughout Hadza country (Woodburn 1982: 442–44).
14. On average, a Bantu patron hands over to his Baka hunter between 25 and 30% of the cash money that he has negotiated with a Muslim trader for the ivory. This payment does not include the initial investment by the patron, who normally provides and maintains his hunter with ammunition, food and tobacco, while the latter is out hunting in the forest.
15. The pockets of Baka trousers merit a story for themselves. They have either been torn out, are riddled with holes or simply in shreds. Anything small and of value goes into a small bag called *sàwàlà*, containing tobacco and lighting equipment, or a larger leather bag, *njele*, both used for walks in the forest. In town and without either of these bags a man will put money, cigarettes and the like in the best-kept pocket of his trousers or jacket, with rather unpredictable results.
16. A frequent comment on the prevailing 'economic crisis' was: 'there is no money!' ('*il n'y a pas d'argent!*'). Bantu also noted that 'money has gone back to its producers!' ('*l'argent est rentré chez les producteurs!*'), or specified that 'money has gone back home to the whites! Is it not true that it is you who produce it?' ('*l'argent est rentré chez les Blancs! C'est vous qui en fabriquent, n'est ce pas?*'). As much as these statements say 'we have no money, we are poor now', they also give expression to a vision of money as a commodity to be kept in circulation rather than accumulated.
17. Althabe speaks of a 'minimal objective importance' of money, but of its 'essential psychological value' (1965: 570). He relates the interesting phenomenon that the role of European currency as an all-purpose medium of payment and exchange – especially banknotes of high value, i.e., Francs CFA 1,000 – was secondary to its role in Baka bridewealth exchanges, where it circulated in a very similar fashion to indigenous iron currencies among their Bantu neighbours. Cameroonian Baka did earn money and receive European objects for work on Bantu plantations, but apparently they reserved the big notes for bridewealth exchanges and

spent the smaller ones on imported European consumer items, which they bought from Muslim merchants during periodically organised, dry-season markets. However, all local exchanges with Bantu of food, iron tools and other local produce – except labour – took place as barter or gifting, and without the use of money (ibid.: 571, 575–76).

18. This emphasis on actors' practices rather than on abstract macro theory has been succinctly defended by Karl Polanyi, according to whose polemic the basic differences underlying substantivist and formalist theory is, that 'the latter derives from logic, the former from fact' (1957: 243).
19. I am drawing here on the analytical distinctions elaborated by Price (1975) between 'reciprocity' and 'sharing', by Woodburn (1982) between the 'competitive egalitarianism' of tribal societies and the 'noncompetitive egalitarianism' of band societies, and by Bird-David (1990, 1992) between 'gifting' and 'giving'. These distinctions underlie to a great extent the ideal-type socioeconomic differences between local Bantu and Baka. It has been particularly Bird-David's (1990) suggestion not only to distinguish between commodity and gift economies, but also to recognise a third type – the economy of giving/sharing – a concept whose authenticity she later explored in 'local models' of the 'cosmic economy of sharing'. Ingold (1986) has extended the basically distributive aspects of Sahlins's principle of generalised reciprocity to include all economic activities, from production to distribution and to consumption, pointing out that it characteristically encompasses the totality of economic and social involvement with the world. Such an unbounded extension of egalitarian exchange is better expressed in the concept of sharing. Sharing is an 'experience' rather than a behavioural code or a rule of prescriptive altruism and covers both the distributive aspect of 'sharing out' and 'the principle of unbounded inclusion' in productive and consumptive 'sharing in' (Ingold 1986: 113–17, 239).
20. This statement has to be qualified, however. Spending money instead of keeping it may also, as we have seen, be related to ideas about modern-day bigmanship and the prestige gained through conspicuous redistribution or consumption. It may also have to do with social pressure and the problem of concealing money resulting from a transaction that everyone in the community knows about. Less important sums of money are obviously saved for particular purposes. In Bidoumo II, for instance, where I hardly ever saw money changing hands, I was privately given money on more than one occasion when I was leaving to go to Souanké Town. These sums of Francs CFA 500 upwards to 3,000 were usually given to me by young men who wanted clothing. On my return I had to hand over the article(s) in question under equally private circumstances, so as not to arouse any suspicions about favouring anybody with presents or to give away that someone had secretly been saving money.
21. Humphrey has argued that 'barter *in the present world* is, in the vast majority of cases, a post-monetary phenomenon (i.e. it coexists with money), and that it characterises economies which are, or have become, de-coupled from monetary markets' (1985: 49, original emphasis). A corollary of barter is, of course, that it prevents the accumulation of money. Humphrey also proposed that an insistence on the immediacy of barter is an expression of economic and political autonomy when confronting market integration and monetisation (ibid.: 65, 67), which confirms what Hart (1978) and Ichikawa (1991) have suggested for the Mbuti insistence on barter-trade in a politically and economically highly unstable situation.
22. The UN Convention on International Trade in Endangered Species.
23. Ingold has pointed out that personal autonomy depends upon the commitment to society as a whole (1986: 223), and that sharing is the expression and continuous confirmation of this commitment and the very condition of such autonomy (ibid.: 116). In their complementarity, Baka socioeconomic practices demonstrate precisely such a commitment to wider social integration.

References

Althabe, G. 1965. 'Changements Sociaux chez les Pygmées Baka de l'Est Cameroun'. *Cahiers d'Études Africaines*, Vol. V, 20(4): 561–92.

Austen, R.A. and R. Headrick. 1983. 'Equatorial Africa under Colonial Rule'. In: David Birmingham and Phyllis M. Martin (eds), *History of Central Africa*, Vol. II, pp. 27–94. London and New York: Longman.

Bahuchet, S. and H. Guillaume. 1982. 'Aka-Farmer Relations in the Northwest Congo Basin'. In: Eleanor Leacock and Richard B. Lee (eds), *Politics and History in Band Societies*, pp. 189-211. Cambridge and New York: Cambridge University Press.

Bird-David, N.H. 1990. 'The Giving Environment: Another Perspective on the Economic System of Gatherer-Hunters'. *Current Anthropology*, 31(2): 189–96.

—— 1992. 'Beyond "The Original Affluent Society". A Culturalist Reformulation'. *Current Anthropology*, 33(1): 25–47.

Bloch, M. and J. Parry. 1989. 'Introduction. Money and the Morality of Exchange'. In: J. Parry and M. Bloch (eds), *Money and the Morality of Exchange*, pp. 1–32. Cambridge: Cambridge University Press.

Bourdieu, P. 1977 (1972). *Outline of a Theory of Practice*, trans. Richard Nice. Cambridge: Cambridge University Press.

Carrier, J.G. 1997. 'Introduction'. In: J.G. Carrier (ed.), *Meanings of the Market. The Free Market in Western Culture*, pp. 1–67. Oxford and New York: Berg.

Coquery-Vidrovitch, C. 1972. *Le Congo au Temps de Grandes Compagnies Concessionaires, 1898-1930.* Paris and La Haye: Mouton & Co.

Delobeau, J.-M. 1984. 'Les Pygmées dans la Colonisation'. *Afrika Zamani-Revue d'Histoire Africaine* (Yaoundé), 14 and 15: 115–33.

Fernandez, J.W. 1982. *Bwiti. An Ethnography of the Religious Imagination in Africa.* Princeton, NJ: Princeton University Press.

Gudeman, S. 1986. *Economics as Culture. Models and Metaphors of Livelihood.* London: Routledge and Kegan Paul.

Guilbot, J. 1951. 'Le Bilaba'. *Journal de la Société des Africanistes*, 21(2): 163–74.

Guillot, B. 1977. 'Problèmes de Développement de la Production Cacaoyère dans les Districts de Sembé et Souanké'. *Cahiers O.R.S.T.O.M.*, Série Sciences Humaines, XIV(2): 151–69. (Paris).

Guyer, J.I. 1986. 'Indigenous Currencies and the History of Marriage Payments. A Case Study from Cameroon'. *Cahiers d'Études Africaines*, Vol. XXVI, 104 (4): 577–610.

—— 1993. 'Wealth in People and Self-Realization in Equatorial Africa'. *Man* (N.S.), 28(2): 243–65.

Hart, J.A. 1978. 'From Subsistence to Market. A Case Study of the Mbuti Net Hunters'. *Human Ecology*, 6(3): 325–53.

Horner, G.R. 1962. 'The Bulu Response to European Economy'. In: Paul Bohannan and George Dalton (eds.), *Markets in Africa*, pp. 170–89, Evanston, Il.: Northwestern University Press.

Humphrey, C. 1985. 'Barter and Economic Disintegration'. *Man* (N.S.), 20(1): 48–72.

Ichikawa, M. 1991. 'The Impact of Commoditisation on the Mbuti of Eastern Zaire'. In: Nicolas Peterson and T. Matsuyama (eds), *Cash, Commoditisation and Changing Foragers.* Senri Ethnological Studies, 30, pp. 135–62. Osaka: National Museum of Ethnology.

Ingold, T. 1986. *The Appropriation of Nature. Essays on Human Ecology and Social Relations.* Manchester: Manchester University Press.

Klieman, K. 1999. 'Hunter-gatherer Participation in Rainforest Trade-Systems: a Comparative History of Forest vs. Ecotone Societies in Gabon and Congo, c. 1000–1800 A.D.'. In: Karen Biesbrouck, Stefan Elders and Gerda Rossel (eds), *Central African Hunter-Gatherers in a Multidisciplinary Perspective: Challenging Elusiveness*, pp. 89–104. CNWS: Universiteit Leiden.

Köhler, A. 1999. 'The Forest as Home: Baka Environment and Housing'. In: Karen Biesbrouck, Stefan Elders and Gerda Rossel (eds) *Central African Hunter-Gatherers in a Multidisciplinary Perspective: Challenging Elusiveness*, pp. 207–20. CNWS: Universiteit Leiden.

Kopytoff, I. 1986. 'The Cultural Biography of Things. Commoditization as Process'. In: Arjun Appadurai (ed.), *The Social Life of Things. Commodities in Cultural Perspective*, pp. 64–91. Cambridge: Cambridge University Press.
Mukito, W. and Mudimba M. 1990. 'Les Pygmées de la Localité de Mbau. Leurs Conditions de Vie et leurs Perspectives de Developpement', Unpublished MS, University of Kisangani, Zaïre.
Peacock, N.R. 1984. 'The Mbuti of Northeast Zaire. Women and Subsistence Exchange'. *Cultural Survival Quarterly*, 8(2): 15–7.
Peterson, N. 1991a. 'Introduction. Cash, Commoditisation and Changing Foragers'. In: N. Peterson and T. Matsuyama (eds), *Cash, Commoditisation and Changing Foragers.* Senri Ethnological Studies 30, pp. 1–16. Osaka: National Museum of Ethnology.
—— 1991b. 'Cash, Commoditisation and Authenticity. When do Aboriginal People stop being Hunter-Gatherers?' In: N. Peterson and T. Matsuyama (eds), *Cash, Commoditisation and Changing Foragers.* Senri Ethnological Studies 30, pp. 67–90. Osaka: National Museum of Ethnology.
Polanyi, K. 1957. *The Great Transformation.* Boston: Beacon Press.
Price, J.A. 1975. 'Sharing. The Integration of Intimate Economies'. *Anthropologica*, 17: 3–27.
Robineau, C. 1966. *L'Évolution Économique et Sociale en Afrique Centrale. L'Exemple de Souanké (République du Congo Brazzaville).* Paris: O.R.S.T.O.M.
Simmel, G. 1978 [1907]. *The Philosophy of Money.* London: Tavistock.
Stoecker, H. 1986. 'The Conquest of Colonies. The Establishment and Extension of German Colonial Rule. Cameroon, 1885-1906'. In: H. Stoecker (ed.), *German Imperialism in Africa. From the Beginnings until the Second World War*, pp. 62–82. Berlin: Akademie-Verlag.
Terashima, H. 1987. 'Why Efe Girls Marry Farmers? Socio-Ecological Backgrounds of Inter-Ethnic Marriage in the Ituri Forest of Central Africa'. *African Study Monographs*, Supplementary Issue 6: 65–83.
Turnbull, C.M. 1965. *Wayward Servants. The Two Worlds of the African Pygmies.* London: Eyre and Spottiswoode.
Vincent, J.-F. 1963. 'Dot et Monnaie de Fer chez les Bakwele et les Djem'. *Objets et Mondes*, III(4): 273–92. Paris: Musée de l'Homme.
Woodburn, J. 1982. 'Egalitarian Societies'. *Man* (N.S.), 17: 431–51.

3

Whose Forest Is It Anyway? Mbendjele Yaka Pygmies, the Ndoki Forest and the Wider World

Jerome Lewis

Introduction

This paper introduces the way the Mbendjele Yaka Pygmies of the Ndoki Forest in Northern Congo talk about their forest and its resources, and the way they conceptualise property relations more generally. This will be contrasted with the way local farming people and the national government talk about property and ownership. Recent developments in global capitalism have converted the Mbendjele's forest into floral and faunal assets that are distributed by central government to multinational organisations. The paper examines how this situation came about and what the implications are for the Mbendjele and other Yaka people.

The Ethnographic Context

The Mbendjele Yaka (Pygmies) live in the forest between the Sangha and Oubangui Rivers in northern Congo-Brazzaville and some parts of southern Central African Republic. This area of forest is increasingly referred to as the Ndoki forest.

The vast majority of Mbendjele often spend more than half the year hunting and gathering in forest camps and some part of the year near or in agriculturalists' villages. In addition to hunting and gathering, here they will trade, labour or perform services for villagers in return for food, goods, alcohol or money. However, the situation varies greatly from place to place. Mbendjele near the Central African Republic are evangelised and relatively sedentary. Those living near logging towns may spend long periods working outside the forest. Others further south spend most of the year in the forest, with some groups not coming out to villages for years at a time.

The same group or family may spend a year in a logging town followed by the next few years mostly in the forest, or vice versa. Annual variation in movements is very common, but the number of places visited is limited. Thus over several years most people will move between well-known resource centres (*ebende ya benda*) within their traditional territories, and sometimes beyond these areas. Such resource centres may be salt licks popular with large game, areas rich in wild yams, seasonal caterpillars, fruit trees, rich fishing sites, abandoned palm-nut plantations, farmers' villages, logging towns, or prospecting camps. Mbendjele travel light and their movements are as likely to be opportunistic as planned in advance.

The Mbendjele clans with whom we lived[1] have established exchange relations with four different groups of farmers: the Bongili, Kabunga, Sangha-Sangha and recently with the Bodingo. They are all speakers of Bantu languages. In addition to those just mentioned, I came across Mbendjele in relations with a great variety of different farmer groups: the Kaka, Ndongu, Ngando, Enyelle, Pomo, Yekinga and Yasua. All these various groups are referred to as 'Bilo' by the Mbendjele. The term Bilo is used by the Mbendjele to make a meaningful distinction between non-Yaka Africans and Yaka (Pygmy) people that is based on perceived racial, ideological, knowledge and economic differences. Instead of Bantu, farmer or villager, in this paper, as elsewhere, I follow their lead and use Bilo.

Mbendjele say they belong to a larger group of *bisi ndima* (forest people) whom they also refer to as Yaka people. Indeed Mbendjele more often refer to themselves as Yaka (*Moaka* in the singular and *Baaka* in the plural) than with the name Mbendjele. Mbendjele is used to distinguish themselves from other Yaka groups they are aware of, such as the Mikaya of Mokeko district, or the Ngombe (Baka) of Cameroon.

Despite a variety of relations between different Yaka groups, ranging from hostility to intermarriage, their shared identity is based on common descent from the first forest dwellers, a shared past, oral tradition, ritual styles and marriage relations – and not on the exchange of goods or trade.[2] This contrasts with Yaka peoples' relations with Bilo or 'Whites' (Mindele), which are predominantly based on trade and exchange. All Yaka groups are hunter-gatherers to varying degrees and each has its own exclusive area of forest. This contrasts with Bilo- and 'White'-owned land that is superimposed over the rights of the different Yaka groups.

Yaka and Bilo

The Mbendjele describe their relations with Bilo with many similarities to the opposition between coloniser and colonised that informs the worldwide indigenous rights movement. Mbendjele describe village people as recent arrivals to the forest who discriminate against them, attempt to exploit them, claim rights over their land and labour, and make aggressive claims to own farmland, rivers, forest and even other people. Mbendjele elders often emphasise that it is their transience in the forest that makes Bilo claims vacuous and therefore not to be taken seriously.[3]

There exists a developed oral tradition that elaborates and entrenches cultural stereotypes differentiating Yaka forest people from Bilo village people through accounts of the past. These numerous and widely told stories attest to the enduring and elaborate nature of the opposition between them. The cultural significance of the contrast between forest people and village people has been commented on by other ethnographers in Central Africa as one of the most fundamental markers of ethnic difference in forested regions (see for instance Turnbull 1966; Bahuchet and Guillaume 1982; Waehle 1986:392; Grinker 1994; Kenrick 2000; Lewis 2001; Kenrick and Lewis 2001; Köhler and Lewis 2002). Even where forest people no longer have access to forest, and may even speak the same language and have many similar cultural practices and beliefs to their farmer neighbours, these oppositions do not break down. Indeed, they can become more entrenched as segregation and discrimination increase, as has happened to the Twa Pygmies of the Great Lakes Region (Lewis 2000).

In northern Congo local Bilo perceptions of the differences between Yaka and Bilo people were expressed to me with many similarities to Woodburn's (1982) distinction between 'immediate-return systems' and 'delayed-return systems'. A young educated Bilo man expressed this in the following way:

> Despite production being for subsistence, the Kabunga organise themselves to make reserves of food for the future. Using elementary conservation techniques, they preserve food from the harvest, fishing and hunting. In contrast, the Yaka will always consume all the food they have before going to look for more. The Yaka is a most sociable person, their whole lives, and all activities, are carried out in groups. Their lives are in eternal communion with each other.
>
> In contrast, the Kabunga, whose life has evolved, is inclined to a solitary existence, each man for himself, God for all. While the Kabunga wastes his time making politics, organising himself, seeking to uplift his land and village, the Pygmy is totally preoccupied with the politics of the bush. He searches to discover all the possible procedures to trap or capture wild animals in the bush. From the point of view of education, the Kabunga orientates his children towards schooling, the Yaka, to the domain of the bush.
>
> There is much conflict between the Yaka and Kabunga. Most quarrels are caused by the Yaka refusing to work. There are also quarrels caused by capricious acts committed by the Yaka, such as theft, abuse of confidence, and refusal to honour debts. (Moise Taito, Kabunga chief's son and second year psychology student at university, aged twenty-six, 1996)

Woodburn's distinction is valuable to anthropologists because of this correlation with local perceptions. The 'immediate return' orientation to life is enduring and indigenous among the forest hunter-gatherers of Central Africa. Woodburn (1982) stressed that his distinctions between immediate- and delayed-return systems, although using economic criteria as a starting point, extend most importantly into social relations and politics, much like Moise Taito quoted above. Similar observations in different places have caused other anthropologists to elaborate distinctions of their own. For example, Barnard's contrast between the 'hunter-gatherer mode of thought' and 'accumulation modes of thought' (2001), or Lee's concept of 'communal foraging relations of production' (1981). Ingold argues that hunter-gatherer sociality is such 'a radically alternative mode of relatedness' (1990: 130) that the term 'society' is inappropriate.

Woodburn characterised this radical difference in his discussion of egalitarianism (1982). People in immediate-return societies do not depend on others for access to vital resources. Goods are not accumulated or conserved for longer than it takes all present to consume them. 'Demand-sharing'[4] is crucially important in assuring the relative equality of all the members of a group by guaranteeing that individuals do not accumulate more than others. Sharing is central to Mbendjele understanding of peoples' relations to material objects, and demand-sharing the process by which they oblige others to let them take what they need. From their point of view property relations are all about sharing relations. In order to contextualise and understand Mbendjele talk about the forest it is therefore necessary to look at Mbendjele sharing in more detail.

Demand-Sharing

> If I have two shirts and someone asks me for one I should give it to them. I can't refuse anyone, family, friend or stranger. Especially if you love people properly, then how could you refuse anyone? (Mongemba, 50-year-old Mbendjele man, Pembe, November 2000)

Bilo use of the term *konza* (in Lingala and many other local languages) conforms in many respects with the delayed return or capitalist notion of 'owner'. Following Barnard and Woodburn's (1988: 13–14) definition of property rights, the 'owner' of some 'thing' should have the ability, through rules, sanctions and a legitimising ideology, to restrict other peoples' enjoyment of the same 'thing'. This fits most Bilo uses of the term *konza,* including certain contexts where the *konza* may be a corporate group.

Mbendjele also use the term but explicitly contrast their meaning with the Bilo use of the same term. The different spellings I use for what is often glossed as the same word, *konza* (Bilo version) and *konja* (Mbendjele/Yaka version), distinguish between Bilo and Mbendjele pronunciation and the different interpretations each has of the concept of 'ownership'.

In Yaka tradition, the closest people get to accepting notions of ownership similar to those of Bilo or capitalists is in relation to certain ritual and mystical knowledge (intellectual property) that will be denied to ineligible people.

Thus spirit-controllers (*konja ya mokondi*) or healers (*ngaŋga*) may refuse to share certain knowledge with other people. These strings of knowledge have been inherited, even bought and sold between Mbendjele and other Yaka groups, over long periods and great distances.

Of material items, only certain personal possessions like a woman's basket (*yukwa*), her pots (*banjoŋgo*), clothing (*betobo*) and machete (*bunu*) and a man's bag (*ngamata*), his weapons – spear and knife (*goŋgo na yobɛ,*), tools (notably the *djombi* – axe) and clothing are recognised as belonging to named individuals, often the person who made, found, took or bought the item. The *konja* has priority over others' claims to the item. But in contrast to ritual and mystical knowledge these items, when not in use by the *konja*, should be shared on demand. Mbendjele relationships are based on the principle of sharing material items.

For most material items need determines who is the *konja,* especially of consumable goods. In the Mbendjele context owning something is more like a guardianship or caretaker role until someone else needs it. For instance, when the Mbendjele recognise the *konja* (owner) of an animal, it is only significant to ensure the *konja* gets his hunter's meat (the 'owner' is by definition the hunter that first wounded the animal), thus ensuring his future hunting success. This, however, gives him no right to refuse anyone an equitable share of the carcass he 'took out of the forest' (*a mu bila nyama ya ndima*). Mbendjele compare their notions of *konja* with those of the Bilo clearly in this context:

> A Bilo *konza* is different. When they say they are the owner of an animal they will refuse people! Even if they are very hungry, they still refuse them. Their way is different, their path is bad." (Mongemba, 50-year-old Mbendjele man, Pembe, November 2000)

Demand-sharing creates and sustains social relations of equality and affection. The importance of affection in defining sharing relations has consequences for spatial organisation. There are 'circles' of sharing depending on the quantity and type of food or other good, and the degree of affection between people.

The Mbendjele household (*mongulu*) is the basic unit of sharing. A typical household might consist of a young married couple with small children, the wife's mother and unmarried younger siblings, all sleeping in the same liana and leaf house (*mongulu*). Another common household type is based around a mature married couple with a wide age range of children living with them. These children will often include some of their own but also some of their siblings' and others' children.[5] Children, like adults, are able to change their residence freely and easily should they desire to. In this way affection is vital to keeping members of a household together. Within this context any household member consumes whatever enters the household freely and normally without restraint.

Normally only people who like each other live together in the same camp (*laŋgo*) since avoidance is a common way of resolving disputes. Any large amount of food brought back by a camp member will be shared equally among all the households in camp. In situations of temporary high population density (such as during dry-season ceremonies, or when feasting on large game, or when visiting Bilo villages) Mbendjele often group their houses together with those people they particularly like and will tend to share more with them than those further away. When numbers get over about sixty people Mbendjele often make several separate camps close to each other in order to respect peoples' differences. There only tends to be sharing between camps when there is great abundance or great scarcity.

The next level of sharing is rare and occurs in only two contexts – big-game hunting and *massana* forest spirit ritual performances. When an elephant is killed Mbendjele in the area will hear about it and go rapidly to where the carcass is lying. Large camps will be set up and feasting and dancing go on until the elephant has been consumed. During long *massana* ritual performances when forest spirits are summoned into camp, especially the three-day performance of *Ejengi*, people from all around will come and participate. In particular *eboka* commemoration ceremonies to end a period of mourning after a death will draw people from many neighbouring areas. In addition to sharing out the spiritual benefits of the forest spirits these *massana* performances also share out prized consumables– such as meat, honey, wild yams, alcohol, tobacco and marijuana, and other goods, including money. Initiations often take place during extended *massana* performances and initiation fees will have to be paid. These fees are immediately redistributed among all present. In the past people would pay with coils of metal, alcohol and food. Now they also use money.

Similarly to men's and women's different but complementary roles in *massana* forest spirit performances and in food collecting, Mbendjele men and women share in different ways. This is related to gender roles and their different productive activities. Women's gathering activities are geared to exploiting labour-intensive but dependable food sources for the regular provisioning of food for the family. These commonly include various wild yams, edible leaves, ground-growing vegetables like mushrooms and certain fruit, small fish and crustaceans. If women have collected a large amount of food they generally share it among themselves in the forest before returning to camp. Once in the camp women will prepare the food and share it again when cooked by sending plates to the men's area (*mbanjo*), and to their friends and relatives. Women's production is rarely shared out on arrival in camp, as the men's is.

Men specialise in obtaining foods with potentially large yields, like wild animals, honey, occasionally large fish, and seasonal fruit and nuts that must be climbed for. These foods are rarely found every day and men only share if they find such food in great abundance. In such cases they will have the bundles of meat or honey they are carrying taken from them even before they enter the camp. If they are carrying a carcass someone else will take it from them, supervise the butchering and ensure the sharing is done equitably. The man who killed the animal is given the hunter's meat that guarantees his future hunting success. Apart from this, the hunter gets an equivalent share to that received by others.[6]

Money Economies and Demand-Sharing

It is interesting to note how traditional sharing patterns are reacting to the introduction of money and wage labour. For instance, in modern contexts of hunting for sale to Bilo or logging workers, Mbendjele will announce to the camp that they intend to sell some meat for such and such a reason (often to pay a fine, clear a debt, or seek medicines when ill) and will only share half the animal with the camp. However, this is controversial. People with such intentions tend to camp in small groups so as to avoid the tensions this can create when people get hungry. They will not be able to stay in the same place as the others unless they share what they have:

> We have to share things or other people get angry. They will throw their eyes at us. So you have to be intelligent when you share. If you kill a small animal then just share it with your *moŋgulu* (hut) and send a few plates around to your friends nearby.
>
> Don't do the same with money. Just share it with your family if you have a lot. When you have worked hard and got lots of money in your pocket you must use your intelligence. You don't share it around as we do with pigs. You keep it with intelligence! Wait until you have problems [and must pay a fine], or if there is great sorrow [someone dies and alcohol will be required for the commemoration ceremony] and then get your money out. Or if someone in your clan needs money badly, get it out. Give it to them. When they have some they'll give you some. (Phata, 65-year-old Mbendjele man, Pembe, December 2000)

Money has also entered marriage relations. Marriages nowadays frequently involve the payment of a small amount of cash to the bride's father, often around Franc CFA 2,000–3,000 (US$4–6, a nominal fee) by the groom's father. This is a recent change. Coils of metal and spearheads were used in the past. Bilo introduced bridewealth in their efforts to justify their claims to authority over Mbendjele. Paying it enabled Bilo to claim rights over the couple whose marriage they had financed and also over any children the couple might produce. Mbendjele have accepted bridewealth among themselves to prevent Bilo claiming they are not 'properly' married and so that the Bilo can be denied any claim to rights over the couple and their children. Far more important for the Mbendjele than bridewealth are the brideservice obligations of the groom to his affines.

Marriage relations provide an important avenue for the circulation of goods and knowledge. Brideservice obligations require the boy to stay with his affines and share his labour with them for a number of years, or until their first child can walk. Thereafter he will be expected to share regularly with his affines and to make an effort to meet up with them and bring them things. These long-term affinal relationships circulate goods, news and knowledge very widely between different Mbendjele communities in different parts of the forest.

The Forest

Each group of Mbendjele associates itself with a particular area of forest delineated by rivers, marshes and Lac Telle. As part of my research I mapped these territories and found that the forest in the Sangha–Oubangui triangle between 1 degree and 3 degrees 30 minutes north of the equator, and 16 degrees and 17 degrees 30 minutes east of Greenwich is recognised as being the territory of particular family groups of Mbendjele (Lewis 2002: 72). These areas range in size between 174,000 hectares and 596,000 hectares and are composed of named rivers, lakes, salt licks, marshes and areas of firm land. These geographic features are the orientation markers Mbendjele use to move through the forest and they are all named. Unnamed areas between named places are associated with the named places. Border areas between different Mbendjele groups are often claimed by both groups, but this does not cause conflict since Mbendjele forest is open to all Mbendjele.

In most cases Mbendjele territories are also claimed by local Bilo groups; some Bilo groups even claim exclusive rights and dispute that Mbendjele have any rights whatsoever. Territories were delineated during the colonial period to discourage local-level warfare and to define the area of forest from which villagers were obliged to collect products like copal resin, rubber and duiker skins with which to pay their taxes. The colonial authorities never officially recognised hunter-gatherer land use as a legitimate claim to rights over the areas so used. However, they did recognise Bilo agricultural usage and accepted that this gave them rights over land. This discrimination against hunter-gatherer land usage is continued today by the post-independence governments.

Despite some newcomers' claims to the contrary, the Mbendjele consider all the forest to be theirs. Their rights to go where they wish and use whatever they like in the forest are a birthright that they consider inalienable. The forest is considered totally abundant and always capable of sustaining Yaka people. Komba (God) created the forest for Yaka people to share, and encouraged them to live in a certain way that includes a system of forest management and certain key social values, such as sharing. Thus the Mbendjele and other Yaka people have been willing to share the forest with others, and in practice rarely deny anyone access to the forest.

They call the area in which they were born, where they do most of their hunting and collecting, *ndima aŋgosu* (our forest). This is a collective claim, not an individual one. No one can claim exclusive ownership of the physical world. The notion that an individual, apart from Komba (God), could own land, rivers or forest evokes suspicion, incomprehension and mockery.

Mbendjele forest is best described in ecological terms as an 'equatorial mosaic forest'. This emphasises the great floral and faunal species diversity found per hectare of forest. The variety of different forest types that occur within it are more or less ignored in the most common ways outsiders classify the forest. Most often forest areas are simply classified as flooded forest, semi-flooded forest or forest on firm land. These classifications relate closely to issues of accessibility from an outsider's point of view. Although Mbendjele make these distinctions they are not the basis for a more generalised structuring of forest types. Rather, at the most general level Mbendjele divide the world (*yombo* or *mokilli*) into forest (*ndima*) and open space (*vulli*). The Mbendjele associate *vulli*, places without forest canopy cover, with discomforts such as heat, noise and danger, whereas the shady forest (*ndima*) is associated with coolness, peace and safety.

Ndima and *vulli* are discussed in terms of different landscapes, each with its own distinctive qualities and associated resources. Thus in *ndima* (forest) the *mooko* is the firm ground where it is nice to camp, dig yams and a place popular with duikers. The only type of mono-specific forest that grows in northern Congo is called *bemba*. Thus *bemba* is an area of Gilbertodendron trees popular with large game, pigs and antelopes. *Ndima ya bisedja* literally means 'forest of thorns' and describes areas dominated by seemingly impenetrable thorny undergrowth. Small muddy areas in forest on firm ground are called *djutu*. *Djamba* is marsh forest, where trees are shorter, making the often very abundant honey easier to collect. Pigs love marsh forest because of the stands of raffia palms (*moleŋge*) that grow there. An area of forest on firm ground occurring in a marsh is called *diko,* and an area of encapsulated forest on firm ground between two streams and their associated marshes is called *tanda*. *Ndobo* refers to a covered forest stream, and is associated with women's dam fishing and good drinking water while contrasted with *ebale* (river), which is a *vulli* or open space, and so on.

Vulli are by definition places where there is no forest canopy cover. The huge rivers in northern Congo create great gaps in the forest canopy. The *mokii* (riverbank) is a marginal space, being at the edge of the forest and open river where fishing and trading opportunities exist. *Mbumbu* (grasses) are similar in that they mark the transition from open village or fields to forest cover. *Vulli* are often places Mbendjele, especially men, go to get things. In the village (*mboka*) forest produce can be traded or casual employment found. Farmers' fields (*kuba*) ˜are *vulli*. In *pbai* (salt licks around a small stream that has been cleared of forest trees by elephants), or *esobe* (small encapsulated savannahs), or in *eyaŋga* (openings in the forest with still water in the centre) where visibility is good Mbendjele men go looking for game to hunt.

Ideally Mbendjele women like to give birth to their children in the forest just outside camp. The forest is idealised as the perfect place for people to be. Everyday Mbendjele conversations are obsessed with the forest, with different tricks and techniques for finding wild foods, on stories of past hunting, fishing or gathering trips, or on great feasts and forest spirit performances (*massana*) that occurred or will occur in the near future. Importantly, the forest links people to the past. Different areas in the forest are talked about in terms of the remembered ancestors who spent time there and the events that occurred. It is these memories that underpin people's claims to areas of forest as 'our forest' (*ndima aŋgosu*), and defines them as descended from the first forest people and hence 'Yaka'. When Mbendjele die they believe they go to another forest where Komba (God) has a camp. They will remain in Komba's forest camp until they are told to take another path and are born into this world again.

Mbendjele cannot conceive of their lives, or deaths and afterlife, without the frame of the forest around them. They express their dependency on and the intimacy of their relationship with the forest in the proverb, 'A Yaka loves the forest as he loves his own body.' The forest inhabits the Mbendjele as much as they inhabit the forest. They are inseparable, part of each other, like an organic whole. Like their bodies, the forest is considered inalienable, so long as one remains alive.

Forest Land as Property

> At first we were all alone in the forest. No one else was here. Then we stayed in *zimo* [abandoned Bilo plantations]. Sometimes we would visit the Bilo to get tobacco and *minjoko* [iron and bronze coils used to make blades]. Then we made friends and would even stay near their villages. (Phata, 65-year-old Mbendjele man, Pembe, January 2001, provides a time-collapsing history of Yaka occupation of the forest)

Yaka forest has multiple claims made over it by different groups. Today, international organisations have added their claims to those made by the Bilo. Other people's claims to the forest differ markedly from Mbendjele claims that rest on birth and occupancy. Newcomers' claims focus on the transformation of forest into habitations or other buildings, farms, plantations and, increasingly today, logging concessions, mines or wildlife parks. These claims to land rights are recognised in national laws because the forest had been transformed. They are frequently presented as exclusive rights, and, at least in theory, people not respecting them can be severely sanctioned. This emphasis on transformation (or destruction in many cases) of forest in order to claim land rights over it effectively rules out Mbendjele claims to rights unless they renounce their hunter-gatherer lifestyle.

In contrast to Mbendjele, conquest is positively valued by Bilo, and is used as an important justification for their claims to authority over land, people and goods. Bilo claims to ownership over the forest land they found during their migrations are based on the legitimising ideology of conquest, of both the forest and the people they found in it. Authority over, and the right to restrict, certain others' access are central concepts in Bilo ideas of an 'owner' (*konza*), whether this be a stream containing fish, a tree with a wild-bee hive in it or a cultivated field. Bailey's et al.'s (1992) account of property relations in Central Africa eloquently expresses this Bilo perspective on land. However, it is mistakenly presented as also the Pygmies' perspective. It seems clear that their use of Bilo translators during research, in addition to their close association with Bilo research assistants, has favoured a Bilo view that is contrary to the Mbendjele point of view. This is an aspect of what Brody has called the 'silencing of tribal people' (2000: 6), a process that pushes them to the remotest margins of the nations they live in, and is often used to deprive them of their richest resources and deny them rights to their heritage:

> Close relations between pygmies and farmers extend to their perceptions of their rights to land. Each farmer clan has rights recognised by all neighbouring farmer clans to a specific area of forest, which they may clear for crop cultivation or where they may hunt, fish, gather and extract required raw materials. The clan of pygmies traditionally associated with that same farmer clan also has recognised rights to exploit the same area of forest. The farmers assist their pygmy partners in maintaining exclusive rights to this area, and violations by either pygmies or other farmers are contested through negotiation, or sometimes violence. (Bailey's et al. 1992: 205)

Describing land rights in this way invests Bilo claims to own Pygmy peoples' lands with legitimacy and gives their claims to control the displacement of Pygmies more credibility. Most farming communities, like other colonists arriving in the Central African forests, have divided up areas of forest between themselves. They have done the same with clans of Pygmy people over whom they attempt to exert control by limiting their mobility to defined areas. It is precisely this mobility that gives Pygmy peoples a significant degree of autonomy despite attempts to dominate them. Forest-orientated Yaka groups I have met in northern Congo and southern Cameroon resent representations of their relationship with their forest that are based on Bilo models. It has no relation to their perception of an abundant forest that Komba (God) wished all creatures to share. Mongemba explains:

> It is the Bilo who say they own the forest. Yet we are all in the same place. If they try and go into the forest alone they easily get lost. They can't go anywhere in the forest without us. So, speak as much as they like, they depend totally on us to get into this forest of theirs.
>
> We are the first people of the forest; we are the real *konja* (owners/guardians) of the forest. Bilo took our things with the strength of their mouths, with anger. That is why they say they have our forest. But it is rubbish, how can they if they get lost just walking a little beyond their farms? It is the strength of their mouths. (Mongemba, 50-year-old Mbendjele man, Pembe, January 2001)

It is unfortunate for Yaka groups like the Mbendjele that their conception of land rights are so easily negated by responsible academics in favour of a literal presentation of Bilo ideological justifications for their attempts to dominate Yaka groups and claim ownership over forest occupied by Yaka people. The impact of Bilo being present when questions over forest ownership are being asked was clearly expressed by Giemba. I had asked him about comments from some loggers involved in negotiating with local communities in areas about to be logged that even if the Mbendjele are present during discussions they never complain about the intrusion of the foresters or seek compensation as the Bilo do.

> If you [a white man] ask a Yaka who owns the forest they will say the Bilo own the forest. They say this because they fear Bilo witchcraft. They do not want to tell the truth to whites when Bilo are present because they know that as soon as the whiteman has gone fury will overcome the Bilo and the strength of their mouths will start killing us [they will curse us]. (Giemba, 40-year-old Mbendjele man, Pembe, January 2001)

The fear of being cursed by Bilo looms large in the Mbendjele psyche. Bilo regularly and verbosely curse Mbendjele by wishing that their worst nightmares should befall them – that their genitals should rot, that they be bitten by a snake, fall out of a tree, or get charged by dangerous animals, and so on. Deaths are often attributed to the malicious activities of Bilo. Mbendjele even sing about it: *Motoko aŋga Bilo a di budi ya passi!* (The noise [speech] of the Bilo is hard and causes suffering!).

Thus the Mbendjele see themselves in a situation that common sense shows them to be in control of, yet in which they see the advantage of paying lip-service to Bilo claims in order to maintain safe access to Bilo goods. The potential for anger and violence from Bilo when their claims to authority over things are not respected frightens Mbendjele enough for them to acquiesce to Bilo claims when in the presence of Bilo. However, the Bilo's total dependence on the Mbendjele to move around in the forest is what makes Mbendjele confident that this acquiescence holds no danger to their vital interests. Bilo claims are ideological because they depend crucially on Mbendjele cooperation if Bilo are to enjoy the rights they claim to possess. Bilo efforts to coerce the Mbendjele critically fail due to this dependence on Mbendjele collaboration and support.

While visiting the Mbendjele again in 2001 I was interested to observe that following the announcement of hunting restrictions in forest claimed by the Sangha-Sangha Lino it was the Lino (Bilo) who protested vigorously. Mbendjele using the same area of forest made no such fuss. The Mbendjele concerned explained to me that they were confident that no one can stop them going where they like and doing what they want in their forest. To them it was all just 'village people' politics. How can people who hardly set foot in the forest they so vigorously claim as their own be serious?

Similarly, when I present ecologists' concerns about increasing faunal scarcity in order to explain their response of closing areas of forest off from human extractive activities, Mbendjele feel somehow exempt from such restrictions. Bird-David's observation about gatherer-hunters' relations with their farming neighbours that '(t)he differences between them relates to their distinct views of the environment that they share' (1990: 194–95) is also applicable to distinguish conservation discourses premised on notions of scarcity and the gatherer-hunters' view of their ecological relations in terms of an abundant and 'giving environment'.

From the Mbendjele point of view the forest has always been – and will eternally be – there for them. It was created for Yaka people. Mbendjele have an unswerving faith that the forest will always be able to provide them with what they need. In order to maintain this state of abundance the Mbendjele must share properly, and have a complex ritual life in which, among other things, forest spirits are enlisted to support and assist the Mbendjele in satisfying their needs. From their point of view, bad hunting and gathering are related to jealousy (due to improper sharing) or to the activities of malicious spirits, rather than to inadequacies in human skill or the environment's ability to provide. People recognise each other's skills but it is impolite to refer to them; rather hunting success is talked about in terms of personal and mystical relationships.[7] This is related to the Mbendjele's egalitarian ethic, in which individual ability is downplayed, and perceived of as a consequence of an individual's conduct in relationships with other people and mystical agents.

The idioms Mbendjele use for discussing the efficacy of food-gathering activities may seem odd but they are practical. If taken as a body of practices it could be argued that they form a system of forest management. For instance, in areas of forest where hunting is consistently unsuccessful, Mbendjele hunters will place leaf cones stuffed with earth on all paths leading into that area of forest. This warns other Mbendjele that the forest is populated by voracious spirits or has been cursed, and that they should not attempt to find food but turn back or simply pass through. Despite a non scientific reasoning, the effect of this allows degraded areas of forest to be left in order that their resources increase to sustainable levels again. However, Mbendjele idioms for understanding the forest and its resources have not yet adapted to the rapid change brought about by the increasingly intensive exploitation of forest resources by outsiders. The sophisticated balances their traditional lifestyle has with the forest are being dramatically shaken by the immense power of modern technology to transform and degrade the environment, and the Mbendjele are only just becoming aware of it.

Mbendjele are protected from Bilo accessing their forest by the latter's dependence on the Mbendjele to guide them. This was also true of other outsiders, such as loggers, wishing to enter the forest. However, multinational companies now use sophisticated navigation and positioning technology that allows them a degree of independence from the Yaka that was impossible in the past. The ability of chain-saws to cut trees and bulldozers to make roads for extracting forest resources have accelerated and facilitated turning the forest into wealth.

Increased activity in the forest has led to large urban developments around the activities of logging companies, the intensive development of road networks throughout the forest, and the opening up of previously inaccessible areas to commercial exploitation, mostly by professional hunters supplying urban centres with bushmeat. The impact of these various uses of the forest by outsiders is that local people – both Mbendjele and Bilo – see their resource base diminishing and increasing numbers of strangers coming into their lands.

In practical terms for local people their forests have been converted into floral and faunal assets that have been traded or rented out by the national government under pressure from international financial institutions. Some local people said that the government had traded forest rights to 'the whites' (i.e. multinational companies). Despite increasing concern about this, local people such as the Mbendjele are unsure how they can resist the determination of central government and the forest exploiters to achieve profit.

Since colonial times hunter-gatherer rights have been largely ignored by those extracting wealth from the forest. Since independence national laws continued to ignore them by investing all control in the state. Now the state obtains an important income from permitting multinational corporations and conservation projects to impose top-down development in the areas they operate in and claim exclusive rights over forest resources.

From French Colonial Structures to Bilo Colonial Structures

Despite independence for French Equatorial Africa in 1960 there is 'a remarkable continuity of interest, reflecting also the political continuity, between the colonial and post-colonial eras' (Colchester 1994: 12). Part of the reason for this striking continuity was the degree of acculturation of the local African elites. By the time of independence they had absorbed French culture, values and tastes to the point that most regarded indigenous traditions as valueless and an inhibition to 'development' (Colchester 1994: 19).

This continuity is also apparent in the perpetuation of some of the colonial concessionaire companies that began in the 1880s and are still active today, or directly passed their rights on to other foreign enterprises. It is apparent in the way in which Congo's, like Cameroon's, land tenure law follows French norms in considering 'vacant and without master' all land that shows no signs of permanent occupation, and defines it as state land. As Burnham (2000) points out, concepts such as 'state lands' were a convenient way of facilitating the acquisition of local people's lands by the colonial authorities by effectively nullifying any 'traditional' claims that local people may have had.

In addition to the continuation of French administrative practices by the newly independent government of the Congo, social policies continued many of the aims of the colonial period. Ideas about 'development' and what directions it should take continued to follow the French lead even during a long period of Marxist-Leninist government. Colonial policies like that of '*regroupement*' were continued by some post-independence leaders. This policy was used by the colonial government to resettle the dispersed and mobile Bilo communities in order to facilitate tax collection and forced labour regimes, as well as to prevent rebellions.

Such policies of forced relocation had several negative consequences in northern Congo. Some Bilo groups were made destitute by being relocated to land belonging to rival ethnic groups. This created land conflicts, such as that between the Pomo of Gatongo and the Yasua of Ngandzikolo, that remain a problem today, in addition to disrupting traditional farming systems based on forest plantations. Relocations were often coercive and justified with claims that they would benefit local people, making it easier to provide health care, education and other services. These resettlement policies continued into the 1970s in the Congo and were aimed at both Bilo and Yaka populations of the north.

Another sign of the continuity between the French and post-independence governments was the 1970 Land Code. This law proclaimed all land to be the 'property of the people represented by the State' and abolished all titles and customary rights to land, leaving only the ill-defined 'right to enjoy the use of the soil'. Thus all traditional territories remained state lands. Only land that had permanent buildings on it or was cultivated could be claimed. This definition of land ownership remains in place today and effectively discriminates against Mbendjele land use and claims over land, since the majority of their lands will appear unoccupied at any given time.[8] In this legal context Mbendjele seem to have no right to claim forest land.

This lack of official recognition of Mbendjele rights to forest land and resources is compounded by the government's lack of interest in supporting the Mbendjele's right to represent themselves in the same way as other communities in the Congo– namely through their own 'village committees'. Despite Mbendjele having some permanent campsites with mud and thatch huts that have been occupied for over thirty years, none of their communities are officially recognised by local authorities. This is demonstrated by the total absence of any recognised Mbendjele village leaders (*Président du village*) or any attempts to conduct elections in order that an officially recognised village committee is established, as is done in every Bilo village.

Mbendjele are growing increasingly resentful of this situation. As previously mentioned, the Mbendjele have been willing to share their forest with outsiders because of their strong ethic of sharing, but whether they will be so willing to share in future remains to be seen. Those communities that have experienced loggers coming and going feel cheated – the huge machines and extensive infrastructure of towns, roads and slipways impress the Mbendjele but also raise their suspicions. How could so much power be used without huge profits?

Loggers and Conservationists

Although Congo-Brazzaville was the fourth largest oil producer in sub-Saharan Africa in 1999, the country remains highly indebted to international financial institutions and debt arrears continue to escalate. The country does not qualify for international debt relief, although international donors met in October 2000 to discuss the situation. They indicated that, if the country follows stringent macroeconomic policies, including further privatisation, developing the non-oil sectors, particularly forestry, and fiscal management, as well as commencing work on a 'Poverty Reduction Strategy', this would take the country one step nearer to qualification for debt relief. Multilateral creditors have also been encouraging timber exports and they are now the country's second major source of export revenues after oil. Additionally, the forestry sector provides 10 percent of formal employment and forestry's contribution to GNP increased from 1 percent in 1982 to 5 percent in 1996 (Forests Monitor 2001). This explosion of activity in the forests began in the late 1970s.

During the late 1970s and 1980s the forest was divided into large concessions called UFAs (Unités Forestières d'Aménagement) in order to attract investment from foreign companies willing to exploit forest resources. This strategy was effective. By 1988 60 percent of Congo's 13 million hectares of exploitable forest were under concession (Colchester 1994: 38). As Colchester further points out, this system resembles the colonial concessionaire system, both in the scale of the areas involved and in the total disenfranchisement of local people's rights over their land and resources.

The northern forests cover 17.3 million hectares, of which 8.9 million are deemed exploitable. Before 1996, 2.1 million hectares of northern forests had been allocated as concessions. The relative isolation of the region previously limited forestry activities, but this has been changing rapidly through the intense development of roads. In 1996 alone, 3.2 million hectares were allocated for timber exploitation and, since 1998, President Sassou Nguesso has been actively seeking multinational logging companies to take over the exploitation of the remaining unallocated northern forests (Forests Monitor 2001).

Today all the UFAs have been attributed to multinational logging companies, except for the UFA of Nouabale-Ndoki, which was given to the Wildlife Conservation Society and is now the Nouabale-Ndoki National Park. Like the logging companies they replaced, the wildlife protectionists impose their presence on local people without meaningful consultations. Only Bilo communities are approached for their agreement and also occasionally to receive compensation.

There seems to be a causal relationship between loggers and conservationists. When loggers get exclusive rights to cut trees in part of the forest there are numerous consequences. For instance, logging communities need feeding, so supplying bushmeat to the salaried workforce becomes a gold rush attracting professional trappers who can hunt out a whole zone of forest using hundreds of cables. The roads used to evacuate the logs also serve the bushmeat traders. As the roads disenclave remote villages, people flock to the logging town to seek their fortune or begin intensive hunting or farming to supply the town with food. The opening up of the forest also draws wider attention to it from international environmentalists, who take an interest in the impact of logging on forest resources. The impact is great, and the environmentalists quickly begin searching for funds to begin conservation.

Images of a dire threat to 'pristine rain forest' are effective at raising funds and have been a popular banner for many conservation organisations working in the area.[9] There is clearly a threat to the environment but by mythologising the forest and ignoring the role of people's long-term presence in it conservation NGOs have tended 'to ignore or misunderstand the social realities of African rainforest environments (and this) serves the interests of no one in the end' (Burnham 2000: 51). According to the logic of the pristine rain-forest myth, local people must be excluded. Only government officials, privileged non-African conservationists, or the occasional high fee-paying Western tourist may now enter protected areas. Commercial bushmeat traders and farmers can go elsewhere, but for Yaka people it is much more difficult since each zone will have important seasonal wild resources not necessarily available elsewhere in the territory they normally live and travel in.

The implications of this dual occupation of the forest by loggers and conservationists are potentially very serious for the Mbendjele. Their forest is becoming increasingly 'modern'. Outsiders can now enter the forest independently of them, using compasses and geographic positioning systems. They can dissect it on maps made using aerial photography or satellite imagery and decisions taken in offices hundreds or thousands of kilometres away can be instantly communicated using mobile communications equipment, to be enacted by the chain-saw and bulldozer criss-crossing the forest with grid-works and roads. As international capital draws more and more of the forest's resources out of the forest, international environmentalists will begin isolating increasingly large areas of forest and excluding local people.

Thus local people, particularly Yaka people, will be the 'easy victims' of those outsiders extracting resources and those 'protecting' resources. In the meantime the real causes for the long-term abuse of resources will remain unaddressed. The severe problem of the unsound management of Congo's forest resources is not technical but political. As Colchester bluntly concluded:

> In sum foreign companies, national politicians and government officials are engaged in what amounts to massive fraud, whereby the countries' forest heritage is being exploited for personal gain at the expense of local people and the nation as a whole, and their chance of sustainable development. (1994: 43)

Traditional Land Rights

The concept of 'traditional land rights' has some de facto recognition in the Congo, but only considers Bilo groups to possess them. These 'traditional rights' were first attributed to Bilo as part of the colonial effort to extract as much forest produce as possible from local villagers. Prior to the colonial influence Bilo groups were highly fluid and mobile. This mobility was related to territorial expansion, political competition for long-distance trade links and considerable local-level warfare between neighbouring groups. It was only after the First World War that colonial 'pacification', land tenure rules, forced resettlement and forced labour stabilised populations and created permanent villages (Burnham 2000: 43).

Observing the mobility of Bilo communities over time has caused the Mbendjele to view them as outsiders, essentially transitory occupants of the forest. Maybe surprisingly, to many who think of the Mbendjele as constantly on the move, the Mbendjele contrast their own long-term and permanent occupation of the forest with the Bilo's migrations and temporary occupation. In conversations about Bilo, Mbendjele elders often remark that 'they are passing by', or that 'they have arrived but are not yet gone', or 'they came into the life but will go again'. Examples of abandoned villages or logging sites and the population reduction in rural Bilo communities are cited as examples of this movement.[10]

This perception of the Bilo by the Mbendjele is an accurate one. In recent years the boom-and-bust economy of logging has led to unrealistic expectations and unsustainable habits developing among Bilo, especially young people, whilst a logging company is operational. When the loggers go the money dries up. This contributes significantly to the rural exodus of young people in search of their former affluence in towns and cities. By 1990 52 percent of the Congolese population (and 85 percent of men between 25 and 29) were concentrated in just two cities – Brazzaville and Pointe Noire. Overall 70 percent of the population is urbanised, despite an absence of large industry to sustain them in most towns (Colchester 1994: 45).

The lack of historical depth when considering traditional land rights has failed to recognise the priority and permanence of Yaka people's occupation of the forest in contrast to Europeans or Bilo. As such it fails to address their sense of being a colonised people. Mbendjele, like other Yaka groups, continue to be treated as inferior citizens, unworthy of the same rights as other people. Discrimination against forest hunter- gatherers is widely reported (see Barume 2000; Lewis 2000: 13–19 and 2001; Kenrick and Lewis 2001; Luling and Kenrick 1998 for some examples) and is part of wider, and very serious, discrimination against hunter-gatherers throughout Africa, as Woodburn (1997) has clearly shown.

It is rare that either Northerners or Congolese question the discrimination against Yaka people, indeed many seem to perceive of it as understandable if not acceptable, since it is mostly unchallenged in public by Yaka peoples. It is also more convenient for international organisations such as logging or mining companies, animal protectionists and safari hunters to think they only need be accountable to Bilo communities in their spheres of influence. Bilo communities get the benefits of consultation and compensation payments if these occur. International organisations conveniently ignore Yaka communities and are frequently encouraged to do so by local Bilo who claim to represent the Yaka and who will resist efforts to deal directly with them. I have seen threatening letters written by workers' union representatives in a logging town to expatriate staff of the logging company who were said to be employing too many Yaka. Some even received letters from local government officials admonishing them.

Increasing respect for international human rights laws relating to indigenous peoples has provoked many 'conservation' organisations to try to show that they are undertaking activities towards supporting indigenous people. A recent, and growing, trend is to create 'village environmental management committees' in villages in or around areas under some form of protection. The formation of these committees is intended to demonstrate that the organisation is inclusive and is allowing local people to participate in managing their environment. However, these committees mostly act to reinforce Yaka marginalisation and dispossession of their rights to forest land because they are only being created in Bilo villages, with Bilo leaders and predominantly Bilo membership. The organisation of such associations is often very bureaucratic and members are assumed to be literate. In these and other ways Yaka people are marginalised from participation.

Investigations of local people's traditional territories often exclude any consideration of Yaka groups' traditional forest and land use patterns, but simply ask Bilo with whom researchers can converse, and locate, relatively easily. In Congo in early 2001, expatriate conservationists mapping out local land use and 'traditional territories' completely ignored Mbendjele areas. When I asked why the Mbendjele were not included, an American conservationist told me, 'Aaa, but they are everywhere in the forest.' These attitudes at once discriminate against Mbendjele land rights by not marking them out, while also drawing on basic Mbendjele assumptions about their ubiquity in the forest guaranteeing their right to use it.

The current lack of respect for or promotion of, Yaka forest rights is linked to the confusion surrounding their status as 'Indigenous People' who can benefit from the international human rights legislation supporting Indigenous People. The problem stems from the development of the indigenous rights movement in opposition to European colonialism, notably in the Americas and Australasia. Thus criteria such as maintaining traditional links with the land and specific cultural traits are sufficient to distinguish indigenous people from migrants coming from other continents. Applying these criteria to Africa serves to exclude European, Asian and other 'bluewater' migrants but ignores the complexity of Sub-Saharan Africa's long history of internal migration and conquest preceding, during and after the colonial period.

The focus on white – black or European – native distinctions in definitions of indigenous peoples has confused many commentators in Central Africa. Thus Burnham scorns the perception of Pygmies as indigenous people of the African forest. To illustrate his claim that such concepts are controversial in Central Africa he proceeds to describe the Beti (a Bilo group) as fulfilling the criteria for an indigenous people of the Cameroonian forest. He goes on to describe how the Beti claim ownership of land as ancestrally theirs, as if they were indigenous, yet in the next moment emphasise their colonising status as having arrived from the savannah with superior civilisation to dominate the more 'backward indigenous inhabitants of the zone' (Burnham 2000: 48).

Such claims are better described as a colonising discourse of Bilo rather than that of an indigenous people. Using Woodburn's concept of 'First People' (2001) instead of 'Indigenous People' would avoid such controversies and confusions in the Central African situation and has the great advantage of being an important indigenous category used by the ethnic groups of the region.

Conclusion

Although the Mbendjele are widely recognised as the first peoples in their area of forest, all later-comers have failed to recognise Mbendjele rights in all but vague and ambiguous ways that do not interfere with their own intentions and interests. Later-comers have imposed themselves in similar ways on the Mbendjele, mostly by force and then later with paternalistic ideologies designed to make Mbendjele more available for work.

The Mbendjele describe these black and white outsiders as arriving with anger and saying they own things. The Bilo came and took what they wanted with anger and said they owned things like forest or rivers. The Europeans did the same. They came with anger and said they were the owners and took what they wanted from Bilo. An angry person is on the verge of violence, and for Mbendjele doing things with anger is synonymous to doing things with violence.

Until recently these various 'angry' claims had no impact on the Mbendjele's ability to maintain their independence. Now, however, with the increasing ease of access for outsiders into Mbendjele forest this has begun to change as areas become hunted out. Thuret (1999) describes a community of Mbendjele near the regional capital, called Ouesso, whose forest is no longer abundant enough for them to remain for long periods away from the Bilo village. As a consequence they have become more and more sedentary, and depend on farmed foods and participation in the cash economy of Ouesso for their livelihoods.

There are some surprising parallels between Bilo colonisation of Mbendjele forest and the French colonial enterprise to dominate Bilo. Bilo continue to perceive of Mbendjele lands as empty and unused, following the colonial definition of state lands. Bilo want Mbendjele to sedentarise in villages and begin farming so that they provide a more accessible labour force. The Bilo now occupy the authority structures left behind by the French, and many emulate their perception of the colonial authorities' activities – of despotic power and corruption. Government and bureaucratic structures – notably the police and civil service – have certain similarities with their colonial predecessors, often enforcing the will of a local 'big' man and protecting his, and their own, interests.

Colonising structures have been doubly stamped over Mbendjele forest rights. First the Bilo imposed their claims to rights in land and other assets over the Mbendjele's forest rights. Then the colonial government and now the national government imposed greater rights over the Bilo claims to rights and the Mbendjele's forest rights. This has had little practical consequence for Mbendjele until quite recently. Now these rights are being sold and traded to multinational companies as rights to specific resources: trees for loggers, minerals for miners, game for conservationists and safari hunters, etc. The original holders of these rights only gain incidental benefits as workers/employees or from infrastructure. Benefits in the forest are hierarchically distributed, with those most recently involved in colonisation getting most benefit; thus the Europeans earn most from logging and mining, then the Bilo (from work, etc) and lastly, if at all, the Mbendjele.

Donor organisation pressure on companies, NGOs and governments to respect indigenous rights has forced some reconsideration of the place of local Bilo. Responsible loggers must develop management plans that show concern for indigenous peoples' rights, yet in practice they tend only to consider and consult Bilo communities. Safari hunters redistribute tiny fractions of their earnings with local Bilo communities. International environmentalist NGOs demonstrate their 'inclusiveness' by creating local environmental management committees in Bilo villages. Maps of traditional territories only label areas with Bilo ethnic names, or mark Bilo villages on official maps. Yaka people are neither consulted with, nor their presence in the forest represented, as other people's are.

Actions aimed at benefiting local people only go one layer of colonialism down – to the Bilo level. Yaka people have yet to be seriously considered. Such activities both reinforce and strengthen Bilo domination of Yaka forest and, critically, further marginalise Yaka people from any future participation or representation in the global processes now dramatically affecting their forests.

Notes

1. Field research was undertaken in the Ndoki forest, northern Republic of Congo, in 1994–97 with generous support from the Wenner-Gren Foundation for Anthropological Research, an Emslie Horniman Anthropological Scholarship and a Swan Fund Scholarship. I am grateful for an Alfred Gell Memorial Scholarship to assist in writing up. A further visit was made from November 2000 to January 2001.
2. A little trade in ritual styles and songs does occur, but not in material goods.
3. Lewis (2002: 198–237) and Köhler and Lewis (2002) provide more details on these relations.
4. Although Peterson (1993) developed the term, I here use it in the manner Woodburn (1998) proposes, which emphasises that demand-sharing is not a form of exchange. Certain individuals consistently produce more than others, and those who are less successful will always demand their excess production. The emphasis is on the obligation of the producer to share and the entitlement of the recipient to demand a share, not on reciprocity or exchange.
5. Sharing children between sets of brothers and sisters or close friends is common, and a childless couple will often be given children to look after for long periods.
6. The taboo against a hunter eating game he has killed, reported among the Aka of C.A.R. (Bahuchet 1985: 375), is not practised by the Mbendjele.
7. The general idiom for discussing success and failure in the food quest or procreation is a term called *ekila*. This is a complex polysemic word that I discuss in detail in my thesis (Lewis 2002: 103–23).
8. For a more detailed account of the relations between land law and hunter-gatherers' land rights in Central Africa, see Barume (2000).
9. Increasingly conservation groups are focusing on the bushmeat trade as the most significant threat to the forest in Central Africa. While enforcing exclusion zones vigorously, and often violently, they do little to address the structures that support members of the local and national elite responsible for organising the most damaging bushmeat trading activities. National elites have taken advantage of the intensive development of roads into the forest and the long-distance routes used to evacuate logs by the logging industry to do the same with bushmeat.
10. Brody (2000) makes a similar point: that farmers are the real nomads, not the hunter- gatherers.

References

Bahuchet, S. 1985. *Les Pygmées Aka et la Forêt Centrafricaine. Ethnologie Écologique*, Ethnoscience 1. Paris: SELAF/CNRS.

Bahuchet, S. and H. Guillaume. 1982. 'Aka- Farmer Relations in the Northwest Congo Basin'. In: E. Leacock and R.B. Lee (eds), *Politics and History in Band Societies*, pp. 189–211. Cambridge: Cambridge University Press.

Bailey, R., S. Bahuchet and B. Hewlett. 1992. 'Development in Central African rainforests: concerns for forest peoples'. In: K. Cleaver, M. Munasinghe, M. Dyson, N. Egli, A. Peuker and F. Wencelius (eds), *Conservation of West and Central African Rainforests*, pp. 202–11. Washington DC: World Bank.

Barnard, A. 2001. *The Hunter-gatherer Peoples. Three Lectures Presented in Argentina.* Buenos Aires: Fundacion Navarro Viola.

Barnard, A. and J. Woodburn. 1988. 'Property, Power and Ideology in Hunting and Gathering Societies: an Introduction'. In: T. Ingold, D. Riches and J. Woodburn (eds), *Hunters and Gatherers Volume 2: Property, Power and Ideology*, pp. 4–31. New York and Oxford: Berg.

Barume, K. 2000. *Heading Towards Extinction? Indigenous Rights in Africa: the Case of the Twa of the Kahuzi-Biega National Park, Democratic Republic of Congo.* IWGIA Document No. 101. Copenhagen: IWGIA/ Forest Peoples Programme.

Bird-David, N. 1990 'The Giving Environment: Another Perspective on the Economic System of Gatherer-Hunters'. *Current Anthropology*, 31: 189–96.

Brody, H. 2000. *The Other Side of Eden: Hunters, Farmers and the Shaping of the World.* Vancouver: Douglas and McIntyre.

Burnham, P. 2000. 'Whose Forest? Whose Myth? Conceptualisations of Community Forests in Cameroon'. In: A. Abramson and D. Theodossopoulos (eds), *Land, Law and Environment. Mythical Land, Legal Boundaries*, pp. 31–58. London: Pluto Press.

Colchester, M. 1994. *Slave and Enclave. The Political Ecology of Equatorial Africa.* Malaysia: World Rainforest Movement.

Forests Monitor. 2001. *Sold Down the River. The Need to Control Transnational Forestry Corporations: a European Case Study.* Cambridge: Forests Monitor.

Grinker, R.R. 1994. *Houses in the Rainforest: Ethnicity and Inequality Among Farmers and Foragers in Central Africa.* London: University of California Press.

Ingold, T. 1990. 'Comment on "Foragers, Genuine or Spurious: Situating the Kalahari San in History" by J. Solway and R. Lee'. *Current Anthropology*, 31: 130–31.

Kenrick, J. 2000. 'The Forest Peoples of Africa in the 21st Century: Present Predicament of Hunter Gatherers and Former Hunter Gatherers of the Central African Rainforests'. *Indigenous Affairs*, 1/00: 10-24. Copenhagen: IWGIA.

Kenrick, J. and J. Lewis. 2001. 'Evolving Discrimination against the Forest People (Pygmies) of Central Africa.' In: S. Chakma and M. Jensen (eds), *Racism against Indigenous Peoples*, pp. 312–25. Copenhagen; Asian Indigenous and Tribal Peoples Network (AITPN) and IWGIA.

Köhler, A. and J. Lewis. 2002. 'Putting Hunter-gatherer and Farmer Relations in Perspective. A Commentary from Central Africa'. In: S. Kent (ed.), *Ethnicity, Hunter-Gatherers, and the 'Other': Association or Assimilation in Southern Africa?* pp. 276–305. Washington: Smithsonian Institute.

Lee, R. 1981. 'Is There a Foraging Mode of Production?' *Canadian Journal of Anthropology*, 2: 13–19.

Lewis, J. 2000. *The Batwa Pygmies of the Great Lakes Region.* MRG Report. London: Minority Rights Group.

—— 2001. 'Forest People or Village People. Whose voice will be heard?' In: A. Barnard and J. Kenrick (eds.), *Africa's Indigenous Peoples: 'first peoples' or 'marginalized minorities'?* pp. 61–78. Edinburgh: Centre of African Studies.

—— 2002. *Forest Hunter-Gatherers and Their World: A Study of the Mbendjele Yaka Pygmies of Congo-Brazzaville and Their Secular and Religious Activities and Representations.* Ph.D. Thesis, University of London.

Luling, V. and J. Kenrick. 1998. *Forest Foragers of Tropical Africa.* London, U.K.: Survival for Tribal Peoples.

Peterson, N. 1993. 'Demand Sharing: Reciprocity and the Pressure for Generosity among Foragers'. *American Anthropologist*, 95(4): 860–74.

Thuret, M. 1999. 'A propos de la situation actuelle des Aka.Mbenzele sédentarisé: un essai comparatif entre le mode de vie baakaa et le mode de vie actuel des Aka.Mbendzele de la région de la Sangha (Nord-Congo)'. In: K. Biesbrouck, S. Elders and G. Rossel (eds), *Central African Hunter-gatherers in a Multidisciplinary Perspective: Challenging Elusiveness*, pp. 241–56. Leiden: CNWS, Universiteit Leiden.

Turnbull, C. 1966. *Wayward Servants: The Two Worlds of the African Pygmies*. London: Eyre and Spottiswoode.

Wæhle, E. 1986. 'Efe (Mbuti Pygmy) Relations to the Lese Dese Villagers in the Ituri Forest, Zaire: Historical Changes During the Last 150 Years'. *Sprache und Geschichte in Afrika*, 7(2): 375–411.

Woodburn, J. 1982. 'Egalitarian Societies'. *Man*, 17(3): 431–51.

—— 1997. 'Indigenous Discrimination: the Ideological Basis for Local Discrimination Against Hunter- Gatherer minorities in sub-Saharan Africa'. *Ethnic and Racial Studies*, 20(2): 345–61.

—— 1998. '"Sharing is not a Form of Exchange": An Analysis of Property Sharing in Immediate- Return Hunter- Gatherer Societies'. In: C. Hann (ed.), *Property Relations: Renewing the Anthropological Tradition*. Cambridge: Cambridge University Press.

—— 2001. 'The Political Status of Hunter-Gatherers in Present-Day and Future Africa'. In: A. Barnard and J. Kenrick (eds), *Africa's Indigenous Peoples: 'first peoples' or 'marginalized minorities'?* pp. 1–14. Edinburgh: Centre of African Studies.

4

The Significance of Trade in an Immediate-Return Society: The Batek Case

Kirk Endicott

Introduction

One of the fundamental questions in all of social science is: What are the conditions that promote or inhibit the rise of economic, social and political inequalities? One way to approach this question is to examine how egalitarian societies deal with cultural features and circumstances that could lead to the development of inequalities. Many, but not all, hunting and gathering societies are egalitarian (Kelly 1995). Egalitarian foraging societies are those with minimal differences among people in wealth, power and prestige, except, in some cases, between males and females and young and old. They often have 'levelling mechanisms' which, by design or by accident, impede the development of such differences. Egalitarian hunter-gatherers are rare in the world today, although they are, or once were, found in many different places. Many of the world's most egalitarian societies – and most of those that are sexually egalitarian – are hunting and gathering societies, which suggests that some features of that way of life, under some circumstances, are conducive to equality in social relations.

What are the conditions that favour egalitarian social relations in hunting and gathering societies? According to James Woodburn's well-known distinction between 'immediate-return' and 'delayed-return' foragers (1982), the most important common feature of egalitarian foraging societies is that they have immediate-return economies, meaning that there is no significant delay between when people obtain food and other raw materials and when they distribute and consume them. Lack of delay prevents the accumulation of property and enduring rights over it that may become the basis of unequal power relations. He says:

> Equality is achieved through direct, individual access to resources; through direct individual access to means of coercion and means of mobility which limit the imposition of control; through mechanisms which allow goods to circulate without making people dependent upon one another. People are systematically disengaged from property and therefore from the potentiality in property for creating dependency. (1982: 431)

By contrast, in delayed-return societies – typified by farmers – people must invest their labour in processes that pay off only much later. To ensure that they gain the benefits of their efforts, they make enduring claims over resources and the products of their labour, which lead to differences in wealth and power, since people may derive power from owning things that are necessary for survival and being able to withhold them from others.

Woodburn, writing in 1982, lists the following societies as having immediate-return economic systems: the Mbuti Pygmies of Zaire, the !Kung San of Botswana and Namibia, the Pandaram and Paliyan of India, the Batek of Malaysia and the Hadza of Tanzania (1982: 433). Today he would probably add the Agta of northern Luzon in the Philippines (Peterson 1978; Griffin and Griffin 1999) and possibly others. However, three of these societies – the Batek, the Mbuti and the Agta – have one striking feature in common, namely, external trade. The trade component of their economies, unlike the subsistence component, is inherently a delayed-return process. Yet social relations in those societies, even between the sexes, are strongly egalitarian.

Why has external trade in these societies not led to a breakdown of equality, as one would predict from Woodburn's theory? In this paper I look closely at the nature of the external trade of the Batek of Malaysia, among whom my wife Karen and I have done fieldwork,[1] to see how it is accommodated within their egalitarian social system. Based on this analysis, I attempt to specify the circumstances under which external trade, despite its delayed-return nature, does not undermine egalitarian social relations in hunting and gathering societies.

Batek Trade

The Batek De' are a language group of Semang, the category of Malayan Aborigines (termed 'Orang Asli' in Malay) traditionally associated with mobile hunting and gathering. In the 1970s and 1980s, there were about 300 Batek in Kelantan state – living in the watersheds of the Lebir, Relai and Aring Rivers – and perhaps another 500 in the adjacent state of Pahang, mostly living along the northern tributaries of the Tembeling River. During that period their home area was covered by lowland tropical rain forest, about 90 percent of which was primary forest and the remainder old secondary forest produced by the swidden horticulture of Malay farmers who once lived along the banks of some of the larger rivers. The Malays were removed by the government during the communist insurrection ('the Emergency') of the early 1950s. Beginning in the late 1970s most of the rain forest outside the

4,340 km² National Park (Taman Negara) was logged off. Now the Batek live inside the National Park, in adjacent selectively logged secondary forest or in government-sponsored settlements. This paper refers to the 1970s and 1980s, when the Batek still lived in relative isolation in the rain forest and before trade became fully monetised, as it is today.

Although the Semang are identified with hunting and gathering, they have a long history of trading forest products to other groups. Probably their ancestors engaged in trade with the earliest horticulturalists in the Malay peninsula, the ancestors of the modern-day Senoi Orang Asli (Dunn 1975; Benjamin 1985). Benjamin hypothesises that the Semang and Senoi deliberately specialised in complementary economic strategies and that trade enabled them both to benefit from the expertise of the other. In recent centuries most Batek trade has been with Malays, farming and fishing people who lived along the major rivers in the area (Endicott 1997: 40–42). The products exchanged varied according to what was in demand at any given time. As in other parts of the country, Malay chiefs or headmen sometimes attempted to control trade with the Batek. The amount of trade ebbed and flowed, depending on whether Batek relations with the local villagers were good or bad, as in periods of Malay slave raiding. In tense times, people sometimes resorted to 'silent trade', in which the parties to the exchange never came into direct contact (Wells 1925: 100; Endicott 1997: 42). When relations between Batek and Malays were good, trade was often supplemented by labour barter, in which some Batek assisted Malay farmers with their agricultural work in exchange for agricultural products.

In the period 1970–90, the products extracted by the Batek gradually changed, as the forest products wanted in the villages and the outside world changed. In the early 1970s Batek on the lower Lebir still provided rolls of thatch to Malay homesteaders, although demand for thatch ceased once the villagers gained access to galvanised iron roofing. There was also some labour barter with Malay farmers. The mainstay of the forest products trade during the whole period was rattan, the stems of various species of climbing palms (*Calamus* spp.; called 'cane' in the furniture trade). Early on there was demand for thin rattans, used by Kelantan Malays in furniture, house construction, fish traps and baskets. Later demand shifted to the thick rattan that is used mostly as frames for furniture. Around 1980 the emphasis shifted to supplying aloes wood (*Aquilaria* spp.; called *gaharu* in Malay), fragrant resinous wood used for incense in South Asia and the Middle East. By 1990, however, most of the suitable aloes wood trees had been found and harvested, and Batek returned to the search for thick rattan.

The products provided by the Malay traders also changed during that period, though not so dramatically. Products continuously in demand included white rice, wheat flour, cooking oil, salt, sugar, tea and tobacco. Manufactured goods – like cloth sarongs, flashlights and steel-bladed bushknives – were also popular throughout that time. Cheap electronic devices, including transistor radios and boomboxes, became popular in the 1980s. By 1990 traders in four-wheel-drive pickup trucks were able to come in on logging roads and bring perishable treats, such as bread, cookies and even ice lollies!

Between 1970 and 1990, very few Malays lived in the Batek home area in Kelantan. Most Batek trade was carried out with Malay traders based in the villages of Kampung Lalok and Manek Urai, on the lower Lebir River. Typically, small groups of traders would come up the river in outboard boats, loaded with the kinds of goods the Batek wanted, looking for Batek camps. The leaders of the trading groups would seek out Batek who wanted to enter into a trade agreement, often people they had dealt with before. These agreements were made between individual traders and individual Batek, both men and women, not between traders and groups of Batek. The prospective trade partners would attempt to agree on the amount of rattan or other produce to be collected, the price to be paid (often stated in terms of Malaysian currency, but delivered in goods), the date the goods would be ready and the location at which the traders would pick them up. Sometimes more than one group of traders would come at the same time, and the competition for Batek services would drive up the price offered. When they reached an agreement, the trader would give his Batek trade partner a partial payment of food and trade goods. Occasionally Batek would stockpile some rattan or aloes wood in anticipation of a later visit from a trader. If no traders were available – say, during the Muslim fasting month – a Batek might try to organise some friends to collect some forest produce and raft it down to the Malay villages themselves. There they would deal directly with the shopkeepers or wholesalers, who were the buyers for the Malay traders. Because the Batek had some choice in whom they would trade with, they were able to get reasonably good returns for their forest produce.

Once agreements had been reached, the Malay traders would return to their villages or set up a camp near the agreed-upon delivery point. Their Batek partners and sometimes their families would then move to an area containing the desired trade goods and begin collecting and stockpiling them. Collecting trade goods involved searching, harvesting and transporting them to the collection point. Thin rattan could be pulled down from the trees supporting the plant, cut into standard trade lengths, bundled up and dragged back to camp or to a stream. To get thick rattan, collectors had to climb the trees and cut the stems loose from the crowns. They then cut the stems into standard lengths, tied them in bundles and carried them out on their shoulders. Usually they would load the bundles of rattan onto bamboo rafts and raft them down to the collection point. Getting aloes wood required cutting down the tree and chopping the trunk apart in order to remove the diseased wood containing the aromatic resin. Collectors would carefully trim away the waste wood and store the valuable resinous wood in pandanus pouches or cloth bundles.

The organisation of the work parties was variable. Usually individuals or small groups would simply go out from the main camp each day, collect the goods and bring them back to camp or a storage place each night. If the source was far from the camp, however, the work group might hive off and form a temporary camp in the area being exploited. Often a few non-collectors – usually spouses, children or friends – would join them. While getting the trade goods, the collectors would live off the rations given by their trade partners and, after those ran out, off wild plant and animal foods. The collectors might alternate collecting expeditions with days of food gathering or they might live off the food obtained by the non-collectors in the camp. Batek recognised that, because of the general sharing obligation, non-collectors would get a portion of their food from the collectors in the early phase of a contract, and the collectors would get food from the non-collectors later on.

When the agreed date arrived, the Malay traders would return to the delivery point. If the contract were for rattan, they would usually hire a few Batek to help build bamboo rafts for transporting the rattan downstream. The traders would then pay the amount still owed to their trade partners in goods and/or cash. The collectors were then free to negotiate a new contract with the same or a different Malay trader. In 1990, however, a few Batek had got into debt, thus shifting the balance of power in favour of the traders. Given the rising importance of trade as wild foods were destroyed by logging and the establishment of oil palm plantations, we may have been seeing the beginnings of a more exploitative relationship. (See Peterson and Matsuyama 1991 for examples of trade leading to exploitation of foraging peoples.)

Ownership and Distribution

The social effects of hunter-gatherer trade depend in large part on ownership concepts and distribution practices. The Batek consider all unharvested resources to be freely available to everyone (Endicott 1988). The person who first finds something with trade value has the right to harvest it, but only then does it become his or her property. The finder may share the discovery with others, in which case everyone who helps in harvesting it gets to keep the portion they harvest. For example, when someone finds an aloes wood tree, the finder usually calls on others to help cut it down and chop it apart. Each worker keeps the aloes wood he or she chops out of the tree. Similarly, once a rattan stem has been stripped of leaves and cut to length, it belongs to the person who harvested it. The owner has exclusive rights to use it or sell it. There is no obligation to share it or give it away. Thus, each bundle of rattan has a known and acknowledged owner, even though it is usually left unguarded on a river bank or at the designated delivery point. Anyone who takes or trades someone else's bundle of rattan is said to have stolen it. This occasionally happens, especially if the owner has a prior debt to the 'thief'. The person taking it would then justify taking the rattan as merely collecting a debt.

Batek consider all goods and money obtained from the traders to be the personal property of the person who collected the forest produce. However, the person's rights and obligations vary with the various types of goods obtained. Non-food items like trinkets, tools, boomboxes and cloth sarongs are personal possessions, much like the things that Europeans and Americans obtain by purchasing them with their own funds. Batek more freely lend and borrow personal possessions than we do, even without asking the owner, but the items remain the property of the original possessor. However, Batek often give things to relatives and friends, in which case ownership of those items is transferred to the recipient. Tobacco is a special case. Tobacco obtained by trade is regarded as the personal possession of the recipient, but people are expected to be generous in sharing it with others.

On the other hand, food obtained by trade must be shared, just like food obtained directly from the forest (see Endicott 1988: 115–18 for details of Batek food sharing). The basic idea is that people have a moral obligation to share any food they obtain with all others in camp who need it. This is not always practical, however. When food is scarce, priority should be given to sharing with children and old people, especially one's parents and parents-in-law. Game animals of any substantial size, say a monkey, should be cut into enough portions that every family in camp, usually between five and ten, receives a piece. Vegetable foods should be shared with as many other families as possible, though parents' first obligation is to feed their own children. Food obtained in trade differs from foraged food in that it is usually obtained in large quantities, for example a sack of rice or flour, it is obtained infrequently, and it is mostly types of food that can be stored for some time without spoiling. Normally the person who obtained the food keeps it, but gradually doles it out according to the daily needs of camp members. This practice implicitly acknowledges that the forest produce collectors received food from others while they were collecting the trade goods. The obligation to share food with fellow camp members is perhaps the strongest obligation in the Batek moral code. Not sharing is considered a profoundly antisocial act, even a sign of insanity. Batek say that a person who persistently refused to share food when others were hungry would be banished from the group, although we never heard of any cases of this actually happening.

Money obtained from trade is considered a personal possession and can be hoarded until it is spent. People may try to conceal the amount of money they have, to deter others from asking for some, but usually everyone knows very well how much money a person has because trade transactions are public acts. Although money may be hoarded, it is useless unless it is used to buy something, and if it is used to buy food, that wealth ends up being shared with the group.

Why Batek Trade Does Not Undermine Equality

On the surface it looks as though forest produce trade could easily lead to differences in wealth and power. Trade would seem to favour young adult males, the group most involved in collection of forest produce, over other categories of people. In most societies people find ways to turn differences in income into enduring differences in wealth and power, but this has not happened among the Batek.

The main impediment to wealth accumulation is the obligation to share food. Collectors of forest produce must eat, and they depend on others in the group to help feed them while they are concentrating on collecting inedible commodities. Although trade is an individual endeavour, it is only possible because of the support of the group. Therefore they are expected to share in turn any food they obtain from trade transactions. People also expect collectors to take some of their earnings in the form of manufactured items that become personal possessions, and no one seems to begrudge them this right. Often young men and their wives acquire more personal possessions than older couples, who are typically less active in collection for trade, but the differences in wealth are usually short-lived. In tropical forest conditions, nondurable things, such as electronic equipment and clothing, quickly deteriorate and are discarded. Like other mobile foragers, Batek also avoid trading for material things that would seriously impede the movement that makes their foraging and collecting forest produce possible. In the early 1980s, at the height of the aloes wood boom, some families had acquired so many possessions that they had to move from one camping place to another by raft. Even with rafts, however, there was a practical limit to the amount of equipment a family could transport.

Why don't collectors use some of their income as capital, which they could invest to produce more wealth? In theory, collectors could use money or goods obtained from trade to hire other Batek to work for them. They could then keep the difference between the wages paid and the income obtained, in classical capitalistic fashion. The main reason this does not happen is that potential employees can easily strike their own deals directly with Malay traders and thus get full value for their produce. There is no incentive for them to work for a fellow Batek instead. In addition, Batek strongly resent being told what to do by others, especially other Batek. (Batek do sometimes work for outsiders for wages if the rewards are sufficient, for example as guides.) They place a high value on individual autonomy and independence. Batek believe that a person who pressures another to do something the latter does not want to do can cause the person pressured to become ill with a depression-like condition called *ke'oy*. Part of the cure is for the offender to make amends to the victim. An offender who refused to do so would be criticised and scorned by the group as a whole. This belief and related attitudes would make it difficult for a Batek entrepreneur to impose discipline on a Batek labour force. One man we knew tried to organise a large-scale contract using friends and relatives as workers, but the enterprise was a failure. Even though the organiser did not expect any extra shares of the proceeds, he found that his 'coolies', as he called them, did not follow through on their promises. The workers happily accepted the food and goods the organiser had obtained as an advance from the wholesaler, but they then found many compelling reasons not to spend their time collecting the promised rattan. They seem to have felt even less obligation to their kinsman than they would have to a Malay trader, who at least would have been able to threaten to withdraw his trade from them in the future. Finally the organiser declared in frustration that he would never again try to do such a thing, as he had no control over his workers and had ended up having to fulfil the contract himself.

In theory, also, collectors could use some of their income to buy a piece of capital equipment and then charge others for using it. For example, a person could buy a boat and outboard motor and then charge others to ride in it. The problem, however, is that there is no precedent in Batek practice for one Batek to charge another for the use of equipment. For example, people freely lend their bush-knives to others whenever they are not using them themselves, and they would never ask for compensation. The one Batek we knew who bought a boat and motor found that his Batek customers baulked at paying any more than a proportional share of his actual expenses (gas, oil, etc.), even though they were used to paying Malay boatmen higher amounts for similar services. The Batek saw using his boat in terms of his obligation to help kin, rather than as a business transaction.

The problem of behaving like a capitalist in a Batek context is well illustrated by the case of a Batek man who almost got rich. In the late 1970s, one energetic, talented and relatively well-educated young Batek man, Limau (not his real name), attracted the attention of local Department of Aboriginal Affairs officials. The Department decided to use him as an example of entrepreneurship for other Batek. With support from officials, he was able to become a middleman in the aloes wood and rattan trade. He obtained a large loan from a buyer in Trengganu state and purchased some goods to offer as advances. He then became a buyer to all the Batek living in the Lebir and Aring River valleys in Kelantan. At first, collectors preferred to deal with him because he was one of them, he gave collectors competitive prices, he gave them advances and credit as Malay traders did, and he was honest in weighing the aloes wood and grading the rattan they collected. However, like any middleman, he paid the producers somewhat less than he got from his buyer, thus making a small profit. In 1981, he had a large plank house at Kampung Macang, on the lower Lebir, complete with linoleum on the floor. He also had two boats and an outboard motor. Later he built a combination sundries shop and café, an oversized plank house with a concrete floor, as recommended by the Department. In 1981, I speculated that he represented the beginning of economic differentiation among the Batek, and I expected this to be a continuing trend (Endicott 1988: 126).

What actually happened was very different. When we returned in 1990, Limau was living on the upper Aring in a lean-to shelter like everyone else, except that he still had a few luxury goods, including a set of china teacups. He had abandoned his eating shop at Kampung Macang. What had happened? According to one of his brothers, people had been eager to trade with him at first. Later they began to get upset with him because they realised that he was getting more for the goods than they received from him, thus getting rich off their labour. They considered this unfair, a breach of the general obligation to help, not exploit, other Batek. The result was that the Batek – even his own family – quit trading with him. As one brother said, 'Limau forgot that he was a Batek.' In 1990, he was still making occasional trips to distant valleys to try to collect from people who owed him money or aloes wood.

Conclusions

According to Woodburn's theory, economic processes involving a delayed return on labour should lead to differences in wealth and power among the members of a society. This is because delayed-return systems 'depend for their effective operation on a set of ordered, differentiated, jurally-defined relationships through which crucial goods and services are transmitted. They imply binding commitments and dependencies between people' (Woodburn 1982: 433). Ingold argues that inequalities are not inherent in delayed-return processes, but that they arise when the delay involves appropriation of resources (1987: 200, 216). He says, 'a delay in the return on labour would only have social repercussions if the initial investment of labour entailed the appropriation of the resource; that is, if it made the resource the object of social relations both among those who can exert claims upon it and between those who can and those who cannot exert such claims' (1987: 216).

Batek trade clearly violates the predictions that would arise from these theories. Batek trade *is* a delayed-return activity. Collecting rattan or aloes wood requires planning, moving camp and stockpiling commodities, processes that may span several months before the final payoff. And Batek collectors *do* appropriate forest products. Batek consider the commodities collected to be the personal property of the collector, as are the goods the collector obtains for them in trade. Ownership of foods obtained from outside traders is qualified by the food-sharing obligation, but other items are considered personal possessions, like things one makes or receives as gifts. One could argue that, in the case of food, this is not really individual appropriation, because the group as a whole has a moral claim to a share of the food. In general, however, Batek speak of food obtained through trade or direct foraging activities as belonging to the person who procured it, even though it is then subject to the sharing obligation. Group members do not pressure collectors to trade only for food. They accept the collector's right to decide what to trade for, although I think they would become resentful if the collector *never* traded for food at all.

Why, then, does Batek trade in forest produce not have the predicted social consequences? The reason seems to be that certain Batek values and practices act as powerful levelling mechanisms, neutralising any economic and social differences before they arise. One such levelling mechanism is the obligation to share food (Woodburn 1982: 442). This ensures that a collector does not accumulate a large supply of trade food and then use it to manipulate other Batek. This obligation gains moral reinforcement from the general feeling that collectors should provide food to those who provided food to them when they were collecting forest products (sharing as 'generalized reciprocity').

Another levelling mechanism is the strong value placed on individual autonomy. This inhibits the development of hierarchical work groups, which could enable some people to profit from the work of others. Members of work groups are independent agents, even though they cooperate in some ways. The circumstances of Batek life also undercut any need for one person to work for another in an unequal relationship. Because natural resources, both foods and commodities, are freely available to all and because anyone who cannot procure food himself or herself can obtain food from others through the sharing network, no one is ever in a position of having to depend on specific others for survival (Woodburn 1982: 434; Ingold 1987: 237). In short, the Batek have the kind of levelling mechanisms that Woodburn sees as characterising immediate-return societies, despite the presence of trade, which is a delayed-return process. (Woodburn recognises that 'there is some delayed-return activity in immediate-return systems', 1982: 449 fn 3.) The dominance of immediate-return social relations effectively neutralises the potential for trade to cause economic, social and political inequalities.

It is likely that in the other egalitarian foraging societies that engage in trade with outsiders, such as the Mbuti Pygmies and the Agta, one could find such levelling mechanisms and circumstances. One feature they seem to have in common is a food-sharing obligation, although the precise form of the obligation varies from one people to another. Other levelling mechanisms may be specific to certain groups. Woodburn mentions that Hadza have equal access to lethal weapons, so one person cannot coerce another physically. The Batek, on the other hand, abhor all interpersonal violence, which has the same effect. I believe that a careful analysis of each of these societies would reveal several values and practices which together neutralise the differentiating potential of trade.

One general conclusion we can draw from the Batek case is that values and social obligations can, in some circumstances, exert control over economic processes and their consequences. Many scholars have noted that food-sharing obligations are so strong among many former foragers that they prevent or seriously hinder the adoption of food production (farming or pastoralism) by preventing successful food-producers from retaining the fruits of their labour (e.g., Lee 1993: 143-44). It is not surprising, then, that food-sharing obligations and other levelling mechanisms can prevent the rise of economic and social differences in foraging societies that engage in trade. When a delayed-return process like trade is embedded in a thoroughly egalitarian social system, it can be made to conform to the system as a whole.

Notes

1. I carried out fieldwork in 1971–72, 1973, 1975–76, 1981 and 1990. I wish to thank the National Institute of Mental Health, the University of Malaya, the Australian National University, the Social Science Research Council, the US Department of Education, the Claire Garber Goodman Fund, and Dartmouth College for financial support for this research. I also thank the Jabatan Hal Ehwal Orang Asli Malaysia for permission and logistical assistance and Dr Lye Tuck Po for her valuable feedback on an earlier version of this paper.

References

Benjamin, G. 1985. 'In the Long Term: Three Themes in Malaysian Cultural Ecology'. In: K.L. Hutterer, A.T. Rambo, and G. Lovelace (eds), *Cultural Values and Human Ecology in Southeast Asia*, pp. 219–78. Michigan Papers on South and Southeast Asia no. 27. Ann Arbor, MI: Center for South and Southeast Asian Studies.

Dunn, F.L. 1975. *Rain-Forest Collectors and Traders: A Study of Resource Utilization in Modern and Ancient Malaya.* Monograph No. 5. Kuala Lumpur: Malaysian Branch of the Royal Asiatic Society.

Endicott, K. 1988. 'Property, Power and Conflict among the Batek of Malaysia'. In: T. Ingold, D. Riches and J. Woodburn (eds), *Hunters and Gatherers Volume 2: Property, Power and Ideology*, pp. 110–27. Oxford: Berg.

—— 1997. 'Batek History, Interethnic Relations, and Subgroup Dynamics'. In: R.L. Winzeler (ed.), *Indigenous Peoples and the State: Politics, Land, and Ethnicity in the Malayan Peninsula and Borneo,* pp. 30-50. New Haven: Yale University Southeast Asia Studies, Monograph 46.

Griffin, P.B. and M.B. Griffin. 1999. 'The Agta of Eastern Luzon, Philippines'. In: R.B. Lee and R. Daly (eds), *The Cambridge Encyclopedia of Hunters and Gatherers*, pp. 289–93. Cambridge: Cambridge University Press.

Ingold, T. 1987. *The Appropriation of Nature: Essays on Human Ecology and Social Relations.* Iowa City: University of Iowa Press.

Kelly, R.L. 1995. *The Foraging Spectrum: Diversity in Hunter-Gatherer Lifeways.* Washington and London: Smithsonian Institution Press.

Lee, R.B. 1993. *The Dobe Ju/'hoansi*, 2nd edn. Fort Worth, TX: Harcourt Brace College Publishers.

Peterson, J.T. 1978. *The Ecology of Social Boundaries: Agta Foragers of the Philippines.* Urbana, IL: University of Illinois Press.

Peterson, N. and T. Matsuyama (eds) 1991. *Cash, Commoditisation and Changing Foragers.* Senri Ethnological Studies No. 30. Osaka: National Museum of Ethnology.

Wells, C. 1925. *Six Years in the Malay Jungle.* Garden City, NY: Doubleday, Page, and Co.

Woodburn, J. 1982. 'Egalitarian Societies'. *Man* (N.S.), 17: 431–51.

5

The Road to Equality? Landscape Transformation and the Batek of Pahang, Malaysia

Lye Tuck-Po

I began this reflection on James Woodburn's contributions with the question: what happens when hunter-gatherers from an immediate-return society use roads to get about? We of course owe the distinction between immediate- and delayed-return political organisations to Woodburn's seminal papers (1980, 1982). There he points to possible trajectories of conflict if and when immediate-return hunter-gatherers are articulated into state systems of governance. In this paper I'd like to extend his insights to the *spatial* context of that articulation. Specifically, I'm concerned with the 'modern' phenomenon of roads. Roads aptly symbolise the encounter–or, rather, the tensions–between immediate- and delayed-return approaches to the environment. We customarily associate immediate-return hunter-gatherers with walking paths rather than metalled roads (Tilley 1994). So when they do use the latter, what happens to the identity of the roads?

Well, perhaps we should first ask: do roads belong to an immediate- or delayed-return system? In framing the question this way, I may be inviting ridicule. Of course roads are the 'property' of those who can mobilise the capital, technology and labour to build them; i.e. they exist *because* of inequality. Most importantly, they are the 'property' of state, part of the state-making enterprise. They serve the standard purposes of promoting commerce, easing communication, establishing governmental presence and maintaining order in frontier regions–of imposing a state-centred vision of 'legibility' (Scott 1999) on the landscape. Unlike the walking paths described in this chapter, roads help administrators to remodel the environment in a shape and form that is highly amenable to centralised governance (see, for example, Ferguson

1990). They are powerful indicators of the relationship between centre and periphery–roads are status and prestige symbols, markers of power and control, and they clearly delineate the limits to equality. The farther one journeys towards a capital city the closer one approaches the delayed-return end of the socioeconomic spectrum. And often the physical conditions of a road will signal which side of the political spectrum its habitual users belong to: a common 'gift' to communities at election time is the building or improvement of roads and other infrastructural facilities. Roads seem to be clear symbols of the delayed-return approach to the environment–especially when we juxtapose them with the walking paths of immediate-return societies like those examined here, the Batek of Pahang, Malaysia. However, roads are also symbols of inclusiveness: the inclusion of far flung places and peoples within the ambit of a state. From the perspective of 'the centre', then, roads are routes to equality, an equality that, in the Malaysia of today, is expressed as access to the benefits of development (Lim 1998). When immediate-return peoples use delayed-return roads, are they colluding in their own demise or placing themselves on the road to full equality? This is the paradox underlying this paper.

Far be it for me to question the vilification of roads (Hood and Hasan 1984; Wadley 1998; Vidal 2001). Yet anthropological denunciation of roads does not stand up to close scrutiny. We use the roads to get to the people (Grinker 1994: 18–20); the people like and make extensive use of the roads. Roads are a great aid to ethnography.[1] And when we do arrive at our field sites, our discomfort with the roads that have taken us there may not be (in my experience, is *never*) matched by local sentiments. We cannot just reject the spectre of roads. For many peripheral peoples, roadbuilding shows that government is turning attention to their needs (Forbes 1999). In Malaysia, the standard practice was to focus development on 'growth poles' (urban nodes): social economic services there (including health care and education) are generally superior to those in less densely populated rural areas (Teh et al. 2001: 230). When I conducted socioeconomic assessments in remote regions of Sabah, East Malaysia, in 1998, the building of access roads ranked high among locals' list of desired developments. Roads, they reasoned, would bring them closer to hospitals, to the children who are boarding at school far away, to the relatives who have migrated out and to the market centres where agricultural products are sold.

Still, none of that brings us closer to understanding the place of these external symbols in the world-view of the Batek. After all: they do not have relatives in the urban centres, children ensconced in school dormitories or produce for village markets. Their perspectives on roads are likely to be different from that of the delayed-return farmers and fisher folk of Sabah. I propose then to consider here, albeit in a preliminary way, how and if roads do enter their property idioms. If roads are markers of social ecological change, cutting up not just space but time, then an examination of how they are assimilated into the cognition and practice of immediate-return hunter-gatherers should provide an insight into the emergence of inequalities. This paper also follows on themes that I've explored elsewhere, on the cognitive and symbolic significance of forest trails to the Batek. Given the centrality of movement in their lives and to their sense of self, it seems only logical to extend the analysis to the new property regimes introduced by roadbuilding.

Immediate-Returners in an Unequal Setting: The Batek

The Batek are one of the twenty or so indigenous ethnic minorities of Peninsular Malaysia, the Orang Asli (Malay for 'original people'–the official administrative label). They live in lowland evergreen rainforests (less than 200 m a.s.l.) in the states of Kelantan, Pahang and Terengganu, in a landscape marked by the alternation of land and water. I estimate the total population to be around 900 or so, with half of that in Pahang.

Government policy on Orang Asli is premised on the need for assimilation, by which is meant assimilation into (Muslim) Malay society (Carey 1970). As with other Orang Asli, the Batek of Pahang regard Islamic conversion with great suspicion. Among many reasons, one is that Malays have always been the ethnic and political majority. Indigenous identities are asserted as *different* from the Malay one (see Benjamin 1966). Assimilationist policies tend to be regarded as a threat and strengthen–not weaken–the Batek's conviction that the lines of identity difference should be drawn as firmly as possible. Following a neoevolutionary paradigm of modernisation, state intervention often begins by promoting a 'higher' form of food procurement (like cash-crop farming), which accompanies a policy of 'not encouraging' the continuance of mobility (JHEOA 1961).[2]

With natural resource exploitation and plantation agriculture fuelling the process of national development, little lowland forest in the Peninsula remains 'untouched' and land security is now the Orang Asli's most pressing need. In Batek experience, large-scale logging and land transformation began in the early 1970s in Kelantan and much of the remaining forest, whether there or in Pahang, is greatly fragmented. However, as long as some forest cover remains, the Batek continue to regard logged-over areas as home (Lye 2000). Over half of the Pahang Batek (about 200–300) spend a majority of time in the 60-year-old national park, Taman Negara (4343 km^2), most of which straddles their traditional territory. All the groups can freely travel in and out of the park.[3] It is now the largest unbroken tract of forest still available to them. For Pahang Batek, mobility remains fundamental (Lye 1997). However, movement patterns have been affected by forest loss. For example: groups might stay longer in a place (though the overall average is about two weeks); groups are not so widely dispersed; camp group populations might also be higher than under conditions of land abundance; they are more conscious of territorial boundaries like those of Taman Negara; and some groups tend to spend more time in semi-permanent settlements, of which there are two on the edges of the national park.

The principal 'immediate-return characteristics' of Batek society that attracted James Woodburn's attention (1980, 1982) continue to persist, albeit in a much altered economic and physical setting. It's hard to avoid the conclusion that, as Woodburn summarised for all 'immediate-returners', equality in Batek society is 'not neutral, the mere absence of inequality or hierarchy, but *asserted*' (Woodburn 1982: 431; emphasis in the original). Elsewhere (Lye 2004: Chapter 4) I have suggested that we can uncover such assertions through a close reading of the mythology. There: complementarity (of male and female; brother and brother; Batek and outsiders) is recognised but inequality is not; strife and conflict are absent and so is the subjugation of 'nature' as a necessary business of cultural evolution. And in everyday statements, Batek will stress that, unlike the Malays, they are not violent, do not have restrictive rules, and they value personal freedoms and autonomy.

In practical activities, their immediate-return approach can be summed up in a single statement: they prefer options that afford the greatest flexibility and the fastest tangible returns (see Endicott 1984 for more details). For example, when Batek men are stranded in the small market towns, they will use up all available cash on an expensive taxi ride rather than wait for the dilatory – but extremely affordable – local bus. Later they will complain about the exorbitant charges: but they will not favour the thrifty – and delaying – option of taking the slow bus home. This preference for the immediate is reflected in the general economic profile. Among all possible economic activities open to them, permanent field cultivation must be the least desirable. Batek recognise that, unlike full-time farmers, they do not – *do not want to* – attend to the daily care of crops. They are rice eaters but not rice growers; they prefer their paddy to come from the store. The main agricultural crops that appear in Batek settlements are fast-growing vegetables and fruits that need only minimum care (maize, cassava, bananas, peppers, papayas, etc.). Thus the tendency, for those who do plant, is to select crops that will not prevent them from switching activities and moving on to other places while the crops are growing.

Like all Orang Asli, historically the Batek combined hunting-and-gathering with forest products extraction (Dunn 1975; Kiew and Hood 1996) and they continue to do so. One reason, I suspect, is that extractive activities are extremely amenable to immediate-return relations with the environment. Anyone, including women and children, can participate at will. They can suspend work whenever they need to – no patron here to dictate working schedules. They can integrate a few hours of 'rattan work' (rattan is the major commercial product today) with food gathering. And the collection cycles (as organised by a Chinese trader) are only three weeks long: they receive payment on the day of shipment and spend most of it right there and then to spend most of their money on the same day. Finally, in view of the spatial dispersal and heterogeneity of tropical forest species, they need to have a certain readiness to search for resource stocks and move locations as new opportunities appear. As Woodburn (1982: 435) phrased it, movement for immediate-return hunter-gatherers is 'not seen as a burdensome necessity but positively as something healthy and desirable in itself'. For the Batek, commercial extraction both builds on their need for freedom of movement and reinforces that need.

From Paths to Roads

The foregoing suggests that new forms of experience tend not to substitute for, but to be defined in terms of, the culturally familiar. Which immediately raises a potential area of conflict. If the Batek emphasise flexibility over structure and select options that bring the fastest tangible returns, we would expect them to embrace the routes of least resistance: to drive rather than to walk and to use roads rather than paths. Let us first examine the social life of the paths before probing this issue in more detail.

An extensive series of pathways traverse over walking trails, rivers and logging roads, criss-crossing the forest and linking it to the world beyond. As with other hunter-gatherers (Tilley 1994; Brody 2001) and perhaps more generally (see, for example, Orlove 2002), paths are important in every sort of way. An idea of a path is indistinguishable from its physical expression in the landscape. The words *halbew* or *harbew* refer not only to the path itself but the notional 'way' or 'route' (hence my definition of *halbew* as 'pathway'). This linkage between the 'thinginess' and the idea of the path is replicated elsewhere. Any stretch of *halbew* may be a path of ascent (*ceniweh*) or of descent (*penisar*) depending on which way you're going. At either end of the journey, you *lew*, which means both to arrive *and* to leave. Every departure implies an arrival as every arrival implies a departure. Directionality, or the movements of the body, is what gives the notional 'way' its physical expression in the 'path'. To rephrase: without the people there is only, to borrow an image from Orlove, 'a web of lines on the land' (2002: 210). And reciprocally without those 'lines' the social life of people would be shaped differently.

From our sedentary perspective, Batek lives can be reduced to the process of moving from camp to camp, all within the surround of the forest. In that movement, however, lies the basis for society. Some campsites have been around a long time; others are established as people discover new resource zones. Thus one is always following on the efforts of the past and discovering new locations. The visitor travelling with Batek groups inevitably comes to hear of other campsites close by. Often there will be stray visitors from these other camps. In the course of the daily round in the forest, the route might bypass or cut through old encampments. The picture begins to emerge of a series of crosshatching and overlapping itineraries, of camp groups meeting other camp groups, of travellers meeting the traces of earlier travellers. The forest begins to look like any busy thoroughfare anywhere, full of paths, projects, schedules, and routines (see Pred 1981).

Many things come together, intersect, and diverge in a camp, then–the physical tracks and trails and the biographies and memories of people. These form social memory. It is only when itineraries merge around a camp that the notion of 'group' assumes a concrete shape. Material from Aboriginal Australia shows that conventional land area boundaries make little sense to hunter-gatherers. Where you journey, there is your country; and that country is marked by the passageways of your trails (Wagner 1986: 21). If land is subject to property concepts, then for hunter-gatherers like the Batek those concepts cannot be divorced from movement and movement patterns in turn enable everyone to claim access but not exclusive rights (see Woodburn 1982: 435–36).

Property considerations do not take us far into the concrete 'actualisation' of the pathways. As Weiner has pointed out: 'Journeying through Hegeso territory on foot is never a matter of merely getting from one point to another' (Weiner 1991: 38). Similarly, a pathway is not just a line between departure and arrival. It is a route to knowledge. The *experience* of moving on a path is the basis for developing concrete knowledge of it. Repetitive, habitual movement over a network of well-defined trails is the method of acquiring familiarity. As Batek recollections show, learning to attend to the important details of the environment is not possible unless it is done consistently and continuously. Understanding is a lifelong process, begun ideally from the first moments of life.

Foraging activities are most focused on trailsides: the *halbew* are often located on ridges and rises from which it is easier to spot useful materials. Batek do not begin foraging trips without a certain route in mind. They prefer the well-trodden trails; then, when gathering or collecting, they will leave the trails, opening up temporary passageways as they comb through the forest in search of materials. As they walk, they actively monitor the world around them. They are looking at changes in the vegetation, spotting animal spoors and traces, indicators of change, swapping information–and affecting the characteristics of the trail by the very act of using it.

With further action and as topography changes (for example, a path is revealed to be too slippery after rainfall), then new pathways are opened up. 'Opening up' may be an extravagant way to describe the practice. The Batek do not cut openings unless the way is impossibly blocked. Typically, they slash a few vines and branches and the vegetation will 'close up' behind them. Following on their heels, it can be hard for an outsider to see where exactly they have pushed through the vegetation unless the passageways already have a well-worn aspect. Path cutting, as with the clearing of lean-to space, is done ever so casually. Often the sharp points of cut saplings stick up at shin level.

Topographic knowledge of the pathways enables individuals and groups to plan their own movements and keep track of others'. Because of the high degree of flux and intercamp visitation, new findings and discoveries about the social and ecological worlds are often shared across vast distances in the form of news and gossip exchange. Additionally, news and gossip serve not just to monitor the resource base, but also to maintain ongoing links between people who are far apart and hence to give everybody a sense of community and belonging.

As the environment changes, so too the routes and the Batek's perceptual bounds. This is shown in a development of terms to describe these newer kinds of paths: *halbew tah* (metalled road), *halbew wing* (logging road), *halbew pelancong* (tourist trail), and *halbew banar* (town road). In these binomials, the secondary words are of foreign origin: *tah* from English *tar[red]*; *pelancong* and *banar* from Malay *pelancong* and *bandar* (the mysterious '*wing*' has not been defined). From this linguistic perspective, a road is just a different type of pathway.

The Social Life of Roads

Events of the past thirty years have complexified Batek life but it shows clear continuities with the past. Batek are fundamentally outward-orientated people: they are, as Kirk Endicott wrote, foragers of ideas as well as of food (1979: 221). External communities, their ways of using and representing the landscape, are not new to the Batek (Lye 2004). In Benjamin's words, Semang[4] 'have worked the fields for Malay farmers, served as porters for forest travellers, sold or bartered forest products with outsiders, and even desultorily cultivated their own swiddens' (Benjamin 2002: 34). There are good reasons for thinking that this pattern–of drawing on external resources for social reproduction–has been integral to Semang economies. Roads rank among the most recent of these resources, affording a different way of experiencing time and space.

The path-to-road relationship was established in the early decades of the twentieth century, when the first roads were built on the site of old walking and bridle paths (Ooi 1963). In the Batek landscape, they probably have made their strongest impact from about the 1970s onwards. That period of time saw the first 'opening up' of many remote areas: first to extract timber then to establish plantation estates. In the following decades, road improvement and other infrastructural changes (like township expansion or establishment) became an ever-present feature of rural life in Malaysia. On the Pahang side of the Batek territory, there is only one major highway, that leading from Kuala Lipis (capital of Lipis district and the former state and royal capital) to Gua Musang in the northeast. The highway is an expansion and improvement of the old trunk road in the same location and part of its route runs parallel with a 70-year-old railway line. But there is also an elaborate network of main and feeder roads (all called *halbew tah* by the Batek), and the forest bounds are criss-crossed by a sinuous network of logging and access roads ('earth roads'), which are now indispensable elements of the landscape.

Before going further, I should clarify that Batek movement is predominantly on foot. Unless men are going out for day-labouring jobs in Malay villages, all work activities involve walking out from camp to the place of foraging (known generically as *cîp bah-hep* 'to walk to the forest'). When moving camp, the walking distance is about one to two hours. Such travels normally occur in the forest away from road networks. In logged-over forest, the Batek paths may intersect or branch off the logging roads; occasionally people may hitch a ride from a passing vehicle but this is not the general norm (traffic volume being low in the forest). They use the roads under two principal conditions: when they go shopping downriver (thus approaching village roads) and when camp groups are disbanding (every three or four months; after about a season's worth of being together). On the latter occasion, splinter groups may decide (following a historical pattern) to disperse to other river valleys. Moving on foot, with children and elders in the group, and following the contours of the land, such a move might take up to a week or even longer. Further, some resource zones outside the national park are no longer connected by corridors of forest. The Batek could circumscribe movement within a smaller area of forest, or extend it by recourse to vehicles and public transport. Roads do promote mobility and therefore cultural continuity.

As we saw above, the Batek have simply extended the meaning of their word for the path, *halbew*, to this new travelling phenomenon. The concept of roads is not totally strange to them. Surfaced roads are different in structure to the forest paths: they are more uncomfortable to walk on, tending to lack shade and to be open to the blinding tropical heat, they are less sinuous and, following a common pattern in Malaysia, they increasingly follow the models of efficiency and economics rather than the topography. Yet roads are similar to paths *notionally* in that they afford immediate rewards on travelling energy: they help the Batek to maintain relations with places and relations far away and they get the travelling done faster. In that sense, road use can be said to aid in the reproducing of the immediate-return approach to the environment.

But what about the 'delayed-returners' who make the most use of the roads? Unlike them–and the farmers and fisherfolk of Sabah I mentioned earlier–the Batek cannot claim that the roads were built *for them*. The roads serve, rather, the broader purpose of national development, nationbuilding, and symbolising the presence of government in remote areas. For most villagers in Malaysia, the past few decades have seen radical change: and they have not been slow to claim new opportunities for social and economic advancement (Tsubouchi 2001). Government policies have tended to privilege urban over rural, and village over forest: to focus development on the strongest – and politically most compliant – portions of the population. Partially as a response, there has been a rapid depopulation of the interior; the proportion of the population living in urban areas registered an annual growth rate of 4.8 percent from 1995 to 2000. Just over a quarter of the population was classified as 'urban' in 1970; now, that number exceeds 60 percent. For the average Malay villager, to be as close to the roads as possible is to hug the highest land values. Emigration is a common pattern. It does not behove villagers to remain at the forest margins. Roadside demography, in other words, reflects what's happening throughout Malaysia. What all this means is that the Batek's landscape is desirable mainly for its natural resources (timber) and its potential for generating wealth (export-oriented agriculture; tourism). It is not desirable socially, or even culturally.

We see then the broad patterns of change. The introduction of new roads and the urban expansion that they afford open up new areas for the Batek to explore. On one hand, this happens by default: the Batek might have more land than before simply because forest-edge populations are declining. On the other hand, their willingness to take to the roads means they can move much farther and retain the land-extensive nature of their dwelling practices. They are in the process of gathering new knowledge of the landscape, discovering new niches, and, counterintuitively, *extending their territory*. What happens to the roads when 'immediate-returners' use them, I asked earlier? The answer seems evident: these symbols of the delayed-return approach to the environment are appropriated and become assimilated into the immediate-return property regime. Thus, as always, the distinction between immediate- and delayed-returns comes to seem less and less clear-cut.

Cognizing Roads and Paths

The foregoing does not suggest that there is no change in Batek society or that change is unimportant. My argument, rather, is that the directions of change – the emergence of possible inequalities and shifts in property regimes – may not take obvious directions. One kind of change, as suggested by landscape fragmentation, can only be suggested here: cognitive.

As mentioned already, knowledge of the trails is not possible unless you are moving on the trails constantly. The basic framework of the trails may remain marked in cultural memory, but the individual features, which are used as orientation and direction markers, are constantly changing. Such details need to be 'updated': when a log-bridge falls, for example, it will not be useful as a direction marker and travellers may need to reorganise their image of the route using a different landscape feature. When one's pathways change, and one does not return for years to a spot, trails become overgrown, young saplings have become mature, trees have fallen and begun to rot, elephants and other animals have left new openings in the forest–the trail is unrecognisable. So if one does not use the trail constantly, the knowledge becomes 'rusty'. Were the Batek to further their pursuit of roads, likely some among them, at least, will become detached from this body of landscape knowledge.

Another possible change has to do with their perception of the landscape more generally. Traditionally, when the Batek came out to the forest margins, they encountered agrarian landscapes dominated by smallholdings. The traditional Malay *kampong* (village) was not spatially distant from the forest and in layout 'composed of a number of houses commonly strung along the sides of roads, footpaths, river, canals and along beaches. The houses are usually set well apart from one another, and there is little tendency for Malay kampongs to assume a compact form' (Ooi 1963: 159). As I argue elsewhere, in view of the Malay tendency to 'take' useful materials from the forest and towards tree-crop horticulture, they reproduced the forest in village bounds – i.e., created an image of the forest in the village (Lye 2004). Malay villages were botanically and geographically integrated with the forested landscape; the difference between village and forest was one of degree rather than kind. Now, in place of small farm dwellings, there are huge monocrop estates. These are culturally unfamiliar and signify the imposition of an alien property regime on the landscape. Thus, increased contact with such areas is likely to enhance the Batek's sense of their marginality and inability to influence the powers-that-be (see Lye 2004 for more discussion).

The conventional image of roadbuilding usually evokes the metaphor of 'opening up' the interior. To some degree, this has happened. New actors have arrived on the scene, bringing with them new constraints and opportunities, and affording new sources of information (and new fodder to fuel the Batek's ethnological endeavours): loggers, merchants, land speculators, immigrant estate labour, tourists – and anthropologists. And yet, when we examine the identity of these new actors, we find that most of these people are also mobile. In fact, they are a great deal more mobile than the Batek. They have no attachments to this landscape and fit more closely the profile of the postmodern idol, the 'traveller' (Robertson 1994). Individually, their impact on the Batek's social consciousness is not great. Timber concerns, for example, tend to be migratory enterprises; they leave physical destruction in their wake but the *people*, the loggers and their bosses, do not stay.

Collectively, though, the impact is different. As I discuss elsewhere (2004), Batek discussions of the landscape often include words that reflect acknowledgement that a 'price' has been put on the world. There is a broader history of losing place and learning to calculate about it. For example, the *denya'* (world) can be perceived as an item of exchange, something concrete that can be held back, given away, subject to struggles over control – it can be '*rugi'*' and '*geh*'. In the shaman Tebu's words: '*Heh geh denya'. Jangan heh rugi' denya'*' ('Let's not give up the world. Let's not lose it'). The most familiar connotations of both words relate to the circulation of material objects. *Rugi'*, of Sanskrit origins, is most likely borrowed through Malay (*rugi*); it is a common Malaysian epithet to describe 'loss' or nonphysical 'injury'. When someone *rugi*, that means he's lost out: either been at the weaker end of a deal or lost the opportunity to profit. *Geh*, a Batek word, is used in material transactions (the giving and taking of things): its straightforward meaning is 'don't want to give'. Though the original meaning of *denya'* is abstract – the world in which we live – it is perceived as having value that is independent of it, that can be conferred or withdrawn. Which suggests that there are two sides to the transaction. One side would stop the world from ending, would *geh* it or refuse to surrender it, and another side – those who 'kill the world' – would try to take it and therefore make everyone else *rugi'*.

The Batek are worried that the forest is being liquidated for development and that they are losing ground. They recognise that they are 'poor' in relation to folks like me and that their values of the forest are denigrated and not considered by decision makers. Thus one effect of roads is to expose the Batek to more objects and symbols of others' wealth and thus reinforce their belief that they are at the marginal end of things. Not only is the forest devalued but the people of the forest distanced from the state. But they do not say, 'give us the land and we'll do a better job of managing it than you'. This is one symbol of authority that they are not coveting. Despite all that's happened, the Batek have not lost their sense of the forest as being unowned and really unownable (Endicott 1988). It is a place to live in, not to be parcelled out to individuals. Rather, what they want is to send the message to those who do have legal powers to reconsider what *they're* doing to the forest. At any rate, other than the physical evidence of degradation, which everybody can see and experience, through their encounter with the 'road traffic' they are keeping themselves informed about the inequalities of state.

In sum, roads have led to a mix of conflicts. On the one hand, the Batek have taken willingly to the new opportunities of improved transport networks. Roads may exist because of inequalities in the larger world around them. It is government's attempt to address these inequalities that may sometimes instigate the building of roads. When the Batek take to the roads, are they, to recall my earlier question, colluding in their own demise: putting themselves on the road to a future outside the forest? I think not. I think, rather, that the roads are simply expanding the possibilities of the pathways: taking the Batek farther, allowing them more direct experience of the inequalities of the delayed-return landscape around them. And this, rather than drive a wedge between the new and the old, may serve the purpose of enhancing identity-construction, of underlining the rightness of following their own pathways through modernity.

Some Tentative Conclusions

I began writing this paper by reflecting on how the immediate-return orientation affects people's use of roads. The remaining question is: what happens to this property regime? There are, clearly, some issues, and I would not commit myself to obvious solutions. However, the impact of the state should not be discounted, especially with regard to the provision of land. The idea of land ownership, and indeed, the entire bureaucratic and political process to acquire it, follows the terms set by the state, and therefore can never be approached on equal terms. For Batek, land is not considered property that can be traded or exchanged. More important is their relationship with the forest. However, given the lack of official recognition of this, their lack of territoriality may pose a major structural problem if they were to organise themselves as a political entity. They may now have more access to 'emptied land' but they have no official title to any of that. Legally, they are little more than squatters. How this tension will work itself out is open to question. So the response to the question I posed at the outset is: roads are a delayed-return phenomenon but, as used by the Batek, they become a bridge between immediate- and delayed-returns, and therein lies the tension and a fruitful source of continuing inquiry.

I'd like to end with an anecdote that phrases the question of property accumulation in a slightly different idiom. I was shopping with some men on an afternoon in 1996. We were walking on a ridge along Gua Musang highway, from which a Malay farmhouse could be seen in the dell below. The owners had plainly just come into wealth. In place of the standard wooden framehouse of the area, there stood a brick-and-concrete house, newly renovated. We stopped for a moment to look at it. All-round silence. As we moved off, one of the men sniffed: 'Very nice. But sooner or later they'll die'.

Acknowledgements

The road to insight is a long and circuitous journey. I would like to record here my great debt to Michael Dove, who first challenged me to cultivate a broader perspective on these issues. To the many Batek friends who put up with my grumbles and discontent as we trekked through punishing logging roads, my debt is inexpressible. Finally, I thank Thomas Widlok for inviting me to the workshop where this was first presented.

Notes

1. As indeed, to history: for a fascinating study of how interior-exterior movement helped to foster the emergence of nationalist consciousness amongst people who had hitherto not had the means of communication, see Anderson (1991).
2. Coerced sedentarisation is not part of this policy. The usual practice with the Batek of Pahang seems to be 'gentle persuasion', which the Batek consider to be unwanted interference in their lives.
3. Official policy (which is not a statutory provision) is to permit the Batek to continue living in the park, but not to harvest forest products, including fauna, for sale (DWNP 1987).
4. The ethnolinguistic term for the cluster of hunting-and-gathering Orang Asli.

References

Anderson, B. 1991. *Imagined Communities: Reflections on the Origin and Spread of Nationalism*, 2nd edn. London: Verso.

Benjamin, G. 1966. 'Temiar Social Groupings'. *Federation Museums Journal* (N.S.), 11: 1–25.

—— 2002. 'On Being Tribal in the Malay World'. In: G. Benjamin and C. Chou (eds), *Tribal Communities in the Malay World: Historical, Social and Cultural Perspectives*, pp. 7–76. Leiden: IIAS, and Singapore: ISEAS.

Brody, H. 2001. *The Other Side of Eden: Hunter-gatherers, Farmers and the Shaping of the World*. London: Faber and Faber.

Carey, I. 1970. 'The Religious Problem among Orang Asli'. *Journal of the Malayan Branch of the Royal Asiatic Society*, 43: 155–60.

Dunn, F.L. 1975. *Rainforest Collectors and Traders: A Study of Resource Utilization in Modern and Ancient Malaya*. Kuala Lumpur: Malayan Branch of the Royal Asiatic Society.

DWNP (Department of Wildlife and National Parks, Malaysia). 1987. Taman Negara Master Plan. Ministry of Science, Technology and the Environment, Kuala Lumpur.

Endicott, K. 1979. *Batek Negrito Religion: The World-view and Rituals of a Hunting and Gathering People of Peninsular Malaysia*. Oxford: Clarendon Press.

—— 1984. 'The Economy of the Batek of Malaysia: Annual and Historical Perspectives'. *Research in Economic Anthropology,* 6: 29–52.
—— 1988. 'Property, Power and Conflict Among the Batek of Malaysia'. In: T. Ingold, D. Riches and J. Woodburn (eds), *Hunters and Gatherers, Vol. 2: Property, Power and Ideology*, pp. 110–27. Oxford: Berg.
Ferguson, J. 1990. *The Anti-politics Machine: Development, Depoliticization, and Bureaucratic Power in Lesotho.* Cambridge: Cambridge University Press.
Forbes, A.A. 1999. 'The Importance of Being Local: Villagers, NGOs, and the World Bank in the Arun Valley, Nepal'. *Identities* 6: 319–44.
Grinker, R.R. 1994. *Houses in the Rainforest: Ethnicity and Inequality among Farmers and Foragers in Central Africa.* Berkeley: University of California Press.
Hood, H.S. and Hasan, M.N. 1984. 'Roads are for Development? Some Aspects of Jah Het Social Change'. *Development Forum,* 14: 19–27.
JHEOA (Jabatan Hal-Ehwal Orang Asli, Malaysia). 1961. Statement of Policy Regarding the Administration of the Orang Asli of Peninsular Malaysia. Department of Orang Asli Affairs.
Kiew, R. and Hood HS. 1996. 'The role of Rattan in the Economy of Orang Asli Communities'. *Akademika,* 48: 3–20.
Lim H.S. 1998. 'Towards Vision 2020: Law, Justice and the Orang Asli'. In: Hasan M.N. (ed.), *Warga Pribumi Menghadapi Cabaran Pembangunan [Indigenous Peoples Confronting the Challenge of Development]*, pp. 118–42. Bangi, Selangor: Occasional Paper no. 8, Department of Anthropology and Sociology, Universiti Kebangsaan Malaysia.
Lye T-P. 1997. Knowledge, Forest, and Hunter-gatherer Movement: The Batek of Pahang, Malaysia. Ph.D. dissertation, University of Hawai'i at Manoa.
—— 2000. 'Forest, Bateks, and Degradation: Environmental Representations in a Changing World'. *Southeast Asian Studies,* 38: 165–84.
—— 2004. *Changing Pathways: Forest Degradation and the Batek of Pahang, Malaysia.* Lanham, MD: Lexington Books.
Ooi J-B. 1963. *Land, People and Economy in Malaya.* London: Longman.
Orlove, B. 2002. *Lines in the Water: Nature and Culture at Lake Titicaca.* Berkeley: University of California Press.
Pred, A. 1981. 'Social Reproduction and the Time-Geography of Everyday Life'. *Geografiska Annaler,* 63B: 5–22.
Robertson, G., et al. (eds) 1994. *Travellers' Tales: Narratives of Home and Displacement.* London: Routledge.
Scott, J. 1999. *Seeing like a State: How Certain Schemes to Improve the Human Condition Have Failed.* New Haven, CT: Yale University Press.
Tsubouchi, Y. 2001. *One Malay Village: A Thirty-year Community Study.* Kyoto: Kyoto Area Studies on Asia Vol. 2, Center for Southeast Asian Studies, Kyoto University.
Teh T-S, Voon P-K, Chan K-E, Tan W-H., and Tan L.S. 2001. 'Geography of Malaysia'. In: Chong Ah Look and P. Mathews (eds), *Malaysia: National Response Strategies to Climate Change,* pp. 203–46. Kuala Lumpur: Ministry of Science, Technology and the Environment, Malaysia.
Tilley, C. 1994. *A Phenomenology of Landscape: Places, Paths and Monuments.* Oxford: Berg.
Vidal, J. 2001. 'Road to Oblivion'. *The Guardian (London)* June 13 <www.guardian.co.uk/print/0,3858,4203058-103680,00.html>. Accessed 11/2/04.
Wadley, R.L. 1998. 'The Road to Change in the Kapuas Hulu Borderlands: Jalan Lintas Utara'. *Borneo Research Bulletin* 29: 71–94.
Wagner, R. 1986. *Symbols That Stand for Themselves.* Chicago: University of Chicago Press.
Weiner, J.F. 1991. *The Empty Place: Poetry, Space and Being Among the Foi of Papua New Guinea.* Bloomington: Indiana University Press.
Woodburn, J. 1980. 'Hunters and Gatherers Today and Reconstruction of the Past'. In: E. Gellner (ed.), *Soviet and Western anthropology.* London: Duckworth.
—— 1982. 'Egalitarian Societies'. *Man,* 17: 431–51.
World Wide Fund for Nature, Malaysia. 1986. The Development of Taman Negara. World Wide Fund for Nature, Malaysia.

Yong, F.S.K. 1992. 'Environmental Impact of Tourism on Taman Negara National Park Malaysia'. In: *Proceedings of the International Conference on Tropical Biodiversity 'In Harmony with Nature'* [*Malayan Nature Journal Golden Jubilee Issue*, 45 (1–4)], pp. 579–91. Kuala Lumpur: Malayan Nature Society.

6

Equalising Processes, Processes of Discrimination and the Forest People of Central Africa

Justin Kenrick

Introduction

The first half of this paper examines the way in which our habitual attempts to counter discrimination tends instead to reinforce that discrimination. It examines the situation of the Forest People of Central Africa in the light of Woodburn's writing on discrimination and in the light of what could be called the 'Catch 22' of discrimination.[1] The situation of the Bagyeli in the context of the Chad–Cameroon oil pipeline, and the perspective of researchers working for the pipeline company, the World Bank and the EU, are examined as further examples of the way in which this habitual Western approach closes down the theoretical space for understanding different ways of relating, and as a consequence closes down the social and physical space for manoeuvre for these people on the ground.

The second half of the paper turns to the particular predicament of the Mbuti of the Ituri Forest, Democratic Republic of Congo, and to Woodburn's analysis of equalising processes amongst immediate-return hunter-gatherers. Drawing on the author's fieldwork, Turnbull's analysis of Mbuti--Forest and Mbuti–Bila villager relations is questioned. Turnbull's analysis has played a central role in the development of anthropological theory on hunter-gatherers, from Sahlins's 'original affluent society' (1968) and Woodburn's 'egalitarian societies' (1982), to Bird-David's 'cosmic economy of sharing' (1992) and Ingold's 'hunting and gathering as ways of perceiving the environment' (1996). This paper rejects his central analysis, reassesses Mbuti–Forest and Mbuti–Bila relations, and in doing so seeks to use Woodburn's understanding to demonstrate the need to focus on both equalising and disempowering processes if we are to understand either.

What is crucial here is to recognise that Mbuti equalising processes are inclusive: extending to and implicating villagers, tourists, anthropologists, conservationists and others whom anthropologists tend to consider as the 'other' to hunter-gatherers. Likewise, disempowering processes are 'penetratingly exclusive', in that they seek to forcefully persuade those being disempowered that they can have no agency except as agents of this same process of division and discrimination – a process which can implicate and persuade Mbuti as much as villager or anthropologist that it is the only game in town. Where Turnbull's work has tended to be either accepted unquestioningly (e.g. Bird-David 1992; Ingold 1996) or rejected completely (e.g. Frankland 1999, 2001), this paper argues that what is needed instead is a drastic reappraisal of Turnbull's work and Mbuti society and context, in order to expand our theoretical space to support people like the Mbuti in a way which engages with, rather than undermines, their agency.

Discrimination

Looking at the situation from a 'discrimination perspective', one can say that the vast majority of Forest People[2] (or 'Pygmies') of Central Africa continue to experience daily discrimination against them by their farming neighbours. When governments and other organisations intervene to help Forest People, it is almost always to continue this discrimination in other ways. This is an example of the 'Catch 22' nature of discrimination, which is to say that in situations where discrimination against a category of people is entrenched in a dominant society, those who think they are opposing the discrimination are very often actually reinforcing it in what would appear to be a more benign but is actually an equally destructive way.

To highlight this process, the first half of this paper briefly outlines examples from indigenous peoples in South America and colonised Africa, and from gender relations in Europe and America. It then summarises Woodburn's analysis of discrimination against hunter-gatherers in Africa, and applies both Woodburn's analysis and the 'Catch 22' analysis outlined below, to the experience of the Bagyeli of Cameroon and the way in which anthropological research can itself be used to close down the space for the egalitarian and inclusive processes which are central to such people's existence.

The 'Catch 22' of Discrimination

This section takes a crude but, I hope, accurate look at general processes of discrimination in three situations with which we are all familiar. In the conquest of South America, the majority of the conquerors perceived the indigenous peoples of the continent to be creatures who deserved no moral consideration and could be treated in much the same way that Europeans today treat animals. They should be subjugated and could even be slaughtered without consideration. It was in opposition to this that Catholic evangelists, the Spanish Crown, and eventually the ruling Pope decreed that Amerindian people should not be treated in this way since they had souls that could be converted and 'saved' (Bennett 1978: 29, Lomnitz-Adler 1992: 265, 269).[3] Consequently, those who claimed to care about indigenous peoples' souls made great efforts to ensure that such individuals were 'saved' rather than simply annihilated. The extermination of their culture and way of life was, however, often a consequence of both approaches. Both approaches were based on a fundamentally discriminatory attitude that saw no value in indigenous peoples' culture and sought to either crush it beneath, or convert it into, the dominant culture.

A similar evolving process can be seen in many situations of discrimination – for example, in the actions of European colonialists in Africa, or enduring responses to the position of women in the West. In the context of the slave trade and colonisation of Africa, a great number of European traders and colonists saw Africans as a raw material to be exploited like any other, not as people with equal rights to themselves. Missionaries and humanists reacted to this and sought to curb the barbaric excesses of colonialism, but in its place would normally embark with great zealousness on the 'civilising mission'. This was often more benign than military conquest and subjugation, but the results were similar. The ways of life of the cultures they encountered were ultimately seen as an obstacle to 'civilisation', to native people's adoption of Christianity and their becoming as similar as possible to Europeans.

In relation to the position of women in the West, there is a similar process. Where formerly the values associated with men included, for example, the public realm, being rational, and going out to work, the values associated with women included staying at home, being emotional, bringing up children (Jordanova is one of many who has looked at the historical emergence in the West of this binary opposition between men as culture and women as nature [Jordanova 1980]). This provided a major justification for confining women to the home, for resisting giving women the vote, for unequal pay and promotion prospects at work. The reaction to this has tended to involve increasing the possibilities for women to work, providing childcare,[4] and equal rights legislation seeking to ensure equal pay and promotion prospects. However, although this can obviously be of enormous benefit to women individually, it fails to question the fundamentally discriminatory attitudes that value the world of work, the public domain and the intellect above the home, childcare and the emotions. In fact, it does far more than continue this process: it evolves, turning the recognition of discrimination of one realm by another into a new attempt to absorb and continue the devaluation of the values identified with the discriminated realm. Rather than giving equal status and value to the different domains of 'men's' and 'women's' work, and enabling the barrier between the realms to be dismantled to the benefit of both women and men, women are simply given better access to the dominant 'male' domain, whilst the 'female' domain remains discriminated against.

These examples show the importance of fully recognising the ways in which discrimination evolves. Where discrimination against a certain category is firmly entrenched, those who claim they are opposing it may simply transform the paradigm of discrimination into new forms. By seeking to alleviate the suffering individuals endure from the dominant group's perspective, rather than by respecting and learning from the values of the discriminated group, efforts are made to 'liberate' them from their former way of life and, in the process, the alternative value system is often attacked. Although this may be presented as humane paternalism, it remains a form of discrimination that can be equally effective at discriminating against, and potentially destroying a way of life. This happens because the fundamental assumption giving rise to the discrimination is not questioned by those attempting to counter the discrimination. Thus those being discriminated against are offered 'help' that simply reinforces the basis for their discrimination by transforming it into more acceptable forms.

This 'Catch 22' experience of severe discrimination is one endured by the Forest People of Central Africa. They continue to experience discrimination not only at the hands of their agriculturalist and capitalist neighbours, but also as a result of national and international policies and actions aimed at 'helping' them, which build on and strengthen the preexisting discrimination against them evident amongst their agriculturalist neighbours.

Woodburn's Analysis of Discrimination Against Hunter-Gatherers in Africa

Woodburn (1997) summarises the forms of discrimination experienced by Central African hunter-gatherers as involving negative stereotyping, a denial of their rights, and segregation. He argues that all over sub-Saharan Africa there is a tendency for differences in modes of subsistence to be represented as ethnic differences and, conversely, that people who consider themselves ethnically distinct often present this as a difference in mode of subsistence. Thus, in Burundi or Rwanda, for instance, Tutsi and Hutu may both be mixed agriculturalists and pastoralists yet will identify themselves as one or the other. Likewise, even where hunter-gatherers are no longer hunting and gathering and are effectively excluded from their forests (as with the Batwa in Uganda), they continue to view themselves, and are seen by others, as primarily hunter-gatherers.

Woodburn points out that ethnic identity in Africa is very flexible, people of different groups expect to eat together, drink together, intermarry; 'in total contrast to India, group identities for most Africans are not rigid and exclusive but tend to stress the mixed origins of groups' (1997: 348). He points out that the situation of hunter-gatherers in Central Africa is very unusual for Africa, since although there has always been rivalry and conflict between different ethnic groups in Africa, the situation of people such as the Batwa of Rwanda has not been like this since they are numerically such a small minority, posing no political threat to anybody, and yet rigid barriers have been drawn up against them, excluding them from normal dealings with other people. The Batwa of Rwanda and Burundi are treated by both Hutu and Tutsi as completely inferior. Eating, drinking and intermarrying with the Batwa is unacceptable to the vast majority of Hutu and Tutsi; even sitting and talking with them is often forbidden, and they have frequently been dispossessed of whatever land they held without this being seen as theft. The 1994 genocide in Rwanda resulted in the death of around 14 percent of the total Rwandan population. The Batwa make up between 0.3 and 0.4 percent of this total yet it is estimated that around 30 percent of the Rwandan Batwa died as a result of this war (Lewis and Knight 1995: 93).

Woodburn's description of the discrimination suffered by the Batwa of Rwanda and Burundi, although extreme, is equally applicable to much of the discrimination suffered by other Forest People throughout the Central African rain forest region. He describes the negative stereotyping as involving open and publicly asserted stigmatising characterisations of hunter-gatherers as ignorant, stupid, primitive, lacking in proper culture and not fully human. From this perspective, any denial of hunter-gatherer rights by non-hunter-gatherers is justified since they are not properly human nor living as people should. This denial of rights, widely contested by Forest Peoples themselves, often takes the form of claiming that Forest People should not have control over their own labour, their lands or their marriages. They are denied rights to the land they hunt and gather over and 'are freely, even casually, dispossessed of the land by agricultural and pastoral people' (Woodburn 1997: 350).

Actions like these are based on the highly discriminatory notion, often supported by national governments and international agencies, that agriculture constitutes legitimate land use and confers some level of rights to land, whereas hunter-gatherer usage confers no such rights. This can easily lead to hunter-gatherers being denied the right to hunt and gather and to their being excluded from their forests without adequate consultation or compensation, if any is even offered (see, for example, Kenrick 2001 on the Batwa of Uganda). If compensation is offered, Forest People are given much less than their farming neighbours. Forest People are also frequently not granted any rights or sustained support from governments, missionaries and development agencies, unless they are willing to give up their way of life, settle by the road, engage in agriculture and send their children to school.

When such changes are carried out forcefully, they continue to embody a fundamentally discriminatory attitude that denies, and can potentially destroy, a people's way of life in a similar manner to the way in which Europeans sought to destroy indigenous cultures in North America and Australasia. Similarly, the agencies and people engaged in such fundamentally discriminatory activities towards the Forest People of Central Africa often believe that their assimilationist attitudes and practices are generous and paternal rather than recognising that they are a denial of hunter-gatherers' fundamental human rights.

In looking at the reasons for this discrimination by their neighbours, Woodburn suggests that these hunter-gatherers are politically weak since, more than in any other human societies, they stress egalitarianism and work hard to minimise social differentiation of power, wealth and status. Their lack of property and wealth accumulation means that they appear poor by the standards of their farming neighbours, neighbours whose security lies in accumulating resources. For Forest People, their security lies in high mobility and a rich natural environment, in a social system where people share with others what they have hunted, gathered or bartered for, in the ritual forms through which Forest People ensure that relationships between themselves, and those with their forest environment, are based on cooperation, harmony and abundance. The processes that ensure equality – demand-sharing, nomadism, the high valuation of personal autonomy, equalising rituals and practices which can involve much hilarity, ridicule, shouting and improvised singing, storytelling and music – are in sharp contrast to farmers' values of authority, politeness and deference to seniors. This can mean that farmers are unable to understand the values and strengths of Forest People's cultures, and see them instead as uncivilised or threatening (Woodburn 1997: 352–53). Here Woodburn's analysis of discrimination and his analysis of equalising processes comes together most directly and fruitfully, and yet I hope to show in the second part of this paper that the existence of equalising processes is not just one more reason for agriculturalist discriminatory attitudes and actions but is also, paradoxically, an effective process for including others (such as villagers) and subverting these very processes of discrimination.

However, in relation to these processes of discrimination, there are two key points to make. One is that Forest People can be willing to participate in (everyday and ritual) relations with their farming neighbours in which they appear to be destitute, subservient or clients. Forest People do this partly in order to gain access to goods that farmers have, and often describe such behaviour in idioms normally used in hunting. The difficulty and suffering they may experience as a consequence of discrimination during interactions with farmers can be equated with the hardships of the hunt. However, wherever Forest People retain their forests and sufficient wild resources, they have little difficulty in maintaining their autonomy and, from their own point of view, maintaining relationships of equality with their neighbours. In these situations (contra Turnbull 1965) they may participate in everyday and ritual relations for far more complex reasons than simply to access village goods. Forest People's central rituals are ones that celebrate their knowledge of and relationship with the forest and, as such, are at variance with what would appear to be the dominant values of their neighbours. Such central rituals include the Ejengi ritual of the Baka and Aka, and the Molimo ritual of the Mbuti (Kenrick 1999). However, the supposed gulf between villager and hunter-gatherer rituals and values may not, at least from an Mbuti point of view, be so unbridgeable (Kenrick 2002); in fact the dynamic of inclusiveness at the heart of the central value of egalitarianism is focused precisely on bridging the divide those seeking to assert their power attempt to create.

The second key point is that Forest People are seen as the first inhabitants of the Central African forests. Farming groups' origin stories are all about arriving from non-forest areas into the forest and then clearing forest for their villages. In contrast Forest Peoples' origin stories begin in the forest and remain there. They see themselves, and are seen by their neighbours, as the autochthons or 'First People' in the Central African forests. Their neighbours commonly see them as the custodians of fertility, whether it is to make crops grow, animals multiply or women conceive and give birth. These aspects of Forest People's identities are recognised in certain farmers' rituals. However, often during these rituals this recognition is subverted by the ritual dispossession of the Forest People's rights over their land through portrayals of their forest-orientated lifestyle as animalistic and debauched, and the investment of rights over the forest in the real people – the farming group (Kagabo and Mudandagizi 1974: 77; Woodburn 1997: 354–55). Despite this history, these widely recognised aspects of their identity are today becoming a potent way for Forest People to assert their rights through the international Indigenous Peoples' movement. However, unless those in the West, who are supporting Forest Peoples' participation in such a movement, can recognise that Forest People have not simply been victims in such rituals but have also participated enthusiastically in them as a way of enabling interdependence in the face of such rituals apparent attempts to assert one group's dominance (as in, for example, the nkumbi circumcision ritual of the Mbuti and Bila of the Ituri, DRC, see below), then we too will remain focused on discrimination in a way which fails to engage with and support Forest People's processes of inclusiveness. If Forest People are supported to fight against discrimination only in opposition to their neighbours, then the fight will be on the terms of what Jerome Lewis has called 'white and black "village people"' (Lewis 2001: 76), involving structures of representation and leadership which will undermine the very equalising processes which are at the heart of such people's social worlds.

Discrimination Suffered by Central African Forest People

Discrimination is nowhere more evident than in relation to land rights. Woodburn argues that discrimination against hunter-gatherers' land rights is based on the notion that agriculture constitutes legitimate land use and confers rights to land, whereas hunter-gatherer usage confers no such rights. Thus, both under colonialism and since independence, traditional territories became state lands unless they were built on or farmed. This meant Forest People's landuse and claims over land could be ignored since their lands will appear unoccupied at any given time (see Barume 2000). This situation has been worsened since the granting of huge forestry concessions in the 1980s, and the increase in Western-controlled wildlife reserves in the 1990s (Lewis 2001: 64–5).[5]

Villagers' attempts to assert their dominance over Forest People is maintained in this context, a context in which governments perceive their hunter-gatherer way of life as primitive and shameful, yet celebrate their forest knowledge, singing and dancing (Lewis 2001: 65). Similarly, conservation bodies and logging companies make use of their forest skills whilst either excluding them from their forests or destroying the biodiversity upon which their nomadic hunting and gathering depends (Kenrick and Lewis 2001). Their skills and knowledge are put to use but the social processes which gave rise to them are devalued, and concerted attempts are made to destroy those very processes through enforced sedentarisation and assimilation policies, which are framed in terms of the need to control, civilise and develop these 'backward' people (Lewis 2001: 65–6).

During the enforced 'villagisation' programmes of the 1960s and 1970s, many Forest People were forced to settle beside roads for a time. Most soon moved back to a lifestyle that involved spending part of the year working farmer's fields and the rest moving through the forest hunting, gathering and trading forest produce. Almost all interventions by governments, missionaries or development organisations have been directed at settling Forest People and stopping their hunter-gatherer lifestyle in favour of farming. This is presented as a benevolent attitude and charitable activity rather than one that is fundamentally discriminatory. Forest People are rarely seen as equals, and officials arriving in Forest People's areas will invariably seek out and deal with farmer communities rather than the Forest People. When these visits are offering benefits to the population, they are easily monopolised by the villagers (Lewis 2001: 66).

A good recent example of this is the experience of the Bagyeli hunter-gatherers in southwestern Cameroon. Here, the consequence of the preliminary cutting through of the pathway to mark where the World Bank-funded Chad–Cameroon oil pipeline is going to run has led not to the alleviation of poverty, as claimed by the World Bank, but to the entrenchment of inequality. Bagyeli land, which they have been cultivating for years, as well as places where they live, have been formally claimed by literate villagers in order that the villagers can obtain the compensation due for its damage by the pipeline (Nelson, et al. 2001).

This small example of discrimination needs to be seen in its wider context. The Bagyeli have been dispossessed of these lands only because they have created fields there. In contrast, there is no legal way of framing as dispossession the way in which the construction of the pipeline will disrupt their forest and their ability to hunt and gather in it because Bagyeli rights to the forest are not even recognised in the first place. The daily discrimination they experience at the hands of their neighbours is encouraged and made possible because the ongoing discrimination by the colonial and now post-colonial state against their way of life is so firmly established and accepted that it seems almost invisible (Nelson, et al. 2001).

Thus, when consultations with the Bagyeli were held (as required by the World Bank Indigenous Peoples' policy) to determine what measures should be taken to safeguard Bagyeli welfare in the context of the pipeline being established, the Bagyeli were shocked that it was being carried out by academics who belong to those very same farmers' groups they experience as dominating and discriminating against them. Furthermore, what the survey concluded was not that the Bagyeli needed land rights and their forest, but rather it sought to establish various inadequate forms of compensation which (as the earlier example shows) have easily been siphoned off by farmers. For example, the survey still stresses the need for the Bagyeli to become fully sedentarised in order to 'benefit' from the development opportunities it appears to offer. This, even though it acknowledges that Bagyeli nutrition in the forest is very good and that it deteriorates rapidly with sedentarisation. The survey failed to take into account Bagyeli wishes and needs, rather it assumed to know what these were (Nelson, et al. 2001), an approach firmly based in the 'Catch 22' nature of discrimination described above.

Where their forests have been destroyed, or where they are forcibly excluded from them, ongoing discrimination against the Forest People of Central Africa is often presented as if it will oblige them to benefit from 'modernisation' and 'development'. In reality, however, there is no such benefit: the process simply subjects them to increasingly severe poverty and continued discrimination. Such discrimination can only be subverted and dissolved by dismantling the process by which one category or realm is made to be inferior to another. If, instead, members of the dominated group are given help to become like those who dominate them, this does not alleviate the discrimination suffered, it intensifies it.

This is evident in the practice of much anthropological and social science research when it is being funded by, and therefore answerable to, organisations such as the World Bank, Exxon and the European Union. The recent summary report from APFT (Avenir des Peuples des Forets Tropicales) is a good example of this, with its extraordinary statement that 'there is and must not be "a Pygmy problem"'; it goes on to say that 'It is crucial to take into account the interdependent relations between Pygmies and their neighbours if a further interethnic conflict is to be avoided' (Bahuchet et al. 2001: 16). The dynamic nature of those relations and the way they are shaped by colonial and neocolonial forces remains unexamined, and the document's description of 'Tropical Forest Peoples Today' in Central Africa largely obscures the part played by Western power in the environmental and social devastation there. This is coupled with a refusal to acknowledge the particular situation of people such as the 'Pygmies' and an emphasis on Western development and democracy as the only cure for the situation. Some of the institutions involved in producing this report have also played their part in the research which has been the basis for the compensation plans and Indigenous Peoples' plans which neither recognise nor analyse the particular nature of Bagyeli relations with their neighbours, and which have consequently intensified the reasons for neighbouring farmers to discriminate against the Bagyeli in order to benefit from the compensation available as a result of the Chad–Cameroon pipeline, a development which these researchers appear to see more as an opportunity for the Bagyeli to become like others, than as a threat to their well-being.

In these and other ways, international players can collude with national governments and local authorities in intensifying the discrimination and denial of basic rights of the Forest People by their villager neighbours. On the one hand, the lack of representation of Forest People at the local and regional levels in Central Africa shows how effectively the discrimination they experience prevents effective representation. On the other hand, seeking to counter this situation in 'village people' terms, simply by assimilating Forest People into such positions of 'representation' as currently exist, would simply intensify the process of discrimination against Forest Peoples' forms of social organisation. Thus, although 'discrimination' is a useful lens through which to analyse the problem, it does not provide a way of seeing the solutions which are already evident in Forest Peoples' own practices; practices which the second half of this paper examines.

Egalitarianism

The first part of this paper questioned the dominant colonial and postcolonial response to discrimination against Central African hunter-gatherers by their farming neighbours, suggesting that it intensifies rather than alleviates their experience of discrimination. In a similar vein, this half of the paper questions the hitherto dominant anthropological ways of understanding the relationship between these hunter-gatherers and their neighbouring farmers, suggesting that it ultimately blocks rather than enables these hunter-gatherers to claim equality with their neighbours. Although I am here questioning many of the anthropological accounts of the relationship between Central African Forest People and their neighbours, I will limit my analysis mainly to the writing of Colin Turnbull.

Colin Turnbull's writing on the Mbuti of the Ituri (1965, 1983) – along with James Woodburn's on the Hadza (1968, 1970, 1979) and Richard Lee's on the !Kung (1968, 1972, 1979) – has been central to three of the fundamental shifts in anthropological understandings of hunter-gatherers. The first outlined a theory of hunter-gatherer affluence (Sahlins 1968); the second outlined a theory of assertive egalitarianism amongst immediate-return hunter-gatherers (Woodburn 1982); and the third turned our focus to these hunter-gatherers' 'cosmic economy of sharing' (Bird-David 1992).

All three writers have grappled with key questions concerning what is distinctive about hunter-gatherer social organisation and sociality. They have also, implicitly or explicitly, used their analysis to reexamine the nature of Western social organisation and sociality, and by juxtaposing the two forms have suggested the possibility of our engaging in a different kind of sociality. As Thomas Widlok (2001: 180) has said of Tim Ingold's writing, 'When Ingold encourages us to understand hunter-gatherers in accordance with their view of the world as inhabited by "undivided centres of action and awareness, within a continuous life process" (1996: 15), he really urges us to see ourselves and all human evolution in this way'. Drawing strong contrasts between Western and hunter-gatherer perspectives does not simply illuminate what is possible for hunter-gatherers but also questions dominant Western ways of interpreting Western experience. When Sahlins writes about 'scarcity' (1972: 4), Woodburn about 'equality' (1982: 448), or Bird-David about 'abundance' (1992: 32), all three are commenting not only on hunter-gatherer sociality, but also on Western experience.

Turnbull was very explicit in doing exactly this. His attempt to use his research to make statements about the West has always proved uncomfortable for other academics. This may, in part, account for the fact that although Turnbull's writing – along with that of Woodburn and Lee – has been central to the three fundamental shifts outlined above, his work has been strangely unexamined. It has tended to be accepted unquestioningly or else dismissed out of hand (the latter, partly as a result of his infamous study of the Ik, [1972]). The only serious and comprehensive evaluation of his work in the Ituri has been by Grinker (1990, 1994), whose invaluable reflections are hampered by the fact that he is basing his evaluation of Mbuti–Bila relations on his work with the neighbouring Lese famers and Efe hunter-gatherers, rather than on work with the Bila and Mbuti who are the subject of Turnbull's studies.

There are three purposes to the reevaluation of Turnbull's work and of Mbuti–Bila relations attempted in this half of the paper. Firstly, to move beyond an unquestioning acceptance or complete rejection of Turnbull's work – however attractive both options may be – and so sketch a more accurate understanding of Mbuti sociality. Secondly, to move from a dualistic analytical approach which sets up opposing categories to one which stresses dynamic processes, and in doing so to question the understanding of Forest People–Village People relations evident in much writing on Central African hunter-gatherers, and so question the understanding of hunter-gatherers evident in the analysis of writers such as Bird-David and Ingold. Lastly, to suggest that if we move away from oppositional categories and instead focus on discrimination as a process of exclusion, and on egalitarianism as a process of inclusion (see Woodburn 1982: 448 cited above), then we may be in a better position to help create the theoretical and political space for Forest People to engage with processes of change on their own terms.

Reassessing Turnbull's Understanding of the Mbuti–Bila Relations

There are two central aspects to Turnbull's analysis of the Mbuti. The first concerns the nature of their relationship with their Bila village neighbours, and the opposition he seeks to establish between the world of the village and the world of the forest. The second concerns the nature of their relationship with the forest itself.

Turnbull's notion of a structural opposition between the Bila and the Mbuti (Turnbull 1961, 1965, 1983) has become the defining feature of Forest People–Village People relations in most subsequent long-term studies in the Central African forests (e.g. Waehle 1985; Grinker 1990, 1994). From the villagers' point of view Grinker describes Lese villagers of the Ituri Forest as basing their relationship with the neighbouring Efe hunter-gatherers on a Lese perspective 'in which the village is made to represent everything good, while the forest represents everything bad' (1994: 76). Grinker agrees 'completely with Turnbull that this pervasive and ever-present opposition between the village and the forest is one of the most fundamental components of the culture and society of these [Mbuti and Bila] foragers and farmers, as well as for the Lese and Efe' (Grinker 1994: 9).[7] Waehle writes, of Lese beliefs concerning the Efe, that 'the Efe are savages and sub-human (likened to chimpanzees or forest hogs); they are thieves; the forest is the contradiction to the village (almost as nature to culture)' (1985: 392). These authors' findings thus appear to repeat in other contexts Turnbull's original description of Bila villager and Mbuti hunter-gatherer relations as being based on a structural opposition in which each side is utterly opposed to, and seeking either to control or outwit, the other. One could easily gain the same impression from Lewis, when he writes that Bilo 'village people are portrayed' by the Mbendjele 'as the archetypal "other", so fundamentally opposed to human values that they are really animals that resemble people' (Lewis 2001: 68). However, unlike Turnbull, Lewis is at pains to point out the historical context of economic decline and Bila dependence on Mbendjele labour: a context which has diminished relations of inclusivity and emphasised relations of opposition between the two groups (Lewis 1999).

What I am suggesting is that focusing only on an 'oppositional' analysis, as for example Turnbull and Grinker do, while accurately conveying an important aspect of Mbuti--Bila relations, obscures equally powerful inclusive processes. More than this, if we ignore these inclusive processes then we ignore the very ways in which we can support Forest People's agency and instead only intensify Forest People's experience of being excluded and dominated.

Turnbull's classic study of the Mbuti is built on the notion of a structural opposition between the Mbuti hunter-gatherers, living in harmony in the world of the forest, and the world of the road, where the Bila village farmers are described as fearing the surrounding forest and forever battling against their forest environment in order to survive. In Turnbull's eyes the Mbuti's fragile forest of Eden will inevitably be broken by the intrusion of modern forces (1993: 9). Turnbull makes an absolute opposition between Mbuti and Bila cosmologies (e.g. 1965: 21). He sharply differentiates between the Mbuti's pure experience of their sacred forest, which he says they regard as both mother and father to them, and the Bila villagers' superstitious ancestor worship and fear of the forest (Turnbull 1961, 1965, 1983, 1990, 1993).

However, from rereading Turnbull and listening to Mbuti today it is clear that accusations of sorcery, and fear of evil spirits, have been important aspects of life not only for the Bila but also for the Mbuti. It is equally clear that Bila are and have been able to be at ease in the forest, and that both people share important beliefs concerning their ancestors as both inhabiting and being the forest. Their beliefs and experience concerning the forest can be in direct opposition to each other, but equally they can converge: sometimes in the sense that Mbuti as well as Bila experience fear and distrust in the forest, sometimes in the sense that Bila as well as Mbuti experience the forest as benevolent and somewhere where they are at home.

The direct contradiction between Turnbull's claim that 'the pygmies practise no sorcery or witchcraft' (1961: 205) and my experience of Mbuti fear of sorcery accusations and sometimes their attempt to assert power through sorcery accusations, would appear to be due to Turnbull's reading all Mbuti behaviour in the light of his idealised opposition between village and forest. If an Mbuti appeared to believe in witchcraft, in Turnbull's eyes they were therefore either peculiar individuals, or they meant something else. He puts Mbuti accusations of sorcery down to following 'the custom without following the belief' (1965: 209); or describes them as happening because 'they already had a grievance against a certain person and chose this way of expressing it' (1965: 75). When he hears 'several pygmies accuse old Sau' of being a witch, he says that 'although they used the village word they meant something quite different by it. They meant no more than that she was accused of making trouble' (1961: 205). This may have been the case, but under different circumstances the same accusation may carry much more hostility, with sometimes fatal results. During my fieldwork in one Mbuti camp an old woman was beaten to death after being accused of sorcery. The intention had been to frighten her out of her supposed malevolence rather than to kill her, but fear of sorcery was pervasive at a point when the camp was under severe pressure from a corrupt regional chief.

Where Turnbull seeks to highlight the opposition between Mbuti and Bila experience, his ethnography is actually full of instances where it is obvious that both peoples can become enmeshed in becoming dominated by fear and attempts to coerce others, and both can maintain relationships of trust and intimacy with the forest and each other. For example, Turnbull describes the 'legend of double trickery' to illustrate the use Mbuti make of tales of sorcery to frighten the Bila from entering the forest, or to account for why they have no meat for their exchange partners (1965: 241–43, 303–37). In fact the story also demonstrates that villagers were not frightened of the forest world but were happy to go far into the forest, and it demonstrates that Mbuti could fear being cheated by the spirits of their dead in the forest. Sometimes Mbuti tales of spirits are told to amuse themselves and to mock the villagers; at other times the same person will believe in sorcery and evil spirits, and the same Mbuti who is lauded for deceiving villagers may at another moment be chastised for attempting to deceive other Mbuti. For example, the same Cephu who was applauded for cheating a villager (Turnbull 1961: 125) was later punished for seeking to deceive his fellow Mbuti (1965: 197). Deception, as well as belief in evil spirits and sorcery, clearly crosses the divide, which

Turnbull saw as unbridgeable, between the world of the forest and the world of the road.

The fear, or attempt to assert power, involved in sorcery accusations, sometimes seems more like play-acting, and sometimes carries a real sense of threat. During my longer fieldwork period[8] it was clear that sorcery was a powerful feature of daily life for everyone from the Mbuti in forest camps to the Bila in the village, from gold panners in the Ituri River to Mobutu in Kinshasa. The same person – be they Mbuti, Bila or Nande – can laugh at people for believing others possess such powers; can describe the reality of such powers and their abhorrence of them; and can also claim that they have such powers.

Turnbull argued that the contrast between villagers' fear of – and Mbuti respect for – the forest, and villagers' fear of – and Mbuti contempt for – sorcery, has nothing to do with historical circumstance and everything to do with the essential nature of these two cultures. Turnbull's research, however, coincided with the most effective period of Belgian colonial domination which treated the villagers and the Mbuti very differently. The Mbuti were allowed to move through the forest freely, while the Bila were forced to move their villages to the roadside and to pay taxes in the form of maintaining the roads, feeding immigrant labourers, and growing cotton to pay as a form of tax (Turnbull 1983: 60). Having to manipulate the Mbuti into working their fields to help produce the required cotton was the last in a long chain of exploitative extractive relations emanating from commercial decisions made in Europe, and made possible by colonial control.

With central government weak or nonexistent, economic relations between Mbuti and villagers today are not shaped by the tax demands of colonisation, but are mediated through the meat trade. Village traders spend long periods of time in Mbuti hunting camps exchanging trade items and produce from their fields, for antelope hunted by the Mbuti. The traders' success often depends on how intimate and personal their relationship is with the Mbuti in camp; and this system, whereby everything which the Mbuti want but cannot obtain from the forest is transported in by traders, enables the Mbuti to stay in the forest for very long periods of time. Although Mbuti–Bila relations under Belgian rule can be seen as being largely shaped by the Bila's desperate need for Mbuti labour in their cotton plantations to meet tax demands, and by Mbuti refusal to be drawn into this subservient role, in fact this perspective denies the importance of agency in terms of how people chose to relate to each other. For example, those Bila chiefs who were desperate to control Mbuti labour to help harvest cotton, were unable to find and control them; whereas those chiefs who maintained relations of autonomy had no such difficulty. Turnbull (e.g. 1965: 41) shows how, despite the immense pressures on the Bila to exploit the Mbuti to meet tax demands, Bila benefited from maintaining relationships of equality and interdependence with the Mbuti just as meat traders in the central Ituri do today.

The relations between Bila and Mbuti are better understood by looking at the processes whereby relationships are established – on the basis of inclusion and equality, or on the basis of domination and inequality – rather than by assuming some underlying cultural given of opposition. A preoccupation with Turnbull's structural opposition obscures the dynamic movement between forest and village that is central to the Mbuti and Bila today, and was clearly evident in Turnbull's day despite his attempt to reproduce the impact of colonial divisiveness as if it represented underlying mutually exclusive cosmologies.

The Example of the Nkumbi Circumcision Ritual

One of the clearest examples of the way in which a preoccupation with the opposition between Bila and Mbuti obscures the reality of cross-cutting ties of relatedness is in Turnbull's examination of the apparently villager-dominated nkumbi circumcision ritual. Based on a reexamination of Turnbull's writing and on my own fieldwork, there are two key points to make here.

Firstly the ritual contains all the elements described in the first half of this paper as exemplifying villager discrimination against the hunter-gatherers. In it the Mbuti are acknowledged as the initial inhabitants of the forest, just as women are acknowledged as the originators of the nkumbi; before the Bila men assert that they wrested the nkumbi from the women, and that they taught the Mbuti sociality. Furthermore, the hated dominant regional chief, the new and resented Bila village chief, and the Mbuti 'chief' (as recognised by the administration) attempt to assert their authority. Such a description fits Turnbull's analysis that the Mbuti only pretended involvement in the nkumbi; and fits with his assertion that Bila opposition to the Mbuti and the forest is played out in the nkumbi in a fruitless attempt to establish supernatural domination over the Mbuti. He argues that the Mbuti are unaffected by the whole process (1965: 69) and simply participate in order to establish exchange relations with villagers (1961: 203–4; 1965: 63–5).

However, the second point is that Turnbull's simple picture of attempted domination by the Bila on the one hand, and pretended participation by the Mbuti on the other, does not reflect the complex intense nature of the occasion. The Mbuti at my particular fieldwork site entered into the whole process of the nkumbi as reluctantly or as fully as their Bila neighbours. Here it is women who form the core, and carry the greatest authority, both in the Bila village and the Mbuti camps associated with it. For the Bila, this isn't simply a matter of personalities in the present but also of recent and mythical history, in which it is women and not men who established the village and are seen as its strongest defenders; and it is women who control who enters the circumcision camp. Here dependence is acknowledged as cutting both ways: Bila being dependent on Mbuti and Mbuti on Bila. The Bila account of the first meeting between a Bila and an Mbuti tells of how the Bila learnt the most basic essential necessary for group survival from the Mbuti, sex, and how the Mbuti (in Bila eyes) learnt sociality with other people from the Bila. Bila sense of dependence on the Mbuti is also acknowledged in stories about how they survived colonialism and the Simba rebellion, and how they would survive the present warfare by hiding with and depending on the Mbuti.

Here the Mbuti 'chief' being controlled by corrupt authorities seeks to control other Mbuti, but is too afraid to enter the circumcision camp because of the levelling of all those present that occurs there. The Bila chief's attempt to manipulate the timing of the circumcision is rejected; and the corrupt regional chief passes through briefly because he walks in fear of his life, whereas the popular traditional regional chief he usurped participates fully. The belief that such a ritual is essentially about the attempt to legitimise hierarchy is simply the perspective of those seeking to assert their power when they are engaged in such an attempt: it is only one aspect of the diverse experience of social interdependence, the expression and exploration of which is the motivating force for individuals' participation in the nkumbi. The nkumbi provides the chance for people from distant camps and villages to come together, tell stories, dance and socialise; and underlying it all, for eligible young Mbuti and Bila, is the fact that this is the place where they are most likely to be able to impress a member of the opposite sex with their dancing, this is the context in which many of them meet their partners. Opposition and solidarity, especially in the form of meals and dances, cross-cut in different ways at different times: sometimes relating more to gender, sometimes to ethnicity. In the nkumbi, conflict happens within a context in which the interdependence between the different groups is heightened.

The key point is that perceiving the interaction only in terms of opposition, especially opposition between Bila and Mbuti, obscures the complexity, excitement and interdependence experienced on the occasion. Just as Mbuti can always become part of a camp by claiming real or fictional kinship with those in it, so Bila (unlike the Lese) are always keen to stress affinal relations, are always keen to expand the strength of their village by welcoming in newcomers. Processes of interdependence and inclusiveness underlie processes of domination and opposition, and these opposing processes battle it out in the nkumbi, in the molimo and in everyday relations. The fundamental opposition here, from the point of view of those who are not intent on attempting to control others (which includes almost all Mbuti and most Bila, most of the time), is not between Bila and Mbuti or Village and Forest but is between these processes of inclusion and these processes of domination.

Reassessing Mbuti–Forest Relations

Over the last decade Turnbull's contrast between Bila and Mbuti ways of relating to the environment has been invoked as evidence of the supposedly sharp contrast between hunter-gatherers' and farmers' cosmologies, to suggest that such hunter-gatherers experience the forest as a sharing partner (e.g. Bird-David 1992), and to suggest that hunter-gatherers' relationship with each other and with the forest is characterised by trust (e.g. Ingold 1996).

In considering the environment as a living rather than an inert entity, Ichikawa makes the important point that Bird-David's portrayal of a hunter-gatherer 'cosmic economy of sharing' with their environment fails to include Mbuti experience of the negative aspects of 'nature': 'while the forest may sometimes be called "father" or "mother" and described as a "womb", it is also conceived to be a place where dead ancestors roam' (Ichikawa 1992: 41). Although Ichikawa highlights the broad range of Mbuti experience of the forest, rather than recognise the importance of the 'ancestors as forest', he instead leaves them to occupy simply a negative intrusive role. However, for the Mbuti (as well as for many Bila) the different aspects of the forest – such as paths, places, streams and old camps – carry the memory of particular ancestors and events which are seen as still potent and present, still embodied in those places. They address the forest and the ancestors in the same breath because they are, for them, the same being, as evident in Mbuti statements such as: 'The spirits of the ancestors are in the forest. Spirit and forest are one, inseparable, one always'.

Ichikawa's division between the ancestors and the forest has parallels with a tendency in the West to make an absolute distinction between the living and the dead, and assume that an ancestor will be treated in a qualitatively different way to a living elder. 'The term "ancestor" sets up a dichotomy where there is a continuum. By conceptually separating living elders from ancestors, we unconsciously introduce Western connotations to the phenomena' (Kopytoff 1971: 140). For the Suku of southwestern Zaire, for example, ancestors are simply elders who are no longer alive but are still present, and are treated similarly to elders (Kopytoff 1971: 138; but see also Kopytoff 1987 and McFall 1995: 258–65).

For the Mbuti, restoring harmony in their relationship with the forest inevitably means restoring harmony among themselves: for the forest is inhabited by the living and the dead, it is alive with those who are living and those who are now both ancestor and forest and who dialogue with the camp through the molimo or in dreams. Thus – to take Kopytoff's argument a step further – the division we habitually make between people (whether ancestors or living) and their environment (in this case the forest) does not hold for the Mbuti, and to a certain extent it does not hold for the Bila either. Although the Mbuti experience ambivalence in their relationship with the forest/ancestors, they generally work within the molimo to make the relationship good.

The Example of the Molimo

Rather than seeing the forest as a separate 'god-head' whom they worship and seek blessings from (Turnbull 1961), it is seen as continuous with human life. There is no division between a supposedly transcendent forest and the human realm; rather when they are calling the forest *ema*, *epa*, *tata* (mother, father, grandparent) they are to a certain extent calling on their own ancestors who are the forest. For this reason Mbuti relations with the forest mirror their relations with other humans. When their relations are dominated by distrust, this will be evident in both their relations with the forest/ancestors and with other living humans. For example, the Mbuti 'chief' in my fieldwork site was so caught in relations of domination and fear that he sought to use both sorcery accusations and the molimo to coerce others. Although he was always ultimately unsuccessful in his attempt to use the molimo to assert dominance, the point is that the molimo offered a forum within which he could attempt it. The way in which this man was being exploited by the corrupt regional chief who sought to create, and benefit from, disharmony in this Mbuti camp, demonstrates the way in which disempowering processes are 'penetratingly exclusive', in that they seek to forcefully persuade those being disempowered that they can have no agency except as agents of this same process of division and discrimination. Such processes are not only evident in Bila villages but can be an aspect of what is attempted through such Mbuti rituals as the molimo.

The molimo usually involves night-long singing between the camp and the voice of the forest/ancestors that arrives in the form of a trumpet (usually a hollowed-out tree) and can take place nightly in Mbuti hunting camps. It tends to either emerge out of a relaxed and abundant state in camp, or be a response to conflict, to a poor hunt, to a death, or to disharmony (often caused by someone not being willing enough to share). As it progresses it tends to gradually draw the camp deeper and deeper into more complex harmonies requiring and echoing the complex cooperation required in the hunt. Rather than being about transcending and controlling the forest or other people, the molimo tends to be about restoring cooperative relationships between all members of the camp and between the camp and the forest/ancestors, to ensure the camp's well-being and to ensure a good relationship with the forest as well, something which is seen as inevitably leading to a good hunt.

Thus for most Mbuti, and for many Bila, the aliveness of their environment is experienced and expressed through their interaction with it, and through the awareness of their ancestors inhabiting the forest both in the past and in the present, a form of inhabiting in which they and the forest become indistinguishable. In a key passage describing Mbuti religion, Turnbull himself hints at this interpretation when he describes *keti* as 'spirits, human and animal, who are not necessarily the spirits of the dead but may be independent manifestations of the forest, and who are disembodied only in that they are invisible to the Mbuti' (1965: 249). The ambiguity in this passage – about who the *baketi* are – mirrors Ichikawa's insistence on broadening our understanding of Mbuti experience. The implication of Turnbull's ambiguity here is in strong contrast to the sharp and explicit distinction he customarily makes between fearful village ancestor worship and trustful Mbuti forest worship. In this passage the spirits of the forest are *both* human and animal, *both* spirits of the dead and independent manifestations of the forest, *both* invisible and embodied.

Just as Turnbull's opposition between the village and the forest is only one aspect of Bila–Mbuti relations, so a relationship of trust is only one way of characterising Mbuti interaction with the forest. Where Mbuti are dominated by distrust, either in their enduring relationships with particular ancestors or in relation to others in the present, then this will be reflected in their experience of the forest and their use of the molimo. Thus it is far more useful to examine the Bila–Mbuti and Mbuti–Forest relationships in terms of understanding particular processes of domination or of inclusiveness, rather than in terms of culturally given immutable categories which cannot offer the breadth and flexibility needed to embrace the wealth of actual Bila–Mbuti–Forest relations. If, in place of Turnbull's rigid opposition, we take a process-orientated approach then there are very clear theoretical and practical implications. Theoretically, we need to move away from the dualism inherent in setting up opposing cosmological categories (whether Bila and Mbuti, or Western and hunter-gatherer) and instead pay attention to the relational processes of domination or inclusion which flow both ways. Practically, we need to consider how to support Forest People's practices of inclusiveness and how to refrain from insisting on structures of representation and leadership which will undermine the equalising processes which are at the heart of such people's social worlds.[10]

Demand-Sharing and Mbuti Inclusiveness

Turnbull's reason for stressing an opposition between the mutually exclusive categories of Village People and Forest People described above was entirely understandable. He was trying to counteract the then prevalent view (e.g. Schweinfurth 1874: 146; Schebesta 1936: 105) of the Mbuti as dependent servants. Likewise those working with Central African Forest People have tended to either follow him in seeking to draw a sharp line between the Village People and the Forest Peoples, in order to emphasise the Forest People's autonomy, or have effectively followed Schebesta in stressing Forest Peoples' dependence on Village People (see Bailey et al. 1989 on ecological dependence; see Grinker 1994: 9 on social organisation).

The argument that Forest People are dependent on, and dominated by, Village People, is used by national and international development agencies to justify the assimilationist policies outlined in the first half of this paper. However, the argument that Forest People survive that attempted domination by retaining a completely distinct culture in opposition to their neighbours implies that they cannot engage with other people without losing the qualities which define them as Forest People (a point further explored in Kenrick 2000: 23–24, and Lewis 2001: 76). In this perspective the gap between Forest People and others is so big it is unbridgeable; all that is possible is a rearguard action as such cultures are inevitably absorbed and destroyed (see Turnbull 1961 [1993]: 9).

Thus in both perspectives contact leads to cultural disintegration, whether seen positively, by development agencies seeking to improve such people's 'standard of living', or seen negatively, by those who see a state of 'original affluence' being destroyed. This is because the contact is happening on 'village people's' exclusive terms, in which some are given more importance than others, not on the inclusive terms preferred by hunter-gatherers, an inclusiveness based on a process of assertive egalitarianism. When contact happens on 'village terms' then attempts to empower Forest People to stand up to discrimination inevitably backfire. Take, for example, the case of an articulate Bagyeli man who became a spokesperson for Bagyeli concerns and travelled to Washington DC to speak for the Bagyeli to the World Bank about the proposed oil pipeline. When he returned he could either tell everyone about the trip and would be seen – in this cultural context where equality is asserted – as bragging, as attempting to assert his power, or he could just tell people slowly in a more modest way. However, many Bagyeli voiced their disapproval of him, complaining that he had told them nothing. He couldn't win either way, because the 'delayed-return' game of representation and accountability is not acceptable to an 'immediate-return' way of ensuring equality. Attempting empowerment based on representation and on opposition to their village neighbours can only fail.

The key point here is that the analytic notion of assertive egalitarianism (Woodburn 1982; Barnard and Woodburn 1988; Woodburn 1998) has tended to be applied only to the 'internal' political and economic aspects of such immediate-return hunter-gatherers' experience. However, the inclusive approach at the heart of this equalising process is not one which hunter-gatherers adopt in the forest world but have to abandon when in contact with others. It is fundamental to their relations with others as well. Just as Mbuti use social occasions such as the nkumbi to build relations, and join Bila in undermining those attempting to use the occasion to dominate others, so they use demand-sharing to assert equality amongst themselves but also with everyone else. What can be seen as begging by outsiders is actually just another form of demand-sharing: an insistence that whoever has more of something than they need must share it with those that don't.

Demand-sharing means that any Mbuti who clearly has an excess of something will be obliged to share his excess with others or be subject to ridicule and general disapproval. This might involve being singled out in one of the evening speeches made by an elder in camp, mocked in one of the hysterically funny performances by one of the older women, or possibly becoming the subject of ridicule by the molimo's 'fool' when the molimo trumpet arrives in camp at night. Demand-sharing is embedded in an attitude of inclusiveness which informs their relations with everybody. Woodburn's description of Hadza inclusiveness is also true of these Mbuti:

> Hadza society is open and there is simply no basis for exclusion. Equality is, in a sense, generalised by them to all mankind but, sadly, few of the rest of mankind, so enmeshed in property relations, would be willing to extend parity of esteem to hunter-gatherers who treat property with such a lack of seriousness. (Woodburn 1982: 448)

One point which follows from this is that Mbuti claims on property of villagers or anthropologists is essentially no different from the claim they make on any Mbuti who appears to possess more than they immediately need. Likewise the 'Mbendjele ideal of their relationship with Bilo is based on friendship, sharing, mutual aid and support, and on equality and respect for one another' (Lewis 1999: 13), on the idea that Bilo should behave as Mbendjele do and simply give Mbendjele whatever they demand. In return Mbendjele will provide Bilo with things they demand (Lewis 1999: 13). During some periods in Mbuti camps I experienced endless demands when I had much more of many things than anybody else. Although this could be taken as evidence of Turnbull's split between people of the forest and those of the village, as evidence of the Mbuti always seeking to exploit outsiders, or of some innate and 'rational' human desire to maximise possessions; these would all be superficial readings of the situation. Demands on fellow Mbuti with conspicuous excess were at least as strong as demands on villagers or myself: objects acquired from me would quickly and easily be passed on to others who, in their turn, had demanded them.

For this reason, it is more appropriate to see Mbuti responses to tourists, anthropologists, villagers and conservationists, not as happening in a different world to their responses to each other, but as being an extension of the inclusiveness that characterises their relations with the forest, the ancestors and each other. 'Inclusiveness' is perhaps a misleading term if it is understood in terms of the current political jargon of 'inclusiveness' – in the West the term is currently used by those with power as a benevolent promise to enfold the excluded, a promise which appears to serve to bolster the positions of those with power by asserting their centrality through protesting their good intentions to reach out to those on the edge. This form of 'inclusiveness' is an attempt to assert patronage and undermine agency, a strategy which can be employed by villagers when they are seeking to engage Mbuti in wage-labour by promising them both material benefit and also promising that they are the ones who care about 'their' Mbuti's well being. For the Mbuti 'insisting on being included in' is the form that inclusiveness takes, an inclusiveness that stresses rights to a share and the primacy of the individual's agency and autonomy. Endless demands are an aspect of the inclusiveness Woodburn describes: an inclusiveness which subverts any attempt by someone with power and possessions to maintain a position of power through giving gifts to those with less and thereby seeking to establish in them a sense of indebtedness.

Conclusion

In attempting to identify processes of disempowerment and processes of inclusion, the second part of this paper has concentrated on demonstrating that the notion of an unbridgeable opposition between Forest and Village is only one way in which Mbuti and Bila frame what is also experienced as a relationship of interdependence.

When Lewis writes that Mbendjele talk about their relations with villagers 'using hunting vocabulary to describe their scams, transactions and encounters' (Lewis 2001: 68), this could be understood in terms of their entering a strange world and treating villagers completely differently to the way they treat each other; and this is the interpretation of Mbuti–villagers' interactions stressed by Turnbull. However, as Lewis points out, the Mbendjele ideal is that their relationship with the Bilo should be based on 'friendship' and the practice of demand-sharing. Likewise, Mbuti descriptions of getting goods from villagers in ways similar to the hunt is evidence of their treating the village world in the same way they treat the forest and each other. Where we might see an unbridgeable opposition between Mbuti and Bila, this is not the way the Mbuti or the Mbendjele experience it. Their central value of egalitarianism is focused precisely on bridging the divide those seeking to assert their power attempt to create between one world and another. Mbuti making demands on villagers is simply one way of engaging in this inclusive process, entering fully into the nkumbi is another. If we only support Forest People to fight against discrimination in opposition to their neighbours, then we only undermine their inclusive equalising processes and intensify the discrimination.

Thus the need is not only to identify the processes of discrimination and domination present within and between both peoples, but also to identify and support equalising processes of inclusion. The second half of this paper has tended to examine this from the point of view of the Forest People, but it could also be examined from the Villagers' perspective. Grinker, although he is very clear that in his work he is concerned primarily with the denigration of the Efe by the Lese, nevertheless notes that 'the Lese do not always characterise the Efe in negative terms' (1990: 113), and further that 'neither side of an opposition entirely constitute lived social relations ... the Lese oscillate between approximations of love and hate in their feelings toward the Efe. They live between tendencies that pull in the direction of either side' (1990: 126).

Neither assimilating Forest People within 'village people's' development schemes, nor seeking to establish an unbridgeable divide between the two peoples, reflects or makes use of the breadth of relations that exist between these peoples or the possibilities present in supporting Forest People to build on the inclusive equalising processes so evident in their relationship with the forest, each other, and those they seek to establish relationships of equality with. In place of attempting to 'develop' or 'empower' such people, we could instead recognise and support their own effective processes of asserting and achieving equality by identifying and defusing the processes of disempowerment and distrust which in large part emanate from Western notions of development, scarcity and control – whether in the form of oil pipelines and unequalising processes of compensation, or in the form of conservation areas that seek to impose controls on such people's relations to their environment.

If, in place of exclusive and opposing categories, we can begin to take a processual approach – one which identifies processes of mutual disempowerment and supports processes of inclusiveness and equality – then we can begin to engage in such situations in a nuanced and intuitive way that does not rely only on oppositional ideas and categories but is alert to the complexity and possibilities inherent in the processes which shape real relationships. Taking this approach, the problems to be addressed can be approached differently. They are not about something lacking in Forest People – who need 'developing' or 'empowering' or 'training' – nor about there being something inherently wrong in their relation with their farming neighbours – requiring that Forest People either *become* like Village People or be supported in their struggle *against* Village People. The problem is instead revealed as historically specific processes of disempowerment.

Today, in most of the cases that affect Central African Forest People, these processes are either the consequences of Western colonial policies, or emanate from the dualistic and scarcity-driven impact of Western development and conservation projects. Supporting, and seeking support from, Forest People and Village People to resist the disempowering impact of such processes, enables a more realistic and nuanced way of countering the domination involved – something which may involve us all in learning from, and engaging with, the equalizing processes of inclusiveness which Woodburn has highlighted for immediate-return hunter-gatherers, and which this paper has sought to begin to sketch as being processes which implicate their immediate neighbours and us all.

Notes

1. Much of the substance of the first part of this paper, on 'Catch 22' and the Bagyeli predicament, is drawn from sections I contributed to a recent article, 'Evolving Discrimination against the Forest People ('Pygmies') of Central Africa' by Kenrick and Lewis (2001). The section on Woodburn's analysis of discrimination is mainly drawn from a similarly named section in the same article put together by us both, and largely summarises Woodburn's 1997 article.
2. The use of 'Forest People' rather than 'Pygmy' is a direct translation of the label many Pygmy peoples in Central Africa prefer to give themselves.
3. Axel Köhler (personal communication) notes that it was Bartolomé de Las Casas who came up with this argument against Indian slavery, an idea which the Spanish Crown eventually supported. Lonmnitz-Adler (1992: 265, 269) points out that, in contrast to this view of Amerindians, black slaves were seen as being lost and having no chance of redemption, which was why they could be enslaved.
4. For example, unemployed single mothers in the USA are obliged to put their children into childcare so that they are available for work.
5. The first three paragraphs and the last paragraph of this section summarise my own, and mostly Jerome Lewis's, contributions to our article 'Evolving Discrimination' (Kenrick and Lewis 2001), mentioned in note 1 above.
6. See also Kenrick (2000) on the Baka of southeast Cameroon and Kenrick (2001) on the Ugandan Batwa.
7. Grinker's understanding differs from Turnbull's in that Grinker sees the forest–village opposition as an ethnic division in which the Mbuti define themselves in terms of the Bila (Grinker 1994: 4–9).
8. Fieldwork in the Ituri was conducted in 1992–93 and 1994–95, funded by the ESRC; rights-based work with the Batwa of Uganda – in 2000, 2001, 2002 – and Bagyeli in 2001 has been funded by the Forest Peoples Programme.
9. The Nande are recent incomers from the Kivu region that lies to the east of the Ituri Forest.

10. There is not space here to examine the implications for the theoretical understandings of hunter-gatherer and Western perceptions and cosmologies such as those evident in Ingold's and Bird-David's work (but see Kenrick 2002).

References

Bahuchet, S., F. Grenand, P. Grenand and P. de Maret 2001. *Tropical Forest Peoples Today. Volume 1: Tropical Forests, Human Forests: An Overview.* Brussels: APFT – ULB (Avenir des Peuples des Forets Tropicales).

Bailey, R., G. Head, M. Jenike, B. Owen, R. Rechtman and E. Zechenster 1989. 'Hunting and Gathering in Tropical Rain Forest: Is It Possible?' *American Anthropologist,* 91: 59–82.

Barnard, A. and J. Woodburn. 1988. 'Property, Power and Ideology in Hunter-gathering Societies: an Introduction'. In: T. Ingold, D. Riches and J. Woodburn (eds), *Hunters and Gatherers Vol 2: Property, Power and Ideology.* Oxford: Berg.

Barume, K. 2000. *Heading Towards Extinction? The Expulsion of the Twa from the Kahuzi-Biega National Park, Democratic Republic of Congo. A Study of Indigenous Rights in Africa.* Copenhagen: IWGIA and FPP.

Bennett, G. 1978. *Aboriginal Rights in International Law.* Royal Anthropological Institute of Great Britain and Ireland, Occasional Paper No. 37.

Bird-David, N. 1992. 'Beyond "the Original Affluent Society": a Culturalist Reformulation'. *Current Anthropology,* 33(1): 25–34.

Frankland, S. 1999. 'Turnbull's Syndrome: Romantic fascination in the rainforest'. In: Karen Biesbrouck, S. Elders and G. Rossel (eds), *Challenging Elusiveness: Central African Hunter-Gatherers in a Multidisciplinary Perspective,* pp. 59–73. Leiden: CNWS (Research School for Asian, African and Amerindian Studies).

—— 2001. 'Pygmic Tours'. In *African Studies Monograph,* Supplement Issue No. 26.

Grinker, R.R. 1990. 'Images of Denigration: Structuring Inequality between Foragers and Farmers in the Ituri Forest, Zaire'. *American Ethnologist,* 17: 111–30.

—— 1994. *Houses in the Rain Forest: Ethnicity and Inequality among Farmers and Foragers in Central Africa.* Berkeley: University of California Press.

Ichikawa, M. 1992. 'Comment on Nurit Bird-David's "Beyond 'the Original Affluent Society': a Culturalist Reformulation"'. *Current Anthropology,* 33(1): 40–41.

Ingold, T. 1996. 'Hunting and Gathering as Ways of Perceiving the Environment'. In: R. Ellen and K. Fukui (eds), *Redefining Nature: Ecology, Culture and Domestication.* Oxford: Berg.

Jordanova, L.J. 1980. 'Natural Facts: a Historical Perspective on Science and Sexuality'. In: C.P. MacCormack and M. Strathern (eds), *Nature, Culture and Gender.* Cambridge: Cambridge University Press.

Kagabo, J.H. and V. Mudandagizi, 1974. 'Complainte des gens d'argile, les Twa du Rwanda'. *Cahiers des Etudes Africaines,* 14(1) Cahier No. 53, pp. 75–87.

Kenrick, J. 1999. 'Reflections in the Molimo Pool: Gender, Ritual, Economics and the Mbuti of Zaire'. In: K. Biesbrouck, S. Elders and G. Rossel (eds.), *Challenging Elusiveness: Central African Hunter-Gatherers in a Multidisciplinary Perspective,* pp. 153–68. Leiden: CNWS (Research School for Asian, African and Amerindian Studies).

Kenrick, J. 2000. 'The Forest Peoples of Africa in the 21st Century: Present Predicament of Hunter Gatherers and Former Hunter Gatherers of the Central African Rainforests'. In *Indigenous Affairs* 2000/2: 10–24. Copenhagen: IWGIA.

Kenrick, J. 2001. *The Batwa of South West Uganda: World Bank Policy on Indigenous Peoples and the Conservation of the Bwindi and Mgahinga National Parks.* Manila: Tebbatebba.

Kenrick, J. 2002. 'Anthropology and Anthropocentrism: Images of Hunter-Gatherers, Westerners and the Environment'. In: H. Stewart, A.Barnard and K. Omura (eds), *Self- and Other Images of Hunter-Gatherers,* SENRI Ethnological Studies, Special Issue. Osaka: National Museum of Ethnology.

Kenrick, J. and J. Lewis 2001. 'Evolving Discrimination against the Forest People ('Pygmies') of Central Africa'. *Indigenous Affairs.* Copenhagen: IWGIA.

Kopytoff, I. 1971. 'Ancestors as Elders in Africa'. *Africa,* 41: 129–42.

Kopytoff, I. 1987. *The African Frontier.* Bloomington: Indiana University Press.

Lee, R. 1968. 'What Hunters Do For a Living: or, How to Make Out on Scarce Resources'. In: R. Lee and I. DeVore (eds), *Man the Hunter*, pp. 30–48. Chicago: Aldine.
—— 1972. 'The !Kung Bushmen of Botswana'. In: M.G. Bicchieri (ed.) *Hunters and Gatherers Today*, pp. 326-68. New York: Holt, Rinehart and Winston.
—— 1979. *The !Kung San: Men, Women and Work in a Foraging Society.* Cambridge: Cambridge University Press.
Lewis, J. 1999. *Gorillas, Pigs and People: Yaka Pygmy Conceptions of Outsiders.* Paper presented at the Seminar on Anthropological Theory, LSE.
—— 2000. *The Batwa Pygmies of the Great Lakes Region: The Problem of Discrimination.* London: Minority Rights Group Report.
—— 2001. 'Forest People or Village People: Whose Voice Will Be Heard?' In: A. Barnard and J. Kenrick (eds), *Africa's Indigenous Peoples: 'First Peoples' or 'Marginalised Minorities'?* Edinburgh: CAS.
—— and J. Knight 1995. *The Twa of Rwanda: Assessment of the Situation of the Twa and Promotion of Twa Rights in Post-War Rwanda.* Copenhagen, World Rainforest Movement and IWGIA.
Lomnitz-Adler, C. 1992. *Exits from the Labyrinth: Culture and Ideology in the Mexican National Space.* Berkeley, Oxford: University of California Press.
Nelson, J., J. Kenrick and D. Jackson 2001. *Report on a Consultation with Bagyeli Pygmy Communities Impacted by the Chad–Cameroon Oil-Pipeline Project.* Moreton-in-Marsh: Forest Peoples Project.
Sahlins, M. 1968. 'Notes on the original affluent society'. In: R. Lee and I. DeVore (eds), *Man the Hunter*, pp. 85-89, Chicago: Aldine.
—— 1972. *Stone Age Economics.* London: Routledge.
Schebesta, P. 1933. *Among Congo Pigmies.* London: Hutchinson & Co. (reprinted 1977 by New York: AMS Press Inc.).
—— 1936. *My Pygmy and Negro Hosts.* London: Hutchinson.
Schweinfurth, G. 1874. *The Heart of Africa: Volume 2.* New York: Harper and Brothers.
Turnbull, C.M. 1993. *The Forest People.* London: Pimlico.
—— 1965. *Wayward Servants: the Two Worlds of the African Pygmies.* London: Eyre & Spottiswoode.
—— 1972. *The Mountain People.* New York: Touchstone.
—— 1983. *The Mbuti Pygmies: Change and Adaptation.* New York: Holt, Rinehart & Winston.
—— 1990. 'Liminality: a Synthesis of Subjective and Objective Experience'. In: Richard Schechner and W. Appel (eds), *By Means of Performance: Intercultural Studies of Theatre and Ritual.* Cambridge: Cambridge University Press.
—— [L. Rigdol]. 1993. 'An Anthropologist Monk'. *The Tibet Journal*, 18(1): 20–26.
Waehle, E. 1985. 'Efe (Mbuti Pygmy) Relations to Lese-Dese villagers in the Ituri Forest, Zaire: Historical Changes During the Last 150 years'. Paper presented at the international symposium: African Hunter-gatherers, Cologne, January 1985.
Widlok, T. 2001. 'The Illusion of a Future? Medicine Dance Rituals for the Civil Society of Tomorrow'. *African Studies Monograph.* Supplementary Issue 27, pp. 165–83.
Woodburn, J. 1968. 'Stability and Flexibility in Hadza Residential Groupings'. In: R. Lee and I. DeVore (eds), *Man the Hunter*, pp. 103–110. Chicago: Aldine.
—— 1970. *Hunters and Gatherers: the Material Culture of the Nomadic Hadza.* London: British Museum.
—— 1979. 'Minimal politics: The Political Organisation of the Hadza of Tanzania'. In: P. Cohen and W. Shack (eds), *Politics in Leadership: a Comparative Perspective*, pp. 244-66. Oxford: Clarendon Press.
—— 1982. 'Egalitarian Societies'. *Man* (N.S.), 17: 431–51.
—— 1988. 'African Hunter-gatherer Social Organization: Is It Best Understood as a Product of Encapsulation?'. In: T. Ingold, D. Riches and J. Woodburn (eds), *Hunters and Gatherers Vol 1: History, Evolution and Social Change.* Oxford: Berg.
—— 1997. 'Indigenous Discrimination: the Ideological Basis for Local Discrimination against Hunter-gatherer Minorities in sub-Saharan Africa'. *Ethnic and Racial Studies*, 20(2): 345–61.
—— 1998. '"Sharing is not a form of exchange": an Analysis of Property Sharing in Immediate-return Hunter-gatherer Societies'. In: C.M. Hann (ed.), *Property Relations: Renewing the Anthropological Tradition*, pp. 48–63. Cambridge: Cambridge University Press.

7

Delay, Return and Hierarchy: Six Aboriginal Marriage Systems Compared

Ian Keen

Introduction

For Claude Meillasoux, the differences between their farming neighbours and a hunting and gathering society as typified by Mbuti people derived from their mode of exploitation of the land. For Mbuti land was a 'subject of labour' in Marx's terms: people made no attempt towards 'maintenance and reclamation'. For want of investment in land, labour yielded an 'instantaneous' yield through independent and discontinuous undertakings of a limited duration, where the product was obtained 'immediately at the end of each venture'. Cooperation in hunting ended with the division of the product. In the absence of a redistributive system, centralisation of product and 'deferred' distribution, sharing was not delayed but instantaneous (Meillasoux 1973: 192–94).

In the case of farming, land is an instrument of labour 'by the incorporation into the land of a sum of labour whose output is deferred'. Cooperation in production is prolonged and continuous. The future becomes a concern, and so the reproduction of the production unit becomes a problem to be solved through modes of descent and marriage (ibid.:198). For Meillasoux, then, delay in returns is incurred through the cycle of production in farming, and the investment of labour in the land in the forms of cultivation, planting, weeding and harvesting, and through storage and redistribution. Such features provide the foundations for the construction of centralised and enduring political power absent in hunting and gathering societies. In the latter, men and women enjoy relative equality, and kin relations remain diffuse. Agriculture, in contrast, supports a hierarchical structure based on age or authority (Meillasoux 1973: 101).

James Woodburn has shifted the boundary between 'immediate-return' and 'delayed-return' across the distinction between hunter-gatherers and farmers, classifying some hunting and gathering societies with farmers as delayed-return societies. By implication, hunters and gatherers with delayed-return systems are more hierarchical than those with immediate-return systems, who tend to be assertively egalitarian. Woodburn classifies Australian Aboriginal societies as delayed-return systems, and describes such systems in this way:

> - Activities are oriented to the past and the future as well as to the present.
> - People hold rights over valued assets of some sort, which either represent a yield, a return for labour applied over time or, if not, are held and managed in a way which resembles and has similar social implications to delayed yields on labour.
> - In delayed-return hunting and gathering systems these assets are of four main types, found separately or in combination: valuable technical facilities used in production; processed and stored foods or materials; wild products which have been improved or increased by human labour; assets in the form of rights held by men over their female kin who are then bestowed in marriage on other men. (Woodburn 1988: 32)

Here, the investment is not in land itself but in technical facilities, the improvement of wild products, and in marriage bestowal. These hunter-gatherers, *contra* Meillasoux, do plan futures. But I would add that Aboriginal people certainly invested time and labour in the management of country to enhance productivity, mainly through the use of fire, as well as proto-agricultural practices such as replanting of tubers after harvesting and seed dispersal (Tindale 1974: 96).

Woodburn has also suggested that:

> In a world of hunter-gatherers, the interaction of adjacent societies with each other, particularly in ritual and ceremonial exchange, might tend to reinforce the ideological basis for delayed-return. This would be particularly significant for systems like those of the Australian Aborigines in which the delayed-return element is based largely in men's ritual labour and the control of ritual assets and of assets in the form of rights held by men over women rather than in the mundane subsistence economy. (Woodburn 1988: 58)

With a focus on marriage, this chapter takes up two themes arising out of Woodburn's revision of Meillasoux: first, the relationship between the degree of delay, the amount and nature of the return, and hierarchy; second, and more briefly, the effects of encapsulation. Drawing on a wider study of variation in Aboriginal economy and society (Keen 2004) it explores variation in Aboriginal kinship and marriage, returns in the form of polygyny, and the association of the variation with difference in power. (The wider study compares the economy and society of seven regions of Australia as they were at the threshold of British colonisation, reconstructed from the reports of early ethnographers, as informed by more recent studies.) The peoples and regions of this comparison are:

- Kûnai people of Gippsland, eastern Victoria;
- Pitjantjatjara people and their neighbours of the Western Desert;
- Wiil and Minong people of the south coast of the southwest region of Western Australia – Minong people lived near the coast while Wiil were their hinterland neighbours;
- 'Sandbeach' people (speakers of Umpila and related languages) of eastern Cape York Peninsula;
- Ngarinyin and their neighbours of the northwest Kimberley; and
- Yolngu of northeast Arnhem Land.

In the context of the concept of delayed-return, marriage in Aboriginal societies can be seen as an investment by various parties. The investment by the potential husband often took the form of a long process of negotiation and a series of gifts and services, most commonly in the form of hunting for meat. From the point of view of the potential wife's kin the daughter or sister was an asset, access to whose sexual, productive and reproductive powers could be exchanged. Potential wives had complementary expectations, and in some regions at least they made reciprocal gifts to the potential husband. However, young first wives were less active in the process, and in the case of infant or prenatal bestowal, not at all active initially. The 'return' on the husband's investment was the formation of a domestic unit or the addition of a wife to an existing one, status as a married man (in the case of a first marriage), access to the wife's product, the identification of children of the marriage with his own group or category (in the case of patrilineal descent or patrifiliation), and the possibility of begetting daughters with the expectation of a return for bestowing them in marriage. Under certain conditions such as patrifilial organisation, then the more wives the greater the return.

Marriage was not just a matter of investment in the expectation of future returns in the form of labour and productivity; it had a variety of implications – for the structure and reproduction of domestic groups, wider political structures and dynamics, and the structure of social networks. But the main questions I address here are: how long was the delay and how great the return in Aboriginal marriage systems? And, how did differences in delay and return relate to power differences? I suggest, to put it simply, that *the greater the delay the greater the return*; and *the greater the return the greater the power differences* in the society.

'Levels' of polygyny in the case studies range from 'low' to 'very high'. These levels have a degree of association with modes of kin classification, and with marriage strategies. The high and very high levels of polygyny among Ngarinyin and Yolngu people respectively were related to asymmetrical terminologies and marriage rules. They also had an association with long periods of time between a bestowal and cohabitation, and in the Yolngu case, where polygyny was highest, marriage involved negotiations among long chains of kin, affines and potential affines.

I will now outline kin classification and marriage in the six regions of the study.

Kûnai Kinship

The Classification of Kin

Kûnai people had a relatively simple system of kin classification with 'Hawaiian' or generational features in Ego's generation and the child's generation (Ives 1998: 100). Four kinds of kin were distinguished in the grandparents' generation, and terms had a bifurcate merging structure in the parent's generation. All relatives in one's own generation were 'brothers' and 'sisters' but differentiated by relative age. Affinal terms were distinct from the kin terms. Some areas of the terminology are hazy; for example it is not clear what the terms were for the spouses of grandparents' siblings. (On Kûnai kin classification and marriage see Smyth 1878: 46; Fison and Howitt 1880: 199–204, Howitt 1904; Scheffler 1978: 111–12; Bulmer 1994).

Marriage

Kûnai people did not pick out narrowly defined classes of relatives as potential spouses. Nor did they organise marriages between exogamous totemic categories, except to the extent that one should not marry a person of one's own patrifilial guardian totem (*je-ak*, 'flesh'). Most important, a spouse had to be a very distant relative, which in practice probably meant not related by a known genealogical link. Since genealogical memory was probably short, it is likely that second cousins (who share a common great-grandparent) and closer relatives could not marry (Bulmer in Curr 1887: 546, Papers MV B10 F5 xm922: 46, see also Fison and Howitt 1880: 199; Bulmer 1994: 8).

Kûnai discouraged geographically close marriage, and expressed the ideal that people of the same local group (a 'division' of a 'clan' in Howitt's terminology) and its estate or country should not marry. In some cases people apparently prohibited marriage of a man to a woman of his mother's local group. As mentioned, a person was not supposed to marry someone of the same patrifilial guardian totem (Bulmer 1994: 15). Some people even rejected those of the same broad regional identity (Howitt's 'clan') as partners even though they were not closely related (Bulmer in Curr 1887: 546). Each of the five regional identities consisted of several hundred people The reported pattern of marriages between named localities shows, however, that people with the same regional identity did often marry (Howitt 1904: 272).

The ways of marrying in Gippsland included bestowal, leviratic and sororatic marriage, elopement and raiding. According to Bulmer, a man could always get a wife if he had sisters. He would bestow his sister, or his female 'cousin' (classified as a 'sister') if she had no close brother of her own, in exchange for a wife for himself. Men thus exchanged 'sisters'. In such a case a man might negotiate directly with the intended spouse rather than her brother. Sometimes, however, a woman's or girl's father and father's brother bestowed her as a wife. A woman might put on at least a show of resistance to a bestowed marriage, and indeed to leviratic marriage (Fison and Howitt

1880: 200n, 220; Bulmer 1994: 9, Papers MV B1 F4 xm77–78, 10 October 1878, xm98 undated).

The ethnographers do not represent only men as agents in marriage arrangements. For example, young women provoked young men to fight, and sometimes a young woman used stratagems, building on beliefs in magic, to induce her family to accept a relationship (Bulmer 1994: 9).

Howitt took 'elopement' to have been the norm except among Brabrolung and Krauatûngolung people. If two young men each had an unmarried sister they might arrange for each to abscond with the other's sister. But Bulmer also writes that a man with no sisters to exchange would have to 'win the heart' of a woman and elope (Fison and Howitt 1880: 200n, 204; Bulmer 1994: 19–20). Would-be partners typically chose the occasion of a ceremony to run away together, especially the Jerra-eil male initiation which people from a wide region attended, the girl's parents supposedly unaware of the proposal. Young women would sometimes take the initiative, according to Howitt, and provoke the young men by killing birds of the male totem (*yiirûng*, Emu wren). The youths provoked the girls in turn, then after the ensuing fights some couples would pair off. Howitt reports (in Latin) the occurrence of group sex on such occasions between a girl and a group of initiation mates (*brogan*) (Fison and Howitt 1880: 202).

A young man could call on a singer of love-magic songs (*bunjil-yenjin*) to induce the woman to run off against her parents' consent. He gave the singer presents of weapons, skin rugs or other items in return. For their part the parents might perform or commission magic to find the eloping couple (Howitt 1904: 275–77). An elopement provoked the opposition of the girl's family, leading to the man having to fight her brothers, and a beating or spearing in the feet for the girl. In some cases a couple would have to elope two or three times, or the girl would have to become pregnant, before the woman's family consented (Fison and Howitt 1880: 200–201, 202; Howitt 1904: 276; Bulmer 1994: 9).

After the death of a husband, the senior brother had the first claim on his widow. If there were several widows then brothers claimed in order of seniority. However, a widow might refuse to go to her husband's brother and choose someone else, in which case he had no remedy except 'by endeavouring to kill her by bulk, that is, by witchcraft' (Fison and Howitt 1880: 204; Bulmer 1994: 10). It seems that among people of some regions in Gippsland people practised sororatic marriage either subsequent to a wife's death, or concurrently. The ostensible reason was that the wives' parents would obtain a double supply of food through the obligation of the son-in-law to provide for them (Fison and Howitt 1880: 203).

Kûnai men also obtained wives in raids against *brajerak*, 'strangers.' abducting the younger women. In return, men of other regions, such as the Monaro tablelands to the northwest, sporadically raided Kûnai country for wives (Fison and Howitt 1880: 199–200).

Polygyny appears to have been comparatively low in Gippsland, with about 17 percent of married men having two wives and 3 percent with three wives, according to the early census data.[1]

Pitjantjatjara and Their Neighbours

The Classification of Kin

The Pitjantjatjara terminology was simpler than Kûnai in that there were only two categories of kin in the grandparents' generation, distinguishing male from female grandkin. But in a similar way to Kûnai kinship, a person referred to most relatives of his or her own generation as 'brother' or 'sister.' differentiated according to relative age as well as gender. Unlike the Kûnai terminology, however, the children of one's *distant* mother's brothers or father's sisters were not siblings but *watjirra*, 'cross-cousins.' the category of the preferred spouse. After marriage, Pitjantjatjara people applied distinct terms to relatives who became affines (see Elkin 1939-40; Scheffler 1978; Dousset 2003 on Pitjantjatjara kin classification).

Marriage

Marriage in this region had links with male initiation, specifically circumcision (which neither Kûnai nor Sandbeach people practised). Circumcision resulted in a contract between the man (or men) who carried out the operation and the young man on whom he operated. As compensation for the injury, in which the circumciser symbolically 'killed' the initiate, the circumciser promised to give the young man his daughter or brother's daughter as a wife. After the operation the circumciser became the young man's *umari* or *waputju*, 'wife's father', and they had to avoid one another. This bestowal initiated a prolonged series of gifts between the families of the circumciser and the young man, as well as relations of restraint and avoidance. The daughter's husband gave food to his wife's mother, and gifts to his wife's mother's brother who had a role in making the marriage arrangement. He gave his wife's father food, but did so through his wife, for the men had to avoid one another (Elkin 1939–40: 341–43; Tonkinson 1991: 65).

As among Kûnai people, marriage ideally took place between people who were not closely related (preferable beyond second cousins), and who were from somewhat distant countries. People of the same or alternate generations (the same generation moiety) could marry. The potential wife's father was likely to be a distant 'mother's brother' (*kamaru*) of the boy, while the wife's mother would have been a 'father's sister' (*kurntili*) (Elkin 1939–40: 218–9; Tonkinson 1991: 64; Dousset in press).

There were other ways of marrying. As an alternative to bestowal, in the west of the Western Desert region at least, a suitor might simply make an indirect request to a girl's parents, by sending meat and other gifts over a number of years through intermediaries (Tonkinson 1991: 98). In another strategy an older man married his wife's younger sister as a second wife, and 'grew her up' with gifts (Elkin 1939–40: 342). Bestowal and marriage could be reciprocated by a return bestowal: Dousset (personal communication) reports the exchange by men of sisters and daughters.

The level of polygyny was low or low to moderate in the Western Desert, and, as the Berndts point out, the age difference between spouses was concomitantly lower than in a region such as northeast Arnhem Land, with girls marrying later and young men earlier (Berndt and Berndt 1945: 50). While the majority of married men had one or two wives, there is a single man with four wives in Long's records, and Munn's genealogies record a man with three. However, Long points out that these may have been serial marriages (Munn 1965; Yengoyan 1967; Long 1970).

Wiil and Mi<u>n</u>ong People of the Southwest

The Classification of Kin

Wiil and Mi<u>n</u>ong kin classification was broadly 'Kariera'-like in that siblings and parallel cousins were classified together – differentiated by gender and relative age, while cross-cousins were distinct (Hassell 1936 Bates 1985: 84–85). However, different terms applied to close and distant cross-cousins. Age difference in the parent's generation was carried down to one's own, so that father's younger brother's child was distinct from other siblings. The sources show no evidence of a skewing rule. In the grandparents' generation the terminology distinguished four kinds of grandkin, who appear to have been grouped into those of the 'father's side' as against the 'mother's side.' indicated by similarities and differences in the terms:

Father's side:	FF/FFB *demman*	FM/FMZ *dem*
Mother's side:	MM/MMZ *murran/moora*	MF/MFB *moorr*

Marriage

Wiil and Mi<u>n</u>ong people married in the range of ways familiar from other regions: infant bestowal, the levirate, elopement, and raiding. Mi<u>n</u>ong people of King George Sound preferred marriage between distant relatives, preferably someone from a distant community. Potential spouses perhaps included relatives of the 'distant cross-cousin' category, distinct from 'close cross-cousin'. A person found their cross-cousins in the opposite matri-moiety, and among Mi<u>n</u>ong at least, in the two opposing semi-moieties. The ethnographic sources do not tell us whether alternative marriages were permitted or if people of alternate generations could marry (Barker journals 31 January 1831, cited in Le Souëf 1993: 11; Nind 1831: 44; Bates 1985: 83).

People bestowed a girl on a young man as an infant, or even before her birth – in effect bestowing a woman on a man as a potential wife's mother. According to Nind, girls appeared 'to be at the disposal of their father' (Nind 1831: 38; Hassell 1936: 682). The husband's gifts were directed more to the father than the daughter, and the 'trifles' she received were generally transferred to him. Gifts to the daughter included game or other foods, while the father might receive a cloak, spears or other implements (Nind 1831: 38; Hassell 1936: 682).

The Wiil *barlee* ('armband') marriage involved a prolonged period in which the potential husband had to provide food to the potential wife's parents, notionally for the child, whom he 'grew'. He had to care for the girl if her parents died or the mother was captured, and she came under the protection of his female relatives. At the time of consummation the man plucked hairs from his wife's head and bound them through his *barlee* arm band in the presence of witnesses, then the wife accompanied him to his hut. After a day or two they went off together for a 'bush walk' (Hassell 1936: 682). (At King George's Sound it was customary for a man to go on a long prenuptial walk (Barker journals 1 January 1830, cited in Green 1989: 48).

The potential husband had an obligation to marry the girl to whom he was promised; if he did not want to then he was supposed to find a substitute husband among his own kin. Conversely in the event of the wife absconding men of kin group joined in taking redressive action. This gives the appearance of a contract between the wife's kin and a *group* of men, not just an individual (Hassell 1936: 682–83). Apart from the exchange of goods, kin groups exchanged women as wives at King George's Sound. This is consistent with the prevailing semi-moiety organisation (Nind 1831: 38).

Both Wiil and Min̲ong people practised leviratic marriage, usually the husband's younger brother succeeded at King George Sound. Nind describes an arrangement in which an old man would negotiate with a younger man who would marry his widow when he died; the younger made gifts to the husband and the wife. People carried out the arrangement, called '*tarra-manaccarack*.' with some tact, so as not to upset others and make the husband jealous (Nind 1831: 39). In the event of his wife eloping with another man, the injured husband might release her after negotiations and gifts (Barker journals 23, 25 April 1830 cited in Green 1989: 20; Nind 1831: 29, 38; Hassell 1936: 684; Le Souëf 1993: 14).

Polygyny seems to have been low among Wiil people at Jerramungup; Hassell remarks that while most men had one wife, some men had two. In some cases the wives were of very different age, but usually great friends, the senior helping the younger with childbirth and child-care, the younger caring for the older if she were sick (Hassell 1936: 682). Min̲ong men at King George's Sound practised a moderate level of polygyny, with older men having up to four wives. (The grandfather of a man living at King George's Sound in 1830 was reputed to have had ten). The old men had not only several wives, Nind remarks, but of all ages (Nind 1831: 39). Polygyny occasioned a great deal of conflict among men, for many of the disputes recorded in observers' accounts arose from young wives running away with young men, leading to retaliation in the form of attempted spearing.

Sandbeach People

The Classification of Kin

Sandbeach kin classification was also broadly Kariera-like. Ideally, the various kinds of relatives could be sorted into those of one's own (and one's father's) patri-moiety (*kaapay* or *kuyan*), and those of the opposite moiety, one's mother's.

In the Sandbeach system, first cross-cousins (MBC, FZC) (opposite moiety) are classified together and distinguished from parallel cousins (MZC, FBC etc.), who are one's 'siblings' (own moiety). Certain second cousins are classified with the first cross-cousins, and others with the parallel cousins/siblings. (Where the linking grand-relative is of the same gender as the following linking relative then the cousin is of the same kind of cross-ness as the linking grand-relative; so that for example MMBSC is a parallel cousin and so a 'sibling.' while MMBDC is a cross-cousin.)

In a second general feature the relative age-differences marked in the parent's generation carries down to one's own, as in Wiil/Mi<u>n</u>ong kin classification. So, the children of one's father's elder brother are all 'elder brother' and 'elder sister.' while the children of one's father's younger brother are all one's 'younger brother' and 'younger sister'.

A third feature was Omaha skewing. Sandbeach people regarded a person's close female cross-cousin (*ngami*, senior and *thaatha*, junior) as 'like a mother.' and consequently not marriageable. This feature did not apply to a more distant cross-cousin, who was a potential spouse.[2] Conversely, father's sister's child was like a woman's or sister's child. These skewing features appear to have been 'secondary' in that their application was limited and their potential consequences for other kin relations were not followed through (Scheffler in Thomson 1972; Thomson 1972; Chase 1980; see also Alpher 1982).

A separate set of terms applied to relatives by marriage. A man applied the term *wulumu* to cross-cousins (*ngami* or *thaatha*), who were potential spouses. These were usually, though not always, *distant* cousins. Before marriage a man had to avoid his *wulumu* (intended wife), and relations with other potential affines required the use of the in-law respect vocabulary (*nguunki*, talking 'one side'), as well as an obligation to look after and supply food to that relative. Only after a man's wife's mother (*yaami*) placed a spear thrower on the man's head should he talk to his wife (Chase 1980: 177).

Marriage

Among Sandbeach people one's potential spouses were somewhat distant or 'outside' cross-cousins (*ngami* and *thaatha*), preferably whose country and/or place of residence were geographically close. Spouses ideally came from the same language group. The skewing rule reinforced the requirement to marry a distant cousin. Some marriages did occur between close cross-cousins; but because any two people were related in different ways through different relatives, a close relationship could be represented as a more distant one in order to justify a marriage (Scheffler in Thomson 1972: 6). Sexual relations and marriage between people of the same moiety, as well as between very close relatives, were incestuous and punishable by death (Chase 1980: 175–77).

The ethnographic reports do not reveal the kinds of negotiations involved in the arrangement of marriage or the range of relationships involved. Nevertheless, it is clear that bestowal often took place before the intended wife was born or even before the intended wife's mother was pregnant. The prospective wife's mother was normally the young man's distant 'FyZ' (*piima tali*). Relatives with the greatest interest in the proceedings included the prospective husband, wife, wife's mother, wife's father, and wife's mother's father. Others involved in bestowal ceremonies included the intended husband's mother or sister. Three rituals, conducted in no particular order, formalised betrothal (Thomson 1972).

Bestowal and marriage involved obligations of gift exchange and service, in the main from the prospective son-in-law to his potential affines, from the formalisation of the betrothal until the husband and wife lived together (Thomson unpublished field notes File 213, undated). If the prospective daughter's husband failed to feed his prospective wife's father and mother there was a danger that she might be given to another man (Thomson 1972: 13). After the marriage the obligations were as follows: a daughter's son gave food to his wife's father but the gift was not reciprocated; a son's wife gave food to her husband's father, who could make gifts in return, although certain foods (perhaps with sexual connotations) were restricted; a husband's mother was under a strong obligation to look after and to feed her son's wife, and they might exchange gifts of food. Obligations to a wife's father increased if he was widowed, when the son-in-law ought to get food and water for him. These obligations seem likely to have been strongest in the early years of marriage, and were practicable only when parents and married children were residing in the same camp (Thomson 1972).

Umpila and Kuuku-Ya'u polygyny was low to moderate, with most men in Thomson's genealogies having one or two wives (one had three and one had four concurrently). Published records do not show the extent of leviratic marriage, but a younger brother would be expected to marry his older brother's widow. Concomitantly, women often married serially (Thomson unpublished field notes MV File 215). As elsewhere, the main condition for polygyny in this region was the age difference between husbands and wives: Thomson remarked on the fact that 'so many young girls are married to old men' among Kuuku Ya'u people, presumably at Lockhart River Mission (Thomson unpublished field notes MV File 213; Thomson 1972: 7).

Ngarinyin Kinship and Marriage

The Classification of Kin

Like Sandbeach and Wiil/Miṉong kinship, the system of kin classification of Ngarinyin people and their neighbours merged parallel cousins with siblings, and distinguished them from cross-cousins. But in some ways the terminology resembles the 'Aranda' type of Radcliffe-Brown's (1930–31) and Elkin's typologies (Elkin 1954: 70). It distinguishes MM and MMB from FFZ and FF, MF from FMB and MFZ from FM. Furthermore, first and certain second cross-cousins (e.g. MBD and MMBDD) are distinct. However, a skewing rule in conjunction with preferred asymmetrical marriage (between a man and his FMBSD, his 'father's mother') transformed the terminology into something like the asymmetrical 'Karadjeri' type of the Yolngu.

One way to represent the terminology is as 'lines' of kin terms traced through men. From an individual's point of view other patri-groups contained relatives belonging to each of these 'lines'. But terms in each line would have been applied to members of a number of groups, and some patri-groups would have contained relatives of more than one line, especially where it consisted of more than one lineage. The lines included the following relatives:

MM, MMZ, MMB, WM, WMB	*gayangi, wolmingi/rambarr*
FM, FMZ, FMB, WF, WFZ, 'wife'	*aringi, wayingi*
MF, MFB, MFZ, M, MB	*mamingi, ngadji, garndingi*
FF, FFB, FFZ F, FB, FZ etc	*lalingi, ngolingi, amalngi, idja*
wC/ZC , H, ZH, FFZH etc.	*arlangi, wuningi*
FZC, FZSC (DH)	*marlangi, wuningi*
wDC, ZDC	*gayingi, wolmingi*

The marking of relative age appears to have differed from the other systems. For example, if one's father's brother married before one's birth, then all his children were one's 'elder brothers' and 'elder sisters' (Lucich 1968: 99–100).

Elkin reported that the Ngarinyin terminology had an unusual feature in that kin terms applied in one generation were extended to all members of a patrilineal group – so all in one group were a person's 'mothers' and 'mother's brothers' all in another were one's 'father's mothers' and 'father's mother's brothers' and so on. Alan Rumsey (1981) has shown more recently that the extension of kin terms in this way depended on context – on whether a person was referring to relations to and between groups, or to and between individuals.

In contexts in which people were talking about group relations the terms for 'mother' (*ngadji*) and 'mother's brother' (*garndingi*) were extended down the generations to denote mother's brother's children, relatives in the generation below that (MBSC), and up to include MF and MFZ. Conversely, one's father's sister's child and FFZC became one's 'child' (w.s.) or 'sister's child' (*marlangi*). However, in contexts in which relations between individuals set the context, one's MF and MFZ were distinguished as *mamingi*. By the same token in contexts of group relations one applied the terms for 'mother's mother' and 'mother's mother's brother' (*gayingi*) to all the latter's patrilineal descendants. In other contexts one referred to MMBS and MMBD as *rambarr* or *wolmingi* as (in the case of a man) potential wife's mother and wife's mother's brother. All patrilineal descendants of one's father's mother's brother (*wayingi*) were all *wayingi* or *marringi* ('FM') regardless of context. The implication of this 'skewed' terminology for marriage seems to be that men could marry a woman of an adjacent generation as well as their own and alternate generations in the opposite moiety (Elkin 1932: 315; see also Love 1936: 94; Lucich 1968: 102–3).

Ngarinyin people and their neighbours projected kinship and marriage relations on to patri-groups as wholes. From the point of view of a person in a particular patri-group, other patri-groups were classified as 'mother's mothers.' 'mother's fathers' and 'father's mothers.' 'fathers' fathers.' 'women's children.' and 'women's daughters' children'. People of a given patri-group regarded some groups as wife-yielders, some as daughter-receivers, some as wives' mothers (*wolmingi*). A man's 'wives' mothers' were in his 'father's mother's mother's' patri-group (Blundell and Layton 1978: 234). Alternative kin terms in Worrorra, recorded by Lucich (1968), classify together 'mothers' mother's,' 'mothers' fathers' and 'fathers' mothers;' 'fathers' fathers,' 'women's children' and 'women's daughters' children'.

Marriage

A person had to marry someone of a different patri-group to his or her own, and of the opposite patri-moiety. The preferred marriage took place between a man and a woman whom he classified as 'father's mother' (*maringi*), which included people of his own, adjacent and alternate generations. He was her 'son's child'.

A marriage between a man and a woman of his father's mother's patri-group repeated the marriage or marriages of his father's father, and so repeated the link between the two patri-groups two generations later. A man could claim the daughter of his wife's brother as a second wife – she was also his 'father's mother' (*marringi*).

In an alternative marriage a man married a second cross-cousin on his mother's side – the daughter of his mother's female matrilateral cross-cousin ('MMBDD'). However, one's FMBSD could also be one's MMBDD. According to Lucich (1968), other unions (among Worrorra people at least) attracted sanctions, from mild to severe. A man was not supposed to marry a person of his own mother's patri-group, while marriage to a distant 'mother' (*ngadji*) attracted only mild sanctions. These also applied to marriage between first cross-cousins (FZS and MBD) and distant 'mother's brother' and 'sister's daughter'. Lucich shows that the children of a wrong marriage applied kin terms as if it were correct, and the son inherited marriage rights accordingly

(Lucich 1968; see also Elkin unpublished field report, cited in Scheffler 1978: 406).

Ngarinyin and their neighbours discouraged sister-exchange on the part of men, although not apparently with very strong sanctions. So sister's husband's sister and brother's wife's brother were not supposed to marry (Lucich 1968). Indeed, such a marriage would break the asymmetry of marriage ties between patri-groups. Scheffler interprets the ethnography to assert that only distant relatives married. This seems to be incorrect. Rather it seems that people had a degree of choice as to how close a relative to marry, at least in the case of a man's marriage to 'father's mother' (Lucich 1968: 48). Elkin recorded no marriages to an actual FMBSD, whereas Blundell recorded two (Blundell and Layton 1978: 234; Elkin unpublished field report, cited in Scheffler 1978: 406).

According to Love and Elkin it was a girl's father who bestowed her on a young man. The bestower was the potential husband's *wayingi* (FMB). Love says that an important older man was likely to be favoured at the young man's expense (Elkin 1932: 314; Love 1936: 99). The man then entered 'upon a long period, even a life-long period, of indebtedness to his future father-in-law'. Love describes the kinds of gifts: for his wife's father kangaroo fat, new spears, belts and ornaments that he in turn acquired, honey gathered by his mother, (or a new billy-can bought in Broome). For his wife's mother, kangaroo meat and other gifts. In return, she made gifts of hair string. However, a man also owed service to his wife's brother, who looked after him during initiation (Tony Redmond personal communication). The girl went to her husband's camp at about the age of ten years in Love's opinion, where the older wives instructed her (Love 1936: 96, 129).

As in the other case studies, Ngarinyin and their neighbours practiced leviratic marriage. Sometimes a younger brother inherited an elder brother's widow much older than himself. A man could also inherit his father's father's (or FFB's) widow, but not of course his actual father's mother (Elkin 1932: 314; Love 1936: 95, 96; Lucich 1968: 48).

As Blundell and Layton point out, the net result of the preference for a man to marry his 'father's mother,' and the prohibition of a man's marriage to a woman of his mother's patri-group, was that men of each patri-group had to get wives from at least two other patri-groups, and women of a patri-group married men of at least two others. Marriages between two patri-groups were ideally repeated in alternating generations; a man 'gives his daughter to a man in the same clan as the man to whom his own FF gave his daughter'. However, the skewing makes the alternating generations pattern more complex than in Blundell and Layton's representation – a lineage could only receive wives from the same lineage in alternating generations, but one could give women of any generation to men of a given generation in a wife-receiving group (Blundell and Layton 1978: 232). The result was an asymmetrical marriage network, in which women's marriages 'flowed' in one direction between patri-groups, linking them in chains and circles. However, the alternative and 'wrong' marriages led to some reciprocal marriage relations between patri-groups. Ngarinyin people also expressed marriage as an inter-moiety exchange.

Love points out that polygyny resulted from leviratic marriage, as well as the marriage of older men to young women (Love 1936: 95). In the early decades of the twentieth century most older men had two wives, some had more. One Worrorra man called Ambula had four wives while another had seven wives, most of whom were young. In many cases younger men remained unmarried before marrying an older man's widow.

Comparatively, then, the level of polygyny was high, and this implies that the average age difference between spouses was considerable, as anecdotal evidence bears out (Love 1936: 100). Men frequently quarrelled and fought over women, and there were frequent love affairs between young men and the wives of older men, as well as elopements (Love 1936: 31–36).

'Father's mother' marriage constituted one of the conditions for the high level of polygyny recorded in the region. Marriage between a man and his FMBSD tended to reproduce the average age difference between potential spouses down the generations (as is the case with matrilateral cross-cousin marriage, as we shall see in the next case study), implying that women in whom a man had the strongest claim as wives tended to be of an appropriate age to marry, given infant bestowal. I surmise that the prior claims of older brothers of a set of siblings in women to whom they had rights as their *marringi* ('father's mothers'), in conjunction with leviratic and other modes of marriage, resulted in some such men marrying many wives.[3]

It may be that the sons' sons of a highly polygynous man were themselves potentially more polygynous than others. A grandson could look to his several 'father's mother' patri-groups for wives, as well as inheriting his father's father's widow. If so, relative 'success' tended to be reproduced down the generations, as among Yolngu people.

Yolngu of Northeast Arnhem Land

The Classification of Kin

Yolngu kin classification sorted grandkin in a different way from previous terminologies, distinguishing MM/MMB from FF/FFZ (like Ngarinyin), but putting together FMB with MF, and MFZ with FM (unlike Ngarinyin but like Sandbeach). The terminology can be arranged in five 'lines' as traced through men, and in some regions seven 'lines' (although Shapiro denies that such lines or sequences are emic constructs) (Warner 1937: 59; Shapiro 1981: 42; Keen 1994: 80). To take just the terms in the grandparent and grandchild generation:

MMMBS, MMMBD	*ngathiwalkur, mumalkur* (not distinguished from relatives in line 3 in some regions)
MM/MMB	*ma:ri* , and descendents through males
FM/MFZ, MF/FMB	*mumu, ngathi,* and descendents through males

FF/FFZ	*ma:ri'mu*, and descendents through males
wSC, ZSC	*gaminyarr*, and his or her fathers (*waku*) and father's fathers
wDC, ZDC	*gutharra*, and his or her fathers (*gurrung*) and father's fathers
FZDDC	*dhumun.gur* (not distinguished from relatives in line 1 in some regions)

Terms for women in line 1, on the right of the conventional diagram (Warner 1937: 59), were ideally the wives of males to whom Ego applied terms in line 2; terms for women in line 2 were ideally applied to wives of males of line 3 and so on. Each woman's 'husband' in the diagram is her patrilateral cross-cousin and each man's 'wife' is his matrilateral cross-cousin (to his right on the diagram). People also traced three sequences of terms through women, cutting across the patrilineal 'lines' of terms (Keen 1978: 106; Shapiro 1981: 52).

Many of these features of Yolngu kin classification were related to the organisation of marriage. Rather than skewing, kin terms were repeated in alternate generations in the male line. This widened the field of a man's potential marriage partners to cross-cousins two generations down, as in Ngarinyin marriage (Keen 1994: 88).

Also as in Ngarinyin marriage, the strict moiety exogamy ensured that a person would find certain kin only in his own patri-moiety, and others in the opposite moiety. A man's potential wife's mother and a woman's potential daughter's husband were of their own patri-moiety, while spouses were of opposite moieties, as in other cases with moiety organisation.

Yolngu grounded marriage in ancestral law in a particularly vivid way. As with Ngarinyin, Yolngu patri-groups, their countries, sacra and ancestors, stood in notional kin relations one to another, so that one country was the 'mother' of another, and so on. These ideal relations came about because of the repeated marriages of one group and another down the generation. An individual could also talk about his or her kin relations *to* a country, its sacra and ancestors – one country was the person's 'father place.' another his or her 'mother's mother place' and so on. In Yolngu doctrine marriages 'followed' the kin relations between sacred objects – 'marriage follows the *rangga*' (Keen 1994: 110). Men looked to people of their 'mother' country and sacred objects for wives, and their *ma:ri* ('mother's mother') country and sacred objects for wives' mothers.

Marriage

Yolngu preferred a marriage between genealogically *close* cross-cousins (male *dhuway* and female *galay*, in a relation of FZS–MBD, and/or MFZDS–MMBDD and related kin-types). They were, by implication, of patri-groups whose countries were geographically close, and of opposite patri-moieties. A marriage contract could involve relatives across several generations and between several lineages, implying long spans of time between the contract being made and brought to fruition. Exchange obligations, particularly on the part of the potential husband, lasted many years.

A number of strategies were open to a young man and the other people who helped arrange his marriage, such as his father and mother's mother's brother (*ma:ri*). He had a strong claims in *galay* (MBD, MMBDD etc.) of his mother's patri-group – the daughters of his mother's close brothers. A man might negotiate with his mother's close brother (*ngapipi*, *gawal*) and mother's brother's wife (*mukul rumaru*) for their daughter as a wife. He also had a strong claim in his close *mukul rumaru* (MMBD, MMMBDD) as wives' mothers. Among them were the daughters of his mother's mother's brothers (*ma:ri*). But they were not necessarily wives of his actual or even close mother' brothers, although they could be. In this strategy the man's MMB (*ma:ri*), as the 'father' of the man's potential wives' mothers, was a key mediator between him and his potential in-laws.

Alternatively, a young man might look first to his *ma:ri* and the latter's wife (*mumalkur*, 'MMMBD') to arrange for their daughter (*mukul rumaru* 'MMBD') to be his future wife's mother, and give him her daughter (who may not yet have been born) as a wife. In all this *maralkur* ('MMBS'), the brother of *mukul* and potential wife's mother's brother, was usually a key figure, for brothers had considerable control of the productive and reproductive powers of sisters. A young man's father and brothers might have taken part in the negotiations on his behalf, and indeed sometimes a father took the young man's promised wife first, and then handed her on. From a woman's point of view the key kin were her patri-cross-cousins (*dhuway*, FZS) and their matrilineal kin, who included her close or distant father and mother's father, their mother's brother (her 'father); and second, her own matrilineal kin (her brothers, mothers and mothers' brothers, mother's mothers and their brothers). In his 1937 ethnography Warner tends to stress the first strategy – negotiation between sister's son and mother's brother, while Shapiro, in his 1981 ethnography notes both relations with a potential wife's father, and relations with her mother, mother's mother and mother's father (Warner 1937: 108; Shapiro 1981: 51).

A short ceremony in which the future husband marked the future mother-in-law on her belly with nasal sebum, sealed the marriage contract (Shapiro 1981: 48). In return, the future husband, helped by his father and brothers, had to provide gifts and services for many years to his future affines, before and after the wife had matured and they began to share a hearth. The wife or potential wife and her kin made reciprocal gifts to the husband's or potential husband's kin; a woman would make gifts to her father's sister (*mukul ba:pa*) as the mother of her future husband. These exchange relations were transmitted to the next generation.

The system was capable of even greater elaboration. By a neat trick, the daughter of a man's female *dhumun.gur* (FZDDC, the reciprocal of *mumalkur* and *ngathiwalkur*) could be designated as *mukul rumaru*, potential wife's mother, closing the circle and paving the way for exchange across five generations, in which a man bestowed his ZDD on to his *ngathiwalkur*, who had given the man *his* ZDD. This closure was rather rare, although both Howard Morphy and I found one or two examples in our genealogies recorded in the mid 1970s (Shapiro 1968; Keen 1978: 115; Morphy 1978: 216).

Some alternatives to bestowal were open to a couple. One was elopement, and the levirate was another means, with younger brothers inheriting the widows of older brothers or being given a wife or wives by an older brother. A third alternative was raiding. In all this, because of her youth a potential wife had little control of her destiny. However, women gained more power in marriage negotiations as older widows, and as potential wives' mothers.

Polygyny

The Yolngu had one of the highest rates of polygyny recorded for Australian Aborigines. Warner (1937: 77) records a case when a man had seventeen wives, Thomson records twenty-six (unpublished field notes, Museum Victoria). Even in the mid-1970s two older men living at Milingimbi had married ten and eleven wives respectively (Keen 1982). The oldest of a group of brothers with the same matrilateral connections had prior claims in the their *galay* as wives, and indeed older brothers tended to be the most polygynous. Sons of polygynous men were advantaged by having many 'mothers' to whose groups they could look to for wives, although strongest claims were in a man's actual mother's group (Warner 1937: 77–78).

Warfare undoubtedly had its effects on the male population (Warner 1937: 155–56), but the average age difference was more important in making polygyny possible: between husbands and wives it was about thirteen years in the mid-1970s, comparatively quite high (Keen 1982: 634). The demographic properties of the Yolngu system tended to ensure that the women in whom a group of brothers had the strongest marriage claims tended to be of an appropriate age, so that the average age difference tended to be reproduced down the generations (Keen 1982).

Conclusions

The Greater the Delay the Greater the Return

The case studies form a series from low polygyny associated with a generational terminology, through low to moderate polygyny associated with Aluridja and Kariera-like terminologies, high polygyny associated with an Aranda-like terminology modified by Omaha skewing, to very high polygyny associated with an asymmetrical Karadjeri-like terminology. The asymmetry of the last two systems involved marriage of a man to his father's male matrilateral cross-cousin's daughter (Ngarinyin and their neighbours), or to his matrilateral cross-cousin (Yolngu).

The most striking contrast lies at the extremes. Kûnai marriage included institutionalised elopement as well as father–daughter and brother–sister bestowal, and sibling exchange sometimes initiated by women. There were no long chains of bestowal relations here. The return on marriage among Kûnai people was the least delayed, especially in the case of institutionalised elopement, and polygyny was low. The greatest delay occurred with the exchange of sisters' daughters' daughters among Yolngu people – a mode of exchange across five generations in this society with very high polygyny. Indeed, modes of exchange provide something of a measure for the degree of delay.

A complex relation holds in the connection between return in terms of the potential numbers of wives and the amount of 'delay'. In one kind of connection, the higher the polygyny and the more older men monopolised women as wives, then the more a young man's marriage had to be delayed, and some young men married older widows. This delay, and the bestowal of very young women on older men, was consistent with (secondly) the long chains of bestowal relations in which a man's potential wife's mother's mother, her father and brothers were involved in her bestowal as a potential wife's mother. The long-delayed marriage required a potential son-in-law to make gifts over an extended period. A third kind of connection in Yolngu marriage consisted of the exchange of sisters' daughter's daughters by two men. This simply meant that a marriage at a given time gave rise to a return marriage much later, across five generations.

The nature of the potential 'return' varied with the social organisation. Polygyny did not constitute such a useful resource for men in the absence of patrifilial groups, for it does nothing to increase the strength of a matrifilial group. In the Yolngu and perhaps Ngarinyin cases, high to very high levels of polygyny engendered fast-growing and declining groups, and a wide range of size between patri-groups, with consequent competition among men, and processes of succession to countries whose groups were dying out.

Degrees of Hierarchy

I suggested at the beginning of the chapter that in Aboriginal marriage systems not only the greater the delay the greater the return, but the greater the return in terms of wives, then the greater the degree of hierarchy. If greater marriage returns were associated with greater inequalities, then of what order?

No recorded Aboriginal society possessed anything like social classes between which power differences were reproduced. Many have been described as 'gerontocratic' (Hiatt 1985) and analysts have given some emphasis to gender inequality. In one view men exploited women, especially in relying on women's labour to 'finance' exclusive male domains in regional ceremonies (Bern 1979). In another (Hamilton 1980, 1981) differences in polygynous marriage provided one measure of gender inequality; low polygyny tended to reflect the existence of a somewhat independent female sphere of 'homo-sociality'. The comparison set out here casts power differences in a somewhat different light.

Male leadership among the low polygyny Kûnai, drew on personal magic as a resource, as well as the role of *birraark* 'shamans' who invoked the ghosts of the dead in séances and helped to direct Jerra-eil initiation ceremonies. The bases of their powers were not patri-group position and birth order but the achieved powers of personal magic and shamanic skills. The ethnography gives the impression of local 'bosses' who, as *mûlla-mullûng* sorcerer/magicians, deployed competing magics such as the power of a lizard familiar or command of the west wind. Certainly male elders could act in consort to impress young men in initiation ceremonies (Maddock 1972: 156), exercising an aggregate power. But individuals could not build very powerful factions through marriage; the social networks caught up in fights and feuds were those of cognatic kinship and affinity, identified by locality and broad region (Fison and Howitt 1880: 216–24).

It is my impression that gender relations among Kûnai people had more of an egalitarian character than among Yolngu. A supporting piece of evidence is the institutionalised 'moral violence' (Sansom 1980) perpetrated by women on male adulterers who, according to report, had to run the gauntlet between women wielding digging sticks or clubs (Bulmer 1994: 15). A second piece of evidence is the very prominent role played by women in the public phase of the initiation of males (Fison and Howitt 1880: 195).

Male leaders among the highly polygynous Yolngu were the 'first-born' males of patri-groups, and as the oldest of their sibling set they were likely to be the most married of men (Keen 1994: 96). They sat at the nodes of the exchange network as the recipients of marriage-gifts from potential and actual daughters' husbands, and as donors to their own wives' kin. Much married, they led lineages and patri-groups which were growing at the expense of others, so blessed with the political support of sons as well as brothers. The results were at least temporary differences of power between patri-groups and the social networks that centred on them, with implications for the control of ritual, succession to land, and the kinds of warfare recorded by Warner (1937: 155–90). People identified protagonists in feuds in terms of patri-group identity (Keen 1982).

Yolngu leaders did not exercise exploitative power but rather genetic power – the ability to generate offspring that replaced the potential offspring of other men. Genetic power gave rise to daughters who could be bestowed in return for gifts and support from daughters' husbands, just as one's sister's marriage generated the obligation of support from wives' brothers. Their power had a segmental rather than a hierarchical form, somewhat like the power of a faction – the ability to take up more social space and so dominate affairs in that way. Displacement of other segments occurred by marrying at others' expense, and expanding the number of offspring at the expense of others. Sons provided military support, obliged by the gift of a relic to avenge a wrong against a father, brother or mother's brother (Warner 1937: 178). If twentieth-century genealogies are a guide then polygynous sons tended to follow polygynous fathers, reinforcing the weight of growing the lineages (Warner 1937: 77–78).

But Yolngu 'name-bearing' (*ya:kumirri*) men also possessed redistributive power in exchange relations. The recipients of many gifts from actual and potential daughters' husbands, and unable to consume them all, they were in a position to redistribute them to their own kin and affines. As leaders of powerful patri-groups they had the say over the performance of major ceremonies and played host to visitors. In community debates they had the final word (Williams 1987: 44).

The political economy of Ngarinyin and their neighbours bore some similarities to the Yolngu one; patri-group leaders dominated exchange of spouses, sacred objects and goods in the *wurnan* exchange system, in which exchanges were supposed to follow a set order among patri-groups. The high level of polygyny among Worrorra people suggests a similar dynamics of growth and decline among groups. Unlike Yolngu, however, the role of *barnman* sorcerer/healer complemented that of patri-group elders (Lommel 1997), and a distinct leader position had less emphasis (Tony Redmond personal communication).

In between, the societies of the case studies with moderate levels of polygyny (except perhaps Sandbeach people) combined roles of patri-group elders with influential sorcerer-healer-magician figures. As in some societies of New Guinea, the role provided an alternative basis for male power.

All this is somewhat reminiscent of the distinction made by Melanesianists between 'great men' and 'big men' (Godelier 1986). In Godelier's formulation the power of men in great-men societies rests on inherited or ascribed powers, especially ritual powers, in contrast with the achieved powers of big men. However, Yolngu leaders combined many of the properties Godelier ascribes to both great-men and big-men. The oldest of a group of male siblings had prior rights in women as wives, and tended to be among the most polygynous. As an older brother he was likely to be a leader of his patri-group, or at least of a lineage, and prominent in the organisation of rituals. A leader had the prerogative of having the last word on when and whether a ceremony would take place. As polygynists they sat at the nodes of exchange networks.

I think it possible to relate the extremes among the above differences in part to isolation (if not exactly encapsulation) within societies of rather different kinds, for the case studies at the extremes formed social peninsulas. A notable feature of the Kûnai social and geographical environment was their isolation; they were cut off to the west and north by difficult terrain and enmities, although they did have social intercourse with people to the east and northeast. The Yolngu region lies in a geographical and social peninsula, with sea to the north and east, and peoples with very different languages and cultures to the west and south – although shared institutions, intermarriage and linguistic diffusion (Heath 1978) modified the immediate differences. The other societies with notably high polygyny were isolated as inhabitants of large islands, such as the Tiwi of Melville and Bathurst Islands (Hart and Pilling 1960), and Wa<u>n</u>indiljaugwa of Groote Eylandt (Rose 1960). It may be that social and geographical barriers provided conditions for the development of rather idiosyncratic and extreme forms of institutions in the Kûnai and Yolngu cases, whereas institutions of people who lived in the middle of extensive social and cultural networks were moderated by influences from and interactions with neighbours. However, relative isolation does not readily predict the direction which institutions took – low polygyny and relatively egalitarian relations on the one hand, and on the other, very high polygyny and gender asymmetry. I have argued elsewhere (Keen 2003, 2004) that relatively high population density in regions of rich resources provided one condition for high to very high polygyny. Kûnai people lived in such a region but lacked the institutional means for high polygyny, namely asymmetrical kin terminologies and associated forms of marriage.

The chapter began with James Woodburn's revision of Meillasoux's argument about the relationship between, on the one hand, immediate and delayed-return, and on the other, the boundary between hunter-gatherer and farming societies, as well as the implications of delayed-return for hierarchy. I have argued, first, that there is an association between the length of the 'delay' in marriage bestowal and the size of the return for males as measured by the level of polygyny. Second, the level of polygyny bears a strong relationship to the degree and kind of power differences in the Aboriginal societies discussed here. Within this 'continent of hunter-gatherers' the delayed-return systems varied, and with that variation so did the forms of power.

Notes

1. The census of a camp by Thomas at 'Moody Yallock' on 11 October 1857 records eleven married couples, all monogamous, eleven single men, and seven children (Thomas, Papers, Box 14). Out of twenty discernible marriage relations in his 1860 census, seventeen are monogamous, there are three cases of men with two wives, and one of a man with three wives. Bulmer records one man with three wives, and two with two (Bulmer, Papers MV B10 F5 xm931: 18).
2. Female cross-cousins' children were classified as 'younger siblings' (*ya'athu*) in the case of senior cross-cousin's child, and 'sister's daughter's child' (*kamityu*) in the case of junior cross-cousin's child (see Thomson 1972; Chase 1980; see also Alpher 1982). Another extension rule applied to the children of male cross-cousins, reclassified two generations up as 'mother's younger sister' and 'mother's younger brother'. The extension of kin terms to relatives two generations lower or higher is a common feature of Aboriginal modes of kin classification and often has to do with the possibility of marrying a spouse two genealogical generations below one's own (and often much younger), as among Ngarinyin and Yolngu people.
3. If the average age difference between father and child was forty, and the average age difference between mother and child was twenty-five years, and so the wife was fifteen years younger than the husband on average, then the average age difference between a man and his FMBSD can be computed as follows: Ego – F (+ 40), F – FM (+ 25), FMB – FMBS (–40), FMBS – FMBSD (–40), total –15 years, reproducing the average age difference between father and mother. My speculation about the claims of older brothers is extrapolated from Yolngu marriage practices (see below). Marriage to alternate generations widened the scope.

References

Alpher, B. 1982. 'Dalabon Dual-Subject Prefixes, Kinship Categories, and Generation-Skewing'. In: J. Heath, F. Merlan and A. Rumsey (eds), *Languages of Kinship in Aboriginal Australia (Oceania Linguistic Monograph No. 24)*, pp. 19–30. Sydney: University of Sydney.

Bates, D. 1985. *The Native Tribes of Western Australia.* Canberra: National Library of Australia.
Bern, J.E. 1979. 'Ideology and Domination: Toward a Reconstruction of Australian Aboriginal Social Formation.' *Oceania,* 50(2): 118–32.
Berndt, R.M. and C.H. Berndt 1945. *A Preliminary Report of Field Work in the Ooldea Region, Western South-Australia.* Sydney: Australian Medical Publishing Company.
Blundell, V. and R.H. Layton 1978. 'Marriage, Myth and Models of Exchange in the West Kimberley'. *Mankind,* 11(3): 231–45.
Bulmer, J.M. 1884. 'Papers'. Museum Victoria, B1 F2 (11.3. 1884), BI F4, B10 F5.
—— 1994. *Victorian Aborigines: John Bulmer's Recollections 1855-1908.* Melbourne: Museum of Victoria.
Chase, A.K. 1980. 'Which Way Now? Tradition, Continuity and Change in a North Queensland Aboriginal Community' (Ph.D. dissertation, University of Queensland).
Curr, E.M. 1887. *The Australian Race: Books 3 and 4.* Melbourne: John Ferres.
Dousset, L. 2003. 'Accounting for Context and Substance: the Australian Western Desert Kinship System.' *Anthropological Forum,* 12(2): 193–204
Elkin, A.P. 1932. 'Social Organisation in the Kimberley Division, North-western Australia.' *Oceania,* 2 (3): 296–333.
—— 1939–40.'Kinship in South Australia.' *Oceania,* 10(2, 3): 196–234, 295–349.
—— 1954. *The Australian Aborigines – How to Understand Them.* Sydney: Angus and Robertson.
Fison, L. and A.W. Howitt 1880. *Kamilaroi and Kurnai: Group-Marriage and Relationship, and Marriage by Elopement.* Melbourne: George Robertson.
Godelier. M. 1986. *The Making of Great Men: Male Power and Domination among the New Guinea Baruya.* Cambridge: Cambridge University Press.
Green, N. 1989. *Aborigines of the Albany Region 1821–1898.* Nedlands, W.A.
Hamilton, A. 1980. 'Dual Social Systems: Technology, Labour and Women's Secret Rites in the Eastern Western Desert of Australia.' *Oceania,* 51(1): 4–19.
—— 1981. 'A Complex Strategical Situation: Gender and Power in Aboriginal Australia.' In: N. Grieve and P. Grimshaw (eds), *Australian Women: Feminist Perspectives,* pp. 71–85. Melbourne: Oxford University Press.
Hart, C.M.W. and A.R. Pilling 1960. *The Tiwi of North Australia.* New York: Holt, Rinehart and Winston.
Hassell, E. 1936. 'Notes on the Ethnology of the Wheelman Tribe of South Western Australia'. *Anthropos,* 31: 679–711.
Heath, J. 1978. *Linguistic Diffusion in Arnhem Land.* Canberra: Australian Institute of Aboriginal Studies.
Hiatt, L.R. 1985. 'Maidens, Males And Marx: Some Contrasts in the Work of Frederick Rose and Claude Meillassoux'. *Oceania,* 56(1): 34–46.
Howitt, A.W. 1904. *The Native Tribes of South-East Australia.* London: Macmillan.
Ives, J. 1998. 'Developmental Processes in The Pre-Contact History of Athapaskan, Algonquian and Numic Kin Kystems'. In: Godelier, T. Trautmann and T.S. Fat, (eds), *Transformations of Kinship.* Washington DC: Smithsonian Institute Press.
Keen, I. 1978. 'One Ceremony, One Song: An Economy of Religious Knowledge among the Yolngu of Northeast Arnhem Land' (Ph.D. dissertation, Australian National University).
—— 1982. 'How Some Murngin Men Marry Ten Wives: The Marital Implications of Matrilateral Cross-Cousin Structures'. *Man,* 17(4): 620–42.
—— 1994. *Knowledge and Secrecy in an Aboriginal Religion.* Oxford: Oxford University Press.
—— 2003. 'Seven Aboriginal Marriage Systems and their Correlates'. *Anthropological Forum,* 12(2): 145–58.
—— 2004. *Aboriginal Economy and Society: Australia at the Threshold of Colonisation.* Melbourne: Oxford University Press.
Le Souëf, S. 1993. 'The Aborigines of King George Sound at the Time of Early European Contact: An Ethnohistorical Study of Social Organisation and Territoriality'. In: B.K. de Garis (ed.), *Portraits of the South West: Aborigines, Women and the Environment,* pp. 1–56. Nedlands: University of Western Australia Press.
Lommel, A. 1997. *The Unambal; A Tribe in Northwest Australia.* Carnavon Gorge, Queensland: Takarakka Nowan Kas Publications.

Long, J. 1970. 'Polygyny, Acculturation and Contact: Aspects of Aboriginal Marriage in Central Australia'. In: R.M. Berndt (ed.), *Australian Aboriginal Anthropology: Modern Studies in the Social Anthropology of the Australian Aborigines*, pp. 292–304. Nedlands: University of Western Australia Press.

Love, J.R.B. 1936. *Stone Age Bushmen of Today*. Glasgow: Blackie and Sons.

Lucich, P. 1968. *The Development of Omaha Kinship Terminologies in Three Australian Tribes of the Kimberley Division, Western Australia*. Canberra: Australian Institute of Aboriginal Studies.

Maddock, K.J. 1972. *The Australian Aborigines: A Portrait of their Society*. London: Allen Lane, Penguin Press.

Meillasoux, C. 1973. 'On the Mode of Production of the Hunting Band'. In: P. Alexandre, (ed.), *French Perspectives in African Studies*, pp. 187–203. London: Oxford University Press.

Morphy, H. 1978. 'Rights in Paintings And Rights in Women: A Consideration of Some of the Basic Problems Posed by the Asymmetry of the "Murngin" System.' In: J. Specht and P. White, (eds), *Trade and Exchange in Oceania and Australia (Mankind 11, Special Issue)*, pp. 208–11. Sydney: University of Sydney.

Munn, N. 1965. 'A Report on Field Research at Areyonga, 1964–5'. Australian Institute of Aboriginal Studies, document 65/2.

Nind, S. 1831. 'Description of the Natives of King George's Sound (Swan River Colony) and Adjoining Country'. *Journal of the Royal Geographical Society of London*, 1: 21–51.

Radcliffe-Brown, A.R. 1931. *The Social Organization of Australian Tribes (Oceania Monograph No. 1)*. Sydney: University of Sydney.

Rose, F.G.G. 1960. *Classification of Kin, Age Structure and Marriage amongst the Groote Eylandt Aborigines: A Study in Method and a Theory of Australian Kinship*. Berlin: Akademie.

Rumsey, A. 1981. 'Kinship and Context among the Ngarinyin'. *Oceania*, 51(3): 181–92.

Sansom, B. 1980. *The Camp at Wallaby Cross: Aboriginal Fringe Dwellers in Darwin*. Canberra: Australian Institute of Aboriginal Studies.

Scheffler, H.W. 1978. *Australian Kin Classification*. London: Cambridge University Press.

Shapiro, W. 1968. 'The Exchange of Sister's Daughter's Daughters in Northeast Arnhem Land'. *Southwestern Journal of Anthropology*, 14: 346–53.

—— 1981. *Miwuyt Marriage: the Cultural Anthropology of Affinity in Northeast Arnhem Land*. Philadelphia: Institute for the Study of Human Issues.

Smyth, R.B. 1878. *The Aborigines of Victoria: with Notes Relating to the Habits of the Natives of Other Parts of Australia and Tasmania, Compiled from Various Sources for the Government of Victoria*, 2 vols. Melbourne: Government Printer.

Thomas, W. 1849-1860. 'Papers.' Museum Victoria, Box 14.

Thomson, D.F. 1935, undated. 'Unpublished Field Notes.' Museum of Victoria, MV Files 213, 215.

—— 1972. *Kinship and Behaviour in North Queensland*. Canberra: Australian Institute of Aboriginal Studies.

Tindale, N. 1974. *Aboriginal Tribes of Australia: Their Terrain, Environmental Controls, Distribution, Limits and Proper Names*. Canberra: Australian Institute of Aboriginal Studies.

Tonkinson, R. 1991. *The Mardu Aborigines: Living the Dream in Australia's Desert*. Fort Worth: Holt, Rinehart and Winston.

Warner, W.L. 1937. *A Black Civilization: A Social Study of an Australian Tribe*. New York: Harper.

Williams, N.M. 1987. *Two Laws: Managing Disputes in a Contemporary Aboriginal Community*. Canberra: Australian Institute of Aboriginal Studies.

Woodburn, J. 1988. 'African Hunter-Gatherer Social Organization: Is It Best Understood as a Product of Encapsulation?' In: T. Ingold, D. Riches and J. Woodburn, (eds), *Hunters and Gatherers Vol. 1: History, Evolution and Social Change*, pp. 31–64. New York: Berg.

Yengoyan, A.A. 1967. 'A Comparison of Certain Marriage Features Between the Pitjandjara and Other Groups of the Western Desert With the Northern Groups: Also Some Comments on the Red Ochre Ceremonies'. *Journal of the Anthropological Society of South Australia*, 5(4): 16–19.

8

The Power of Women in an Ostensibly Male-Dominated Agro-Pastoral Society

Jean Lydall

Introduction

If you were to visit Hamar in southern Ethiopia, you would probably gain the impression from what you see and hear that this is a relatively egalitarian yet also male-dominated society. The elders appear to be equals, each self-sufficient and independent, and no one being noticeably wealthier than another. You would be received as a guest in so-and-so's homestead, the son of so-and-so. Your host would order his wife and daughters to lay out a cowhide for you to sit on, put on coffee for you to drink, and make fresh food for you to eat. If it is evening, he would call his son over and instruct him which cow to milk for you, and which goat to bring for you to slaughter and eat.

When the wife has made the coffee, she will first serve some into her husband's gourd bowl, which she keeps by her side while serving coffee to the guests. Once her husband's coffee has cooled enough, the wife offers the bowl to him with her right hand, lowering her head and body in a submissive pose as she does so. Her husband does not look at his wife directly and only slowly condescends to take the bowl. The husband and other elders who are present individually spray coffee from their lips and invoke health and good fortune for the home, the neighbourhood and the whole country, before they begin to drink. The wife does not drink coffee but sits at the hearth, breast-feeding her infant and refilling the bowls whenever they are handed to her. Meanwhile the elders talk animatedly about this and that.

Next morning your host may take you to visit his neighbour to drink coffee. At the neighbour's homestead you get the same kind of treatment and observe the same kind of behaviour as at your host's home, only this time it's the neighbour's mother who serves coffee, as his wife has already gone to work in her field. The neighbour's mother serves herself coffee before serving the others. She gives her son his bowl in the same way she hands coffee to the other elders, looking him in the eye and telling him to take the bowl. You may not notice, but before she drinks from her own bowl, she spills a little coffee at the hearth; it is for her deceased husband. As well as drinking with the elders, this woman also joins in the conversation. She does not spray coffee or obviously call forth good fortune, but in an undertone she echoes the phrases uttered by the elders.

The view of Hamar as an egalitarian society corresponds to that characterised by James Woodburn for delayed-return societies, viz.:

> the community of political equals is usually a community of property-holding household heads whose relations with their wives and female kin and with their junior male kinsmen within the household are far from equal. Intergenerational inequality and especially the inequality of holder and heir is usually stressed. The household head has the right and the duty to maintain and control the assets held by the household and to direct the labour of its members. (Woodburn 1982: 446)

James Woodburn assumes here that household heads are male.

In Hamar, however, if one looks a bit closer behind the rhetoric of naming, ritual, gesture and speech, one gets to see another reality in which women also act as household and homestead heads, maintain and control assets, and direct the labour of household members. In short, behind the apparent male domination, we find a hidden, but none-the-less effective, female power. This is what I want to demonstrate in this paper.

Household and Homestead Heads in Hamar

In Hamar, a distinction is made between household (*ono,* house) and homestead (*dele,* livestock enclosure). Houses and their hearths are associated with individual women and those who depend on them for food and drink. Although her husband is acclaimed the household head (*ono-imba,* house-father), a woman is also acknowledged as the female household head (*ono-imbano,* 'female house-father'). A homestead consists of one or more households making use of a semi-permanent cattle and/or goat enclosure. A married man can establish a homestead in his own name only once his father and his father's wives are dead. As in the case of households, both a man and his senior-most wife are recognised as heads of homestead, the one male, the other female. When a man dies, his senior-most widow becomes his female successor, *djalattono,* and her senior-most son becomes his male successor, *djalatta.* The homestead will continue to be called the homestead of the deceased man, but his widow and her son, if or when he is married, become the homestead heads. Until her son gets married, a widow may share the homestead with a younger brother of her husband, or with an unrelated lover. When a widow dies, her junior co-wife, if she has one, or the senior-most wife of her senior-most son, becomes her successor and the female head of the homestead. Households of junior co-wives or junior brothers are usually incorporated into their respective senior co-wife's or older brother's homestead. Households that are not yet able to establish their own independent homesteads may temporarily attach themselves to other people's homesteads. In some cases a wife may be estranged from her husband and attach her household temporarily to someone else's homestead. Given these regulations, how does it look in practice on the ground?

Dambaiti 1973–83

Dambaiti is the settlement area in Hamar where Aike Berinas resided, and where Ivo Strecker and I built a house so we could live in Aike's proximity and benefit from his friendship and teaching. Dambaiti encompasses a ridge of land about 2 km wide and 3.5 km long, lying between two tributaries of a sandy riverbed, the Mulmule, and the middle reaches of another riverbed, the Pere.

In 1973 and again in 1983, I made a survey of all households residing in Dambaiti. In 1973 there were 52 households incorporated in, or attached to, 17 homesteads. By 1983, 9 of these homesteads had been disbanded, the homestead heads having moved away from Dambaiti, and 10 new homesteads had been established. All but one of the new homesteads were established by people whose households were formerly attached to Dambaiti homesteads, or by people who were previously dependants of Dambaiti households. Although there were more homesteads by 1983, 18 instead of 17, there were fewer households, only 40 instead of 52.

Dambaiti households, headed by:	**1973**	**1983**
married man with wife/wives	21	12
widow	29	27
widower	0	1
estranged wife	2	0
Total number of households	52	40

Dambaiti homesteads, headed by:	**1973**	**1983**
married man with wife/wives	4	5
widow with married or widowed son	8	6
widow with husband's married younger brother	2	2
widow with unmarried son or husband's unmarried younger brother	3	5
Total number of homesteads	17	18

What is remarkable about these data is that in 1973 as well as 1983, there were more widow-headed households (29 in 1973, and 27 in 1983) than ones headed by a married man and wife (21 in 1973, and 12 in 1983), and two to three times more homesteads were headed by widows, either alone or together with junior married men, (13 in 1973 and in 1983) than were headed by married men with their wives (4 in 1973, and 5 in 1983). In other words, there were many more women in positions of authority than one would have expected in such an ostensibly male-dominated society. How does this come about, and how do these women wield their authority in a world where men are supposedly dominant? Following James Woodburn (see Woodburn in Volume 1), I suggest the answer can be found by exploring the rights to property and the ideologies linked with such rights.

Hamar Country and Subsistence Economy

The mountains, hills and lowlands of Hamar lie between the rift valley of the Woito River in the East and the Omo River in the West, in southwest Ethiopia. Rainfall is low, unreliable and usually unevenly distributed across the country. In this environment, the Hamar have developed an economy of mixed subsistence involving pastoralism, slash-and-burn cultivation, apiculture, hunting and gathering.

Most of Hamar country is covered by thorny bush scrub, which is particularly suitable for keeping goats. Grass depends on rain, and is scanty except in the low-lying areas on the outskirts of the country. Cattle, goats and sheep are kept in small numbers in the hills and mountains where slash-and-burn cultivation takes place. Additional animals are kept in shifting camps in the outlying grazing areas.

Sorghum, maize, beans and pumpkins are cultivated in small quantities, on a shifting slash-and-burn basis, in gullies and alongside sandy river courses. Up until the mid-1980s cultivation was done by hand with the use of metal hoe and wooden digging stick, a task undertaken primarily by women. Ploughing with oxen has since been adopted by more and more people, and is undertaken primarily by men.

Hamar country is good for bees, especially in the middle altitudes where flowering acacia bushes proliferate. Here young men make beehives and collect honey. The outlying lowlands used to be well stocked with game, and until recent years there used to be plenty of small antelope and wild pig in the hills and mountains, which men could hunt for meat. At certain times of year leaves, fruits and roots can be gathered from the bush as a further source of food. Gathering is mainly a female activity.

Control of Material Assets and Labour

Land and its Products

People say land is and should be free. There is little incentive to own cultivation sites on a permanent basis. When a man and/or woman abandon one field they do so because the land has become exhausted or overwhelmed by weeds. The old field is left to revert to bush for up to ten years, when it may be suitable for cultivation again. The former users retain a preemptive right to reuse it, but only if they assert this right actively, otherwise someone else can use it. The important thing for anyone is not to retain exclusive rights in abandoned field sites, but rather to have access to unused land that can be made into fields.

Land is also free for pastoral activities. Pastures get worn out, water gets scarce or animals get sick, and herds have to be moved to new areas to graze, water or recover health. No one is interested in having exclusive rights in pasture or water holes. Married men are associated with named territorial areas, usually where they have been born and their grandfathers have been buried. In critical times, such as severe drought, these men may oblige others associated with other territorial areas to move their livestock out of the area. Control of access to land in such cases is only possible on a communal basis, never on an individual one.

Hunting, gathering and bee-keeping activities as practised in Hamar do not entail exclusive rights in land. Firewood, timber and grass for house and kraal construction, stones for grinding stones, clay for plastering houses or making pottery, herbs for medical treatment, water for human consumption, and many other useful products of the bush and land are all regarded as free for whoever makes the effort to collect them. Ownership only begins once someone has collected something, cut or stacked it, or put it into a container and brought it back to their house, homestead, field or camp.

Livestock and Labour

Unlike land, livestock is not free but is owned and controlled in various ways. Labour is also controlled. The control of livestock and labour are closely linked, as I will clarify below. There are, of course, many other material assets besides land and livestock, which could be considered, such as rifles, houses, clothing (both skin clothes of women and cloth of men), beads, metal tools, etc. I will, however, concentrate on livestock because it is the most important property, the control of which underlies the whole social organisation. In December 2000, while making the documentary film, *Duka's Dilemma*, I conducted many interviews with the main characters of the film: Duka, the daughter of our special friend, Aike Berinas; Sago, her husband; and Sagonda, her mother-in-law. In one conversation, Sagonda expressed the importance of livestock in the following way:

> You've all grown up, look after the goats well, the cattle well, if the goats are many, the cattle are many, your name will be big, Sago, your name will be big. Sorghum, even if you grow stacks and stacks, you have no name. It's just shit. White things – goats and cattle – raise your name. 'Bargar's son, Sago. Bargar's son, Sago.'

General Division of Labour

Individual family units try to be self-sufficient, using their own labour to engage in all forms of production: pastoralism, slash-and-burn agriculture, apiculture, hunting and gathering. Regular labour is employed in three distinct spheres: in the fields where sorghum and other crops are cultivated; in grazing areas in the vicinity of the fields and homesteads where herds of goats and milk cows are kept; and in distant grazing areas on the outskirts of the country where mixed herds, dry stock as well as milk animals, are kept. Women and girls provide the regular labour required in the fields. Boys provide regular pastoral labour required in the vicinity of the fields and homesteads, teenage boys being chiefly responsible for herding goats. Young men provide regular pastoral labour required in the distant grazing areas, their main job being to defend the herds against dangerous wild animals and raiders from neighbouring groups (e.g. the Dassenech who are sometimes friends and sometimes enemies, or the Mursi who are now friends and used to be enemies). These young men, in their turn, go from time to time on raids hoping to bring back livestock to augment the herds, or go hunting for meat or glory. Raiding and hunting are immediate-return activities. Some young men also put up beehives in tall trees, and collect honey when it's available. Older men engage in both agricultural and pastoral activities in all three spheres, providing labour required on an occasional basis, such as cutting and burning off the bush to make a new field, repairing the thorn bush fencing around the fields, checking beehives, or collecting livestock from debtors. Women and girls combine their regular agricultural activities with immediate-return activities such as daily food processing (grinding grain and cooking), fetching water, or seasonal gathering of wild fruits, as well as innumerable other jobs, like sweeping clean the goat kraal, curing skins for clothing, plastering the house, etc. Children from an early age are involved in daily tasks such as looking after kids and calves, scaring away birds from the fields, carrying younger siblings, or running errands.

Work Parties

Local work parties are organised by individuals for accomplishing certain agricultural jobs such as weeding or harvesting, or for other tasks such as constructing the roof of a new house. When a woman invites her neighbours to join her work party for which she has brewed beer, or will slaughter a goat, she should invite each person personally or send someone in her stead.

Those invited should not refuse to participate unless they have an acceptable excuse, such as sickness. Participation in a work party is a moral obligation, and even if you are never likely to hold a work party yourself, you are obliged to go or send someone from your family in your stead. As James Woodburn says about the sharing of meat among the Hadza (see Woodburn 1998), participation in work parties in Hamar is obligatory and does not necessarily imply reciprocation. In this sense it cannot be seen as a form of exchange. The participants in a work party are given food and drink which is an immediate return for their efforts. A person's work party may be boycotted if they have offended the local community in some way, e.g. because of not participating in preparations for a local initiation. To gain the forgiveness of the locals, the offender has to admit his or her offence and offer compensation, such as giving a goat or brewing beer. The construction of a goat enclosure and the erection of a roof must be done together with the neighbours. This obligation gives the local people a way of accepting or rejecting someone as a full resident. Although land and residence is free in theory, local people can ultimately decide on whether newcomers are fully accepted or not. Since local people have to participate in crucial rituals, such as a child's naming ritual, it is only possible for someone to remain in an area in the long run if they have gained local acceptance.

Joint Herding Units

Joint herding units, both in the settlement areas and in the distant grazing areas, are common, allowing families to pool their limited livestock and labour resources. The owners of livestock held in joint herding units are often close kinsmen or age-mate friends, but may also be unrelated. There is constant movement of personnel and livestock between the camps and the settlement herds, as well as changes in the composition of joint herding units. In the dry season when there is no agricultural work to do and no grain left to eat, whole families and their livestock may go to the distant grazing camps to survive on a diet of milk and blood. People are always free to segregate their livestock and go their own ways, or join up with other people. In most cases people can avoid conflict in this way. But here we are not dealing with individual persons, rather with individual or composite family units. Members of family units cannot easily operate independently of each other.

The Labour of Sons, Daughters and Grandchildren

As James Woodburn predicts for delayed-return societies, the division of labour in Hamar involves a high degree of interdependence within family units. It is the heads of family units who want a division of labour in the first place, and who want to control other people's labour, especially that of their sons. This was clearly expressed by Sago when I interviewed him in March 2000:

Sago: I said, 'May I have many boys' The reason I want many boys is the goats and the cattle. One can go after the cattle, another after the goats, one to the field, and another to the beehives. Boys set a person up within one day. Girls, growing up, eventually join their husbands. I was my mother's only son; for the cattle – I, for the goats – I, for the beehives – I. Then my father died, and I had to struggle on. 'What can stop me from struggling? Could it be my wives? If I marry wives they'll give birth and that will relieve me of my struggle on the cattle path, the goat path, the field path.' Saying this, I married two wives so I could have many boys. Ulde is my only brother, and our mother has no one else with her, that's what makes me struggle. 'May fortune grant me many boys' That's what I thought.

Jean: Now Bona and Marro [two of Sago's daughters] ran to your mother's field.

Sago: They ran. They run errands for their grandmother, down in the field. If Bona and Marro weren't there, now that my mother has gone to get injections, there'd be no one to stay in the field would there? Now these, her son's children have grown up, they are the ones who stay in her field and guard it against the cattle, baboons and pigeons, and then come back to me in the evening. Later when their grandmother returns, Marro is her girl. She'll go to her grandma and keep the cattle away, and throw stones at the pigeons in the field.

Parental Control of Sons' Labour through Control of Livestock

Sago wants sons so they can relieve him and his wife of the struggle they have doing all the jobs needed to make the fields, herd the livestock and collect honey. How can he control the labour of his sons? What will prevent them from going their own way? The answer is simple: he and his wife will do the same as their parents before them, control their son's access to livestock and his ability to found an independent family unit, thus making him totally dependent upon them until they allow him to marry, possess livestock and have children in his own name. Unmarried sons are rarely allowed to own the livestock they collect by their own effort. There are three categories of livestock that an unmarried man can collect: stolen, exchange and bridewealth livestock.

Stolen Livestock

When a son comes home from a raid driving stolen (*banki,* spear) cattle, he sings a glory song announcing the buttermilk cow he's bringing his mother. If his father is alive, he should hand all the stolen cattle to him, otherwise to his father's heir, his eldest brother. Only if he is his father's heir can he keep the cattle for himself. His father will hand on one stolen cow to his mother's brother or father's mother's brother if he hasn't done so before, as a mark of appreciation for the ritual protection afforded by these relatives. If a son brings home stolen animals on several occasions, his father or older brother will eventually hand him some and he will then also give one to his own mother's brother. That at least is the theory. Even if the son is granted a stolen cow, he cannot do much with it until his father, whether alive or dead, has performed the *erra* (milk and water) ritual. Until this ritual is done a stolen cow cannot be used for marriage payment, or as a *garo* calf, which a man needs for his initiation rite, nor as a *sari* calf, which is slaughtered during mortuary rites to provide a hide to envelop the deceased. By postponing the *erra* ritual a man's father can control his son's use of stolen cattle.

Exchange Livestock

A son can also acquire livestock through exchange of things such as honey for a goat, sorghum for a goat or cow, tobacco for a goat, goats for a cow, or any of these items for money, as happens more and more frequently. If a son acquires such exchange (*shani*) animals he should hand them to his father or his father's successor, i.e. his older brother. The father or older brother may let him keep certain animals if he collects many. A cow bought with goats (*k'uli-wak,* goat-cow) is very special. The first goat-cow acquired by a man should be given to his father or older brother; subsequent ones can be retained but still belong to the father or older brother. A son or younger brother will be told that if he hides bought or stolen animals from his father or older brother, this will bring misfortune, which will be revealed in the intestines of sacrificial goats. Unlike stolen cattle, cattle bought with goats can be used for marriage payment, but this doesn't help a son gain independence from his parents because he can't get married before he is initiated, and his parents control that. As in the case of stolen cattle, a goat-cow cannot be used as a *garo* calf for an initiate, or as a *sari* calf for a deceased person, nor can it be exchanged for goats, before a ritual has been done to free it for these purposes. As in the case of stolen cattle, this ritual has to be performed by a man's father, whether he is alive or dead.

Bridewealth Livestock

An unmarried man can acquire livestock as bridewealth (*kemo,* marriage) from his sister's husband, but if he has an older brother he has to give them to him to administer. These bridewealth animals do not belong to a man's father or mother. The parents of a girl also claim gifts of goats and sheep from their son-in-law, but these are not counted as bridewealth. Bridewealth cattle are not usually reproductive stock unless they are substituted by sheep. Bridewealth animals can be used for further bridewealth transactions, or to purchase a rifle (between eight and fifteen cattle depending on the rifle and the cattle), but they cannot be used as a *garo* or *sari* calf until the bridewealth payment has been completed and a finalising ritual has been performed. Bridewealth payments are not usually completed in a man's lifetime, so this means a son cannot usually use the bridewealth cattle for these purposes. In theory, by collecting bridewealth animals a man acquires the animals he needs to give as bridewealth when he marries. He can only marry, however, once he has leapt over the cattle, an initiation rite he can only perform when his parents allow him to. Since he's not allowed to marry when he wants, an unmarried son will usually use the bridewealth he collects to purchase a rifle instead, as Sago explained to me in March 2000:

> *Sago*: That's the girls. When I say they are like a bank, it's because of them there will be cattle, and goats. For Bargar and Gadi and Tammo and now Tini, the girls, Bona and Marro and Kaira, are their rifle, their cows, their goats, their honey. If I am poor and don't collect any wealth, Bargar will take a rifle from Bona, from Bona's husband, he'll also take bridewealth cattle. Gadi will take a rifle from Kaira's husband, and take bridewealth goats and cattle. Also Tammo will later take a rifle from Marro's husband, and take goats. When the girls and boys are equal in number, then older brother and younger brother won't squabble. 'You go over there.' For example, if Gadi asks his older brother, Bargar, for a rifle, and he says 'My father didn't collect any cattle or goats, and now my brothers want cattle and goats, where should I get the animals to buy a rifle or marry you to a wife? Go to your in-law and let him give you cattle. Go to Kaira's husband and let him give you cattle.' And so he'll go and collect enough cattle to buy a rifle. That's why I say, girls are a bank. They are worth a lot. Girls are important.

Control of Son's Initiation and Marriage

In order to gain some independence from his parents, a man needs to get initiated, married and have his wife brought in as a bride, for it is only via his wife that he is able to acquire livestock which are his outright property, or as the Hamar say, his *siti* (hair). Let me quote from an unpublished paper I wrote in 1985:

> By going through his transition rites a Hamar man gains the right to marry and the contingent rights to claim children and livestock as his own, i.e. the children his wife bears and the livestock she receives as gifts from his relatives. Unless a man goes through these rites he is not allowed to marry, claim children as his, nor own livestock. But without a wife, children and livestock he cannot normally hope to achieve economic independence, and he is forced to depend on his parents, relatives and neighbours. Even once he has gone through the rites, a man normally has to wait a number of years, frequently up to ten years, before he can fully realise his rights. This is because he depends on his parents to arrange his first marriage, and they usually arrange for him to marry a very young girl. Although he is officially married, yet he has to wait a number of years before his wife is allowed to be brought in as a bride and before she can collect gifts of livestock and bear children for them both. During these years a man remains dependent on his parents, relatives and neighbours. The transition rites can be seen, therefore, as a way of controlling the age at which a man is allowed to gain economic independence.

First and foremost the parents of a man would be interested in keeping him dependent so that he could provide the labour necessary to herd their cattle in the distant grazing areas and protect these herds from theft by enemies, as well as maybe augmenting them by raiding cattle from enemy country. Close relatives and neighbours who don't have adult sons of their own would also be interested in controlling the age at which a man gains independence. In fact the cattle of many economic units are grouped together in order to be herded by available young men in the distant grazing areas. If we take a look at the transition rites we find that they require the participation of all interested parties, i.e. parents, close relatives and neighbours. Any one of these can impede the performance of the rites by refusing to participate. A man cannot perform his rites without the consent of the interested parties, which is demonstrated by their participation in the rites.

Bridewealth Payments and Their Equalising Effect

Once a man's marriage has been settled, his brothers-in-law have the right to claim bridewealth. When Baldambe (Aike Berinas) told Ivo Strecker and me about his country's customs, he explained that the first Hamar elders, having appointed a *bitta* (ritual leader), asked him to tell them how much bridewealth they should give:

> '*Bitta*!'
> '*Woi.*'
> 'The people are all poor, they have no cows, they have no goats. It would be bad if one had to give much to get married. Tell us what to do.'
> 'Do you ask me as the *bitta*?'
> 'We have asked you.'
> '*Eh-eh.* My country has mountains only. Over there Irgil Bala, here Mama Dunta, and up there Bala Kuntime. Give twenty-eight goats plus one male goat and one female goat."
> 'Good. What about the cattle?'
> The *Bitta* said: 'Both rich and poor should give the same; eighteen head of cattle, plus one 'stone cow' and one 'cloth bull' which makes twenty altogether.' (Lydall and Strecker 1979: 5–6)

If the Hamar were poor, it seems at first odd that the *bitta* should have stipulated such a high bridewealth. It is very difficult to calculate how many cattle and goats people possess in Hamar; livestock should not be counted, and people like to be vague about how many animals they own. The surveys made by Ivo Strecker and myself suggest, however, that in 1973 there was at least one head of cattle per head of population, and three or more head of small stock. Unlike Mursi bridewealth, which is 'fixed by negotiation in advance of marriage, (and) is paid in a lump sum' (Turton 1980: 90), Hamar bridewealth is fixed at a set sum for everyone, and paid in instalments, the size of which are negotiated each time the bride's brothers and cousins claim an instalment. The bride's husband may seek contributions for the bridewealth from his brothers and patrilateral cousins, or collect outstanding bridewealth from his sister's and cousin's husbands. Whatever the case, there will be a limit to how many animals he can provide in any one instalment and he remains indebted to his in-laws for the rest of his life, a debt his sons and grandsons may even inherit. The wife's brothers or their successors return again and again to claim bridewealth whenever they need animals and believe the husband or his successor has animals to spare. The high bridewealth debt which men incur upon marriage can be seen to have a levelling effect on livestock holdings because whenever a stock-owning unit acquires more than the usual number of animals, members of their wife's brothers', mother's brothers' or father's mother's brothers' patriline will come and claim outstanding bridewealth debt. As a result, no man in Hamar can remain wealthy for very long.

Choice and Control of Son's Wife

A man's parents not only determine when he gets initiated but they also decide whom he should marry and when his wife will get brought in as a bride, and finally, when she will be given to him. Even when his wife has been brought in as a bride, an event in which he has no role to play, his parents, especially his mother, continue to assert control over him and his wife. He only gets to sleep with his bride several months after her arrival, when his mother thinks fit and his bride has completed the rituals his mother does with her in order to prepare her for bearing a legitimate child. When Duka became a bride in 1990, Sagonda, her mother-in-law, explained to me that Duka was now her child, would work for her and give her first child to her:

> *Sagonda*: When she was in her father's home she grew up and ground flour. But this is our Hamar custom. Now I have given birth to her anew, like her father gave birth to her before, just as I gave birth to Sago before. I have given birth to her and rubbed on butter, just as one rubs butter on a newborn child. As one feeds a baby with butter and breastfeeds him, I will feed her with food, cook good food for her, milk the cattle and feed her with milk. I'll rub butter on her and tell her to sleep, putting her down to sleep. She will be like a child, and then I will bring her up and when she has grown up after three or two months, I will give her to her husband saying, 'She's grown up now.' Now I have covered her with butter she is my child, and this month she won't do any grinding, she won't fetch water, she won't come down from the loft, she won't fetch firewood, she won't sweep up the goat droppings. The same goes for the next month. Then I will say, 'You should sweep up the goat droppings a little', and in the night she will get up and sweep the goat droppings and spill them away, then return to the loft. I will keep cooking food for her and give it to her, and she will keep being my child. She will only sweep up goat droppings. Then she will put the kids away and bring the goats away and the calves, and the next month she will go and fetch green fodder for the kids and fetch firewood for me, but she will not fetch water, she will not grind the grinding stones. When the last month is over, I will advance her by doing her rituals. Didn't I tell you the other day about how her hands will be rubbed with water and then I will give her to her

> husband? Then she will grind for me, and she will put on coffee for me. I won't prepare coffee anymore. I won't grind and cook anymore. She will do the grinding and will feed me. She will put on coffee for me. I will cultivate my field and when I come back I will call out, 'Hey, children, have you put on coffee for me?' 'Old woman, we have put on coffee for you.' 'Then serve it up and give me some. I want to drink coffee.' Also food will be given me so I can eat. A cowhide will be put out for me. 'You are old,' they will say, and I will rest. Then my child, the one she gives birth to, she'll give him to me. Then she will have grown up and I will hold her child while she goes to fetch water, to fetch fire wood, and when she is doing these things I will say, 'I am now old', as I breast-feed her child, holding him. If the child keeps crying I'll call out, 'Come and feed your child, he is starving', and I will give him to her. That's the way we do it. Her first child, when I lie down I will have the child by my side. My son's eldest son, that's mine. I am the one to bring him up. He's called the grand-mother's child. The next one she gives birth to will be hers.

Sagonda clearly states here how she expects her daughter-in-law to work for her, how she supervises her daughter-in-law's rituals and how she intends to take her daughter-in-law's first child for herself. It is by supervising her daughter-in-law's pre-conception rituals, as well as those involving her children – the naming (*gali*) ritual, the necklace (*katchi*) ritual and the band-tying (*gor*) ritual – that a woman asserts control over her daughter-in-law and her son. In December 2000, Duka explained this to me as follows:

> *Duka*: It's our Hamar ritual isn't it? If Sagonda had left without doing the ritual [naming ritual for Duka's baby] what could we do? If she refuses to do the *gongolo* [ladle] ritual, it's bad, if she refuses to do the *gali* [naming] ritual it's bad. She wouldn't have refused if we hadn't done wrong. If we wives, when she got sick, had ground flour and given it her, collected firewood and given it her, fetched water and given it her, then when she came for the ritual, she wouldn't be cross with you. When she was laid up sick, we just looked, her son did nothing, we wives did nothing. When my husband told me to ask her to do the ritual, 'You abandoned me when I was sick, I will die. Let your husband do the *gali* ritual, let him do the *gongolo* ritual, or find some one else to do them.' That's the anger of an old person. After she brought in her son's bride and brought her up, when she then bears children, she gets angry on those occasions when you have rituals to do. 'Who ties the bands for your child? Who does the naming? Brewing beer for the bands, and taking it to the phallus man's home, who showed you what to do? Sitting down, 'So-and-so's home, please tie the bands for my children'. Only once I've told you, can you go.' Because of that she was angry with her son. 'Your wife doesn't fetch water for me, doesn't collect wood for me, doesn't grind flour for me.' If she says this and Sago says, 'Why didn't you do these things?' you think about it and do the things for her. 'Ah, my son's wife fetches water for me, collects firewood for me, cures goatskins for me, I won't refuse to do her rituals, won't refuse to do her child's *gali* ritual,' and quietly she does it. If you are angry with her, don't fetch her water or collect wood for her, then she'll be angry at the ritual, saying: 'Let her learn something. If the *gali* ritual is not done, once that child has been weaned, will she give birth to another child?' If a child's naming ritual is not done, once the child is weaned, another child shouldn't be born. For us Hamar such a child would be unclean,

> and the newly born child as well as the previous one will be thrown away. Because of this trap we attend to the old woman. It's the same for the *katchi* [necklace] ritual.

As these texts reveal, a mother-in-law controls her daughter-in-law by way of managing the rituals that legitimise her daughter-in-law's reproduction, and by promoting an ideology that sanctions these rituals and her own indispensable role in their performance.

Acquisition of Livestock in Own Right

Once a man has been initiated, has married and his bride has been brought in and given to him, he can finally acquire livestock in his own name and with full ownership rights, which he shares with his wife. To do this, however, he depends on his wife, who has to claim the livestock from his parents, other kinsmen and his parents' cattle bond-friends. His wife, on the other hand, can claim such gifts even after her husband has died! These gifts are distinguished into two general categories, those called 'bowl' (*sherka*) animals, so called because they are given with the presentation of a bowl, and those called 'drawn out' (*buls*) animals, so called because they are drawn out from other homesteads.

'Bowl' Livestock

'Bowl' livestock are reproductive animals, mainly female, which a woman can claim from her husband's senior patrilineal kinsmen and their wives or widows, especially her father-in-law, mother-in-law, husband's eldest brother and his wife. A man's mother controls the occasions when her daughter-in-law can claim gifts of 'bowl' livestock. When a woman is brought into her husband's home as a bride, she can refuse to enter the homestead before she is given a gift of a female goat. In Duka's case, because her father-in-law was dead and Sago has no elder brother, it was her mother-in-law, Sagonda, who presented her with such a goat. When the bride's *bingere* (neck band, which shows she is her husband's first wife) is put on, she can claim further gifts. Sagonda granted Duka a female cow on this occasion. When a bride's rites are completed and she is handed to her husband, she may claim further 'bowl' gifts, which are referred to as the 'dung' goats, in reference to the goat droppings she sweeps up as a bride. Further, whenever a woman bears a child and the child's *gali* (naming) ritual is performed, and later his/her *gor* (tying-on-of-bands) ritual, she can claim further gifts from her husband's patrilineal seniors. These patrilineal kinsmen are those to whom her husband has had to hand over any livestock he collected by his own effort. In so far as this is the case, 'bowl' gifts can be seen as reciprocation. The senior patrilineal relatives cannot be forced to make these gifts, and they only give them when claimed in person by their kinsman's wife. A man cannot claim these gifts on his own, but his wife can do so even after his death. Needless to say, all the occasions when a woman can claim 'bowl' livestock are ones where her mother-in-law is in charge, so long as she is still alive.

'Drawn out' Livestock

Once a woman's bridal rites have been completed and she has been given to her husband, he will go with her to visit his relatives and his parents' cattle bond-friends to introduce her to them. The woman can use this occasion to claim *buls* (drawn out) gifts of reproductive livestock. The main relatives whom she claims gifts from are her husband's mother's brothers and his father's mother's brothers' sons, or their widows. Since these relatives benefited from the bridewealth they received for their sisters, and gifts of 'spear' cows from their sisters' sons, these gifts can be seen as reciprocation. However, the mother's brothers and father's mother's brothers cannot be forced to give against their will, and they only grant gifts if the woman claims them in person. A woman may also claim gifts from her father-in-law's sisters' sons or her husband's brothers-in-law, but in these cases the gifts are counted as bridewealth gifts. The bride may also claim gifts from her parents-in-law's cattle bond-friends. In each case the woman has to claim gifts in person, and may do so even if her husband is dead. The donors only grant gifts if they have appropriate animals to spare, but they may promise future gifts when they become available. They cannot be forced to make gifts against their will, although they may feel morally indebted to the woman's husband because of previous bridewealth or stolen cows received.

The 'bowl' and 'drawn out' gifts of livestock are reproductive stock, both cattle and small stock and maybe donkeys, and form the basis for a couple's herds. Because the wife can claim further 'bowl' gifts each time she bears a child and performs the naming and tying-on-of-bands rituals, this basic herd can be increased as the family also increases. The overall effect of the 'bowl' and 'drawn out' gifts is the continuous redistribution of livestock from those who have livestock to spare, to those who are in need of them.

'Inheritance' Livestock

Far less important than the pre-inheritance gifts just described, are the inheritance (*gos*) gifts a man can claim when his father's or mother's brother's mortuary rites are performed. When an elder dies, those animals he acquired through his own efforts ('spear' cattle and 'goat' cattle) cannot be alienated from him and transferred to others as outright property unless special rituals have been completed, so these rituals are the first to be done during the mortuary rites. There are many people who can claim some of the dead man's livestock. Those cattle bond-friends to whom he gave cows on loan, will probably want to continue keeping the cows. If the widow and eldest son of the man, i.e. his successors (*djalattono* and *djalatta*) agree to extend the loan, the son performs a ritual in which he blesses the bond-friends and the cows, which remain the property of his father and, therefore, his mother. On the other hand, the widow of a deceased man will want to retain the loan cattle she has from her husband's bond-friends. In December 2000, Sagonda told me how she persuaded her husband's bond-friends to let her keep the loan cows:

> *Sagonda*: Sago, your father died when you were still a child [i.e. not yet married]. Keeping the cattle bond-friends, I put coffee on for them, brought out beer for them, cooked fine food for them, and when they had eaten, they said, 'I came to reclaim a cow.' 'Oh, my husband has died, how shall I bring up my children? I have no cow to give.' 'I have drunk coffee, it was good, and I ate good food. Indeed, how can she bring up her children? She herds the cows for me, may they reproduce.' So the bond-friends went home empty, and I could feed my children with milk. My home is full of orphans: my sister's sons and husband's younger brothers. I am the only one. What to do? Going on like this, I transferred the cattle to Sago, transferred the goats to Sago, married him to a wife, 'Now let your father's bond-friends come to you. Haven't you taken over your father's beehives?' 'I've taken them.' 'Have you received goats?' 'I have.' 'If you go on a trip, let your wife look after the goats, may she shout at the children to look after the cows and goats. Now I have brought you up.' That's how I concern myself about things.

The wives and daughters-in-law of a man have the right to claim 'bowl' gifts whenever a child's naming or tying-on-of-bands ritual is performed. For this reason these rituals are performed as part of a man's mortuary rites before livestock is distributed as inheritance. Then the sisters' sons and daughters' husbands can claim livestock as inheritance (*gos*). Before doing so they come singing their praises of the deceased, and then perform special rituals for him. The dead man's male successor, his eldest living son, distributes gifts to these claimants. Finally the sons and daughters of the deceased can claim animals, if any remain, as inheritance. They too sing their praises of their dead father, and sacrifice oxen or goats in his honour. The eldest son of the dead man does not give away livestock that his mother has collected as 'bowl' and 'drawn out' gifts without her consent. A young widow will need to keep most of her property to support her family that will continue to grow even though she is not allowed to marry again. The timing of a mortuary ritual is decided upon by a dead man's widow and son and can be postponed for many years.

A Widow's Control over Her Married Son

Even after his father's death, a man remains dependent on his widowed mother, especially if he is the eldest surviving son. Both mother and son may try to control the other, which may lead to conflict, but in the end the mother has the upper hand because she has the power to curse her son, or, by refusing to do the rituals for his son's wives and children, to doom his children, as Duka explained above. In December 2000, Sago's mother refused to do the naming ritual for Duka's newborn son. The local elders, who had come to take part in the ritual, intervened and persuaded her to do the ritual. Then a discussion ensued in which Sagonda and Sago aired their complaints about each other, and the elders reconciled them, giving them their advice. Here I present the essential parts of this dispute.

> *Sagonda*: Banna rituals are different [i.e. from Hamar rituals], now the girl [Sago's second wife] will her mother say she wants to grow up with her daughter [i.e. stop bearing children when her daughter starts] by throwing the goatskin [a Banna ritual]? If she says 'I'm young and will bear children', she should show us her ritual surrogate. Sago said, 'You did the *gongolo* [ladle] ritual for my first wife, why don't you do it for the little one? You left your father-in-law's custom behind [i.e. the goatskin ritual], so you should do the ritual for this wife.' 'No, I won't do it. Aike's daughter [Duka] is Hamar, and in Hamar women are not taken to their father's home, the mother-in-law performs the ritual.
>
> *Banqo* (a local elder): That's what I say, the rituals are different from place to place.
>
> *Sagonda*: The mother-in-law performs the ritual. I do it [for Duka]. I grew up [stopped having children] with my son's wife [Duka] and now I can do rituals for others [as a ritual surrogate]. But in this land [Banna] there is another custom. 'The country you've entered is different.' When I said this, he [Sago] didn't like it. Boro's mother told him she wouldn't throw the skin cape, 'I'm young and will bear children, let Narinda throw the skin cape for me.' Later she'll give her a female cow, won't she? When my daughter married, I was still young and wanted to bear more children, so I put myself behind a ritual surrogate, but now I've stopped bearing children. It was that woman who transferred me over the poles, and she received a female cow.
>
> *Banqo*: The customs are the same, just a little different.
>
> *Sagonda*: That's why, in case Boro's mother gets angry with me, I refrain from doing the *gongolo* ritual. If she wants to do as I did, she should ask Narinda to throw the skin cape. I didn't refuse for bad reasons. Now where should she go for the *gongolo* ritual? I didn't refuse for bad reasons. Now Boro has born a son, and for the boy's *katchi* ritual, because Narinda has died, there's no need to find someone to throw the skin cape. So I, the grandmother, should do it. 'The boy [Tammo] has chewed fresh grain, the cattle [i.e. his teeth] have come up, go now to the child's grandma for the *katchi* ritual.' If this were said, I would do it with my *tiri* [head-dress], putting it on four times. Then his wife may rub on *bodi* [i.e. perform the pre-conception rituals] in order to birth. When her ritual [i.e. menstrual period] comes she'll seek me and I will do the *gongolo* [ladle] ritual, do the 'finishing' ritual, and make all well so she can go ahead and bear a child. Like the *katchi* [necklace] ritual that he did on his own, let him do the *gongolo* ritual for his wife alone. Don't let him send her to me.
>
> *Bona* (a local elder): Just as he did the *katchi* alone. That's a big problem.
>
> *Sagonda*: That's one. Now the house: When Sago got married he had his own house and he built me a house. It's called the 'old one's house'. This coffee should have been served in my house; the *gali* ritual should be done in my house; the *gor* ritual in my house. Now I don't have a house, only my field house. Instead of looking at cattle in the morning, I look at sorghum. There is no gateway. Rituals have to be done at my husband's gateway; the *gali* and *gor*

rituals. Now the head of this house was I, when out of the blue he tells me to leave for my house. Where should I stay? They should come to me to do the rituals. So this house is someone else's now. Should I do the rituals in the house down there? Will he come to me saying 'Mother', or will he go elsewhere to get his rituals done?

Bona: You've told us now why you ran away. The concern people have varies from home to home. Some homes quarrel when an initiation is held, or when there's a work party. When they eat and drink they quarrel, and when they feast. Other homes, when they have a ritual to do, they ask their friends how to do things, and they tell them do this, give that. They tell which goats to give, and which beer. Now this *gali* ritual, like an initiation or other ritual, if she leaves and stays away, the ritual will be left undone, won't it? Why should she abandon it? But she reconsidered and returned, afraid of offending the elders. May *barjo* [good fortune] bless her. Being a woman she has an important role to play.

Sago: Now the *katchi* ritual, I didn't know I'd done wrong. Now I've understood. The problem that led me to send her off to her field house, please straighten it out for me. A son and his mother, the father and his son, if the father and his wife survive they will have their own house, and their young son, the one who cuts the bush and cares for the livestock, will care for them in hunger and sickness. He looks after his mother's livestock and buys his father a blanket. Now her husband has died, she's in her own house, with her own milk cows – the quarrel my mother has in her stomach is quite something else. My word is hot. If a ritual takes place and there is an argument, I don't like it. I believe most people are envious of my homestead. Now since my father and his brothers died, my mother and I have stayed together. Beer makes her crazy. When I say, 'Don't drink', she says, 'I won't stop.' Then, when going to rituals – children go away – later, when going to rituals, being still youthful, there's beer for the locals and the mothers' brothers, or for the girls. There's her husband's younger brother who hasn't leapt over the cattle yet, and there's her son. On the occasion of their initiation there'll be trouble. Since I married and my father died, I haven't initiated anyone. When Tini was initiated, for Kadde's wife and Kasa's wife, she caused trouble. She brought the trouble to the phallus man. There was trouble in the home. If they didn't brew beer or grind flour for the mothers' brothers and the girls, you should ignore it. But she complained, 'You didn't come with beer, you didn't do something, nor something else.' It's the beer causing trouble, a fight and blows. They landed in the phallus man's house. Sagonda had brewed beer and the phallus man took it, and the two chased the other women away. I'm not an incompetent person – but I don't know about women's rituals. I know about working for the community and the welfare of my home. I don't know the details of the *gongolo* ritual she talked about.

[After further discussion Sago made the following comment]: Why doesn't she grow up and stay put. The cows and goats are hers, and when I take a goat to town she can ask, 'Which goat did he take yesterday?' 'One to buy mead.' 'Which goat did he take the other day? Where's he put the honey?'

Sagonda: Where am I when

Sago: Wait, let me finish

Sagonda: Get lost! Where am I to see you take a goat? Where am I to see you put money in your pocket to get the mead I want, or to see you drive a goat? I have lots of goats to get the things I want. Thinking of your mother and buying me mead, saying 'Here, drink this. Brew mead with this honey.' When did you ever do this? When did you give me honey so I can stay at home, or buy me *arike* [gin] to drink at home?

Sago: Stop, you are right, stop now.

Sagonda: Like a wild pig you creep, bringing things to your wives. What have I done to make you lift your nose and say, 'I don't like her going to town'? Of course, when I get the desire for *arike* I'll go to town. Of course, I'll sell my vagina for drink.

Sago: You elders tell us what you think?

Bona: This is not a fight, listen, it's a discussion, straightening things out. [Bona gives an example of a man and his wife who sent their sons away. In time of hunger they had no one to get grain for them Then their children came and slaughtered goats and the couple revived. The man was sorry he had sent his sons away before. Had they stayed he and his wife would not have suffered. That's what will happen if Sago and Sagonda quarrel.]

Banqo: [After a long speech]: If you say bad things it's like a rotten tooth; if you don't pull it out the rot spreads. It's bad talk that destroys the home. Only if you stop will things be all right, and it'll become just a game. As the father said in the past, let the discussion be a game.

Tsasi: [Duka's brother, who was visiting, gave a placatory speech saying Sagonda should be happy she has such good fortune, to which Sagonda then responded.]

Sagonda: True; my fortune is special, my forehead is special. When he was a child Sago wondered, 'Where was my mother born to come to my father's home?' Just like Aike Berimba's child [i.e. Tsasi] has said, I brought the cattle fortune with me. My husband's people only ate chillies. I saw no bleating goat, no mooing cow. When my husband rose up, collecting things and putting up beehives, the Bashada wondered because his father, Ditto, used to steal from beehives. What made him successful? It was my forehead [i.e. fortune]. Full of goats when he was born, full of cows when he was born, lacking nothing, Sago bought gun after gun. Planting sorghum, I put aside grain and initiated him. How many orphans have I brought up? *Barjo* [fortune] made them feeble, otherwise they would have collected cattle for me, and supported my son. Bashada people have mixed origins, Banna have mixed origins. If he had married someone else's daughter, if he'd been married to Likomba's daughter, would this prosperity [*majono*] have reached the homestead? If he'd married Lotchomba's daughter, would this good fortune have entered the home? I rubbed the staffs and gave them to my husband. He had dreamed his father had told him to go to Aike's homestead. Everyone else had been chased away from the Berinas homestead as rubbish. The good fortune was brought by my forehead. When my husband died, I took the staffs and went there. I blessed her [Duka] to fill up the homestead, to give birth like a dog. I am not crooked. Even if I'm not sick, but say I am, won't you slaughter a goat for me? If I long for *arike*, and cry out for mead or *arike*, won't you get me some? Won't you ask, 'How are you doing?' The house is the topic. He should leave this house and make another for his wives. All the cattle and goats are mine, the ones my husband collected. There are no animals that he and his wife have collected. When I lay suffering rheumatism, he and his wives stayed here. No one came to ask how I was. I want to tell the elders this first so they can judge. That's part of doing rituals.

Abo [the senior-most elder present]: If you forbid your mother to go to town, and forbid her other things [e.g. to drink beer at home], how about the house? She's right to want her own house. She should sacrifice to her husband at her own hearth, not her son's. That's how it is in Banna. In Banna, she spills coffee to placate the dead so the cattle and goats will graze safely. I don't know the customs down there [in Hamar]. In Banna she does that in her own house, not her son's. So build her a house. Next time you do a ritual like this, let her placate her husband there. This is ritual isn't it? Placating the dead and doing rituals. The other stuff is domestic squabble. As for the town, those who stay in town, do they have sorghum or livestock? Away with it! Sago says he has collected the cattle and goats for himself and his wives, but this is not true, they are his mother's. She is the shade for the cattle, the goats, the wives, the children, the sorghum. Look at my older brothers Anombe and Bazabe. The home getting mad, where was there honey [as *bitta* they should have called forth the bees]? Only after Bazabe died and Anombe died have things gotten better. Now there's honey again. Now that they have died, there's no more quarrelling.

Sagonda: Once the house is erected …

Abo: Build the house.

The upshot of this dispute was that Sagonda got what she had wanted: a new house and renewed attention from her son and his wives. Sagonda used the ritual as a source of coercive power over her son and his wives.

A Widow's Control over Her Husband's Younger Brother

A widow can also assert control over her husband's younger brother. If his parents are both deceased, she controls their livestock as well as her own, and her husband's younger brother relies on her to make gifts to his wife when she becomes a bride and each time she bears a child. If he is not yet initiated, she may initiate him and provide marriage gifts and bridewealth for his wife's family. Because he is dependent on her, he is an ideal partner for her to cohabit with and bring up children. In the case of Birinda, a woman in Dambaiti who became a widow before she even became a bride, she was advised by her husband's kinsmen to cohabit with her dead husband's brother, Woro. As both his parents were dead, Woro was completely dependent on Birinda, who bought him a rifle, initiated him and married him to a wife. Birinda then brought Woro's wife in as a bride and gave her gifts of livestock. Meanwhile, Woro sired Birinda's children, looked after her livestock and helped with making and caring for her field. Once he was married and his wife had collected gifts of livestock, Woro tried to make himself independent of Birinda, but she still kept him under her sway by controlling his wife's and children's rituals.

Conclusion

Following James Woodburn's approach, I have explored how property rights and the ideologies (and rituals) that support them explain how Hamar women have so much hidden power in their households and homesteads. In the last resort, property rights and ideologies can be traced back to the exigencies of the Hamar economy. Married couples want to have many sons to provide the labour required for their diverse and dispersed subsistence activities. In order to control the labour of their sons, they control their rights to own livestock, to get married, to be united with their wives, and for their wives to bear children and collect livestock for them. Men's marriages are thus usually delayed, often into their mid-thirties, while girls' marriages are usually contracted while they are still children. As a consequence, the age difference between men and their wives is usually well over ten years. If a man's wife is brought in when he is over thirty years old, and the same happens for his sons, it is unlikely that a man will still be alive when his sons' wives get brought in as brides. Women, on the other hand, becoming brides around the age of seventeen, are more likely to be still around when their sons get their wives. This explains why so many women become widows, some of them already as brides or young mothers (29 out of 52 women in 1973, and 27 out of 39 women in 1983, were widows in Dambaiti). Those women who bear sons bring them up from the start to be dependent on them, and even when their sons are married men, they continue to assert authority over them and their wives, controlling their access to livestock, wives and children, and resorting to ritual coercion if need be.

References

Lydall, J. and S. Strecker 1979. *The Hamar of Southern Ethiopia II, Baldambe Explains*, Hohenschäftlarn: Klaus Renner Verlag.

Turton, D. 1980. 'The Economics of Mursi Bridewealth: A Comparative Perspective'. In: J.L. Comaroff (ed.), *The Meaning of Marriage Payments*, London and New York: Academic Press.

Woodburn, J. 1992. 'Egalitarian Societies'. *Man*, 17(3):431–51.

—— 1998 'Sharing Is Not a Form of Exchange': an Analysis of Property-sharing in Immediate-return Hunter-gatherer Societies'. In: C.M. Hann (ed.), *Property Relations: Renewing the Anthropological Tradition*, pp. 48–63. Cambridge: Cambridge University Press.

9

The Incorporated Ground: The Contemporary Work of Distribution in the Kutubu Oil Project Area, Papua New Guinea

James F. Weiner

It has long been an anthropological truism that public social life throughout Papua New Guinea centres around the mechanisms and activities of distribution of a variety of resources: food, marriageable women, ceremonial wealth items such as pigs and shell valuables, and less material things such as cult formulae, sorcery and magic techniques, and songs. However, the manner in which such traditional distributive mechanisms have responded to the more recent challenge of distributing revenue from resource extraction projects throughout the country has yet to be addressed in as comprehensive a manner. In this paper I outline some of the dimensions of distribution of petroleum revenue within the societies of the Kutubu Joint Venture's Kutubu oil project area. Since I have carried out fieldwork exclusively with the Foi-speakers of this area since 1979, I will restrict my examples to those from the Foi, though I suspect that most of the things I say are applicable across the entire range of longhouse-based societies within the oil project area, and specifically the Fasu, the main land owners within the project area.

The Foi number around 6,000[1] today and inhabit the heavily forested region of the Mubi River Valley in the Southern Highlands Province of Papua New Guinea. Until 1988, their low population density, the inaccessibility of their habitat, and the limited prospects for agri-commercial development in this soil-poor, high-rainfall area ensured that both the provincial and national governments paid little attention to the area. All this changed dramatically when a joint venture headed by Chevron Niugini discovered one of the biggest reservoirs of light sweet crude oil in the southern hemisphere in the region directly to the west and south of Lake Kutubu.

The Chevron Company chose to deal with local land-owner compensation and payment through the mechanism of the Papua New Guinea *Land Group Incorporation Act* of 1974. Both royalty money and equity benefits are paid into bank accounts owned by putative land-owning groups incorporated under this legislation. In fact, since mid-1992 Chevron has incorporated virtually all local clans in the Kutubu oil project area, including local clans who are not in receipt of any petroleum or pipeline revenues. Thus, the *Land Group Incorporation Act* has affected the nature of collective and distributive activity within the entire Kutubu oil project area, and not just for those groups in receipt of revenues.

Since Foi and Fasu clans have become incorporated under the *Land Group Incorporation Act* and have begun to receive royalty payments from the sale of petroleum, there have been numerous applications for new Incorporated Land Group (ILG) status from subgroups already incorporated in the early 1990's. In 1998, thirteen new Fasu ILG applications were lodged, all of them apparently by subgroups within already incorporated clans. The most common reason given was that the income was not being satisfactorily shared by those designated by the clan to control its income. These new ILGs wished to have their own passbooks and receive their income payments directly.

State petroleum policy in Papua New Guinea stipulates that all land-owning groups within a Petroleum Development License (PDL) area shall receive a share of royalties, regardless of whether the wells are located directly on their land or not. Since the royalty payments on the well-head value of petroleum produced each month are a predetermined amount, the more ILGs that are registered within Chevron Niugini's Petroleum Development License Area (PDL-2), the less each single group will receive as regular cash benefit.

The Company interpreted this trend in two ways: as a sign that local clan leaders are dishonest and that clans themselves are unable to act effectively as corporate or collective units for the common interest of its members. It could be, however, that this response of progressive fissioning of royalty receiving groups was the Foi's and Fasu's own way of implementing a distributive mechanism that is considerably more culturally entrenched within this region. I would therefore like to suggest an alternative explanation that is more in line with the way Foi and Fasu and other oil project area peoples conceive of local groups of this sort and their functions in social life. I'd like to first talk about how clans divide in Foi and to question the status of the subclan as a global feature of Foi clan organisation. I would also like to link this description of local organisation with the social function of distribution, both as a mechanism attributable to the way social systems 'work', as a conscious goal of social competition which importantly centres around its verbal forms, and as a more narrow focus of Foi concerns these days, when the distribution of petroleum revenues in various forms, not entirely understood by them, is the most pressingly important issue for them.

Given the fact that between 97 and 99 percent of the land in Papua New Guinea is held under local customary land tenure, Chevron's decision to employ the ILG mechanism might seem to represent the most practical and culturally empathetic fusion of Western corporatism with Melanesian customary resource management. It may occur to some readers that an anthropologist might very well approve of the enshrining of local custom and the power of indigenous decision making in this way. But I reserve the option of distinguishing between the domain of local clan and land-owner politics and values, and the less culturally entrenched liberal democratic institutions which a developing non-Western country such as Papua New Guinea could be expected to put in place to make such local custom continue to work. The main conclusion of this paper is that the very reasons why the incorporated land groups are so successful in serving as recipients of land-owner benefit are the same reasons why they cannot provide a firm base for broader, more long-term democratic, representational political life in resource development areas. I'd like to make a case for a foundation for revenue distribution policy that makes a clear distinction between the domain of land-owner custom and politics, and a separate domain of representational organisations not tied to land-owner interests per se, as the best way of managing the Solomonic task of balancing land-owner[2] and non-land-owner benefit in resource development areas.[3]

Western and New Guinean Forms of Sociality

Let me first try to draw a broad contrast between the way people of the Kutubu oil project area and we English-speaking Westerners 'do' social life. Our own English-derived western notion of social life starts with the irreducible 'individual', the 'given' of social life. The individual is thought to be born as a unique organism – genetically, temperamentally, and in terms of history and identity. We Westerners then pose 'society' as a matter of deliberate, conscious, rational 'contract' between discrete individuals, a contract entered into by those individuals for their common good. The social contract stipulates that it is in the interest of the individual to forego some of his/her passions, drives, strivings, and so forth in order to forge a functioning and positively valued social system in which the individual can pursue his/her interests with the maximum amount of freedom and yet also (under ideal conditions) serve the community or public interest as well. To sum up, we see the individual as 'natural', or 'God-given', and society as a human artifice set up to mediate the innate strivings and drives of the individual (in broad terms, self-preservation and the maximisation of property and comfort).

For many Papua New Guineans such as those within the Kutubu oil project area, this scheme is exactly reversed. People are born not as unique and discrete individuals, but as already-connected[4] – through bodily substance, ancestral intervention while in the womb, in terms of the series of debts and obligations that attended the marriage of one's mother, by being nourished on the same land – to others within their social field. What is 'natural' or 'given' in social life is this web of connections. If this is the case, what then do people consciously and deliberately 'do' themselves? Under these conditions, Papua New Guineans must consciously and deliberately 'achieve' individuality – it is not a condition that is given to them at birth. They must strive to cut themselves off from others, to preempt the duties of debt and obligation, to make themselves unique and powerful in the face of this convention which connects them to others.[5]

But when one's world is given to one as a total universe of connections, where one connection implies all the others in that world, to break one's self off means to break one's self off from the total world. To make one's self different means finding a different whole world for one's self, with a whole different set of connections. In other words, in the Foi social world, it is all or nothing. A quarrel – over property, over adultery, over sorcery accusation – inevitably leads to the departure of one of the disputing parties to another place, especially if powerful men are involved. Foi and Fasu history becomes the history of disaffected men taking their retinue, that is, the fragment of their social universe remaining to them, leaving their natal residence, and migrating to other places. At these places, they are given access to and control of land and sites so that they can carry out the total range of subsistence tasks.

I think it is important to understand that these quarrels and departures and migrations are the visible form that the *normal state of affairs* takes in this part of the world (see Wagner 1998). They are not aberrations within the theoretically smooth functioning of a social organism, because there is no social organism as such. When people become disaffected from their nominal groups of affiliation, they do not assert their individuality and leave, for individuality is not the "default setting" of non-sociality for Papua New Guineans. Rather, they take a miniature fragment of the social world to which they belonged, in the form of immediate family and other assorted hangers-on and sympathisers, and go off and recreate another, albeit smaller, version of the social whole from which they have detached themselves. Another way of describing this situation in Foi is to say that there are subclans without there being clans: subclans are the effective local unit in this part of Papua New Guinea. Each subclan assumes it is related to other subclans of the same name, even if they cannot specify the actual kin connection. Even if they could, these subclans never act as a single 'clan' in any circumstances.

But even the local subclan is a contingent unit: it is subclan fragments that migrate, immigrate and emigrate, not individuals, and it is sub-clan fragments that are taken in and given land, status and brides *as local sub-clan groups*. The consequences of fragmentation of groups then is not ultimately a set of atomised individuals, but smaller and smaller versions of a single global social totality which only ever achieves a hypostatised ideal form.

Bridewealth

The matter of distribution, in any number of forms, some of which I will mention here, is of central importance to the articulation of Foi social activity. If my characterisation of Foi and Fasu sociality is correct – if, in other words, there can be no decomposition of social groups into component individuals, but only into smaller groups which retain the functions of the original group – then we should be able to confirm this in the kinds of distributive mechanisms associated with these groups.

We can begin to inspect it at its most basic level when we watch a Foi hunting party deciding how to distribute the various portions and cuts of an animal collectively trapped or killed. Considerations of, for example, the ownership of the dog involved, who first sighted the animal, who dealt the lethal blow, who may have been injured during the chase, who did the work of butchering and cooking, all contribute to determining the correct portions allotted to all. In line with what I have said about social convention, in such occasions, the 'rules' of distribution are usually tacit and understood by all and rarely, except in an explanatory passage to the visiting anthropologist, articulated as 'a rule'.

Although I have argued elsewhere that for the Foi what we call law and the quality of being law- or rule-governed is not something that was consciously articulated, the coming of the government administration and missionaries provided them with exposure to the idea that social law and customary action, including these tacit conventions of distribution of resources, were something that could be objectified, codified and altered by human effort, rather than phenomena that were only revealed in the course of humans reacting to otherwise situational and contingent social engagements and encounters. One of the most concerted ways in which Foi experimentation with codification proceeded was in the area of bridewealth. As a result of the influx of large numbers of high-quality pearl shells into the Highlands by Australian administrators after the Second World War, the Foi experienced a great inflationary pressure on what was perceived to be the normal size of bridewealth payments. Along with the appointing of *komitis* of various sorts, each village had, by the time I first arrived in 1979, appointed a bridewealth *komiti* to represent its interests and opinions in this regard. These bridewealth *komitis* met on at least two occasions in 1980 and 1981 to agree upon a standard amount and composition of bridewealth.

Because social rules are not usually overtly articulated, as ethnographers such as Merlan and Rumsey (1991), Goldman (1983), A.J. Strathern (1975), M. Strathern (1974) and more recently Brison (1992) have demonstrated, communal agreement concerning the normative in social life is often reached after a protracted process of public argument and verbal contention. As Marilyn Strathern suggested in an early paper (ibid.), the idea that in a public dispute, all points of view should be aired and made visible, all persons' opinions should be voiced, is very important to achieving an acceptable resolution to a conflict in these areas of Papua New Guinea. We can suggest, again to elaborate on the metaphor I am employing, that points of view must be distributed as widely as possible, at least in these public speech events.

There was never, therefore, a hard and fast rule concerning how much bridewealth one had to give in earlier times; there was only the communal assessment of a bridewealth as being proper or insufficient. Since the obligations of wife-takers to wife-givers was a continuing one, it was likely that agreement as to sufficiency of bridewealth at the time of a bride's transfer did not preclude requests for additional payment in the future. What was important about distributive mechanisms of this sort was not exactly how much material resource was spread out within a social field but rather how wide one could expand one's social network of indebtedness and obligation to others.

On the other hand, the whole institution of bridewealth was perfused with normative understandings, most of which were given quite explicit public acknowledgement in the discussions amongst bridewealth *komitis* in 1980 and 1981 that I attended. The *komitis* and head-men talked for some time about the size of shells, the number of shells, and the people who should be recipients of them. Finally, as the argument went back and forth, and agreement started to converge upon the proper amounts and sizes of items, the opinion was voiced that these agreements had to be written down, sample pearl shells had to be collected and marked with a fixed price to serve as standard, and a pamphlet produced that could be distributed throughout the area, informing everyone what the correct and agreed-upon composition and mode of distribution was to be. In this particular conversation, there was agreement that in the matter of the distribution of a girl's bridewealth, distant relatives should get less, a token amount, while more recognition should go to the man and woman who played the major parental and nurturing role in the girl's upbringing. It was suggested that the mother and father or persons in that role should divide between them a cash payment of 200 Kina (which in 1980 was a large sum in the area), in recognition of the 'hard work' the two expended in nurturing the girl. I'll return to this shortly.

Control of Land within Clan Groupings

Let us now shift our attention to a different side of the issue of distribution in Foi social life – specifically, the relation between clans, people and land. The distribution of Foi villages and their territory, and of component local clan groups within each village territory, is perceived to be such that each person and local clan has access to all types of terrain and resource thought necessary to subsistence and social life: garden land, sago swamps, riverine and creek frontage, hunting areas, access to useful species of trees, and so forth. In some cases there are large-scale discrepancies: Tugiri Village, for example, was situated on the east bank of Lake Kutubu, a long way from its own garden and sago swamp territories to the east and southwest. They had chosen the social and dietary convenience of being on the Lake to the isolation of locating their longhouse close to their horticultural resources (these same considerations ultimately led them to put pressure on the territory of Hegeso Village, which was closer at hand to them and which contained additional sago swamp areas). But in most cases, each village territory contains within its borders ample resources of all types of major importance to Foi subsistence.

This distribution of ecological variation is replicated at the clan level, the largest *nominal* land-controlling unit in the area, and my use of the qualifier *nominal* will be made clear shortly. Theoretically, each clan also controls all types of subsistence resource within its holdings. But here discrepancies are more common, because clans are more mobile, more variable in their size and more prone to division than are longhouse villages. (Longhouse villages came about because of the exigencies of warfare, raiding and blood feud. Their function is not so apparent these days but they nevertheless maintain a stability of regional, if not political, identity.)

The emergence of subclans is a contingent and situational occurrence in Foi and is not a uniform or defining part of Foi clan organisation. The key distinguishing feature here is that the subclans are differentiated by name. According to Charles Langlas, who worked in the Upper Mubi in the mid-1960's, this type of division occurs if the local clan 'has been large in the past, or if part of the segment is descended from an immigrant' (1974: 46–47). Under such conditions, such as occurred within the Aidobo clan of Herebo Village, intermarriage is even possible and did occur, although it elicited disapproval from some clan members.

A man and his sons, however, exercise more immediate control over specific locales and sites within clan territory, just as they exercise decisive control over the bridewealth of their daughters and sisters. These individual 'lines' – and the Foi call them *ira*, meaning 'tree' and which I have previously glossed as 'lineages' – are differentiated by the territory they inhabit, exploit and control. Groups of men related as full brothers or sons of full brothers inevitably find themselves living in and exploiting contiguous areas of clan land, and thus are territorially differentiated from other more distantly related groups of agnatically-related men within the same clan. As I have argued elsewhere, a man and his grown sons are the effective resource exploitation unit in Foi society (Weiner 1986). In Hegeso, those So'onedobo clan men who inhabited territory near the 'source' of the Mubi (the place where it emerges from its underground traverse) were differentiated from those other So'onedobo men whose land was near the site of the Hegeso longhouse. The former called themselves the 'Ibuga' (*ibu*: 'water; stream; river'; *ga*: 'source, head') So'onedobo, and in fact most of these men traced their descent directly from that original group who came down from Nipa via Lake Kutubu, while the latter were known as the *a hua*, the 'longhouse' So'onedobo. There was a similar territorial differentiation made within the next largest clan in Hegeso, the Orodobo clan: there, reference was made to the 'Hesa' Orodobo, who made their homes, gardens and sago stands near the place Hesa along a stretch of the bank of the Mubi near the longhouse, while another group were called 'Yebibu' Orodobo, living somewhat further upstream. Each of these groups centred around a group of full brothers or at most full parallel cousins, and it shows that even within the clan, the local bridewealth and land-owning unit, territorial distinctions were made up of the smallest family units possible. This tendency then, has not been a response to the presence of petroleum revenues, but a mode of differentiation always inherent in Foi and Fasu social differentiation that was given an additional stimulus by the influx of oil revenue. In the 1990s, memoranda within and between both Chevron and the Department of Petroleum and Energy evinced frustration that land-owning ILGs within the Foi–Fasu area were rapidly breaking down into what appeared to be 'family' units, but which were most likely these extended lineage-like *ira*. The point I am making is that the Foi local clan traditionally had only a weakly developed form of corporate identity: those of its members who asserted control over particular tracts of land through long-term habitancy and use were its effective owners. Other clan members could dispute these effective owners' decisions concerning disposal of land, but my point is that the bigger the local clan the less successful it was in reaching clan-wide agreement as to the disposition of its resources and the more likely it was that individual men and/or sets of brothers would arrogate to themselves effective power of disposal.

Further, men kept their land-using activities if not exactly secret then certainly private. Men of the same clan were never certain as to what tracts of land or sites specific men had asserted claims to. It was a father's responsibility to take his sons around and show them all the spots where they had planted permanent tree crops, sago, and where they had set traps, so that the sons could know what spots their father had a legitimate claim to as against other men of the clan. The only time when this total catalogue of inhabited and utilised places was made public was in the public poetic recitation of place names associated with a man after his death (see Weiner 1991).

I make these points if only to suggest that caution should be exercised in assuming that the clan is by definition a corporate group and that it recognises or acts upon a commonality of interest. Clansmen were obligated to each other to provide support in bridewealth, ceremonial exchange and disputes, but the assumption of a commonality of interest is neither a necessary nor sufficient condition for this sense of obligation. The obligations had more to do with blood kinship and affinity rather than clanship as such.

The Distributional Politics of Petroleum

Petroleum is different from surface horticultural resources. Unlike bridewealth, persons and territorial resources, it is not infinitely partible nor is it evenly distributed. Its distribution was determined by the ineluctable processes of geological formation which caused the oil to become trapped within an anticlinal ridge which runs northwest to southeast in the Kikori-Mubi River area along one of Papua New Guinea's major geological fault lines. This line governs topography to a marked extent, and inevitably marks out the geographical boundaries between different language groups. The territories of the Fasu, Lower Foi and Upper Foi are divided by this anticlinal–synclinal boundary and, as luck would have it, the Lower Foi and Fasu inhabit the surface of the oil-bearing ridge while the Foi to the northeast are situated in territory atop its synclinal rise.

There are two broad political phenomena at work in the Kutubu oil project area: (1) the fissioning of revenue-receiving ILGs that I have been discussing so far; and (2) the struggle over regional representation within an area differentiated by revenue-receiving and non-revenue-receiving clans. It could be said that in the 1990s, the arguments between what are now termed the 'land-owners' (that is, incorporated land groups who own land within the PDL) and those who are not all revolved around the attempt to make the oil distribution as random and as equitably distributed as all the other resources, both human and material, which the Foi and Fasu have access to in more or less equivalent degrees.

Historically, a good number of Foi local clans throughout the Lake Kutubu and Upper Mubi River region can trace their origin to Fasu groups. Typically, in the time before colonial control, warfare, homicide, sorcery accusations and the like ultimately resulted in the departure of clans or other groups of people to new homes, sometimes outside of their linguistic territory altogether. Many Foi clans of Lake Kutubu are also connected to the Fasu through more historically proximal affinal and resulting maternal connections. Warfare and a generalised social aesthetic of compensation ensured that movement between villages and regions was a constant feature of interior Papua New Guinea life. Migration and incorporation into a host domain, including the granting of rights in territory, were normal features of local organisation throughout this broad region. Many of the disputes over landowner status within the PDL-2 and the PL-2 have revolved around a consideration of just these historical factors of movement and re-settlement.

Before the discovery of petroleum, the Foi and Fasu were not only jointly administered from Pimaga Patrol Post (as they continue to be today) but also participated (at least nominally in the case of the Fasu) in the Foe–Fasu Progress Association,[6] a non-official organisation designed broadly to promote the development interests of the region, particularly at the provincial level, where they maintained an office in Mendi. Shortly after the petroleum was discovered in Fasu territory, the Fasu abandoned the Foe–Fasu Progress Association and formed their own Namo'aporo Landowners Association, the official representative body of the Fasu petroleum land owners. By and large, its previous and newly acquired functions were coterminous, since all Fasu local clans were land-owners in this sense. The Foe Association was left to represent the Foi alone, though in this case there were many more non-landowning Foi groups than there were land-owning ones.

These land-owning clans are in receipt of a regular payment deriving from petroleum revenues. Their income is bitterly resented by those clans with the misfortune to own neither type of land and who do not share in these payments. The previous Papua New Guinea Organic Law of Provincial and Local Level Government stipulated that all royalty of this kind was to go to the provincial government within which the mining projects are located. Since royalty was redirected directly to land-owners under subsequent legislation, the major problem facing all local leaders became how to arrive at a distributive agreement that provides some participation by all local groups in the receipt of profit from the Petroleum project.

There are several ways in which land-owners within the Petroleum Development License Area 2 (PDL-2) and the oil Pipeline route (PL-2) have received benefits. First, they receive royalties on the well-head value of the petroleum. They receive from the national government a 30 percent share of the royalty paid to the Government, which is 2 percent of the well-head value. The other seventy percent of this amount goes to the Southern Highlands Provincial Government. In the original agreement, 90 percent of the land-owner portion went to the Fasu land-owners and 10 percent went to the Foi land-owners within PDL-2. By the end of 1995, about 10m kina in royalties had been paid to Foi and Fasu land-owners in PDL-2 (Power and Hagen 1996: 769).

Second, land-owners share in equity. The state, through its holding company Petroleum Resources Kutubu (PRK), originally owned a 22.5 percent equity interest in the Kutubu Project. This equity was originally distributed to both the Gulf and Southern Highlands provincial governments and to land-owners in both provinces. Thus, 12 percent of the State's 22.5 percent was originally promised to land-owners after PRK had repaid the oil developers for costs incurred during the project development (Power and Hagen 1996: 756). Of this 12 percent, 7 percent went to the land-owners in the Southern Highlands Province and the remaining 5 percent to land-owners in the Gulf Province. An additional 3 percent share of PRK holdings was allocated to land-owners following renegotiations between Government and land-owners in January 1996. As a result of this agreement, the potential equity value of the land-owner share of the Project is estimated at over 62m kina (Power and Hagen 1996: 767).

The Foi in the 1990s were gripped by a contest between the original Foe Association, claiming to be 'the mouthpiece of the Foe People', headed by Hami Yawari, Sese Vege and Nelson Kigiri, and the Foe Landowners' Association, led by Nixon Mira of Damayu Village, which is more exclusively aligned as a land-owners' organisation and, more specifically, locates its support within Mira's own sphere of influence among Foi PDL-2 land-owners of the Damayu-Fiwaga area. The split between these two organisations began in earnest in August/September 1995 with Mira's formal attempt at the registration of the Foe Landowners' Association on 12 September. Since then, the leaders of the two organisations have been attempting to leverage support from both provincial and national politicians and government officials in the attempt to outflank each other.

Since I have been based at Hegeso Village since 1979, my first accounts of this situation came from Nelson Kigiri, a Hegeso man and an executive member of the Foe Association. This is his account of the equity division that served as a catalyst for the conflict between the two groups: of the total PRK holding, that allocated to the PDL-2 land-owners amounted to 7 percent of the total PDL-2 equity. The original equity arrangement arrived at in 1991–92 allocated this 7 percent to the Southern Highlands Province land-owners in the following manner: the Fasu received 5.4 percent, the Lower Foi received 1 percent and the Upper Foi received 0.6 percent. The advantage of the Lower Foi is explained by the share of equity they receive as pipeline land-owners as well as PDL land-owners. In late 1995 the so-called Kutubu Review took place. The National government increased the 7 percent to 10 percent. Of this 3 percent increase, 1.5 percent went to the Fasu, and 1.5 percent went to the Foi. Hami Yawari, then the Secretary of the Foe Association, in a meeting of 12 February 1997 which I attended, referred to an undated Memorandum of Agreement which was signed by him and the late Henry Kapi Nato of the Namo'aporo Landowners Association, agreeing to divide the additional 3 percent equity granted by the national government to the land-owners between the Foi and Fasu.[7]

In the discussion held on 12 February 1997 two Upper Foi ILG representatives, Thomas Kapi and Kai Daima, observed that the Lower Foi have only twenty land-owning ILGs, while the Upper Foi have sixty-four. They sought to make a division of the additional 1.5 percent which favoured the Upper Foi and which was designed to rectify what they perceived was the inequity engendered by the differing numbers of land-owners in the two regions (the point being that the less numerous Lower Foi land-owners were sharing a greater portion of wealth than the more numerous Upper Foi land-owners). Hami Yawari made the point at that meeting that it was the responsibility of the Foe Association to vote on the distribution of this 1.5 percent. The land-owners have to all agree to it to make the distribution binding. If they disagree, they still have to come together to alter it.

Hami Yaware is from Gesege Village at Lake Kutubu, has historically recent maternal kin connections with a Fasu land-owning clan, and can thus consider himself an oil land-owner himself. Yet in the meeting he seemed to support distribution of equity income to non-land-owning Foi clans. At one point he said:

> If a man kills a marsupial, all the men who went hunting share. The marsupial is the equity money. For the eighty-four landowning ILGs, there is no problem, they all eat. But it's not right that some men eat only bone and skin and the others eat the flesh. All must share all the parts equally. It's not fair that the Lower Foi, who are few in number, receive much more than the Upper Foi, who are numerous. That would be like us eating the bone and skin while the Lower Foi eat all the meat.

The marsupial is the equity money, Hami Yawari said. Sixty-four Upper Foi ILG's and twenty Lower Foi ILG's are involved as either well-head or pipeline land-owners. In the event that an agreement is made by a group of land-owners to redistribute equity, if even one ILG does not sign the agreement, they may bring legal action against the other land-owners. Therefore, he said, the Foe Association cannot make these kinds of decisions in a meeting such as this. They cannot decide to give non-PDL land-owners a share of the equity in this meeting. It is a matter for all the eighty-four Foi land-owning ILGs to get together and decide unanimously. However, the executive then went ahead and proposed a vote on several alternative distributions. Hami Yawari suggested that the division could be 1.1 percent to the Upper Foi, and 0.4 percent to the Lower Foi. A representative from a non-PDL-2 landowning Lake Kutubu Village suggested 1percent for the Upper Foi and 0.5 percent for the Lower Foi. The actual distribution approved was 1.3 percent for the Upper Foi and 0.2 percent for the Lower Foi.

As I have noted, the Lower Foi who are also PDL land-owners receive both pipeline revenue and PDL entitlements, while those outside the PDL still receive entitlements by virtue of being pipeline route land-owners. But when the pipeline revenues were handed out, some of the Lake Kutubu Upper Foi groups who are pipeline route land-owners were left out, and so they felt they had been cheated out of what is their due – this primarily affected Tugiri and Yo'obo Villages at Lake Kutubu. The *kaunsils* of these two villages, Kai Daima (Tugiri) and Thomas Kapi (Yo'obo) made this complaint, and so they opposed any distribution to non-land-owners. Nelson Kigiri's point was that through the Foe Association, non-land-owners like himself and Manitage Yamabo of Barutage Village fought on behalf of the entire Foi area to get the equity percentage raised. Now some of the Foi land-owners wished to exclude the non-landowning clans from the distribution.

What we see here is the same kind of tussle over decision-making that has always characterised intra-clan arguments over control of clan resources at Lake Kutubu: it is true that the clan *should* act collectively in matters of land and property disposal, but *in fact*, those persons residing on and exploiting a piece of land have the last word. It is also important to recognise that in these public encounters that revolve around dispute over distribution, what appears as an attempt to achieve unanimity in decision-making invariably involves the renunciation of conflicting claims by one or more parties (see also Goldman 1983 for an account of similar processes in Huli land disputes). In the same vein, corporatisation might call for Western-style collective decision making, but in the absence of a culture of representation as such, oppositions emerging from differences in control, access and disposition of resource are likely to govern whatever further distribution of revenue land-owners make, just as is the case of resource disputes internal to the clan.

Shortly after this meeting, on 27 February, a different meeting was held by Bai Waiba (Wasemi) and Nixon Mira (Damayu), rivals of Hami Yawari also including land-owners representatives. No executive members of the Foe Association were in attendance, but nevertheless the claim was made that it was speaking for fifty-three land-owning Foi ILGs, though Nixon's area of immediate control includes about thirty of these groups, from Fiwaga, Damayu, Gena'abo and Ibutaba Villages in eastern Foi. At this meeting, at which Chevron company personnel from their External Affairs department were in attendance, a decision was made to divide the 1.5 percent as follows: The Upper Foi, most of whom are not land-owners, were given 1 percent of that equity, while the remaining 0.5 percent was allocated to the Lower Foi. Of the 1 percent granted to the Upper Foi, 0.6 percent was granted to non-PDL land-owners, while 0.4 percent was retained by PDL land-owners among the Upper Foi. At this point I am still not sure which division became the official one or whether indeed any of these decisions were legal in any binding sense. At any rate, it is the decision making process that governs rhetorical confrontations during these encounters which is of more interest to us for the moment.

The faction headed most visibly by Nixon Mira, representing about half of the Foi land-owners, wants a specifically land-owner representative organisation. The other group, representing through the Foe Association most of the Foi villages, is led by Hami Yawari, Sese Vege and Nelson Kigiri, and seeks to continue the Foe Association's charter as the Foi people's official political body. But in both venues, the numerically more numerous Upper Foi forced a redistribution of revenue to which the Lower Foi land-owners were technically exclusively entitled. Historically, the more numerous Upper Foi have always asserted themselves at the expense of their more remote and less numerous Lower Foi neighbours to the south. In the 1990s, and given that some of the Lower Foi are involved as PDL land-owners in their own separate project area at the Gobe field, this resulted in the establishment of a separate Lower Foi land-owner association, the Fukigi Association (the business arm of the Lower Foi land-owners, Tiate Eboda, was also a response to what the Lower Foi perceived to be their lack of executive and shareholder power within Foe Digaso Oil Company, which nominally had been the business arm of the Foe Association but is now restricted to the Upper Foi. The Namo'aporo Landowners Association is similarly linked to the company Iagifu Oil and Gas). In the 1990s we witnessed new, putatively representative organisations such as the Foe Association becoming transmuted into more traditional forms of oppositional and fragmentational social life, because the *Land Group Incorporation Act* enshrines the oppositional culture of clan fragmentation in its own constitution. What this has led to in the Kutubu oil project area is the percolation of land-owner values and loyalties into local and regional politics on a much wider scale than was previously the case in this area.

What might be more desirable, however, is the encapsulation and limitation of land-owner custom so as to allow new forms of democratic, representative culture to fill the expanding political domain. A hypothesis worth pursuing is that more contemporary, representative organisations such as political and land-owner associations are not as subject to fragmentation as more traditional land- and genealogical-based social units such as clans. This is because such associations are founded on a commonality of interest. The clan, however, is not a unit in which commonality of interest is a political underpinning. Its conventions of association are, as I have suggested earlier, only tacit, and are subject to the oppositional manoeuvres of its members.

It is important to understand that the landowning ILGs have interests which are distinct from that of their villages, as politico-residential units. Each village sends a *komiti*, to the Foe Association, but it is the landowning ILGs and not the villages per se, which are represented by Nixon Mira's Foe Landowners' Association. Only two of the men who attended the Foe Association as representatives of their villages also signed their names to Nixon Mira's petition of incorporation for the Foe Landowners' Association as ILG representatives. It is reasonable to consider that members of the revenue-receiving ILGs may feel that they have a stake in both organisations and feel that there is room for both in the total landscape of political functions in the Kutubu Oil Project Area. It is evidently important for the national government to maintain this distinction as well, in the interests of trying to distribute petroleum revenue as equitably and as widely as possible throughout the project impact area. Company and Government encouragement in this direction might prove to have some surprising results.

A final observation I would like to make in this regard is this: if land-owner values affected the development of representative bodies in the oil project Area, the reverse influence is also possible: clans could theoretically become more representative, and achieve a more communal function. Thus, at Wasemi, with the stimulus of a powerful and influential local leader, Bai Waiba, three So'onedobo subclans decided to incorporate as a single ILG, contrary to the trend already identified in the area. Further, a superficial inspection of the Foi ILG lists indicates that nearly all of the separate registration of so-called subclans has occurred in Damayu and Fiwaga villages, where Nixon Mira has his support. It could be that Mira was trying to inflate his nominal representational base, and there are indications that both he and Hami Yawari were engaged in this competitive accumulation of 'on paper' numerical support in their search for provincial and national political allies. The confluence of leadership, representation, and the development of a culture of communal interest needs more careful monitoring in the future.

Some Final Observations

What this comparison of very different yet also procedurally very similar attempts at achieving a convention of distribution leads to is a comment on the different way in which the local groups at Lake Kutubu articulate the relationship between relationality and life activity. Bridewealth accumulation and distribution is a social activity 'from the ground up'. Foi men are actively engaged in it as life activity from the point of acquisition. It is therefore not discontinuous with all of the other life activities they are also simultaneously enmeshed in, which are also social activities with social consequences. As a result, the conventional pressure to keep as many people involved in the affair of bridewealth distribution is great, as many people can claim to be co-engaged with this variegated range of activities from the point of view of the main participants. Participation in conversation, which the Foi see primarily as verbal exchange, and participation in bridewealth transaction, which is exchange of another sort, are central to the task of social distribution upon which Foi place a central value.

With petroleum, however, the situation is markedly different. Here we have a resource the collection of which is not undertaken by the Foi themselves, but by a foreign company and their personnel. The collection of the oil as such is invisible to the Foi and not articulated with their local social activity. It can much more readily be seen in its more important manifestation, that is, in the form of regular royalty payments to which land-owners are entitled. But by that token, it is more 'alienated' and external to their lives, first because the Foi only see and control it in its cash form, and secondly, the *komitis* cannot exercise control over its distribution. This was not the case with the bridewealth *komitis*: they could legislate an alteration in the size, composition and distribution of bridewealth across the Foi area (whether there was any way in which they could enforce this agreement was another matter; people of the villages represented by each *komiti* accepted that they had the prerogative to enter into such agreements on their behalf).

Another point I'd like to pursue here concerns the metaphor between public debate and argumentation over the issue of distribution per se, and the role that distributive mechanisms play in a more broadly viewed social mechanism. The impression on the part of the developer was that an intolerable amount of time was spent at various meetings of land-owners and land-owner representatives arguing again and again over the same issues. I suggest that this can be explained as a distributive mechanism in its own right. In a society still dominated by the oral form of language, in which the written word is still the prerogative of only a privileged few, the public forum is the only place where people can make their opinions known and assess the state of their leaders' intentions and knowledge. It is important to view these often interminable and repetitive encounters as part of what we could analogously label the exercise of local democracy, for everyone has the right to express him- or herself on these occasions. Indeed, they must in order for any consensus to achieve some amount of efficacy. Thus, the bringing to public awareness of these mechanisms of important distributive mechanisms like marriage choices and bridewealth, and subjecting them to conscious manipulation must play some role in the mechanisms themselves, especially when such distributions will ultimately have subsistence and residential consequences for people.

It could be that the division between land-owning and non-land-owning ILGs within the Foe Association will prove to be too great to overcome by appeals to still visible regional, linguistic and cultural cohesiveness, and that the Foi ILGs who are petroleum revenue recipients will realise that their political future is more closely aligned with the Fasu than with the other Foi clans. Some indication that this might be the case emerged in the 'Petrokina' affair. The leader of the Fasu land-owners attempted to replace the current government equity holding body for the Kutubu land-owners, Petroleum Resources Kutubu (PRK), with his own holding company, to be called Petrokina. Part of garnering support for this move involved offering representatives of the Foi PDL-2 land-owners a higher percentage of royalty payments (currently, Fasu ILGs within PDL-2 receive 90 percent of royalty;

Foi ILGs receive 10 percent. The Fasu leader offered to increase the Foi land-owners' share to 40 percent). In any case, the Petrokina move, which was a direct challenge to government management of equity holding through their Minerals Resource Development Corporation (MRDC), failed, and equity for all Kutubu area land-owners remains managed through PRK. However, the control of PRK will remain a target for those who are now competing for sole representational power within the oil project area: in early 1998, it was the stake in Yawari's and Mira's competition for ascendancy among the Foi.

I maintain that what an earlier generation of anthropologists used to refer to as the 'plasticity' and 'lability' of New Guinea kinship have very real distributive and regulative effects on human behaviour vis-à-vis the environment. Modjeska, speaking of the Duna lineage, said:

> Lineage organisation is not simply an effect of the ideological validation of certain pre-existing genealogical ties and distributions of people. Rather, it is a matter of actively creating certain ties and securing others through the exchange of pigs against rights in people, as well as the continuing validation of relations between men within the lineage through reciprocal 'helping'. (1982: 103)

With respect to the present topic, in *The Heart of the Pearl Shell* (1988) I suggested that the coupling of bridewealth inflation and rising population had a qualitative effect on Foi kinship: because there was more bridewealth to obtain, men had to go to more distant relatives for aid in amassing it, and consequently, when their own daughters and sisters married, men had a wider circle of other men to whom they were indebted and to whom they had to reciprocate. This put pressure on formerly 'close' relatives to be actively involved in support and nurturance of children so that they could cement a claim to their bridewealth when they married. The agreement that the bridewealth *komitis* reached in their 1980 meeting was consistent with this emerging recognition of the collapsing of kinship into parentage, something which always modelled Foi kinship but which never totally defined it. The point is both that anyone can 'become' a relative by evincing the proper nurturative and cooperating behaviour towards others, and that the distribution of important tokens of social reproductivity were distributed as widely as possible despite the countervailing tendencies to narrow the social field of recipients. The lability of Foi local clans and the strongly bilateral features of Foi clanship assured that large clans would not place undue pressure on their own resources but would in a pinch have access to that of others.

The 1974 *Land Group Incorporation Act* had no effect on the Foi until the discovery of petroleum. The Foi were then forced to adhere to the convention of incorporation in order to be in a position to deal with both the government and Chevron Niugini.[8] The effect of this is to rigidify the boundaries of a social entity whose most centrally important feature was its porousness and flexibility. The appeals to clan 'solidarity' were always only chiefly rhetorical, since more dispute occurred within the clan than between them. The Foi Incorporated Land Group will find it harder to maintain this porousness which was always a hedge against the intractability of disputes, the porousness that maintained the strength of distributive mechanisms of all sorts. Under the conditions of late twentieth century nationhood in Papua New Guinea, it seems likely that such regulatory and distributive mechanisms will be transferred onto various administrative bodies, both official and quasi-official, of the national and provincial governments, and outside of the primary local arenas of Foi social consciousness. The understandable and legitimate tendency of both Government and Company is to want to deal with land-owner representatives and to turn community and area management as such back over to local and provincial government agencies. But the exigencies of distributive mechanisms I have touched on briefly here, and the pressures on land-owning groups to share income widely within the oil project area, will ensure that this is a difficult if not downright quixotic goal.

Acknowledgements

My thanks to Tony Power, Colin Filer, Chris Warrilow, Mick McWalter, Tim Rowse and the members of the Resource Management in Asia-Pacific Project seminar (RSPAS, ANU) for comments and corrections on this paper.

Notes

1. Despite experiencing an influenza epidemic in the early 1950s, the Foi population has tripled since that time.
2. I employ the term 'non-land-owner' in this context to refer to those groups within the oil project impact area who are at the same time not entitled to petroleum revenues of any type.
3. In this regard, I expand on the recommendation made by Taylor and Whimp (1997: 103).
4. See Strathern (1988).
5. See Wagner (1981).
6. Officially, the Foi spell their name 'Foe', which was the original spelling employed by Murray Rule, the linguist/missionary who first transcribed their language by way of English orthography. I therefore use the term 'Foi' to refer to the culturally distinct language group I have been studying since 1979, and 'Foe' in all the contexts which the Foi themselves use this term as official self-designation.
7. Hami Yawari was elected Regional Member of Parliament for the Southern Highlands Province in the last Papua New Guinea national election.
8. This meeting was chaired by John Giheno and attended by representatives of the Department of Petroleum and Energy.
9. Burton (1991) refers to as 'cadastral' units which come into existence as a result of legislation that identifies them and grants them an interest and function, as is the case with Incorporated Land Groups in resource extraction zones in Papua New Guinea.

   It is ironic that the model of the corporate descent group, for so long a mainstay in the anthropological rationalisation of non-Western social units in places like Papua New Guinea, should be now reintroduced into the ethnographic landscape on behalf of and with the cooperation of New Guineans themselves. During the 1970s anthropologists working in New Guinea, such as Wagner (1974), Strathern (1972) and Kelly (1977), adduced evidence that led to the successful critique of this British social anthropological model and catapulted the social anthropology of Melanesian societies to the forefront of theoretical advance during this period.

References

Brison, K. 1992. *Just Talk: Gossip, Meetings, and Power in a Papua New Guinea Village.* Berkeley: University of California Press.

Burton, J. 1991. 'Social Mapping'. In: P. Larmour (ed.), *Customary Land Tenure: Registration and Decentralisation in Papua New Guinea.* Waigana, Papua New Guinea: IASER Monograph no. 29.

Filer, C. 1997. 'Compensation, Rent and Power in Papua New Guinea'. In: S. Toft (ed.), *Compensation for Resource Development in Papua New Guinea.* Canberra: Law Reform Commission of Papua New Guinea *et al.*

Goldman, L. 1983. *Talk Never Dies.* London: Tavistock.

Kelly, R. 1977. *Etoro Social Structure.* Ann Arbor: University of Michigan Press.

Langlas, C. 1974. 'Foi Land Use, Prestige Economics, and Residence: A Processual Analysis'. Ph.D. thesis. University of Hawaii.

Merlan, F. and A. Rumsey 1991. *Ku Waru: Language and Segmentary Politics in the Western Nebilyer Valley, Papua New Guinea.* Cambridge: Cambridge University Press.

Modjeska, N. 1982. 'Production and Inequality: Perspectives from Central New Guinea'. In: A. Strathern (ed.), *Inequality in New Guinea Highlands Societies.* Cambridge: Cambridge University Press.

National CBNRM Forum Botswana 2000. *Proceedings of the Second National CBNRM Conference in Botswana, 14th–16th of November 2001 and CBNRM Status Report 2001.* Gaborone, Botswana and The Hague, The Netherlands: SNV/Netherlands Development Organization.

Nico, R. (ed.) 2001. Community Based Tourism in Botswana: The SNV Experience in Three Community-Tourism Projects. Gaborone, Botswana and the Hague, The Netherlands: SNV/Netherlands Development Organization.

Power, A. and P. Hagen 1996. 'The Escalation of Landowner Benefits in the Kutubu Petroleum Development Project'. In P. Buchanan (ed.), *Petroleum Exploration, Development and Production in Papua New Guinea: Proceedings of the Third PNG Petroleum Convention.* Sydney.

Strathern, A. 1972. *One Father, One Blood.* London: Tavistock.

—— 1975. 'Veiled Speech in Mount Hagen'. In: M. Bloch (ed.), *Political Language and Oratory in Traditional Society.* London: Academic Press.

Strathern, M. 1974. 'Managing Information: The Problems of a Dispute Settler (Mt. Hagen).' In: A.L. Epstein (ed.), *Contention and Dispute: Aspects of Law and Social Control in Melanesia.* Canberra: Australian National University Press.

—— 1988. *The Gender of the Gift.* Berkeley: University of California Press.

Taylor, M. and K. Whimp 1997. Report on Land Issues and Hydrocarbon Framework Study. Report made to the Asian Development Bank.

Wagner, R. 1974. 'Are there social groups in the New Guinea Highlands?'. In: M. Leaf (ed.), *Frontiers of Anthropology.* New York: Van Nostrand Company.

—— 1981. *The Invention of Culture.* Chicago: University of Chicago Press.

—— 1998. 'Environment and the Reproduction of Human Focality'. In: S. Bamford (ed.), *Identity, Nature and Culture. Social Analysis,* 42(3): 55–66.

Weiner, J. 1986. 'The Social Organization of Foi Silk Production: The Anthropology of Marginal Development'. *Journal of the Polynesian Society,* 85(4): 421–39.

—— 1988. *The Heart of the Pearl Shell.* Berkeley: University of California Press.

—— 1991. *The Empty Place.* Bloomington, IN: Indiana University Press.

10

Sharing the Land: Kalahari San Property Rights and Resource Management

Robert K. Hitchcock

Introduction

A common assumption about property rights among hunting-gathering peoples, including the San of the Kalahari Desert region of southern Africa, is that access to land was relatively equitable and that hunter-gatherers, like other indigenous peoples, 'shared the land' with one another (Johnson and Earle 1987; Durning 1992). Having access to the land or territories of other groups was seen as part of a system of reciprocity necessary to the long-term survival of groups and individuals. Ethnographic research among foraging groups that have been described as egalitarian, however, reveals that in fact individuals and groups had differential access to land and resources, depending on a whole series of variables, including kinship, age, social and marital status, language group affiliation, and personal and group identity.

Among the San of southern Africa, property rights are tied up with what can be described as 'territories.' The San territorial unit is known as a *gu* (G/wi), *g!u* (G//ana), *n!ore* (Ju/'hoan), *no* (Kua), *n//olli* (!Xo), or *nong* (Nharo). The importance of territoriality among San has been emphasised by a number of researchers and development workers (see, for example, Marshall 1976: 71–2, 93, 103, 131–32, 184, 187–89; Yellen 1977: 37–41, 54–64; Lee 1979: 58–61, 117–19, 334; Wilmsen 1989: 168-86; Albertson 1998, 2000). Among the San, a territory is an area over which local people have rights of access and resource use. It is usually a named unit of land that contains natural resources upon which people depend, including water, wild plants, trees for shade, fuel wood, and construction, and materials used in the manufacturing of tools and other goods. In general, the size of the territory is based on the types and amounts of resources it contains, which theoretically at least should be sufficient to meet the needs of a group in an average year.

Research among hunter-gatherer and part-time foraging societies carried out in the past several decades has suggested that there is tremendous diversity in these societies (Lee and DeVore 1968; Woodburn 1968, 1979; Kelly 1995). Significant theoretical insights have been provided by James Woodburn, who has examined the degree to which there is equality in hunter-gatherer societies and how these societies have been affected by interactions with non-foraging peoples (see Woodburn 1982, 1988, 1998). Today, foraging societies are seen as complex entities that employ diverse strategies to survive. Many if not most foraging societies have common property resource management (CPRM) systems. This is not to say, however, that every foraging society or group manages land communally. As will be shown in this chapter, land management and land use among foraging and former foraging societies is diverse, and the ways in which people manage their land and resources varies tremendously both regionally and within specific territorial areas. While land is often held by a kinship-based collective, individuals within that collective do sometimes have rights over specific portions of land, and they often use these areas of land to their own advantage.

The Ju/'hoansi of the Northern Kalahari

The Ju/'hoansi of northwestern Botswana and northeastern Namibia are some of the best known populations on the planet. The Ju/'hoansi, sometimes referred to as the !Kung, are northern Bush-speaking peoples who have been studied for over fifty years by anthropologists (Marshall 1976; Lee and DeVore 1976; Lee 1979; Wiessner 1977; Wilmsen 1989; Biesele 1993; Hitchcock et al. 1996; Lee et al. 1996). Unlike some of the more popular conceptions of the Ju/'hoansi and other San, the peoples of the northern Kalahari are diverse in their adaptations and land and resource management strategies. They have what can be described as a mixed economic system, combining foraging with food production and income generation. They engage extensively in trade and exchange with other groups, and they often work in the formal sector of the southern African economy as miners, herders, truck drivers, road builders, and domestic workers. They also trade on their traditional skills, performing dances, taking tourists on gathering and hunting trips, and selling crafts that they produce for the global market.

As some San and other groups in Botswana and Namibia have noted, there has been a struggle for the land for hundreds of years in southern Africa. Some of these struggles have been between foraging and food-producing societies; there has also been competition within foraging societies for land, especially in those areas where population densities were relatively high. In the colonial period, land was allocated among nonlocal people, with Europeans being given blocks of land, for example, in the Ghanzi Ridge region of Botswana in the late nineteenth century and Afrikaner and German farmers and others gaining rights over land in the Gobabis and Tsumeb Blocks of Namibia. After independence in Botswana, land was allocated to other groups besides the Ju/'hoansi in Ngamiland (North West District), including Batawana and Herero (Lee 1979; Hitchcock et al. 1996). As these changes in land tenure and land use took place, the Ju/'hoansi and other San sought to formalize their rights to land and natural resources. One way that the Ju/'hoansi did this was to reassess their traditional concepts of territoriality and to adapt their land tenure and use principles to contemporary realities.

As informants note, San territories are roughly circular or elliptical areas of land with largely unmarked but known and understood borders. People maintain knowledge about these territories, and they exchange information concerning their statuses. San territories are units of land that also contain sacred sites – the graves of people's kin, places where rituals took place, and localities that have spiritual significance. They are, in other words, the 'homelands' or 'countries' of groups of people.

From a social standpoint, San territories are areas to which people belong, and where they say they are from. The territories are the units of stewardship and management in both a spiritual and material sense. In the past, San, like other former foraging peoples, had clearly defined genealogical ties to areas where they resided and earned their livelihoods. In some cases, people inherited rights to these areas from one or the other or both parents. Leadership was linked to stewardship of the resources of each territory by a core group of siblings. Among San groups, generally there was an elderly man or woman from this core group who was known as the 'owner' (master). This individual, or sometimes several people, had guardianship but not authority over the resources of the area in question. It was this individual from whom permission had to be sought to enter the territory and utilise its resources.

As Marshall (1976: 72) notes, a key feature of Ju/'hoan San territoriality is the possession of resources. Resources in the territories generally were shared among the members of the land-holding group. But it should be stressed that access to the various areas within the territorial units varied according to a number of criteria, including the closeness of association that an individual had with the core group or individual who oversaw the land, the length of time that a person and his or her family had resided in the area, and the place where the person resided.

Within Ju/'hoan territories, the land was subdivided into residential areas, places for hunting or gathering, and places that might be considered no-person's land – areas that were shared between two contiguous territories. The subdivided areas were associated with subunits of the larger group such as families. There are also localities where what some called 'special resources' were found, – places where there were groves of mongongo (*Ricinodendron rautanenii*) trees, patches of morama vines (*Tylosema esculentum*) or baobab (*Adansonia digitata*) trees that were sometimes claimed by individuals or nuclear families. This was the case, for example, with the mongongo groves of Dobe /Oa, north of Dobe in western Ngamiland, Botswana (Yellen 1977: 55, map 4). In the Dobe area in the 1960s, the average range size was 320 km^2 (Yellen 1977:

54). Individuals and groups moved around in these areas, and they crossed into the territories of other groups on both sides of the Botswana–Namibia border. It was not unusual for individuals or families to move into other people's territories, something that was done relatively frequently, depending on what they were doing and whether or not they had kinship or other kinds of connections with the people residing in those territories.

The sharing of resource areas associated with territories is organised along lines of kinship, historical association, and specific local resource availability. In times of stress such as during drought periods, the boundaries of these territories were often observed to a greater degree than in periods of high rainfall and production. Under stress, land and resource sharing became more restricted, and the numbers of people from the outside who would be given access to the areas were limited, if not restricted completely.

The rights of Ju/'hoan territory sub-unit owners are understood to include the right of permanent, exclusive utilisation and occupation. Resource access rights were determined by decisions made by individuals on the basis of their assessment of the conditions of the resource base, the density of resource users, and the kinds of strategies people were employing. It was more likely, for instance, that people who pursued a foraging lifestyle would be allowed access to a resource area than those who possessed livestock and who wished to bring their domestic animals with them. Thus, decisions about resource access were not based on the assumption of equity but rather on an assessment of the environmental, social, economic, and political conditions that exist at the time and on the basis of people's identity and their kinship, marital, economic, historical, cultural, ideological and other linkages.

Among the Ju/'hoansi of northwestern Botswana and northeastern Namibia, a *n!ore (*plural: *n!oresi)* is a named place containing various natural resources (see Figure 10.1). Some *n!oresi* are residential while others are used only for hunting and gathering. Each residential *n!ore* has one or more 'eating

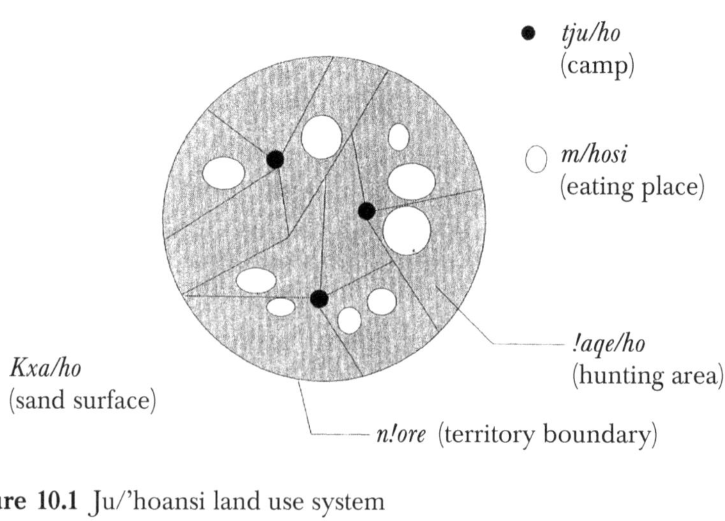

Figure 10.1 Ju/'hoansi land use system

Table 10.1 Community trusts in Botswana's Northwest District and conservancies in Namibia's Tsumkwe District that are involved in integrated conservation and development activities

Name of trust and founding date	Controlled hunting, area, size km^2	Composition of population, size	Project activities
Jakotsha Community Trust, 1999	NG 24: 530 km^2	Mbukushu, Herero and G//anikwe San, 10,000 people, multiple villages	Community tourism, makoro (canoe) poling, basketry and other craft sales
Khwaai Community Trust, 2000	NG 18: 1,815 km^2 and NG 19: 180 km^2	Bugakwe San, Tawana, and Subiya 360 people, 1 village	Ecotourism, craft sales, work at safari lodges, auctioning off of a portion of the hunting quota
Mababe Zukutsama Community Trust, 1998	NG 41: 2,045 km^2	Tsegakhwe San, 400 people, 1 village	Ecotourism, leased out some of the hunting quota to a safari company
N=a Jaqna conservancy, 2002	Tsumkwe District West, 8,457 km^2	!Xun, Mpungu, and Vasekela San, 4,500 people, 24 villages	Ecotourism, leased community-based campsite at Omatako Valley
Nyae Nyae Conservancy, 1998	Nyae Nyae area, Tsumkwe District East, 9,003 km^2	Ju/'hoansi San, 2,200 people, 37 villages	Community-based tourism and safari hunting
Okavango Community Trust, 1999	NG 22: 580 km^2 NG 23: 540 km^2	Bugakwe, Bayei, Hamubkushu, G//anikwe, Dxeriku, BaTawana, 2,200 people, 5 villages	Safari hunting and photo-based tourism
Sankuyo Tshwaragano Management Trust (STMT), 1995	NG 34: 870 km^2	Bayeei and Basubiya, 345 people, 1 village	Ecotourism, safari hunting concession, craft sales, campsite
Teemashane Community Trust, 1999	NG 10 and NG 11: ca. 800 km^2	Mbukushu, Bayei Bugakwe San, G//anikwe San, 5,000 people	Community tourism, campsite, cultural trail, craft sales
/Xai/Xai Tlhabololo Trust, 1997	NG 4: 9,293 km^2 NG 5: 7.623 km^2 (16,966 km2 total)	Ju/'hoansi San, Mbanderu, 40 people, 1 village	Leasing out of portion of quota, crafts, community tourism

Source: Data obtained from Hitchcock et al. (1996); National CBNRM Forum in Botswana (2001); Rozemeijer (2001) and from fieldwork

places' ('*m/hosi)*, which may or may not be shared with contiguous *n!oresi.* A residential *n!ore* also has an associated 'hunting place' (*!aqe/ho*) or direction of usual hunting. These hunting areas are sometimes shared with nearby residential *n!oresi.* Where 'eating places' ('*m/hosi)* are shared, each *n!ore*'s inhabitants has a special, but ultimately non-exclusive, relationship to the portion of the '*m/ho* closest to their *tju/ho* (village). This portion is called a *q/ani,* defined as 'the gathering area that is behind you,' in the sense of 'in your back yard.' As one informant stated in June, 1992 in response to questioning about exclusive rights to resources in his *q/ani:* 'Look, even if bush food is in my back yard, it doesn't belong to me alone; it belongs to all of us.' The rights of *n!ore* owners are understood to include the right of permanent, exclusive possession, with resource access modified by flexible, environmentally modulated sharing with associated neighbours (Megan Biesele, personal communication).

There are two key concepts of land tenure and resource use in the Ju/'hoan *n!ore* system. These are (1) *n!ore* rights and (2) the right of the *kxa/ho* (the larger land area of the region known as Nyae Nyae in Namibia under which *n!ores* are subsumed). The *kxa/ho* (literally, 'sand surface') is all of the land traditionally inhabited by the Ju/'hoansi and all of its water, bushfoods, game, grazing, wood, minerals, and other natural resources. In the past, the Ju/'hoan region extended from what is now the Ghanzi District in western Botswana north to approximately the Tsodilo Hills in Botswana and from an area not far from the Okavango Swamps (Kauri) west to the area around Tjum!kui (Tsumkwe) in Namibia, now the sub-district capital of Tsumkwe District in Otjozondjupa Region (see Figure 10.2). Portions of the ancestral Ju/'hoan territory were lost as a result of decisions by the colonial and post-colonial administrations of Southwest Africa (now Namibia) and

Table 10.2 Data on the N!oresi (traditional territories) of the Dobe area, Ngamiland, Botswana

Name of N!ore	Size km^2	N!ore kxau ('owner')
Chercheraha	144	N?/a
/'Aosha	57	Syndicate (N/haoakxa, Debe, Kxao +Oma)
/'Arin//aho	40	Syndicate (N/haoakxa, Debe, Kxao =Oma)
G/hij'Ahn	244	/Ui /Kaece (manager)
!'Ubi	230	/Ui /Kaece (manager)
N/oa/ho	106	Komtshaa Kha//'au, Boo Kommtsa
N'Abi/hi	–	Not mapped
Dobe	320	Not mapped
Totals: 8 locations (7 mapped)	1,141 km^2 (average size = 163 km^2)	

Source: Data obtained from Albertson (1998) and from Yellen (1977: 54)

Bechuanaland (now Botswana). For example, the Kaudum Game Reserve was declared as a conservation area in Namibia in 1986, an area of some 3,840 km². The government of Southwest Africa also allocated the southern portion of the Ju/'hoan ancestral territory to Herero in 1969 as part of the land rationalization efforts aimed at institutionalising *apartheid* (separate development) in the country.

Figure 10.2 Map showing the Ju/'hoan region

Based on interview data of Ju/'hoansi done in 1987, 1992, 1995, and 2001, the right of the *kxa/ho* is usually exercised in the following ways: (1) the right to drink the waters of the land, particularly in times of drought; (2) the right to travel freely through the land, and to obtain water, hunt, and gather while on the journey; (3) the right to shoot and follow wounded game anywhere in the land; and (4) the right to gather key bush foods anywhere; these include mongongo nuts (*Ricinodendron rautanenii*) and morama beans (*Tylosema esculenta).* Anyone who speaks the Ju/'hoan language and refers to him- or herself as Ju/'hoan is assumed to possess the right of the *kxa/ho.* As one Ju/'hoan man put it, the *n!ore* right and the right of the *kxa/ho* 'have kept the peace among us and served us well.'

The approximately 17,000 Ju/'hoansi of the northwestern Kalahari region have built on these principles in their management of land and resources, and they have used the *n!ore* system as a basis for making land claims in both Botswana and Namibia. With the possible exception of the G/ui and G//ana San, whose lands were protected until recently by the Central Kalahari Game Reserve, the Ju/'hoansi are the San people who have been able to retain the largest portion of their ancestral lands, some 15 per cent.

One of the strategies for coping with drought and climatic uncertainty employed by the Ju/'hoansi was to request permission to move to another group's territory which had sufficient resources to sustain a larger number of people. Usually people asked permission to visit the territories of people with whom they already had social ties, such as those created through marriage (affinal ties) or ones that came about through trade partnerships. In most instances, if the territory 'owners' felt that there were enough resources available in their area, they gave permission for the other people to enter. There were cases, however, when permission was refused, especially in times of extreme drought or when there were other kinds of problems affecting the area, such as die-offs of wildlife and livestock due to diseases such as rinderpest or lungsickness (contagious bovine pleuropneumonia, CBPP). This was said to have been the case in the central Nyae Nyae region in the early part of the twentieth century, for example, around 1933, when a lengthy drought saw large areas affected, so much so, according to Ju/'hoansi informants, that even the large trees along dried-out fossil river beds died off.

Many San employ creative social strategies to deal with potential resource access problems. One such strategy found among the Ju/'hoansi is what is known as *hxaro* (Wiessner 1977: 118ff.). Ju/'hoansi could establish a fictive kinship or genealogical bond through a system of exchanging goods. There is also naming system in which all of the people with the same name are considered kin and thus can be called upon to provide assistance (Marshall 1976: 238–42). The social ties created by the reciprocal although not always equal material goods exchanges and the name-relationship system were important because they facilitated the sharing of information about the state of the environment in various areas; they also resulted in a widespread network of people who had mutual rights and obligations. In many ways, these systems were social mechanisms for risk-reduction. All people who had a name relationship, that is, those who shared a name, were considered to be related. As one Ju/'hoan woman put it to me in 1995, 'it created a sense of belonging.' Another Ju'hoan woman said that the name-relationship and the associations among the Ju/'hoan people through exchanges, both material and social, gave them a sense of identity that was important and comforting to them. Those people who lack these connections, ones who are from other groups, are considered by the people of the Nyae Nyae and Dobe regions to be *ju dole*, strangers.

Methods of Obtaining Land Rights in Botswana

The Ju/'hoansi have a number of different ways in which they can obtain rights to land including (1) inheritance (birth rights), (2) marital ties, (3) borrowing, and (4) clientship, where in which an individual enters a patron-client relationship and is given access to land in exchange for his or her allegiance. In some cases, individuals and groups gained access to land and resources through colonisation, the movement into an unutilised area and the establishment of occupancy. Under Tswana customary law, land and resource rights could be obtained through the investment of labour in the construction of a facility, as occurred, for example, when people dug a well or cleared a field or a residential area.

The primary way that people got land and water in the past in northwestern Botswana was through self-allocation. Beginning in the late 1940s, there were cases were Ju/'hoansi approached the Tswana wardhead (traditional Tswana leader) at !Xangwa in western Ngamiland and asked for land. In some cases, land was granted to these individuals, sometimes on the basis of an agreement that the individual or family would allow the ward head to graze his cattle in their area. According to informants, some of the people in western Ngamiland refused to go along with this stipulation, and they found themselves at odds with Tswana cattle owners.

After the passage of the Tribal Land Act in Botswana, which went into effect in 1970, people were supposed to apply to the Land Board in Maun for plots of land to be used for purposes of residence, arable use, or business. More recently, people in western Ngamiland have had to travel to Gomare where they applied for land. When asked in August, 1999 whether people in Dobe had Land Board certificates for their land, only 30 percent said that they did. The rest of the people to whom I spoke said that they had simply established their homes and gardens on their own, sometimes after having asked the local headman if they could do so. One of the reasons they did not seek Land Board approval, they pointed out, was that they usually were not granted a certificate. When Tawana Land Board members were asked why San were sometimes not given Land Board certificates, they said that it was because there was a possibility that people would be relocated to places away from the present settlements so that the wells and boreholes could be used for grazing purposes. The Land Board members went on to say that if the

Ju/'hoansi were going to be moved, there was not much point in allocating land to them.

This issue of potential resettlement is a tremendously sore point among the San of many parts of Botswana. People in the Tsodilo Hills, for example, noted in interviews that they had been relocated away from their homes close to the Hills in 1995, and that they were having to walk as much as 5–6 km to get water. In the late 1990s, San at Shaikarawe in northern Ngamiland lost their land rights briefly but appealed the decision to the Land Board and the Ministry of Local Government, Lands, and Environment with the help of DITSHWANELO, the Botswana Centre for Human Rights. They won their appeal, and they were able to move back to their land.

While some San advocacy groups felt that this was a precedent-setting case involving land rights for San, since that time other San groups have been removed from their ancestral territories to new localities, and they have been unable to regain their original land rights in spite of legal action brought before the high court of Botswana, as was the case with the G/ui and G//ana San and Bakgalagadi of the Central Kalahari Game Reserve (Hitchcock 2002).

In the 1970s, Ju/'hoan groups in western Ngamiland attempted to dig wells by hand in the hopes that they would be able to claim *de facto* rights to the water and to the surrounding grazing under Tswana customary law. In one case, a group of forty people under the leadership of Qoma Qomquasi began digging for water in 1974 at Xumxgeni (//Gum//geni), a summer water point 30 km south of /Xai/Xai. The *n!ore k'xausi* decided to prevent the digging of the well as he feared he would lose his rights to the *n!ore* (Wiessner 1977: 54–55). This particular effort resulted in land use conflict, when a man who had only vague land rights there decided to dig a well and excluded the major *n!ore k'xau* because he did not wish to work.

Another well-digging effort was initiated at Dobe by Ju/'hoansi in 1975, but when water was struck, the well was taken over by Herero. The people of Dobe attempted to get the Tawana Land Board to grant them rights over the water point and to have the Herero removed from the site but were unsuccessful. The lesson from this situation was not lost on the Ju/'hoansi, who wanted to ensure that they were able to get water and land rights from the Land Board, something that they continued to do over the next two decades.

The period 1995–96 saw major changes in northwestern Botswana as a result of a governmental decision to kill all the cattle in the region in order to contain an outbreak of lungsickness among cattle. Until that time, livestock was an importance source of subsistence (in the form of milk and meat), draft power, and income for a sizable number of households, some of them Ju/'hoansi. Over 320,000 head of cattle were destroyed, and the remains of the animals were buried in large pits that were covered over with sands. People had to turn to other methods of making a living since they could no longer depend on milk and the meat of cattle that had been dispatched or died.

As part of the disease containment effort the Botswana Ministry of Agriculture and North West District officials also constructed additional veterinary cordon fences in order to restrict the movements of animals, both domestic and wild. Some of these fences, such as the Setata Fence that extended east–west from the Namibia/Botswana border fence to the edge of the Okavango Delta, cut across wildlife migration routes. These fences reportedly contributed to the deaths of wild animals, which further affected the subsistence and income-generating opportunities for Ju/'hoansi and their neighbours in the western Ngamiland region. The fences were patrolled and people were stopped from crossing them if they were carrying items such as bags of mongongo nuts or *biltong* (dried wild animal meat). The cessation of movement meant that the people in the region could not exchange goods with other groups, a process that had impacts on their reciprocity systems.

The socioeconomic impacts of the cattle eradication campaign and the establishment of fences and veterinary control activities were substantial. Local people responded in a variety of ways, some of them increasing their foraging and craft production and marketing activities. Others moved across the border to Namibia or east to towns along the edge of the Okavango Delta. Still others became involved in culturally based tourism and safari hunting. A few Ju/'hoansi began working with non-government organizations or with government labour-based relief and development operations in order to generate some food and cash.

In the latter part of the 1990s, some of the Ju/'hoansi in Ngamiland left the settlements where they had been living for two decades or more and went back to their original areas. There they resumed some of their natural resource exploitation activities, collecting wild plants, trapping small game, and hunting the now more abundant larger animals. This was not always easy; some people were arrested and jailed for hunting without licenses; others were pressed into service as border and fence guards, and still others built roads and community centres in exchange for cash from the district council and public works department of the Botswana government.

The Ju/'hoansi realized that they needed to gain greater control over their areas if they were to ensure that they had long-term occupancy and use rights and especially if they were to get *de jure* (legal) rights over land. One way that they chose to do this was to take part in the Botswana government's community-based natural resource management programme (CBNRMP). The Ju/'hoansi discovered that under Botswana's CBNRM policy, they could apply for rights over areas zoned by the North West District Council as community-controlled hunting areas if they formed community trusts or some other kind of representative body and wrote up a constitution. The Ju/'hoansi and Mbanderu of /Xai/Xai, a village of some forty people on the Botswana-Namibia border south of Dobe, formed a community trust known as the /Xai/Xae (Cgaecgae) Tlhabololo Community Trust, which was recognized officially by the Botswana government in 1977. This trust was able to get the wildlife quota for two areas, Controlled Hunting Area NG 4 and NG 5, which together cover an area of nearly 17,000 km^2. The /Xai/Xai Trust decided to enter into a joint venture with a safari operator who agreed to pay the trust a sizable sum, approximately P1,000,000 (a Pula was then worth about US $0.17), and to employ local people in addition to providing meat from the hunts, medicines, and other goods to the members of the trust (Hitchcock et al. 1996; Nico Rozemeijer, personal communication).

Unfortunately for the Ju/'hoansi and others who hoped to capitalize on community-based natural resource management activities, a formal decision was made by the Ministry of Local Government and the Ministry of Lands, Housing, and Environment in January, 2000 that community trusts would no longer have the right to make their own decisions on natural resources or to retain their own funds generated from those resources. The benefits of those resources should instead be, as one government official put it, 'a national resource, like diamonds.' The government decision affected the sixty or so community-based natural resource management projects in the communal areas of Botswana. This policy decision, which had yet to be rescinded officially as of the end of 2003, has had effects on community trusts in which San make up a sizable percentage of the constituents such as those in Dobe, Mababe, Khwaai, and /Xai/Xai in Ngamiland.

In spite of the constraints posed by the uncertainty relating to the Botswana Government's decisions on community trusts and their operation, the numbers of local communities in Botswana that were interested in becoming involved in community-based natural resource management and utilisation was on the up-swing in the 2001–2002. With the assistance of such San organizations as the Trust for Okavango Cultural and Development Initiatives (TOCaDI), Kuru Development Trust (now the Kuru Family of Orgnaizations) in D'Kar, and the Working Group of Indigenous Minorities in Southern Africa (WIMSA), a number of communities organised themselves as 'representative and accountable management groups' and attempted to get themselves registered officially with the Government of Botswana as legal entities.

In the late 1990s, the Ju/'hoansi decided to engage in mapping of their traditional territories as part of a strategy to gain further government and district council recognition of their land rights. They did this through carrying out field surveys with the aid of Geographic Positioning System (GPS) instruments, which allowed them to plot the locations of important places and spatial boundaries. They then applied Geographic Information Systems (GIS) techniques to the data. The teams, led by a skilled consultant, Arthur Albertson, came up with a series of very useful maps of the territories of the Ju/'hoansi in the Dobe and G!oshe areas of western Ngamiland (see Albertson 1998, 2000).

It is useful to look at one place to see the dynamics of how this land mapping and land right application process worked. The community of Dobe, which in 1999–2000 had a population of approximately one hundred people, was a core area for some groups of Ju/'hoansi (Yellen 1977: 53–56; Albertson 1998). Dobe, like other communities in western Ngamiland, had fluctuated in size over time, in part due to the availability of water and grazing and wild foods there, but it remained as a central place where people, both Ju/'hoansi and Herero, resided. Dobe was in essence a kind of core *n!ore*, whereas other *n!oresi* in the areas surrounding Dobe were used primarily during the rainy season when water was available and there were wild resources sufficient to sustain small groups. There was a seasonal movement of people out to the subsidiary *n!oresi* which could be characterized as a kind of decentralization strategy, people later returning to Dobe in order to take advantage of the borehole water and food relief provided by the Botswana government during the dry season.

The Dobe Ju/'hoansi, not content to await national and district-level decisions about their future, sought to further institutionalize their land and resource rights. One way that they did this was through establishing new water sources, one successful one being at !Ubi (Qubi), a Ju/'hoan community that is the most important *n!ore* in the Dobe complex of *n!oresi*, and the only one in which there were residents living year round. The !Ubi *n!ore* is some two hundred thirty km^2 in size, second only to G/hii'ahn, the largest of the eight Dobe *n!oresi* at two hundred forty four km^2 (Albertson 1998).

In the process of applying for water rights in western Ngamiland, individuals have on occasion attempted to out manoeuvre their communities and obtain individualized rights over water points, something that did not sit well with other Ju/'hoansi, some of whom pushed for rights to be given to communities rather than individuals. As several Ju/'hoan informants noted, having land rights granted to communities was much more in keeping with Ju/'hoan traditions and sensibilities. The problem was that some of the individuals who sought to gain individualized rights were some of the same ones who were *n!ore kxausi* and who had long-standing rights over areas in and around Dobe. When asked how they could do this, one man said, 'When the Botswana government changed the rules, it was every man for himself.' When pressed about this perspective, the man said that in his opinion, Ju/'hoan societies were not, in fact, egalitarian along gender and class lines. Rather, he said, men were the ones who had greater rights over territories because, as he put it, it was men who hunted and who ranged over large areas and who were the ones who found the places that they and their wives and families later occupied. He elaborated his points, noting that in fact the *n!oresi* were not group access areas but rather were divided among individuals along lines of gender, status, occupancy order, and length of association with specific places. The core areas of *noresi* belong to individuals, not groups, he said, and it was these groups that in his opinion had preferential rights to land and the resources on that land.

In some areas, as in the case of the Dobe area (NG 3) and the Ncwaagom (NG 10 and 11) areas in Ngamiland, community mapping efforts were undertaken with the assistance of a consultant and local people. These mapping activities enabled local groups to participate extensively in the identification and demarcation of their traditional areas. The impacts of these efforts have been profound. In the case of the Dobe area the community groups have been able to obtain water rights from the North West District Council and Tawana Land Board and have drilled several successful wells (see Albertson 1998; Kuru Family of Organisations 2003).

Admittedly, there have been disagreements within groups about who has the right to claim specific areas. There have also been attempts by individuals to make deals quietly and out of earshot of their fellow community members, with Land Board members. There have also been some inter-ethnic disagreements in western Ngamiland, between for example, Ju/'hoansi and Herero and between Ju/'hoansi and Tawana who were hoping to claim areas of land which originally were in the hands of the Ju/'hoansi, but which have been occupied for generations by members of a number of different ethnic groups. Efforts have been made by the Trust for Okavango Cultural and Development Initiatives to assist San communities in Ngamiland in their efforts to increase their management capacity and to gain a greater control over their own resources.

One of the activities of TOCaDI has been to employ a consultative, participatory strategy in which people have the opportunity to discuss their problems and their needs and to express their opinions about the situations in which they find themselves. This process of empowerment has been instrumental in getting some of the internal conflicts over land and resource rights out in the open. In these contexts, conflict resolution mechanisms are paramount, and the Ju/'hoansi have been more than willing to air their views and put forth their positions. Eventually, agreement is reached by public consensus. This is not always easy when attempts are being made by government officials, wealthy cattle owners, and safari operators to co-opt individuals in the hopes that they will hand over their certificates or offer their customary rights to land and resources in exchange for a payment of some kind. As one Jo/'hoan informant pointed out, the situation today is far different from the ways the Ju/'hoansi describe their traditional land tenure and land use system, and it is more complicated than many skilled analysts and non-government organizations working for long periods in the field in close cooperation with Ju/'hoansi have been able to discern. It is apparent, therefore, that additional research on Ju/'hoan land tenure conceptions and practices is needed, and that a closer look at within-territory variation is warranted.

Conclusions

The Ju/'hoansi of northern Botswana and Namibia, like many other indigenous peoples around the world, are locked in a struggle for control over land. Their opponents are powerful – governments, wealthy individuals, multinational corporations, and other groups. The Ju/'hoansi point to the experience of the Hai//om in Namibia, documented so carefully by Widlok (1999), and the Nharo of the Ghanzi region of Botswana, analyzed by Guenther (1986) and Barnard (1992: 134-55), for lessons as to what happens when people lose out in the struggles for land rights. It is no surprise, therefore, that the Ju/'hoansi and other San are employing innovative ethnocartographic methods and are carrying out detailed efforts in conjunction with advisors and consultants and supportive non-government organizations to map their land and document in detail the ways in which they manage their resources. While the Ju/'hoansi say that they are willing to share their land, they want to make sure that they are able to retain rights to the land and the resources it supports.

The Ju/'hoansi and other residents of the rural areas of northwestern Botswana want to make sure that the following rights, among others, are recognized: residential rights, hunting rights, gathering rights including commercial rights of wild plant (so-called *veld*) products, water rights, grazing rights, arable land rights, rights to do business, and cultural rights (including rights to visit graves of ancestors and to practice traditional and modern ceremonies of significance to local people). The Ju/'hoansi have called for particular attention to be paid to security rights and subsistence rights as well as the right to development. They want to ensure that they get some of the benefits from the tourism and other development-related activities in rural Botswana.

A major concern of Ju/'hoansi and other San in Botswana is the promotion of *security rights. Security rights* include the rights to be free from torture, imprisonment, or execution, in other words, these are rights relating to the integrity of the person. This set of rights is especially important in light of the frequency of allegations of alleged torture and mistreatment of suspected 'poachers' by game scouts, police, and other government officials in Botswana. Ju/'hoansi also want to ensure their continued *subsistence rights* – those rights related to the fulfillment of basic human needs such as water, food, shelter, health assistance, and medicines (Miller et al. 1999). The denial of the right to hunt and gather, according to some people, is an example of restrictions placed on subsistence rights. The Ju/'hoansi, like other indigenous peoples, understand full well the need for conservation of wildlife, plants, and other resources. At the same time, they feel that they should be able to exploit resources as long as they do so sustainably.

The future of the San and other peoples in Botswana and Namibia depends very much on their ability to convince governments, international agencies, companies, and non-government organizations, including environmental and human rights groups, of the importance of social, economic, and cultural rights, which they see as a matter of cultural as well as physical survival. Central to these deliberations over rights is the ways in which the Ju/'hoansi organise and manage their land and resources.

Without an understanding of the complexity of San territoriality and an appreciation of the complex history of land tenures, land use, and resource management, it will be difficult for Ju/'hoansi and the various organizations working with them to be able to make a cogent case for recognition and institutionalization of their land and resource claims. Simply giving land to broadly-defined groups or to individuals could well have the effect of undermining the well-being of some Ju/'hoansi while favouring others. It is crucial, therefore, that greater efforts be made to assess the complexities in the ways in which San share, manage, and utilise the land and resources of the Kalahari.

Acknowledgments

Support of the research upon which this paper is based was provided by the U.S. National Science Foundation, the Ford Foundation, the U.S. Agency for International Development (USAID), the Norwegian Agency for Development Cooperation (NORAD), and the International Work Group for Indigenous Affairs (IWGIA). I would like to thank my informants and the various organizations with whom I worked for the information and insights that they so willingly shared with me. I would also like to acknowledge the important contributions of San support organizations, including the Working Group of Indigenous Minorities and the Trust for Okavango Cultural and Development Initiatives, who have played such important roles in bringing about San empowerment.

References

Albertson, A. 1998. *Dobe Land Mapping Project.* Shakawe, Botswana: Kuru Development Trust.

—— 2000. *Traditional Areas (N!oresi) of the !Goshe Community.* Shakawe, Botswana: Kuru Development Trust.

Barnard, A. 1992. *Hunters and Herders of South Africa: A Comparative Ethnography of the Khoisan Peoples.* Cambridge and New York: Cambridge University Press.

Biesele, M. 1993. *Women Like Meat: The Folklore and Foraging Ideology of the Kalahari Ju/'hoan.* Johannesburg: Witwatersrand University Press and Bloomington and Indianapolis: Indiana University Press.

Durning, A. 1992. *Guardians of the Land: Indigenous Peoples and the Health of the Earth.* WorldWatch Paper 112. Washington, D.C.: WorldWatch Institute.

Guenther, M. 1986. *The Nharo Bushmen of Botswana: Tradition and Change.* Hamburg: Helmut Buske Verlag.

Hitchcock, R. 2002. '"We Are the First People": Land, Natural Resources, and Identity in the Central Kalahari, Botswana'. *Journal of Southern African Studies,* 28(4): 793–820.

Hitchcock, R., J. Yellen, D. Gelburd, A. Osborn and A. Crowell 1996. Subsistence Hunting and Resource Management among the Ju/'hoansi of Northwestern Botswana. *African Study Monographs* 17(4): 153–220.

Johnson, A. and T. Earle 1987. *The Evolution of Human Societies: From Foraging Group to Agrarian State.* Stanford, California: Stanford University Press.

Kelly, R. 1995. *The Foraging Spectrum: Diversity in Hunter-Gatherer Lifeways.* Washington, D.C.: Smithsonian Institution Press.

Lee, R. 1979. *The !Kung San: Men, Women, and Work in a Foraging Society.* Cambridge: Cambridge University Press.

—— M. Biesele, and R. Hitchcock 1996. "Three Decades of Ethnographic Research among the Ju/'hoansi of Botswana, 1963–1996". *Botswana Notes and Records,* 28: 107–20.

—— and I. DeVore (eds) 1968. *Man the Hunter.* Chicago: Aldine.

—— and I. DeVore (eds) 1976. *Kalahari Hunter-Gatherers: Studies of the !Kung San and Their Neighbours.* Cambridge, Massachusetts: Harvard University Press.

Marshall, L. 1976. *The !Kung of Nyae Nyae.* Cambridge: Harvard University Press.

Milner, W., S. Poe, and D. Leblang 1999. "Security Rights, Subsistence Rights, and Liberties: A Theoretical Survey of the Empirical Landscape". *Human Rights Quarterly,* 21(2): 403–44.

Widlok, T. 1999. *Living on Mangetti: 'Bushman' Autonomy and Namibian Independence.* Oxford: Oxford University Press.

Wiessner, P. 1977. Hxaro: A Regional System of Reciprocity for Reducing Risk among the !Kung San. Ph.D. Dissertation, University of Michigan, Ann Arbor, Michigan.

Wilmsen, E. 1989. *Land Filled With Flies: A Political Economy of the Kalahari.* Chicago: University of Chicago Press.

Woodburn, J. 1968. 'Stability and Flexibility in Hadza Residential Groupings'. In: R. Lee and I. DeVore (eds), *Man the Hunter*, pp. 103-110. Chicago: Aldine.

—— 1979. 'Minimal Politics: The Political Organization of the Hadza of Tanzania'. In: P. Cohen and W. Shack (eds), *Politics in Leadership: A Comparative Perspective*, pp. 244–66. Oxford: Clarendon Press.

—— 1980. Hunters and Gatherers Today and the Reconstruction of Their Past. In: E. Gellner (ed.), *Soviet and Western Anthropology*, pp. 95–117. London: Duckworth.

—— 1982. Egalitarian Societies. *Man* 17: 431–51.

—— 1988. 'African Hunter-Gatherer Social Organization: Is It Best Understood as a Product of Encapsulation?' In: T. Ingold, D. Riches, and J. Woodburn (eds), *Hunters and Gatherers I: History, Evolution, and Social Change*, pp. 31–64. London: Berg.

—— 1998. "'Sharing Is Not a Form of Exchange': An Analysis of Property-Sharing in Immediate-Return Hunter-Gatherer Societies". In: C.M. Hann (ed.), *Property Relations: Renewing the Anthropological Tradition*, pp. 48–63. Cambridge: Cambridge University Press.

Yellen, J. 1977. *Archaeological Approaches to the Present: Models for Reconstructing the Past.* New York, New York: Academic Press.

11

The Professionalisation and Commoditisation of the Contemporary Bushman Trance Dancer and Trance Dance, and the Decline of Sharing

Mathias Guenther

The trance dance has undergone some radical changes among some contemporary farm Bushmen. Its move toward commoditisation, and, as a related process, the trance dancer's move toward professionalisation, are due to a number of factors, prime of them the breakdown of sharing, the dance's central mode and spirit. My account of the dance and dancer, in their traditional and contemporary forms, will focus on the element of sharing. I will consider how and why this key ingredient is usurped in the dance's and dancer's present form.

The Traditional Trance Dance and Dancer: Sharing *N/um*, 'Doing God's Work'

The trance dance is the central ritual of the Bushmen (San) of southern Africa, with roots reaching far into the culture's past (as evidenced by literal and metaphorical depictions thereof on rock art panels that were created centuries or millennia ago). The dance is a vigorous curing ritual, held throughout the night around a fire, in which mostly male dancers, either singly or in groups of two to half a dozen, dance to the chanting and clapping of women. They do so in order to reach trance – called *!kia* in !Kung – through which a curing potency – *n/*um[1] – is activated in the dancer's body, which enables him to cure in a variety of ways (Guenther 1999: 184–86). Preceding the trance phase of the dance, at its initial, warm-up period that may last a couple of hours, other people, too, may dance, including women and children. At that point the dance is in its free-for-all 'play' mode. As the ritual dancers near trance the dance becomes more and more solemn and the play-dancers drop out of the dance circle, leaving the floor to the increasingly intense and disassociated trance dancers. They move around to cure the sick person or persons on whose behalf the dance is held, as well as apply general palliative treatment to the other spectators at the all-night ritual event. Eventually a dancer will collapse – or 'die' as the Bushmen refer to this portentous moment – signalling the same with an ear-piercing, heart-rending shriek. As in death, the dancer's spirit will then leave his inert body, to travel to the spirit world, at times in the spirit body of a lion or antelope, braving dangers in an effort to restore health to the sick. The dancer may present an account of his spirit journey after recovering from his trance collapse and then resume his dancing and curing. He may repeat this cycle, of dancing and curing, mounting altered trance state, collapse, spirit travel and confrontation, several times during one night, so that at day break he is left physically exhausted and spiritually drained.

This morally and mystically charged group ritual is a classic rite of solidarity, at which people, from both within and outside a camp or village, participate with a high degree of emotional involvement, for the sake not only of its spiritual and curative benefits but also its entertainment value – 'for the sheer fun of it' (Biesele 1993: 75; see also Guenther 1986: 256–57). Like foraging, trance dancing divides labour by gender, in complementary, reciprocal fashion, as well as with overlap, as the women, the singers, are by no means barred from dancing and trancing, even though this ritual task normally falls to the men. In this way trance dancing is like hunting, a subsistence task to which it is linked metaphorically (Lewis-Williams 1981: 100–183; Guenther 1999: 78, 178, 186–87), as well as morally.

The reason for the moral parallels between trancing and hunting is that the modus operandi of both is sharing: meat distribution – as cogently argued by James Woodburn (1998: 56–57; see also Barnard and Woodburn 1988: 20 and Hunt 2000: 15–17) – is 'directly analogous' to trance dance curing. Both meat and *n/um* are personally owned 'consumables', according to Woodburn, that are shared with the community, that were given as unreciprocated and uncalculated gifts, by the hunter and trancer, the 'Owner of Meat' and the 'Owner of N/um', to people who require them and may demand them. On the basis largely of Lorna Marshall's (1976a: 357, 363, 366) and Polly Wiessner's (1977, 1982) ethnographic work among the !Kung, I would qualify Woodburn's observation somewhat by noting that these sharing qualities actually apply more to healing than to meat distribution. While sharing is the mode of distribution of meat in its primary phase, in its secondary and tertiary phases, and in particular as cooked meat,[2] distribution may include elements of reciprocation and calculation.[3] These two economic sentiments are entirely lacking from *n/um*-sharing, which is thus altogether 'purer' than is meat-sharing.

Indeed, as an instance *par excellence* of the 'pure gift' the trance dance is Bushman culture's most rarified expression of the ethos and practice of sharing (Katz 1982: 197–210; Katz et al. 1997: 48–52, 55–57). *N/um* is like a bursting seed pod, say the Ju/'hoansi, or it is like sparks that leap out in every direction; it 'moves throughout the participants of a dance ... bursting beyond one healer, leaping out to others' (ibid: 52). Healing with *n/um* is sharing not only between humans but also between humans and God, who gives *n/um* or the healing arrows to the dancers as a gift, to be dispensed among humans in the same spirit (Guenther 1999: 112, 189–91). The dancer's rewards for 'giving *n/om*' are not material but moral, consisting of such 'manifold and diffuse' things as 'personal satisfaction, the love and respect of family, and the gratitude of those [he] had saved,' as interviewed healers explained to Richard Lee (1993: 123). All this makes an experienced trance dancer an esteemed member of his community; he is respected for bringing to them health and spiritual well-being (Katz 1982: 197–210) – at his peril, as death by trance and the sojourns to the spirit world are a dangerous business. It brings the dancer in direct contact with dangerous spirits, and also with God (Guenther 1999: 186–90). Healing, in fact, is 'God's work' to some healers (such as the great Ghanzi dancer Tsau, who explained his vocation as healer to me in this way).

Given its centrality within the ritual and social life of the people, the trance dance plays out, in addition to intra- and inter-group sharing, such other values and processes of Bushman social organisation as social and gender equality, exchange and kin networking, conflict resolution, levelling and cooperation (Katz et al. 1997: 48–52). It allows creative and affective expression to the individual and links him and her to the community. In view of this wide range of organisational congruence, the trance dance's 'structure is the same as society itself' (ibid.,48). Like story telling (Biesele 1993; Guenther 1999: 133–40), the trance dance becomes an arena for the moral, emotional and creative interplay between the individual and the community (Katz et al. 1997: 48, see also England 1967).

The trance dance has gained special experiential and symbolic salience among Bushmen living in an ethnically plural setting, marked by political oppression and economic deprivation, such as the Nharo (Naro) on the white-owned ranches of the Ghanzi District (Guenther 1976, 1986: 50–67), the Ju/'hoansi attached to black herders at /Kae/kae in Ngamiland (Katz et al. 1997) and the Khomani of and around Kalahari Gemsbok National Park in South Africa, among whom trance dancing has recently been revived (Isaacson 2002). As the quintessentially 'Bushman thing', as the Ghanzi farm Bushmen refer to it (Guenther 1999: 196), the trance dance and dancer have become a mechanism for revitalising demoralised Bushman communities and filling them with hope and purpose and defining the people's collective identity and advancing their political agendas (as happened recently among the Khomani, after their leader Dawid Kruiper had relearned proper trance dancing from a renowned Ghanzi dancer, to whom he had undertaken a lengthy, quest-like journey [Isaacson 2000: 238–63]). The identity-defining force of trance dancing may be manipulated by Bushman leaders, such as the late John Qace Hardbattle, who underscored his political action group, the *Kgeikani Kweni*, the 'First People of the Kalahari' (motto, 'political survival through cultural revival') by taking a trance dancer or two along to perform at especially strategic meetings with politicians, donors or media representatives. The message is also expressed in 'First People's' logo, which Hardbattle had himself designed, depicting a fire surrounded by a circle of paired footprints, and flanked by a digging stick and an arrow; it expresses one of its principal political survival/cultural revival mottos. These developments, which attest to the political awakening and mobilisation of the Bushmen, have become especially acute in the previous and current decades, in the context of the cultural politics of the region, since the collapse of apartheid in Namibia and South Africa, that have drawn in many Bushman individuals and communities (Hitchcock 1996; Bank 1998, Smith et al. 2000: chapter 10; Lee and Hitchcock 2001).

Let us turn now to a recent parallel development to the process of enhancing the ritual and political salience of the trance dancer and his curing ritual: the progressive professionalisation of the trance dancer and commoditisation of the dance.

The Professionalisation of the Trance Dancer

While a number of the older dancers continue to perform their curing rite in the old fashion – as a communal rite, executed in the spirit of sharing and cooperation – others have brought a number of significant alterations to the dance. Through them the dancers are in the process of differentiating and elaborating their status and role beyond its loose institutionalisation in traditional Bushman culture. Professionalisation is evident in such new or altered features of the dance as collecting payment, rationalisation and instrumentalisation of healing, employment of self-promoting, status-enhancing ritual and mystical props, and the expansion of the healer's repertoire of healing practices (either within or beyond his traditional range of expertise). Some of these developments began to appear among farm Bushmen (Guenther 1986: 262–64) and cattle-post Bushmen (Katz 1982: 198, 254–62) in the 1960s and they have proliferated and intensified over the past decade, especially among the Ghanzi farm Bushmen.

The expectation to be paid – ideally on the spot, on a quid-pro-quo basis – is perhaps the clearest indication of the trance dancer's move towards professionalisation. It is a development that is to be expected, in part, because for a number of dancers healing has become regular work and a source of income on which they depend, in part, because cash, as a medium of exchange and remuneration, has become an established economic concept, in the context of the wage economy into which the farm Bushmen have become incorporated. The idea in the minds of many farm Bushmen and dancers is that trance dancing 'is work' and work is something for which one gets paid (except in situations where a dancer heals his own family members). The party charged is the 'patient' on whose behalf the dance is held; in addition a !Kung trance dancer may expect the payment of a fee from people for just watching his dance (Katz 1982: 261). The fact that the other medical specialists who operate within the pluralist society of Ghanzi (and who are widely sought out by the farm Bushmen), the Black diviner and White nurse or doctor, also charge their patients fees for their services likely sets a model also for Bushman curing and may be another factor in the development of the fee component of contemporary trance curing.

The payment demanded by Bushman healers may be quite high, consisting either of sums of money or of goats, chickens, blankets or clothing, along with the food and firewood the host has to provide, at quite a bit of additional expense. Among the Tyua of northeastern Botswana, most of whom are today agro-pastoralists and wage earners who have for the past one or two millennia interacted with non-Khoisan populations, trance dancers may accumulate cattle herds and even motor vehicles from the proceeds of their curing craft (Hitchcock 1999: 228). Frequently a healer is unable to collect all or any of his fee, especially if it is on the high end of the scale, resulting in acrimony and social tension between the healer and members of his community. It may also put him at odds with the women who danced for him and his apprentices who assisted him, as they, too, may expect some payment from the dancer. Financial difficulties of this sort may lead him to leave his village, in order to practise healing at what he perceives to be greener pastures, for instance the Ghanzi farms, to which a disgruntled healer from /Kae/kae may take his business (Katz 1982: 260, Lee 1993: 123) – only, in all likelihood, to experience much the same frustration, as complaints about nonpayment of fees are constant amongst Ghanzi healers (Guenther 1986: 264, 268).

The reason a healer has difficulty collecting his fee is as much practical as it is cultural. The practical reason is that people rarely have the resources for the full, or even partial, payment and thus cannot and will not pay the healer. The cultural reason is the persistence in some people's minds of the precapitalist hunter-gatherer notion that in an exchange transaction, along lines of sharing or generalized reciprocity, there is either no return payment or its transaction is delayed indefinitely. Trance curing continues to be regarded, more or less implicitly, as an instance of sharing by many people and by some dancers, and as a gift and a calling from God, intended for the well-being of the people, not for the enrichment of the dancer. To charge for the dispensation of *n/um* is criticised by the !Kung, as it 'goes against Ju/'hoan tradition' (Katz et al. 1997: 55). This mercenary element of the contemporary trance dance is probably its sharpest break with the past and with tradition.

The process of rationalisation, through which the healer practises his craft in a more instrumental and pragmatic fashion in order to maximise efficiency, is evident in a number of ways. One is that dances become shorter and more frequent, as well as more routinised; for instance Khã/'e,[4] the eminent trance dancer at D'Kar village in Ghanzi District, may hold as many as three or four performance sessions a day. Dances have become more focused, each on a specific individual – the one who has hired the dancer – with a specific sickness, rather than on all participants at the rite, who before were generally included within the trance dancer's curing purview. The number of participants has decreased, being limited to the patient and his family, and perhaps kinsfolk from nearby huts. The circle of spectators now also usually excludes members from other villages, due to the decline in 'cross-camp healing' (Katz et al. 1997: 103). Healing dances may now be held during the day, with only a handful of women – or none at all – providing the song. Both of these scenarios are influenced also by practical, predominantly financial considerations: wood, for the nocturnal fire, is hard to come by in the overcrowded village and may have to be hauled in by donkey cart a long distance at considerable cost, and women usually expect some form of payment for their song. To get around the latter problem a dancer (for instance Khã/'e) may obtain that service from his wife, who is usually at hand, or he may even, in the event that she and no other women are available, dance and cure to his own singing. Dancing to the vigorous and sustained song of a group of women is still his and everyone's preferred form of curing as dancing and curing are held to be more efficacious if done to the women's song, making trance more readily attainable and *n/um* stronger. As explained to me by Khã/'e , without the women's singing he cannot achieve full-blown trance, with trembling, shaking and vomiting, all of which are required properly to expel the disease from his body, after having absorbed the same from that of the patient. Thus, whenever possible nocturnal dances are still held; however, once again we note a practicality-derived difference from the traditional form: dances now rarely last through the night and usually are over by midnight. The practical consideration to enter into this new night-dance schedule is that principals and participants at the dance may have to get up for work the next morning. Reflecting these various aspects of rationalisation, curing dances have now become informally differentiated and graded among the Ghanzi farm Bushmen into two categories: 'small' and 'big' dances. The ultimate criterion is organisational complexity and expense: small dances are short and inexpensive daytime affairs, while big dances are protracted, all-stops-pulled-out, expensive night-time performances, sometimes with the air of a gala event.

Another manifestation of rationalization is for the trance dancer to modulate his use of *n/um*. Instead of dispensing it widely and freely as before, both to administer cures to specific sick individuals and to cure everyone at the dance palliatively, he is now likely to hang on to *n/um*, to withhold it from 'hopeless' cases (whom 'only God can help'), who might die despite his treatment. Such an outcome may tarnish his reputation as a healer, as well as preventing him from collecting a fee as, by the implicit rules of trance curing, a doctor can collect the same only when his patient gets better. He now husbands his *n/um* and applies it sparingly, primarily to cases that will enhance his reputation and generate compensation (Katz 1982: 264).

A further aspect of rationalization is the need to 'control trance', a point stressed to me by Khã/'e , in a lengthy conversation about his healing activities. While the ability to control this volatile psychological state has always been the hallmark of a competent dancer, and was expressed in prolonging the moment of collapse when engaged in trance curing and in refraining from carrying out (self)destructive actions while in trance and, instead, channelling these into acts of curing (Lewis-Williams 1981: 97; Lee 1984: 113–15; Guenther 1986: 258–59, 1999:183–84), control and competence today covers a wider range of elements of the trance ritual. These include such things as the ability to switch, readily and swiftly, from 'play-dancing' to 'death-dancing', to dance and trance without the women's song, and to be able to trance-cure a patient who is not physically present. The last feat dancers of the past were not able to do as physical contact with the patient is a basic requirement of trance curing.[5] Another manifestation of control is the ability to simulate trance, including the 'death shriek', at play dances, or traditional dance competitions for tourists and other outsiders.

The reason, perhaps, that control and competence have become issues of importance to contemporary professionalised dancers is that the trance experience, in its traditional manifestations, reveals a marked degree of vulnerability in the dancer. This is evident when the dancer is in the grips of trance and his actions and words are strikingly dissociated and irrational and devoid of the control trance dancers usually aspire to. Such vulnerability may be viewed, by the dancer or by his clients and spectators at a curing dance performance, as a kind of exposé and as a challenge to his competence, in a world which has come to expect the same from its high-profile, and highly paid professional dancers (and in which, as to be noted below, agnostic doubt about his mystical experience and curing efficacy is beginning to rear its head in the minds of some contemporary Bushmen).

The fascinating account of the utterances, during trance, of the great traditional Ju/'hoan dancer 'Oma, recorded verbatim by Polly Wiessner and Flemming Larsen (1979) in the mid-1970s, reveal the manifestations of vulnerability and loss of control, and its attendant self-exposing weakness, experienced by a dancer during the numinous climax of the dance. The predominant theme in the dancer's 'calling narratives' – which included utterances of nonsense words – were plaintive calls to the women singers, addressing them as 'mothers' and imploring them to give to him the trance-inducing song, or of 'holding' him (a !Kung child's request to his mother to be picked up by her). Along the same beseeching lines, he repeatedly referred to himself as 'a little child' ('crawling in the sand'), or, switching from generation inversion to species inversion, as 'a little duiker'. His reference to a ten-minute stretch of dancing as 'to my years here' reflect his confused sense of time and expressions like 'I feel like something that is crazy' a sense of impending loss of sanity. This theme is expressed in varying ways, and with mounting fear of being lost and marooned in the spirit world, of not 'jumping off' – back to normal life – and of death ('I feel like a dead thing'). Another theme the expansive narrative dwells on is self-doubt and frustration about his inability to heal the sickness, along with paranoid expressions of dismay about the people around him, whom he accuses of directing hate, insults and ridicule towards him.

Perhaps as a measure to buttress his credibility, a dancer's post-trance 'debriefing' accounts of his spirit journey when in collapse may now be presented to people also outside the trance dance context, as part of the dancer's regular narrative repertoire. The accounts have a ring of self-promotion and bravura, all uncharacteristic for a value culture in which the 'humility ethos' (Lee 1993: 54–56) is a pillar. For some trance dancers these narratives have, I sense, become self-authenticating devices that dwell on the elements of danger and courage which the dancer faced and overcame during his psychological and spiritual trance experience. Dramatic accounts may be presented of lion transformations (Katz et al. 1997: 24–25), or of perilous encounters with the dangerous spirit beings, some of whom hold the healing powers and substances (Guenther 1999: 188–89). These encounters may be especially dangerous to the spirit-dancer in their female form, and the dancer's account to people of her attempts at seducing him add melodramatic spice to his tales from the beyond, all the more so when he repels these, as he – a human – must, resulting in the spurned spirit-woman's unleashing hell's fury on his head, and grievous injury to his body. This is how the exceptionally flamboyant Hai//om trance dancer (and farm worker) /Garugu //Khumob (alias Joel) explained his four-day period of unconsciousness and almost fatal sickness: it was caused by a severe beating he received from //Gamab's wife Kaindaus, after he had refused her advances (Wagner-Robertz 1976: 536–37; Schatz 1993: 8). Like /Garugu, the Nharo dancer Khã/'e also has encounters with a female //Gãuwa, whose great danger was the substance of an elaborate narrative, which Khã/'e presented to me in 1997. He accompanied his story with a striking prop: an actual picture of the female spirit, in the form of a photograph from a well-thumbed Danish variety magazine he had obtained years ago from a European visitor. The photograph depicts a full-figured white woman in a low-cut dress wearing a black leather mask. The moment Khã/'e laid eyes on the picture he recognised the depicted woman as the female //Gãuwa from his dream and trance experiences! He has kept the picture ever since and shown it to many people, as a visual aid for his trance spirit encounter tale. He also uses the picture to help him establish contact with the spirit and her world.

The use of paraphernalia – some established and traditional, some, such as Khã/'e's picture, new and invented – is another trait that distinguishes the professionalised, modern trance dancer from his traditional counterpart, who owned few ritual objects and who was as visually undistinguishable from the other band members as he was socially. The above-mentioned /Garugu //Khumob from the Grootfontein farm region of Namibia again provides the example[6] (Wagner-Robertz 1976: 539–40; Schatz 1993: 11–12) – one somewhat extreme by comparison to the healers known to me from the Ghanzi farms who use such insignia much more sparingly. His trance dancing get-up, which he displays on the photograph featured on Schatz's book cover, is elaborate, as are the narratives he has developed around some of them. Along with a variety of ritual routines, such 'supportive texts' (Schildkrout 1999: 202) provide his paraphernalia with a mystical charge, distinguishing and enhancing this trance dancer's esoteric appeal. Around his neck hang his 'medicinal ornaments', consisting of dozens of strings of beads, made of glass, berries and grass seeds. He wears them on his chest, to prevent evil spirits from entering his body. On his head he wears a colourful glass-bead headband with a crown of ostrich feathers. What Schatz (1993:11) refers to as the *'Allerheiligste'* ('Holy of Holies') in his assortment of ritual props is a small wooden 'medicine drum'; it contains the four 'spirit children' he had received from Kaindaus after she 'had played with his soul' (ibid.: 8) who provide him with his mystical powers of healing. Another prop is a leather pouch containing bone particles and hair from certain animals and a powder he sprinkles over the embers of the trance fire, which help induce trance. He owns and shoots invisible arrows at //Gamab with a flick of his hand and another mystical prop is his snake familiar, with iridescent eyes and the capacity to transform itself into a human or an antelope (Wagner-Robertz 1976: 547). He handles live coals and does push-ups over the fire, without any burn marks on hands or chest. He is required, by virtue of his spiritual constitution, to observe numerous food taboos and he knows a wide variety of medicinal plants. A veil of carefully guarded secrecy shrouds his esoteric knowledge, which he reveals to the author – who is also the wife of the farm on which he resides and works – inside the walls of his hut, every so often interrupting his discourse by stepping outside to drive away possible listeners (Schatz 1993: 1–2). Further enhancing the mystical status of this 'great medicine man' is his reputation as a potential sorcerer, who is capable of using his invisible arrows against humans, ones he dislikes or who have done him wrong, for instance his mother-in-law, whose death was ascribed to /Garugu's sorcery (ibid.: 9).

The last raises another aspect of professionalisation of some contemporary trance dancers: proliferation of healing skills and the requisite esoteric knowledge, in the context of an expanding range of diseases within an ethnically plural society and an existentially stressful life situation. The Bushmen of the farms, government settlements, military tent city (as at Schmidtsdrift in South Africa) and urban shanty townships suffer a higher incidence and variety of diseases than ever before (including HIV/AIDS, which has hit Botswana with a vengeance [Lee 2003: 190–92]). One of these is sorcery (and witchcraft), derived from the Tswana and other black neighbors, and incorporated into the Bushmen's own mystical and medicinal system (Guenther 1992; Lee 2003: 137–40; Vorster 1995; Marshall 1999: 233–40). Some of the 'new diseases' (tuberculosis, venereal diseases) are attributed to contact with Blacks and Whites and are held to be treatable primarily with European medicines (Guenther 1986: 273–74). While most Bushmen healers hold black diviners and European or Western-trained doctors and nurses to be the appropriate medical experts for such ethnically labelled diseases and refer a Bushman patient in whom they have diagnosed such a disease to its respective healer, others have widened their own fields of medical expertise by incorporating the other experts' treatment into their own body of healing skills (Lee 2003: 139). Yet other trance dancers have coopted the other groups' medicinal expertise by directing a Bushman patient they attempt to heal to the Western clinic or Black diviner, making this part of their own treatment (Guenther 1999: 195). Tyua traditional healers, in addition to treating witchcraft cases and casting spells for foreign clients, have expanded their repertoire of ritual skills from curing to providing spiritual guidance to youths in rites of passage. They also take on young men and women as apprentices for extended, ten-year periods, and for a fee paid in goods and money (Hitchcock 1999: 228).

Commoditisations of the Dance

The process of professionalisation of the trance dancer is paralleled by the commoditisations of the trance dance. That is, a monetary value has become attached to the dance; it has become a product and service, the motivation and validation of which, communal, diffuse and indeterminate before, has now become mercenary, tangible and calculable. It is turning into a much more concrete and instrumental enterprise – very much a '*tool* of social and spiritual technology' (Katz et al. 1997: 62, my emphasis) – and less embedded than before within a social matrix. The dance before was for community and kin, presented in the spirit of sharing; dances were widely attended; indeed, implicitly attendance was an expectation placed on all members of a camp (something noted also by Thomas Widlok among the Hai//om of northern Namibia [2001: 170–71]). Attendance today is irregular and entirely optional, reducing the dance's communal and cohesive effects on the community. Dances today are performed, ideally, on a contractual basis, for clients or customers whom the dancer-curer – or just dancer – may not even know. The healing scenario may be that of 'producing for unknown consumers in return for goods and money', two key attributes of commoditisation (Peterson 1991: 4).

The commoditisation of the trance dance plays itself out within two social contexts, the one directed inwardly, towards the Bushman community, the other outwardly, towards non-Bushmen. The former dances follow the basic format of the trance dance and contain the element of curing while the latter, the outside-directed dances, may be substantially altered and may be devoid of curing (and only simulate trance). In the former case the consumers are insiders, for the most part sick Bushman individuals of the village or region seeking the dancers' services, or having them sought on their behalf by kin. The consumers in the outside-directed dances are outsiders; they are either tourists who visit a Bushman village and have a dance performed for them, dignitaries at a political ceremony that contains the performance of Bushman dances, or spectators at traditional dance competitions performed by dance troupes (such as the /Guiba dancers from /Kae/kae [Katz et al. 1997: 77–80; Lee 2003: 201–5]). Another scenario is local Blacks seeking treatment from a trance dancer (Katz et al. 1997: 137; Guenther 1999: 193–94; Hitchcock 1999: 228; Lee 2003: 138–39) or, as happened a couple of generations back, Boer farmers hiring Bushman 'rain doctors' during a drought spell. Apart from the tourists, who visit the Kalahari in increasing numbers (Guenther 2002), other non-San customers for a Bushman dancer may be visiting anthropologists, who might commission and pay for a trance dance or two for study purposes.[7]

The outside-directed dances, performed for customers with cash and a readiness to part with it, provide contemporary trance dancers with a new source of income. It is income that is less encumbered than what he would get from his Bushman clients; that is, income that is more readily and reliably forthcoming, in a balanced economic transaction in which hard cash is presented to the dancer when he performs his dance, then and there, rather than promised and owed for an indefinite length of time into the future – or never paid – by the cure's recipient, because of kinship links between dancer and client, and economic rationales of sharing or generalised reciprocity. These new outside-directed non-trance dances are highly popular amongst the country's dominant Batswana, especially the traditional troupe dance competitions at which Bushman entrants draw the largest crowds and tend to win the top prizes (Lee 1993: 179; Katz et al.1997: 77–79; Guenther 1999: 192–93). They are also standard offerings to tourists at Bushman ethnotourism venues.

One problem such dance performances present to the dancers is the problem of cross-cultural translation, that is, of presenting the dance in such a form that it becomes palatable to the paying outsider. This necessitates such alterations of the dance as shortening its performance, as well as, on most occasions, holding it during the day rather than at night. These alterations parallel and reinforce the amendments of the dance within the intra-cultural context that were mentioned above. This applies especially to the use of paraphernalia and, as an added touch to satisfy the primordialist aesthetics especially of tourist outsiders regarding the Bushmen (Buntman 1996, 2002; Guenther 2002), the cultural performers' use of native dress (or undress), in leather loincloth and beaded skirt and cloak, and bare-chested.

The most significant difference between the intra- and extra-cultural performances of the dance is the absence, in the latter, of genuine – rather than histrionically faked – *!kia*, the trance experience and, of course, also of *n/um* curing. These are the dance's emotional and ideational core, that, in the Bushman context, give to the dance its purpose and meaning, its defining moment. That they are not part, indispensably so, of a dance – or, at best (or worst), simulated – has furthered the scepticism of some farm Bushmen about the mystical and curative powers of trance dancers. However, to others (including the dancers themselves) the trance-free dance is not seen as all that much of a distortion of, or deviation from, the traditional dance, nor as a threat to the integrity of this key ritual and cultural institution. They might point out that the 'real' trance dance has a lengthy 'play' phase to it, at the beginning of the performance, which, while not its core and climax, is nevertheless a regular element of the dance. (A Western parallel might be a simple Protestant church service, one offered without the element of communion, which few congregation members would shun for its lack of the core sacrament of the Christian faith, but would likely regard as a legitimate and spiritually satisfying, truncated variant of the regular service.)

Once the dance has become freed of its distinctive element, and been 'secularized' as a 'play dance' for entertainment, largely of tourists, rather than the 'death dance' for curing of community members, there is wide room for creative innovation. Dances have proliferated; some are derived from the trance dance, others have a different source, and they may be performed for either a Bushman or a non-Bushman audience. Some, following the traditional pattern, are named after an ever-expanding menagerie of animals, echoing the ancient symbolic linkage between hunting and dancing; others have names and dance routines that reflect the modern world, such as 'Policeman' (Schatz 1993: 16), or 'B.M.C'. (Botswana Meat Commission), a favorite dance number of the traditional dance troupes from D'Kar (Guenther 1999: 192).[8]

Because of the high degree of popularity of the trance dance and other Bushman 'traditional dances' among outsiders – both in the country and by international tourists – Bushman dances are in the process of being coopted by entrepreneurially minded non-Bushmen. This development enhances the commoditisation of the dance, as well as adding a new element of competition for the Bushman dancers, who now see themselves pitted not only against fellow Bushman dancers but also non-Bushman ones. These may on occasion control the dance's performance and side-line–or altogether exclude--Bushmen, thereby pushing them off the ritual and cultural performance stage. Unfortunately this has recently happened, at both the regional and national levels. The former case is /Kae/kae, where the Tswana teaching staff are keeping the regalia and prize money of the highly acclaimed /Gwihaba troupe under lock and key at the village school, which had founded the troupe in the early 1980s, and out of the dancers' and the Ju/'hoan community's reach (Katz et al. 1997: 77–80). At the national capital the Mambo Arts Commune, which was founded in the late 1980s, over a thousand dancers – all of them non-Bushmen – have reportedly been trained in trance dance-derived dances. These dancers may be officially appointed to high-profile performances, such as visits from foreign dignitaries or other public ceremonial events, or they may be sent on tours to Europe (Hermans 1998: 284). A similar development at elite Botswana secondary schools is for BaTswana students to form dance troupes that perform BaSarwa dances, with the steps, songs and costumes copied from the Bushmen (Lee 2003: 205). In Bushman communities, too, black trance dancers may appear on the scene, offering traditional Bushman curing dances to the local people (Isaacson 2002: 268–70).

Factors in the Transformation of Trance Dancing

How can we explain the changes the trance dancer and dance have undergone, from a ritual performance carried out in the spirit of sharing and a setting of dense moral interaction, to a rational service, performed for a fee, by a professional for a client? In answering this question, I will consider both external and internal factors, that is, those having to do with recent, outside-derived, or acculturational changes and those factors that reside within Bushman culture.

The former, the extensive economic, social and cultural changes the contemporary Bushmen have experienced over the past decades or century, provide much of the answer. Many of the Bushmen, especially the farm Bushmen of the Ghanzi District or other farming regions of southern Africa (such as the Omaheke District of neighbouring Namibia), have become drawn into a cash economy, as wage labourers on largely white-owned cattle ranches, operated along modern, capitalist lines (Guenther 1986; Sylvain 1998). The pattern of remuneration that applies to farm labour – money for labour services rendered, in the context of a contractual agreement – has become applied to the performance of trance dancing (displacing sharing, its traditional mode of transaction). Trance dancing is regarded by the farm Bushmen as a case *par excellence* of 'Bushman work' – as opposed to work for the whites or blacks – that consists of tasks of great complexity, import and power, requiring skills and cultural expertise held only by a trained Bushman doctor-dancer. As 'work', of importance and skill, trance dancing yields remuneration, in the form, ideally, of money. Parallelling the notion of payment for service is that of payment for goods, especially firewood, home-made beer and meat, usually from a butchered goat. Exchange, of goods and services, before were transacted through sharing – in the case of meat and trance dancing – or through generalised reciprocity – in the case of items of personal property (through *hxaro*, among the !Kung). These traditional practices are continuing to some extent amongst farm Bushmen (Guenther 1986: 163–64) and, as seen above, at times compete with the modern monetary ones (resulting in a dancer not being paid his fee). However, more and more frequently money has become the basis for a growing number of economic transactions within the Bushman community, among a people who have become plugged into a cash economy, which has eroded its sharing ethos and replaced it with a 'saving ethos' (Lee 1979: 412–13). The trance dance, too, is transacted and validated through money, leading-*pace* Simmel[9] (1907/1978) – to an objectification and depersonalisation of the social relations that have traditionally embedded the dance.

These processes are increasingly evident within the relationship between the trance dancer and the people for whom he performs the curing dance. Whereas in the past he was a central and key member of his patients' community – which was sometimes extended through inter-village dancing – today the curer's ties to his patients and their community are generally a good deal more tenuous, as well as more contracted as the treatment given out 'belongs to the individual who paid for it, not to the community at large' (Lee 2003: 139). Khã/'e, the trance dancer at D'Kar village featured above, practices his craft in a village of 1,000. He is attached, by kinship or neighbourhood ties, to only a fraction of the villagers. Thus, it is only on the odd occasions that he conducts a curing dance for family members or friends. Like many other trance dancers of repute, he is also frequently called to other villages, sometimes places in remote regions of the farming district, performing his dance, once again, in a community to which he has few if any ties, to clients who are paying customers, rather than kin, with whom he interacts on a contractual, rather than 'consanguineal' basis.

What also renders the trance dancer less accessible to members of his community is the elaboration and differentiation of his status, as against the recent past, when trance dancing was practised by over half of the men (as well as by many women). This formalises the trance dancer's social role; it renders him distant, as he may now be a figure who is 'respected or even feared', as some Tyua doctors are reported to be (Hitchcock 1999: 228). Because of his social and professional distance from his patient-clients, his relationship to them is more formal, more likely to be contractual and business-like. While not as marked, the Ghanzi farm Bushmen accord a similar status to their trance dancers – the ones of renown – and it would appear that the redoubtable /Garugu among the Namibian Hai//om was held in like esteem. What further contributes towards rendering his status distinct is that today's trance dances, on the Ghanzi farms, tend to feature just the one, professionalised dancer, whereas in the past curing dance performances were usually held by several dancers, who did not differ that much in the degree of ritual expertise they held. The degree of professionalisation and social differentiation and distancing of trance dancers is not uniform and there are individuals who still dance, trance and cure in the traditional fashion.[10]

What has also affected the relationship of the community to their trance dancer, and has injected a quality of wary distance into that relationship, is a new attitude, one absent in the past, scepticism. It is especially marked among the younger people on the Ghanzi farms who, on a Saturday night, might prefer a disco-dance to recorded music blaring from the beer-laden truck of a black entertainment entrepreneur to a trance dance held in another section of the village. Apart from different musical and dance form preferences, the younger generation also question the mystical aspects of the trance dance – animal transformation, extra-body travel – and the curing efficacy of the dancer, echoing the scepticism of their Tswana school teachers, as well as the resident Tswana nurse (Katz et al. 1997: 80–81, 85–89). While for some the bowdlerised dances, because of their popularity and salience, 'could be effecting a renewed appreciation of the value of n/om', for others they are an empty shell, devoid of its 'heart' – which is *n/om* – as it has now become 'transformed into an ordinary entertainment vehicle ... catered to the expectations of the audience' (ibid.: 80). 'Something for tourists', was some of the people's response to Janet Hermans when she questioned them in Ngamiland about the incidence of trance dancing today, a 'spectacle without meaning performed only for money' (Hermans 1998: 283). One might wonder whether the above-described elaboration and embellishment some trance dancers subject their craft to may not be measures to counteract such agnostic doubts and misgivings amongst the trance doctor's clientele.

The relationship of trance dancers to one another also encourages the professionalisation of their role. In the past this was a relationship of cooperation, as at night-long dances several dancers would trance and cure together. The next day, before parting their separate ways, they might sit together and 'talk shop', discussing and sharing practical and esoteric aspects of their trade, with interest and mutual respect (Guenther 1986: 263–64). While this can still be seen at some dances, the relationship among dancers has given way to competition (Katz et al. 1997: 61, 138–39). One way this is evident is that an element of a trance dancer's self-commending discourse that was mentioned above may be to compare himself favourably to other trance dancers, or even devalue their skill (Katz 1982: 263). While cooperation could be expected to bring out commonalities in the logistical and mystical elements of the dance ritual, competition has the opposite effect, of highlighting singularities, developed by each dancer, in accordance with his own level of ritual and esoteric expertise and repertoire of routines and skills. It leads each dancer to develop his own distinctive profile and dance routine, to increase his recognisability.

In sum, five explanations for the move towards commoditisation and professionalisation of the trance dance and dancer have been considered: erosion of sharing ethos through the onslaught of a money economy; depersonalisation of the curer-patient relationship the basis of which has become monetary and contractual; differentiation and distancing of the increasingly professionalised trance dancer from his community; its members' scepticism about his competence; competition amongst trance dancers (both of the latter factors inducing the dancer to prop up and valorize his craft and skills).

The Transformation of Trance Dancing and the Decline of Sharing

Of these explanations, the first, the erosion of sharing, is the most significant factor. As it declines as a practice and value, it deprives the trance curing dance of its basic social form and force, leaving only the instrumental objective of curing a specific sick individual, the dancer's client and the dance's sole *raison d'être.*

While it has not altogether disappeared (especially amongst family members), the demands and obligations of sharing have become increasingly burdensome to people and strategies of shirking the sharing obligation are resorted to by some, while others accept the same, at times with grim and grudging resignation, as one of the unavoidable facts of life (Guenther 1999: 47). The fact that the demands of sharing may nowadays be put as such, demands, exacerbates the irksomeness of this practice. 'Demand sharing' of the asymmetrical, pointed, pressured and unnegotiable sort described by Peterson (1993) and Macdonald (1999) among Australian Aborigines, and Woodburn (1998: 49) among the Hadza, can now also be seen among the farm Bushmen. Traditionally the practice was more attenuated and less institutionalised and found primarily among the elder generation, in the form of a quasi-institutionalised 'complaint discourse' directed to 'no one in particular' (Rosenberg 1990: 32) that was part of the 'entitlement' privilege that Bushman ethos extends to Ju/'hoan seniors (and which 'enables them to live up to the demands of sharing and egalitarianism' [Lee 2003: 91]). It also applied primarily to gifts (Marshall 1976a: 369) – usually between non-*hxaro* partners, whose exchange relationship was generally relaxed and affable – rather than food, for which, in the case primarily of cooked, as well as some raw meat, a potential demander should, according to !Kung etiquette, 'sit at a little distance, not seem importunate and wait to be asked to share' (ibid.: 355) – and if a request is put forward, the wording may be metaphorical and circumspect (Biesele 1993: 24–25).

What has brought about an increase in the incidence and intensity of demand sharing among farm Bushmen is an entrenched condition of social and economic inequality. The latter is both exacerbated by, and exacerbates demand-sharing. The inequality, principally, is between those who have employment and means and those who do not. The latter direct sharing demands to the former (requesting primarily food, clothing and money), activating the more or less implicit 'due' or 'entitlement' component of the sharing process with unrelenting persistence, in a context of economic disparity (Guenther 1999: 45). This makes giving and receiving increasingly and perpetually one-sided, with sharing demands being unrelentingly directed by the badgering 'have-not' recipient to the ever more reluctant 'have' giver. 'Maté' – 'give me' – is one of the most frequently heard sentences in the auditory backdrop of the Ghanzi farm Bushmen. And while 'mate' may in the past, in non-food exchange situations, have been said by one person to another in the context of a previous obligation the person addressed had to the one requesting him to give, today that is unlikely. The requester is likely a poor, hungry, job-, money- and prospect-less hanger-on kinsperson, who, in view of severe underemployment, has never been, nor ever likely will be, in a position to reciprocate and to restore the symmetry between giving and receiving that may have been expected of him in the past. As for the reluctant would-be donor, he is likely to be a wage labourer who may have opted into a capitalist economy, the accumulative, consumerist values of which may tempt him, as he is saving to buy, and aspiring to keep, stock or such expensive consumer items as blankets, clothing, boombox radios, a donkey cart or even a second-hand pick-up truck. Sharing avoidance ploys may be resorted to with increasing readiness and regularity, for instance lying about one's possessions or concealing them or curtailing amounts of food shared and the period of sharing (Guenther 1999: 47, Lee 2003:159).[11] By evading the demander and avoiding sharing demands, the previous levelling effects of sharing cannot take effect and the development of social inequality remains unchecked and becomes more and more entrenched within farm Bushman social organisation.

As sharing declines generally in Bushman economic and social interaction, it declines also in trance dancing, the premier social arena for the display of this premier value and practice. No longer being the moral ground and being for trance dancing, the dancer and dance are now free to move into the trajectories of professionalisation and commoditisation, which the new economic order, of capitalism, wage labour and consumerism, have brought into the land.

However, we must ask whether these external factors, as extensive as they have been, were enough to bring about the decline – within the short period of two or three decades – of something as integral to Bushman society and culture as sharing. I do not think they tell the whole story. Sharing is deeply entrenched and pervasive in that society – for instance in trance dancing and meat sharing, dealt with here, but also in such other patterns as land tenure and resource exploitation, marriage, visiting, (out)adoption, story-telling, all of which, in some way, are instances of sharing, respectively, of food resources, meat (through suitor service), sociability, children, stories. Sharing (along with egalitarianism) is a hard-worked social practice in hunting-gathering societies such as the Bushmen; it is (with egalitarianism) the key element of their sociality and it is an ethos – of cosmic dimensions, according to Nurit Bird-David (1992: 30–31). One would not expect so entrenched a practice and value to be eroded within the span of a generation.

I would suggest that the reason for the erosion of sharing is its downside – the problems and contradictions that surrounded its practice in traditional, precapitalist Bushman society, and small-scale hunter-gatherer societies generally. The basic problem is that the sharing ethos was never quite as unassailable and unequivocal as one might assume it to have been, in view of its adaptive, social and moral importance and centrality in traditional Bushman society. As with the other Bushman values, of egalitarianism, cooperation, even-temperedness, it was surrounded with a cloak of self-interest and of maximisation, stemming from the high degree of personal autonomy accorded the individual (whose individualism might manifest itself in self-centredness and self-aggrandizement [Gulbrandsen 1991]). As in the present, it seems clear from the ethnographic literature that in the past, too, sharing was a matter not just of the heart, or of altruism, but also of the head, or of self-interest, and a matter not only of the dictates of custom, but on occasion also of calculation, the one proclaiming, the other undermining, sharing and generosity. A case in point is the !Kung man Toma observed by Lorna Marshall two generations back, who, when he 'had eland fat to give, took shrewd notice of certain objects he might like to have and gave their owners especially generous gifts of fat' (1976b: 366). Moreover, apart from individuals thinking or acting contrary to the maxim of generosity and sharing, there were those who chafed then – as they do now (albeit more intensively and more frequently than before) – under the demands of this practice. Richard Lee notes that the !Kung 'often gripe about sharing' (1979:

55) and Polly Wiessner reports how people 'browbeat each other constantly to be more generous' and are merciless in their request for gifts, leading one man to exclaim that 'my people kill me for things' (1982: 80). People may lie about gifts to *hxaro* partners from whom they may wish to get disassociated (ibid., 68–69) and hunters may eat up much of the meat of a kill out in the bush, or divide portions amongst close kin before anyone else in other camps can find out (Wiessner 1977: I, 156). Sharing avoidance ploys were thus also a practice of the past.

Elsewhere I have examined[12] the contradictions surrounding sharing, in the context of a wider discussion of value ambiguity in Bushman culture (Guenther 1999: 41–49), prime of them the precarious, ongoing contest between individualism and communalism. I suggest that while sharing is a stated, and practised, value of Bushman moral culture, it is not one that comes too readily or easily to individuals and it is one of the key items in the socialisation regimen for children (Guenther 1986: 166–67). While this works towards making sharing implicit and nonprescriptive (Ingold 1999: 407–8) in members of the society, it is a practice, nevertheless, that may also be violated. It has to be enforced by sanctions, by people who vigilantly observe one another, ready to pounce on their fellows for alleged or displayed 'far-heartedness'.[13] Accusations to that effect are a principal source of tension within the band, and meat-sharing episodes are especially tense, requiring much social finesse on the part of the person handling the distribution, as well as stereotypical displays of self-deprecation and humility (Lee 1993: 54–56, 185–88; Guenther 1999: 42–43).

Today's shift away from sharing, which was triggered by a number of extraneous forces amongst the acculturated, Westernised and monetised farm Bushman dancers, was thus not a radically new development within Bushman social and economic practice and ethos. This may explain the rapidity with which the sharing component of trance dancing, and its incumbent social and moral elements, is giving way to professionalisation and commoditisations, among some farm Bushmen. Self-interest, avariciousness, selfishness and other instances of non-altruistic actions and thoughts were an integral element also of traditional Bushman sociality. While occasionally rearing their heads, they were kept in check through countervailing, altruistic values and levelling practices, deriving from economic, social and ideational institutions and processes of an egalitarian, communal society. These the onslaught of a capitalist economy and value system are in the process of sweeping away, so that self-interest, deprived of its traditional checks and nurtured by a new capitalist social order, is free to hold sway.

Conclusion

I do not want to close on so bleak a note, however: sharing is still practised, especially among family members. Given that these may be flung far and wide and reside in farm villages scattered hither and yon, sharing networks do continue to operate and are activated by farm Bushmen and women (as shown in a recent study by Reneé Sylvain [1998], among the farm San of the Omaheke district in eastern Namibia). The haves and have-nots distinction is as yet incipient and is full-blown only in the larger villages (such as at D'Kar, an ethnically plural village of 1,000 people) and despite resistance and grumbling, and griping and shirking, most of the haves do, in the end, give in to the demands of the have-nots (who, as often as not, are hanger-on kin). The money economy, the most direct trigger for commoditisation, has not as yet taken deep roots within the economic behaviour of the farm Bushmen, because there is so little of it and it is so quickly spent, on food, clothing and blankets, and alcohol. And those few haves who do have enough to target-save, or to buy stock, rarely achieve their targets – or hang on to their stock, or any of its offspring to breed or sell – because they share it out or have demanded it away. As before, individualism-triggered self-interest continues its tug-of-war with communalism-generated altruism.

As for the trance dancers and dances, there clearly is the danger that the processes of professionalisation and commoditisation we find today could lead either to their disappearance as a ritual and curing practitioner and practice, or their transformation into a cultural performer and performance that are predominantly outside-directed, towards tourists, politicians or judges and spectators at national traditional dance competitions, and thus of little practical use to the Bushman community.[14] Yet, not all of today's dancers operate in the individually self-centred and culturally de-centred fashion I have described. Quite a few labour on as before, more or less in the spirit of sharing, doing 'God's work' as before, or returning to 'old time' curing, after a mercenary phase in their career when they were younger and perhaps more ambitious (as did the Ju/'hoan curer Oma Djo, after he had seen the error of his ways [Katz et al. 1997: 55–59]). Others dance – in altered form – in the spirit of self-representation, expressing, to themselves and to fellow-nationals or international visitors, their identity and political aspirations and engaging the modern world and negotiating a presence within it. As the Bushmen's central ritual and purest manifestation of their sharing ethos and their salient expression of cultural distinctiveness, the trance dance, in both its traditional form and as an instance of 'renewed tradition' (Katz et al. 1997: 136), is likely to stay on as an important mechanism for social integration and political change for post-foraging Bushmen of the new millennium.

Notes

1. Alternative, and more recent, spellings of these two !Kung terms are *n/om* and *!aia.*
2. The reason is that the process of cooking has increased the element of ownership that applies to the meat (Hunt 2000: 17), so much so that women, among the Cape /Xam, once they had cooked the meat, had control over its distribution, giving specific portions to specific individuals. The latter, according to Lloyd's informant /Han=kasso, were women and children and excluded men, who 'merely gnaw the back' (Lewis-Williams 2000: 15).
3. Lorna Marshall depicts meat sharing, especially in its second and third waves of distribution, as instances of reciprocal exchange, in terms of 'a web of mutual obligation' (and not without elements of calculation and maximisation) (Marshall 1976a: 357, 363, 366; see also

Silberbauer 1981: 254–55). She likens the exchange of the smaller portions of meat in the later phases of distribution, and of cooked meat, to gift exchange (ibid.: 363–70), of the kind Polly Wiessner was later (1982) to describe as *hxaro*. This exchange relationship does contain reciprocity and calculation, as it is a risk-management strategy in which exchange partners set up a 'relationship of mutual obligation and weigh their advantages and disadvantages and then decide where to go and with whom' (Wiessner 1977: I:, 161). There may be reciprocity also in the first wave of meat sharing, in that the person distributing the carcass may be the *hxaro* partner of the man who actually killed the animal, who, in return for receiving the arrows gave his arrow-giving exchange partner the hunted animal (Lee 1979: 247–48). We might note that Wiessner, too, did not draw a radical distinction between gift and meat distribution. While the former usually excludes food, she notes that a meat donor, in the first, sharing-informed wave of meat distribution, may give a choice piece to a *hxaro* exchange partner (Wiessner 1982: 67; see also Hunt 2000: 17). Thus, in the case of the !Kung, meat distribution does not appear as quite so pure an instance of sharing as it is presented by Woodburn (and is evidently found among the Hadza), that is, as a form of distribution that is devoid of reciprocation and calculation, and that affords the hunter no control over the meat he has procured, and no scope for building up 'social capital'. (See also Price 1975 and Hunt 2000: 15–17.)

4. The name is fictive.
5. Two dramatic manifestations of distance-curing were the attempted treatments, in 1980 and 1996 by a number of Ghanzi farm Bushman trance dancers, of Sir Seretse Khama and John Hardbottle, both of them terminal cancer patients who lay in their hospital beds while the dance was performed a long distance away (in the latter case as far away as Germany [Hermans 1997: 282]).
6. Martin Gusinde already in the early 1960s reported a similar state of ritual embellishment among the Hukwe (Kxoe) 'shamans' of the lower Okavango, leading him to posulate a distinction between a condition of 'real shamanism', of the Hukwe and other 'River Bushmen', and of 'incipient shamanism', among Kalahari Bushmen (Gusinde 1966: 134–35).
7. Or, as in the case of Martin Gusinde, to have the anthropologist's fieldwork cleared with //Gãuwa by a trance dancer. To Gusinde's relief the god, according to the dancer testimony, deemed the Pater's work 'a good thing' (Gusinde 1966: 21).
8. See Lee (1993: 115–29) and Katz et al. (1997: 115–29) for accounts of two new dances among the Dobe and /Kae/kae Ju/'hoansi (the Trees Dance, inspired by the Johannesburg mine compound dances and brought to the region by a Ju/'hoan man after he had worked in the mines, and the older, widespread Drum Dance, derived originally from the Bantu-speaking Mbukushu).
9. See Peterson (1991: 2–5) for a lucid explication of Simmel on this point, and an application to hunder-gatherers.
10. Such as among the /Kae/kae Ju/'hoansi, where, notwithstanding a number of changes of the sort described in this paper, trance dancing, by the late 1980s, was described by Richard Katz and his co-researchers in much the same terms as a generation earlier, as an instance of synergetic 'community healings', performed by the dancer in the sharing spirit.
11. Woodburn (1998: 55, 63) describes these for the traditional Hadza (whom he notes to be 'unenthusiastic' about sharing): not offering to share, but requiring the potential recipient to initiate the demand, concealing things that should be shared, telling lies about their possessions and withdrawing to another residential location, when in possession of shareable items' and, with respect to meat' the dog-in-the-manger action of gobbling up an excessively large amount of meat, which, 'once eaten cannot be shared'!
12. As have others, such as Sahlins (1972: 203–4), Marshall (1976a: 295–303), Service (1979: 21–23), Woodburn (1982: 432), Lee (1982: 53–56), Gulbrandsen (1991), Kelly (1995: 164–66).
13. James Woodburn makes the same point about egalitarianism: like sharing, it, too, does not come naturally to people, some of whom may seek more power or wealth, requiring a group's constant vigilance against such individuals (1982: 432; see also Kent 1993 and Riches 2000).

14. The latter development, the higher incidence of outward-directed dances over inward-directed ones, has been reported at the !Kung community operating Omatako Valley Rest Camp in the Otjozondjupa region of northwestern Namibia. This community-run tourism operation offers these commoditised dances on a regular basis to visiting tourists. Members of the community saw this as a problem, expressing concern over the fact that such cultural performances had come to take precedence over the regular performances of the trance curing dance, to the detriment of the community, who are being deprived of a vital institution of their culture (Brörmann 1999: 40).

References

Bank, A. (ed.) 1998. *The Proceedings of the Khoisan Identities and Cultural Heritage Conference.* Cape Town: Institute for Historical Research, University of the Western Cape.

Barnard, A. and J. Woodburn. 1988. 'Property, Power and Ideology in Hunting and Gathering Societies: An Introduction'. In: T. Ingold, D. Riches and J. Woodburn (eds), *Hunter and Gatherers Volume 2: Property, Power and Ideology*, pp. 4–32. Oxford: Berg.

Biesele, M. 1993. *Women Like Meat: The Folklore and Foraging Ideology of the Kalahari Ju'hoansi.* Johannesburg and Bloomington: Witwatersrand University Press and University of Indiana Press.

Bird-David, N. 1992. 'Beyond "The Original Affluent Society": A Culturalist Reformulation', *Current Anthropology*, 33: 25–47.

Brörmann, M. 1999. Working Group of Indigenous Minorities in Southern Africa WIMSA Report on Activities April 1998 to March 1999, Windhoek: WIMSA.

Buntman, B. 1996. 'Bushman Images in South African Tourist Advertising: The Case of Kagga Kamma'. In: P. Skotnes (ed.), *Miscast Negotiating the Presence of the Bushmen,* pp. 271–80. Cape Town: University of Cape Town Press.

—— 2002. 'Travels to Otherness: Whose Identity Do We Want to See?'. In: H. Stewart, A. Barnard and K. Omura (eds), *Self- and Other-Images of Hunter-Gatherers.* Senri Ethnological Studies no. 60, pp. 65–84. Osaka: National Museum of Ethnology.

England, N. 1967. 'Bushman Counterpoint', *Journal of the International Folk Music Council* 19: 58–66.

Guenther, M. 1976. 'From Hunters to Squatters: Social and Cultural Change among the Ghanzi Farm Bushmen'. In: R.B. Lee and I. DeVore (eds), *Kalahari Hunter-Gatherers*, pp. 120–33. Cambridge, Mass.: Harvard University Press.

—— 1986. *The Nharo Bushmen of Botswana Tradition and Change* (QKF 3). Hamburg: Helmut Buske Verlag.

—— 1992. '"Not a Bushman Thing": Witchcraft among the Bushmen and Hunter-Gatherers', *Anthropos*, 87: 83–107.

—— 1999. *Tricksters and Trancers: Bushman Religion and Society.* Bloomington: Indiana University Press.

—— 2002. 'Ethnotourism and the Bushmen', In: H. Stewart, A. Barnard and K. Omura (eds), *Self- and Other-Images of Hunter-Gatherers.* Senri Ethnological Studies no. 60, pp. 47–54. Osaka: National Museum of Ethnology.

Gulbrandsen, O. 1991. 'On the Problem of Egalitarianism. The Kalahari San in Transition'. In: R. Gronhaug, G. Haaland and G. Henriksen (eds), *The Ecology of Choice and Symbol Essays in Honour of Frederik Barth*, pp. 81–111. Bergen: Alma Mater Forlag AS.

Gusinde, M. 1966. *Von gelben und schwarzen Buschmännern*, Graz: Akademische Druck- und Verlagsanstalt.

Hermans, J. 1998. 'Basarwa Cultural Preservation in Contemporary Botswana: The Dance'. In: A. Bank (ed.), *The Proceedings of the Khoisan Identities and Cultural Heritage Conference*, pp. 281–87. Cape Town: Institute for Historical Research, University of the Western Cape.

Hitchcock, R. 1996. *Kalahari Communities: Bushmen and the Politics of the Environment in Southern Africa.* IWGIA Document No. 79. Copenhagen: International Work Group for Indigenous Affairs.

—— 1999. 'The Tyua of North-Eastern Botswana'. In: R.B. Lee and R. Daly (eds), *The Cambridge Encyclopedia of Hunter and Gatherers,* pp. 225–29. Cambridge: Cambridge University Press.
Hunt, R.C. 1999. 'Forager Food Sharing Economy: Transfers and Exchanges'. In: G.W. Wenzel, G. Hovelsrud-Broda and N. Kishigami (eds), pp. 7–26. Senri Ethnological Studies no. 53. Osaka: National Museum of Ethnology.
Ingold, T. 1999. 'On the Social Relations of the Hunter-Gatherer Band'. In: R.B. Lee and R. Daly (eds), *The Cambridge Encyclopedia of Hunter and Gatherers,* pp. 399–410. Cambridge: Cambridge University Press.
Isaacson, R. 2002. *The Healing Land: A Kalahari Journey,* London: Fourth Estate.
Katz, R. 1982. *Boiling Energy: Community Healing among the Kalahari Kung.* Cambridge, Mass.: Harvard University Press.
Katz, R., M. Biesele and V. St. Denis 1997. *Healing Makes our Hearts Happy: Spirituality and Transformation among the Kalahari Ju/'hoansi.* Rochester, Vermont: Inner Traditions.
Kelly, R. 1995. *The Foraging Spectrum.* Washington, D.C.: Smithonian Institution Press.
Kent, S. 1993. 'Sharing in an Egalitarian Kalahari Community', *Man* (N.S.), 28: 479–514.
Lee, R.B. 1979. *The !Kung San: Men, Women and Work in a Foraging Society,* Cambridge: Cambridge University Press.
—— 1982. 'Politics, Sexual and Non-Sexual, in an Egalitarian Society'. In: R.B. Lee and E. Leacock (eds), *Politics and History in Band Societies,* pp. 37–60. Cambridge: Cambridge University Press, 1982.
—— 1984. *The Dobe !Kung.* New York: Holt, Rinehart and Winston.
—— 1993. *The Dobe Ju/'hoansi,* 2nd ed. Fort Worth: Harcourt Brace College Publishers.
—— 2003. *The Dobe Ju/'hoansi,* 3rd ed. Wadsworth: Thomson Learning.
—— and R. Hitchcock 2001. 'African Hunter-Gatherers: Survival, History and Political Identity'. In: J. Tanaka and M. Kimura (eds), *African Studies Monograph,* Supplementary Issue. 26: 257–80.
Lewis-Williams, D. 1981. *Believing and Seeing: Symbolic Meanings in Southern San Rock Paintings.* New York: Academic Press.
—— 2000. *Stories that Float from Afar.* Cape Town: David Philips Publisher.
Macdonald, G. 1999. 'Economics, Personhood and Demand Sharing among the Wiradjun of New South Wales'. In: G.W. Wenzel, G. Hovelund-Broda and N. Kishigami (eds), *The Social Economy of Sharing: Resource Allocation and Modern Hunter-Gatherers,* pp. 87–111. Senri Ethnological Studies no. 53. Osaka: National Museum of Ethnology.
Marshall, L. 1965. 'The !Kung Bushmen'. In: J.L. Gibbs, Jr. (ed.), *Peoples of Africa,* pp. 241–78. New York: Holt, Rinehart & Winston.
—— 1976a. 'Sharing, Talking and Giving: Relief of Social Tensions among the !Kung'. In: R.B. Lee and I. DeVore (eds), *Kalahari Hunter-Gatherers,* pp. 349–71. Cambridge, Mass.: Harvard University Press.
—— 1976b. *The !Kung of Nyae Nyae.* Cambridge, Mass.: Harvard University Press.
—— 1999. *Nyae Nyae !Kung Beliefs and Rites.* Peabody Museum Monographs no. 8. Cambridge: Peabody Museum of Archaeology and Ethnology, Harvard University.
Peterson, N. 1991. 'Introduction: Cash, Commoditisations and Changing Foragers'. In: Nicolas Peterson and Toshio Matsuyama (eds), *Cash, Commoditisations and Changing Foragers,* pp. 1–16. Senri Ethnological Studies no. 30. Osaka: National Museum of Ethnology.
—— 1993. 'Demand Sharing: Reciprocity and the Pressure for Generosity among Foragers'. *American Anthropologist,* 95: 860–74.
Price, J. 1975. 'Sharing: The Integration of Intimate Economies'. *Anthropologica,* 17: 3–28.
Riches, D. 2000. 'The Holistic Person; or, the Ideology of Egalitarianism'. *Man* (N.S.), 6: 669–85.
Rosenberg, H. 1990. 'Complaint Discourse, Aging and Caregiving among the !Kung San of Botswana'. In: Jay Sokolovsky (ed.), *The Cultural Context of Aging,* pp. 19–41. New York: Bergin & Garvey.
Sahlins, M. 1972. 'On the Sociology of Primitive Exchange'. In: Marshall Sahlins, *Stone Age Economics,* pp. 185–275. Chicago: Aldine.
Schatz, I. 1993. *Unter Buschleuten,* Windhoek: Ilse Schatz.

Schildkrout, E. 1999. 'Gender and Sexuality in Mangbetu Art'. In: R.B. Phillips and C.B. Steiner (eds), *Unpacking Culture: Art and Commodity in Colonial and Postcolonial Worlds*, pp. 197–213. Berkeley: University of California Press.
Service, E. 1979. *Man the Hunter.* 2nd ed. Englewood Cliffs: Prentice-Hall.
Simmel, G. 1907/1978. *The Philosophy of Money.* London: Tavistock.
Silberbauer, G. 1981. *Hunter and Habitat in the Central Kalahari Desert.* Cambridge: Cambridge University Press..
Smith, A., C. Malherbe, M. Guenther and P. Berens 2000. *The Bushmen of Southern Africa: A Foraging Society in Transition.* Cape Town and Athens: David Philips Publishers and Ohio University Press.
Sylvain, R. 1998. 'Survival Strategies of San Women in the Omaheke Region, Namibia'. In A. Bank (ed.) *The Proceedings of the Cultural Identities and Heritage Conference,* pp. 336–43. Cape Town: Institute for Historical Research, University of the Western Cape.
Vorster, L.P. 'The !Xu of Schmidtsdrift and Sorcery'. In: A.J.M. Sanders (ed.), *Speaking for the Bushmen*, pp. 101–15. Gaborone: The Botswana Society.
Wagner-Robertz, D. 1976. 'Schamanentum bei den Hain//om in Südwestafrika', *Anthropos*, 71: 533–54.
Widlok, T. 2001. 'The Illusion of a Future? Medicine Dance Rituals for the Civil Society of Tomorrow'. *African Studies Monograph*, Supplementary Issue, T. Widlok and K. Sugawara (eds), 27: 165–83.
Wiessner, P. 1977. 'Hxaro: A Regional System of Reciprocity for Reducing Risk among the !Kung San', 2 vols. Ph.D. dissertation, Anne Arbor: University Microfilm International.
—— 1982. 'Risk, Reciprocity, and Social Influence on !Kung San Economics'. In: R.B. Lee and E. Leacock (eds), *Politics and History in Band Societies*, pp. 61–84. Cambridge University Press.
—— and F.T. Larsen 1979. '"Mother! Sing Loudly to Me!": The Annotated Dialogue of a Basarwa Healer in Trance'. *Botswana Notes and Records,* 11: 25–31.
Woodburn, J. 1982. 'Egalitarian Societies'. *Man* (N. S.), 17: 431–51.
—— 1998. 'Sharing is not a Form of Exchange: An Analysis of Property Sharing in Immediate-Return Hunter-Gatherers'. In: C. Hann (ed.), *Property Relations Renewing the Anthropological Tradition*, pp. 48–63. Cambridge: Cambridge University Press.

12

From Humility to Lordship in Island Southeast Asia

Thomas Gibson

In this paper, I compare the egalitarian religious images that exist in one of the most hierarchical societies in Island Southeast Asia, the Makassar of coastal South Sulawesi, with the hierarchical religious images that exist in one of the most egalitarian societies, the Buid of highland Mindoro. This comparison will allow me to cast new light on Woodburn's argument that the origin of social inequality in immediate-return hunter-gatherer societies may lie in the appropriation of the religious domain by senior men.

In the first part of the paper, I argue that the Makassar and the Buid formed part of a single regional system in which coastal societies preyed on the members of autonomous tribal societies practising shifting cultivation in the highlands. The depredations of the hierarchical coastal societies spawned an ethic in the highlands in which equality, autonomy and communal solidarity were valued above all else. But even within the coastal societies, the lower orders often developed a set of religious values similar to those of the highlanders, values that rejected the hierarchy, dependency and factionalism of the elite. This rejection was expressed through popular interpretations of world religions like Islam and Christianity. Historically, religions promising spiritual salvation from social bondage often arose in the most hierarchical social orders. I argue that hierarchy and equality, dependency and autonomy, solidarity and factionalism should all be viewed as conceptual oppositions that develop in tandem with one another, much like the concepts of 'free gift' and 'commodity' (Parry 1986).

In the second part of the paper, I approach popular ideas of salvation among the Makassar through an analysis of the Epic of Datu Museng. In reciting this epic, Makassar bards simultaneously recall their experience of Dutch colonialism, express a mystical vision of life as a quest to transcend the social order and reunite with God, and rework a pervasive preoccupation of

Austronesian mythology, the fate of opposite-sex twins. They also reveal a profound ambivalence toward the values of equality and hierarchy, autonomy and dependency, solidarity and factionalism. It is only because Makassar society was based on hereditary ranks, slavery and warfare that Makassar religion could develop such a clear ideal of the wandering saint who transcends all worldly spatial, temporal and categorical boundaries.

In the third part of the paper, I compare the salvation Islamic saints promise the Makassar with the salvation Jesus Christ promises lowland Filipinos. In both cases, the lower orders in a hierarchical society can appeal to the transcendental values of a global religion to circumscribe the power of the local spirits and political elites. I contrast this situation with that of the Buid and the immediate-return hunter-gatherers discussed by Woodburn. In these egalitarian societies, the major threat to society comes not from elites who abuse their power but from individuals who place their own autonomy above the needs of the group. Religious rituals are used to assert the primacy of communal solidarity over individual autonomy. The seeds of inequality lie in a widespread tendency to map the opposition between communal and individual interest onto the opposition between male and female, allowing senior men to assert a monopoly of control over collective ritual.

Equality as a Symbolic Value

The values of social equality, individual autonomy and moral solidarity coexist in most societies with their opposites: hierarchy, dependency and factional loyalty. This claim derives from the simple point that at the level of symbols and meanings every element gains its meaning from its place in a structure of significant differences. For egalitarianism to be a value, people must have some concept of its opposite. The same is true of hierarchy. This means that people who value equality in some contexts must at least have a concept of hierarchy in others. In most societies, the two sets of values govern different spheres of social life. In extremely hierarchical societies, egalitarian and individualistic values may be confined to the realm of religious belief and practice. This is Dumont's argument with regard to religious renouncers who sought individual salvation in Hindu India without regard to hierarchical notions of the relative impurity of social groups like castes (Dumont 1970). In extremely egalitarian societies, hierarchical values may be confined to the realm of religious belief and practice. I have argued that this is the case for the Buid of Mindoro, Philippines (Gibson 1986). Woodburn has made a similar argument regarding the presence of an exclusive men's cult in otherwise perfectly egalitarian hunter-gatherer societies in Africa (Woodburn 1998).

Six Kinds of Society in Island Southeast Asia

In a previous paper comparing attitudes towards violence, domination and aggression among shifting cultivators in Island Southeast Asia, I identified three types of society that value equality in distinctive ways (Gibson 1990a). In the first category of societies, typified by the Buid, equality is *ascribed* to every member of society at birth. At the social level, everyone enjoys equal access to productive resources, personal autonomy in the choice of spouse and place of residence, and the right to share the meat of domestic animals sacrificed by other members of the community. At the religious level, all men enjoy equal access to the spirit familiars that guard against disease, personal autonomy in relation to the spirits of dead ancestors and an obligation to participate in certain collective rituals to appease the spirits of the earth. Women play a less prominent role in interactions with the spirit world. They are not categorically excluded from it, however, and some women do acquire direct access to spirit familiars.

In Buid society, social relations based on long-term indebtedness, moral obligations to genealogical kin and factional conflict are viewed as morally wrong and mystically dangerous to the social whole. Boastful, domineering, possessive and aggressive actions by individuals are stigmatised by society. All these behaviours are vividly exemplified in the religious domain by a host of predatory spirit types. Among human spirit types, the ghosts of dead kin are always greedy for meat, the spirits of the mountain peaks are possessive lovers, the spirits of the forest are irrationally aggressive, and spirits who resemble lowland peasants are cannibalistic. The cosmos as a whole is represented as a food chain in which moral vice is represented by the predatory spirits at the top of the chain who attack humans for their food. Moral virtue attaches to the spirits of the earth and the plants at the bottom of the chain that feed all the rest.

A second category of society views equality as an *achievement*. Access to the status of equal adult tends to be more open for men than for women, and the achievement of such status is often linked to feats of bravery which are precursors to the acquisition of a wife. Marital and parental claims are correspondingly greater than in the first category. But the ideal continues to be a community of equal adults. The clearest example of this type is the Ilongot of northern Luzon (R. Rosaldo 1980; M. Rosaldo 1980). A third category departs from valuing equality of outcomes, but continues to value equality of opportunity in the *competition* for high rank that is not necessarily passed on to the next generation. A famous example of this type is the Iban of Borneo described by Freeman and others (Freeman 1970; Rousseau 1980). Again, men have an advantage over women in this competition because it is linked to success in headhunting and warfare.

In addition to the predominantly egalitarian societies discussed so far, it is also possible to identify the presence of egalitarian values in predominantly hierarchical societies. Many tribal societies in Island Southeast Asia have a system of hereditary ascribed ranks, often glossed as 'noble', 'commoner' and 'slave', which are reproduced through a hierarchical marriage system involving large marriage payments. But significantly, societies in this category retained a large place for *competition between factional leaders* who occupied relatively equal positions in the ranking system and who sought to convert their economic, military or religious achievements into higher social rank. This would appear to be the most typical form of society in the Southeast Asian highlands, where a complex of headhunting and competitive feasting helps to reproduce a stratified social order. Societies of this sort continued to exist into the twentieth century among the Ngaju, Kayan and Kenyah of central Borneo (Schärer 1963; Rousseau 1990).

A fifth category includes those internally ranked tribal societies that developed into even more hierarchical chiefdoms and kingdoms between the fourth and fourteenth centuries CE, often adopting Indic notions of divine kingship. Many of these kingdoms later converted to Theravada Buddhism, Islam and Christianity. These religions brought with them both hierarchical versions centred on the royal court and egalitarian versions centred on popular ritual and *mysticism* (Reid 1993: 132–202). Talented boys could escape their humble origins to pursue careers either within the religious hierarchy or in opposition to it. As Cannell has argued for the Christian Philippines and as I argue for Islamic Indonesia, these global religions made new idioms of equality and solidarity available to increasingly oppressed peasants at the same time that they provided new forms of legitimacy for their masters.

A sixth category includes the societies that fell under the control of Europeans after the Portuguese conquest of Melaka in 1511. The history of the Philippines and Makassar after the imposition of European rule is one of continual anticolonial uprisings, often framed in terms of *millenarian* ideas derived from Christianity or Islam. Colonial rule led to a cleavage between the social, political and religious hierarchies at a very early date. In the Philippines, the pagan tribesmen of the mountains were the only peoples to resist both Christianity and Spanish rule. Their territories often provided a refuge for lowland peasants seeking to evade colonial rule. In South Sulawesi, the Makassar kings of Gowa and Tallo' became the heads of a peninsula-wide social hierarchy during the sixteenth century. They converted to Islam in 1605, making the scholars and saints of Mecca and Medina the heads of the religious hierarchy in the seventeenth century. They were defeated by the Dutch in 1667, making the Governors of the United East India Company (VOC) the heads of the political hierarchy in the eighteenth century.

Southeast Asia as a Regional System

For many centuries, societies falling into all six of these categories constituted a single, loosely integrated system in Island Southeast Asia (Gibson 1990b). This system was composed of units that were both politically autonomous and socially porous. The autonomy and fluidity which characterised societies in the region from prehistoric times until the rise of modern states was facilitated by certain features of the physical and social landscape: the proximity of most land areas to navigable trade routes, low population densities, and an interstitial position between the great civilisations of East, South and West Asia. Local ethnic groups could form, grow into great powers, collapse and be absorbed into their neighbours (see e.g. Warren 1981).

Social fluidity was also facilitated by the fact that societies falling into all six of these categories employed variants of a single underlying cultural model inherited from their common Austronesian ancestors. Elsewhere I have argued that kinship, understood as relations of filiation and descent, and marriage, understood as alliances between distinct kinship groups, are not central to social life in most Austronesian societies (Gibson 1985, 1995). Rather, the social order is based instead on idioms of shared space and activity that allow Austronesian societies to transform strangers into kin over time.

Houses serve as the primary symbol of shared space. Houses provide the basic framework for the most fundamental shared social activities: cooking, eating and sexual intercourse. In addition to structuring people's everyday social and economic experiences and activities, the house draws together many of the models of gender, space and time encountered in myth and ritual. It is androgynous, divided into three levels and oriented according to the movements of the celestial bodies. It integrates celestial, biological and historical time. Finally, houses are a microcosm of the local community, the kingdom and the world. Social groups of widely different sizes can be symbolised by structures that range from humble huts containing a family of slaves to royal palaces that represent entire kingdoms (Headley 1987).

The relationship between co-resident siblings and spouses serve as the primary symbols of shared activity. Sibling sets are internally differentiated by relative age but not by gender. The relation between elder and junior sibling is less hierarchical than that between parent and child and more elastic (cf. McKinley 1981). In the 'bilateral' societies of central Indonesia and the Philippines, one normally marries a cousin, a kinsman of the same generation who is comparable to a sibling. Some marriage rituals are designed to open up a symbolic difference between potential spouses sufficient to avoid the feeling of incest at the time of marriage (cf. Conklin 1964; Bloch 1971). Other rituals are designed to transform those related only by marriage into kinsmen. This transformation can be effected through a 'downward focus' on the common offspring of a marriage through devices such as teknonymy (Geertz and Geertz 1975) or by stressing the relation between co-parents-in-law as stabilised through shared grandchildren (Carsten 1997). The fluidity between the categories of sibling and spouse receives its purest expression at the level of myth, in the story of opposite-sex twins who are separated at birth but ultimately reunite. This is a theme that runs through the Panji tales of Java and Bali and the I La Galigo tales of the Bugis (Rassers 1922; Ras 1973; Pelras 1996: 88–89). It is also one of the themes that underlies the Epic of Datu Museng.

In summary, transitions from one category of society to another could take place in either direction, both in the lives of individuals and in the histories of whole societies. Thus, social inequality in Island Southeast Asia was not the result of a unilinear and irreversible evolution, but of the changing concrete political and economic situations a group confronted in its history. Individuals were able to cross from societies dominated by one set of values to another, either through choice, as when slaves escaped to the highlands, or through coercion, as when highlanders were captured to serve as slaves.

History, Mysticism and Myth in the Epic of Datu Museng

I will now turn to the images of equality and personal autonomy that lie at the heart of religious practice in one of the most hierarchical and predatory societies of Island Southeast Asia, the Makassar of South Sulawesi. These images are contained in written and oral literature inspired by Sufi mysticism and in associated ritual practices. They enabled even the most humble slave to imagine a world in which individual moral virtue outweighed all forms of inherited power, rank and wealth. This form of Islam stood in opposition not only to the hierarchy of the social world, but also in opposition to the official Islam of the royal court.

My first-hand knowledge of Makassar culture and society was acquired during field research in the villages of Ara and Bira, located at the southwestern tip of the peninsula of South Sulawesi. These two villages have enjoyed a regional reputation as boat builders and sailors since at least the sixteenth century and possibly even since the thirteenth century. They appear in the I La Galigo, the ancient mythical cycle of the Bugis people, as the Waniaga, from the Sanskrit term for merchants (Pelras 1996). For most of their history, Ara and Bira have derived a remarkable degree of political, economic and cultural autonomy from their geographical position at the mouth of the Gulf of Bone. This location allowed them to serve both as middlemen on the trade routes between Java and the Spice Islands, and to play the Bugis powers to the north off against the Makassar and colonial powers based to the west.

Between 1530 and 1600, the twin Makassar kingdoms of Gowa and Tallo' took advantage of their privileged access to Portuguese firearms to establish their hegemony over the whole of South Sulawesi. Armies made up of free Makassar from the core of Gowa captured slaves from outlying kingdoms who were put to work building elaborate fortifications and growing rice. The rice was exported to the Moluccas in exchange for spices that were used to obtain yet more firearms in an ever growing spiral. Ara and Bira became vassals of the pagan Empire of Gowa in the 1560s.

In 1605, the ruler of Tallo' looked across the seas for a more cosmopolitan model of royal absolutism than was provided by the local myth of royal descent from heavenly beings. He found it in the Islamic Sultanate of Aceh, ruled at the time by Iskandar Muda. The royal court of Aceh had in turn modelled itself on that of the Mughal Emperor Akbar. Tallo' converted to a version of Islam that placed the ruler at the centre of both the secular state and the religious cosmos. The royal chronicle composed at the behest of Akbar, the *Akbar Nama*, and the royal chronicle of Aceh, the *Hikayat Aceh*, provided a new model for centralised imperial authority in the 'Gunpowder Empires' of Asia (see Hodgson 1974: Volume III, Book 5). Between 1603 and 1611, all the kings of South Sulawesi converted to Islam, either voluntarily or after being defeated by Goa.

In 1667 the Kingdom of Gowa was itself defeated by a coalition of the Dutch and Bugis from the Kingdom of Bone. According to the Treaty of Bungaya, Gowa's outlying vassals were transferred to the VOC by right of conquest. These included the villages of Ara and Bira. The VOC established a permanent garrison in Ujung Pandang just north of Gowa's palace at Somba Opu. The King of Bone also maintained a permanent presence in Ujung Pandang in a fort at Bontoala that had been captured from Gowa. The three greatest powers of eastern Indonesia thus confronted one another in Ujung Pandang throughout the eighteenth century.

In 1727, the villages of Ara and Bira began paying annual tribute to the VOC. After 1737, they were nominally under the authority of a 'Junior Merchant' stationed at Fort Carolina in Bulukumba. Throughout the eighteenth century, the VOC maintained garrisons in many other outlying territories, including Selayar and Bima. The Dutch officials in charge of these outposts assumed the power formerly enjoyed by local chiefs of enslaving people as a punishment for certain crimes or in cases where a miscreant was unable to pay a fine. These officials soon became the primary suppliers of the slaves exported from Makassar (Sutherland 1983). They also frequently intervened in local succession disputes in exchange for bribes. The Governor in Ujung Pandang was often drawn into the matter and had to decide who was the legitimate ruler of a local kingdom. He thus undertook one of the roles formerly played by the Sultan of Gowa, that of confirming local rulers in office, without being able to play his other central roles as the apex of the regional systems of marriage and religion.

The Dutch did not attempt to impose direct rule on villages like Ara and Bira until 1864 and did not do so effectively until the 1920s when native officials were paid a salary for the first time. From 1942 until 1961 South Sulawesi suffered constant turmoil, first from the Japanese occupation, then from the war of independence, and finally from the Darul Islam insurrection which attempted to establish an Islamic state. The grip of the central government on the villages of Ara and Bira only really tightened between 1971 and 1998 under the New Order regime of President Suharto (Gibson, 2000). Thus despite having acknowledged a series of distant overlords over the past 500 years, the villages of Ara and Bira have been able to maintain a remarkable degree of political and cultural autonomy.

The Sinrili' Datu Museng in 1852 as Subaltern History

The Sinrili' Datu Museng seems to have first come to the attention of Europeans in 1852, when versions of it were recorded by two different Dutch missionaries. The first of them, Benjamin Frederick Matthes, arrived in South Sulawesi in 1848 (van den Brink, 1943). In his *Makassarsche Chrestomathie* he wrote that the Sinrili' Datu Museng was obtained 'from the mouth of a renowned singer and transcribed by the hand of a very accomplished Native scribe' (Matthes 1860: 512). The full version contains about 1,150 lines of thirteen or fourteen syllables each.

Version 1: The Sinrili' Datu Museng (Matthes, Goa, recorded c. 1852)

> Datu Museng is a loyal servant of the Sultan of Sumbawa. The Sultan learns that the Datu of Jarewe is in Ujung Pandang and is on the verge of persuading the Governor to recognise him as the legitimate Sultan of Sumbawa. He sends Datu Museng to plead his case. Datu Museng brings his wife Maipa Deapati along. When the Governor learns of her beauty, he demands her as a concubine, offering to exchange forty slave women for her. Datu Museng refuses. Together, he and Maipa decide it would be better to die and reunite in heaven than to submit to an infidel. Maipa washes, prays and allows Datu Museng to cut her throat. Datu Museng discards his protective amulet and fights to the death. The Karaeng of Galesong kills him with a lance and brings his head back to the Governor. (Condensed from Matthes 1860: 529–57)

Matthes linked this version of the Sinrili' Datu Museng to a real succession dispute that took place in Sumbawa in the 1760s. The historical background to this dispute is as follows.

The rivalry between the Kingdoms of Gowa and Bone continued after Gowa's defeat in 1667. Bone's attempt to establish its own hegemony over South Sulawesi was thwarted by the astute marriage politics of the royal house of Tallo' with other royal houses in Borneo and Sumbawa. The continuing ability of the House of Tallo' to maintain its position at the top of the regional marriage system after the fall of Gowa was a source of constant irritation to the VOC in the eighteenth century.

> Sumbawa belonged to the realms where the Makassarese rulers (that is, the Gowanese and Telloese rulers) who were no longer in a position to expand by means of conquest sought to do so by means of marriage alliance; although diminished in power, the Gowanese and Telloese rulers knew how to preserve their prestige so well among the rulers of Celebes, as well as among those of the island of Sumbawa and the east coast of Borneo, that it was repeatedly the case that upon the death of a ruler in one of the realms situated there he was succeeded by the son or daughter of the Gowanese princess he had married, whether or not he had also fathered children in a previous marriage to a woman who, while not Gowanese, was sprung from no less pure noble blood, and whose claim to the throne was thus of no lower standing than of their Gowanese brother or sister. (Ligtvoet [1875] in Noorduyn 1987: 10)

In 1756 Sultan Shafi al-Din of Tallo' died, the last strong ruler the polity of Gowa-Tallo' was to have. In 1763 a struggle for the throne of Sumbawa broke out between the reigning Sultan, Datu Jarewe, and his traditional rival, Datu Taliwang. Datu Taliwang recruited Bugis fugitives from Wajo' to fight on his behalf, while Datu Jarewe turned to Balinese from the neighbouring island of Lombok. Datu Taliwang then enlisted the support of the VOC Resident in Bima, Johann Tinne (1758–64), by promising him 100 slaves. Tinne persuaded the VOC Governor in Ujung Pandang, Cornelis Sinkelaar, to send troops to help Datu Taliwang. In November 1763, three sloops with twenty-one European soldiers arrived under the command of the Resident of Selayar, Jakob Bikkes Bakker (1758–64). The Dutch succeeded in driving out the Balinese, capturing Datu Jarewe, and installing Datu Taliwang as Sultan of Sumbawa. Datu Jarewe was brought back to Ujung Pandang in February 1764 (Noorduyn 1987).

Datu Taliwang's ally Tinne died on 25 June 1764 and the commander of the Dutch expedition, Bakker, took his place as Resident in Bima (1764–68). Fearing that the death of Tinne would undermine his influence with Governor Sinkelaar, Datu Taliwang sent a mission to Ujung Pandang at the end of 1764. It included the current Nene Rangan, another of the five Electors, and the Datu of Busing. The Datu of Busing was the Chief of Re, one of ten districts in Sumbawa proper, and also governor of one of the four districts into which the capital was divided. They arrived too late: Sinkelaar had indeed decided that he had been misled by Tinne about Datu Jarewe's right to the throne of Sumbawa. On 9 February 1765, Sinkelaar signed a treaty recognizing him as the true Sultan of Sumbawa. Sinkelaar then ordered the arrest of the three emissaries of Datu Taliwang to prevent them from returning to Sumbawa with the news. Two of the emissaries surrendered, but Datu Busing resisted. On 4 March 1765, Datu Busing 'ran amok' in Ujung Pandang and was killed by Dutch troops (Noorduyn 1987: 34–35). This was, of course, none other than the Datu Museng celebrated by the Sinrili'.

The second Dutch missionary to record the Sinrili' Datu Museng was William Donselaar. Matthes had visited the former VOC outpost at Bantaeng in 1849, where he found a large Indo-European community, a product of liaisons between the garrison of Dutch soldiers that had been established in 1737 and local women. Neither Muslim nor Christian, they were deeply immersed in a Shaivite cult of Karaeng Loe that probably dated back to the fourteenth century (Goudswaard 1865). Matthes recommended the dispatch of two missionaries who could both minister to the spiritual needs of the nominal Christians on the south coast and study the local languages with a view to carrying on missionary work among the surrounding Muslim population. The Netherlands Missionary Society at Rotterdam reassigned Donselaar from Kupang in Timor to Bantaeng in 1852. In 1853, he published a summary of the Sinrili' as it was then recited in Bantaeng.

Version 2: The Sinrili' Datu Museng (Donselaar, Bantaeng, 1852)

Datu Museng elopes with Maipa Deapati, the daughter of the Datu of Jarewe, a vassal of the Sultan of Sumbawa who is himself a vassal of the Dutch Governor of Ujung Pandang. When Datu Jarewe goes to complain about Datu Museng to the Governor, the latter follows to defend himself. But when he arrives with his wife, the Governor falls in love with Maipa and tries to seize her by force. Maipa tells Datu Museng she would rather die than submit to an infidel. She bathes in consecrated water and offers her throat to his knife. He kills her, wraps her in a shroud and recites the appropriate prayers from the Koran. Then he goes out and fights until he is exhausted. He cannot be shot or stabbed because he is invulnerable. The Karaeng of Galesong finally kills him by striking him in the head with the butt of a rifle. (Condensed from Donselaar 1855)

As we will see, the detail about the elopement of Datu Museng with the daughter of a noble man is central to the version I recorded in Ara in 1988. Already the story is motivated as much by contradictions internal to Makassar society as it is by the uncontrolled power and appetites of the Dutch overlords.

Sufism in South Sulawesi

Although the Sinrili' Datu Museng concerns the fate of a minor noble from Sumbawa who died at the hands of the Dutch in Ujung Pandang, it resonates among all the Makassar whose ancestors suffered under the oppressive rule of the VOC. The versions recorded in 1852 came from the Dutch possessions of Bantaeng and Ujung Pandang. The versions of the Sinrili' Datu Museng I recorded 136 years later in Ara derived from the island of Selayar. Like Bantaeng and Sumbawa, Ara, Bira and Selayar were all intermittently under Dutch indirect rule from 1667 to 1949.

All these areas were also deeply engaged in long-distance networks of Islamic learning from the seventeenth century on. Soon after the conversion of South Sulawesi to Islam between 1603 and 1611, students from all over the peninsula began to embark on the pilgrimage to Mecca, stopping at ports all around the Indian Ocean to study under Islamic teachers. The most important port along the way was Aceh in north Sumatra. The Shaik al-Islam in Aceh from 1637 to 1643 was a man of mixed Hadrami and Gujarati descent known as Nur al-Din al-Raniri. al-Raniri was a key figure in Southeast Asian Islam. He was the descendent of a long line of Shaikhs from the Hadramawt who taught both Islamic law and mysticism all around the Indian Ocean.

Nur al-Din al-Raniri may have been raised specifically to teach a version of Sufism to Malays that Fazlur Rahman labelled 'neo-Sufism' (Rahman 1979: 195). This version rejected the antinomianism and pantheism that had grown up around it in certain circles, but it was still based on Ibn al-Arabi's Neo-Platonic doctrine of the Unity of Being. According to this doctrine, the universe is composed of a series of Grades of Being that descend from the perfect unity of God to a phenomenal world made up of a multiplicity of corruptible entities. It is the task of the Perfect Man to ascend these Grades of Being through mystical exercises and reunite with his Creator. This doctrine made its way into popular Islam in Southeast Asia during the sixteenth century and remains embedded in many popular rituals to this day (cf. Bowen on its presence among the Gayo of northern Sumatra, 1993).

When Sultan Iskandar Thani II came to throne of Aceh in 1637, he made al-Raniri his Shaikh al-Islam, the highest religious office in the realm. He commissioned him to write an encyclopaedic work in Malay on universal history, the *Bustan al-Salatin.* al-Attas lists fifteen other works al-Raniri wrote during his seven-year stay in Aceh. They included basic texts on the rules and regulations applying to worship, and laws on marriage and divorce which were sent to Kedah in 1640 for the correction of the people who had 'lapsed into infidelity and paganism' (al-Attas 1986: 11). He also trained a wide range of students from throughout the archipelago in Sufism and the shariah law, including a number of Bugis and Makassar from South Sulawesi. Many returned to serve as religious advisers to local rulers and to set up their own schools. Although he fell from favour at the royal court of Aceh in 1643 and returned to western India, he continued to teach Indonesian students until his death in 1658.

Around 1650, a Bugis student of al-Raniri settled in Bira. He is known in local genealogies as Haji Al-Shaikh al-Julaij Ahmad bin Abdullah al-Bugisiya, or Haji Ahmad the Bugis. His descendants provided most of the Kalis, or chief Islamic officials, in both Bira and Ara until the twentieth century. These Kalis were trained to recite sacred texts written in both Arabic and Makassar, many of which were written by al-Raniri himself (Gibson, forthcoming). The version of the Sinrili' I will discuss in this paper was recited by a descendent of Haji Ahmad, Dessibaji.

Dessibaji learned the Sinrili' from his uncle Daeng Pagala, who served as the last hereditary ruler of Ara from 1913 to 1915. Daeng Pagala learnt it in Bira from a man called Haji Hae', a man who was originally from Selayar. The mystical dimensions of the ballad can be attributed both to this local tradition of Islamic learning and to the fact that in his youth Dessibaji also studied Islamic mysticism in the village of Cikoang in Jeneponto. One can gain some sense of what was taught from the field research conducted there by Hamonic in the early 1980s.

> Traditionally, we are told, religious education here comprised four degrees: *Angngaji*, apprenticeship in reading and writing the Qur'an; *Assarapa'*, apprenticeship and knowledge of Arabic grammar; *Assarea'*, apprenticeship in Islamic law (*shari'at*) in Arabic and in the Makassar language written in Arabic characters; and finally *Attire'*, apprenticeship in gnosis (*marifat*) and in spiritual truth (*hakikat*). This last degree, which develops the discussion of religious problems relating to the creation of the world and to the figure of the Prophet, presupposes of course the perfect mastery of the degrees which precede it. It thus requires a secret initiation which takes place by word of mouth from master to disciple. . . Finally, the teaching of the principal articles of the faith (*usul al-din*) relies on three works, *Sharab ul-anam*, *Achbar ul-achirah* and *Aqidat ul-'awam*, in the Makassar language transcribed in Arabic characters, and which, like the Ashshirat al-mustaqim, are attributed to a great Muslim mystic who stayed in Aceh in the first half of the seventeenth century, Nur ul-Din al-Raniri. (Hamonic 1985: 179–80)

It is thus clear that mainstream Islamic mysticism has been present all along the Makassar coast for almost 400 years and has entered deeply into local understandings of the person and the cosmos. In Ara today, all Muslims agreed that there are at least two aspects to Islam: the outer form contained in the *syariat*, law, and the inner meaning acquired by pursuing the mystical path, the *tarekat*. Many informants added two further stages after the *tarekat*: *hakekat*, truth and *marifat*, gnosis. The head of the Department of Education in Tanaberu, Muhammad Idris Maming, explained the relation between these four stages with a parable about fishing. Knowing the *syariat* is like knowing that there are fish in the sea. Practicing *tarekat* is like going off in a boat to catch them. Achieving *hakekat* is like actually catching a net full of fish and being able to examine them closely and sort them into kinds. Reaching *marifat* is like eating the fish and making them part of your own body.

Version 3: The Sinrili' Datu Museng (Dessibaji, Ara, 1988)

The version of the Sinrili' Datu Museng recorded by Dessibaji in Ara in 1988 is almost twice as long as the one recorded by Matthes in the early 1850s. The narrative clearly grew in length and complexity between 1850 and 1988. All three versions link Datu Museng to Taliwang and cast the Datu of Jarewe as his enemy. Only Matthes' version retains a reference to the original dispute between Datu Taliwang and Datu Jarewe over succession to the office of Sultan. The other two attribute Datu Museng's presence in Ujung Pandang to the anger of Datu Jarewe over the abduction of his daughter. In all three versions, Datu Museng kills Maipa and allows himself to be slain by the ruler of Galesong to avoid dishonour at the hands of the Christian ruler. The greatest development has occurred in the first half of the Sinrili', when Datu Museng learns the Koran, is rejected by Maipa's father, acquires esoteric knowledge in Mecca, and returns to abduct her. These episodes acquire a status equal to the later episodes set on the boat and in Ujung Pandang.

In the following summary of Dessibaji's version of the Sinrili', I have divided the story into four parts based on Datu Museng's journeys to and from four places: his home in Taliwang, the royal palace in Sumbawa Lompo, the centre of Islam in Mecca and the centre of power in Ujung Pandang. I will argue that Datu Museng's four journeys may be seen as allegories for the four stages of the mystical path and of the human life cycle as understood in Sufi theosophy. At this allegorical level, Datu Museng's Beloved, Maipa Deapati, represents the divine Beloved, from whom we are all separated at birth. His life is a long struggle to know and to reunite with the One Being who underlies all created beings. To provide the reader with a sense of the relative weight attached to each part of the story, I have indicated in brackets the approximate number of lines devoted to each incident.

1. Syariat: union before birth, separation and reunion while studying the Koran
[Lines 1–250] Baso Mallarangang (The Forbidden One) is deeply bound to Maipa Deapati even before he is born, indicating that they are twins who were separated at birth. Maipa grows up in the royal palace in Sumbawa Lompo, while Baso is raised in the remote village of Taliwang by Nene' Rangan, a mysterious being who was delivered in a cave by a tiger shaman and brought up by a snake. [This cave is still well known as a place of mystical power, *karama'*.] When Baso Mallarangang grows up, Nene' Rangan allows him to study the Koran with the Imam of Sumbawa Lompo. In just three days he memorises and understands not only the Koran, but also the poetical Life of the Prophet written by Jaffar al-Barzanji (d. 1766).

Also studying with the Imam is Maipa Deapati, the young daughter of the Karaeng and the most beautiful woman in the kingdom. She has learned nothing after three months, and the Imam tells Baso Mallarangang to tutor her. Impatient with her at pointing to the wrong letters while he is reciting, he slaps her hand, causing her heirloom ring to fall through the floor. Baso Mallarangang retrieves it, but vows to return it only after he has married her. Baso Mallarangang returns to Taliwang and sends a messenger to the King asking for Maipa's hand in marriage. The messenger is rudely rebuffed, since Gallarrang belong to the commoner class and women cannot marry beneath them.

Datu Museng experiences a state of bliss before birth by sharing his mother's womb with his twin sister. He is separated from her at birth, and exiled to Taliwang at the periphery of the kingdom. His task in this life is to reunite with her at the royal centre. Datu Museng is raised by a wild hermit with supernatural powers whose midwife was a tiger. When he reaches maturity, Datu Museng returns to the central palace and pursues the first stage of the mystical path, the acquisition of exoteric knowledge of the Koran and other sacred texts (*syariat*). There he gets to know his twin sister on a superficial level and is irresistibly drawn to her. He now knows that it is his destiny to reunite with her, whatever the obstacles. Datu Museng returns to Taliwang and sends an emissary to the king asking for his Beloved's hand in marriage.

2. Tarekat: separation and reunion using esoteric knowledge learned in Mecca

[Lines 250–1400] Humiliated, Baso Mallarangang sells his buffalo and sails for the Hejaz. He studies the esoteric knowledge that grants one invulnerability in war for seven years in Mecca and seven years in Medina. At the end of his stay, he performs the *hajj* and takes a new, noble name, Datu Museng. He returns to Taliwang on the eve of Maipa Deapati's marriage to her first cousin, the Dammung of Alasa in Lombok. Datu Museng becomes so depressed he forgets to pray. Finally, he rouses himself just in time to go and disrupt the wedding. Datu Museng challenges the Sumbawans to a contest playing raga ball. In order to get Maipa Deapati to look out of the window, he plays the fool until the entire crowd is laughing at him. Then he exercises his magical powers on the ball, making it stay up in the air as long as he wishes. Maipa finally bathes and dresses and sits against the central post of the house before going to the window. Datu Museng catches Maipa looking out the window and casts a spell on her, causing her to faint. He continues outplaying his rival, Dammung Alasa, and mocks his manhood. The Dammung attacks him and soon Datu Museng and Nene' Rangan are fighting the entire army of Sumbawa. Due to their invulnerability magic, they soon put them all to flight.

Before leaving, Datu Museng makes the raga ball descend into Maipa's house, turn into a lizard and enter her belly. Maipa falls grievously ill and none of the healers can help her. Finally, the ruler of the Malays tells her father that only Datu Museng can cure her. He is summoned, enters her bedchamber, cures her with ordinary water, and shows her the lost ring, vowing to return it only after they are married. He goes away, but a week later at midnight casts a spell on her, causing her to awaken and to insist on going down to the well to fulfil a vow. Datu Museng causes her escort to flee by sending down a rain of ashes, and Maipa makes her way to his house. It is dark, but when she enters and sits against the central post it is filled with light. They are married by the Guru Keramat of Taliwang. Datu Museng returns her ring and they consummate their union.

In this section, the hero goes into voluntary exile after being humiliated and pursues the next stage of the mystical path, the acquisition of esoteric knowledge (*tarekat*). He journeys to the centre of the religious world in Mecca and Medina. The mystical knowledge he acquires there from the descendents of the Prophet and the Saints enables him to transcend his original social status as a commoner. He completes the *hajj* and takes a noble name. When he returns home to Taliwang, he uses his mystical knowledge to penetrate the palace in Sumbawa Lompo, abduct the princess, bring her home to Taliwang and physically unite with her.

3. Hakekat: victory in battle, crossing the sea and sacrifice at the hands of a Muslim
[Lines 1400–1750] When her absence is discovered, the Karaeng Dea Rangan sends his army after them, but Datu Museng and Nene' Rangan easily defeat it. Knowing now that Datu Museng's magic is too strong for him, the Karaeng hatches a scheme. He forges a letter from the Dutch Governor of Makassar, known as Tuan Malompowa, The Great Lord, ordering Datu Museng to come to Ujung Pandang and promising to appoint him as his successor. Maipa is fearful it is a trap, but Datu Museng reassures her that his invulnerability magic is such that no blade or bullet can pierce his skin. Datu Museng and Maipa Deapati set out on his great black ship, the I Lolo Gading. During the long voyage, they pledge to remain together in eternity.

The abduction leads to a full-scale military assault on the hero by the king. The hero's mystical knowledge makes him invulnerable to attack by ordinary mortals. The king is forced to recognise him as a social equal and to open negotiations to legitimate his marriage with his daughter. But the normal progression from a successful abduction to a formal marriage is interrupted when the king realises that the hero's mystical power might yet be overcome by the corrupt power of the infidel ruler in Ujung Pandang. He forges a letter summoning Datu Museng to the centre of political power. But the hero has now reached an even deeper level of spiritual understanding. Knowing that the ultimate outcome of his journey across the ocean in a magical boat will be death, he goes willingly because he knows true happiness is impossible in a corrupt world. During the crossing of the ocean, a frequent image in Sufi poetry, he achieves a state of spiritual unity with his Beloved, the state of *hakekat*, ultimate reality.

4. Marifat: perfect union in the tomb
[Lines 1750–2025] They arrive in Galesong where the ruler is his kinsman and settle into a palace. When the Governor sees Maipa sitting in a window, he becomes infatuated with her and sends the Public Prosecutor to offer Datu

Museng forty concubines in exchange for her. Datu Museng indignantly refuses, and Maipa says she would rather die. The Governor sends his soldiers, but Datu Museng and Nene' Rangan run amok and put them to flight. Realising the next morning that she is the cause of scores of deaths, Maipa says she would rather die than cause any more deaths or become the wife of a Dutchman. Datu Museng cuts her throat and arranges her on a chair as if she were still alive. He goes down to the sea and throws his amulets and keris into the water, thereby making himself vulnerable to weapons. He asks his relative, the Karaeng of Galesong, to whip him to death, since his skin can still not be pierced by a blade. When the Governor hears he is dead, he goes to the house and embraces Maipa. When he realises she is dead, he jumps back, hits his head on a post and dies.

The Captain of the Javanese in Ujung Pandang buries Datu Museng by the shore where he fell, but the grave begins to move. After seven nights it lies next to that of Maipa Deapati, so that just as their spirits are reunited in the afterlife, their bodies are reunited on earth. Due to all the knowledge Datu Museng accumulated in Mecca and Medina, these twin graves become a sacred place where devotees implore his intercession with God.

The utter corruption of worldly existence is dramatised by the military power and uncontrolled lust of the Christian ruler of Ujung Pandang. The only true happiness lies beyond the grave in the purity of paradise. The hero and his Beloved purify their bodies for the grave before their physical death. They do not allow themselves to be killed by Christian infidels: Maipa is sacrificed by Datu Museng, and Datu Museng by the Karaeng of Galesong. The sister/wife is buried inland and the brother/husband is buried on the shore, but after seven days, their tombs miraculously merge. Lover and Beloved merge back into the primordial androgynous unity of *marifat*, gnosis.

The tombs of Datu Museng and his 'sister'/wife are popular pilgrimage sites to this day for newly-weds. In a manner that recalls the Merina of Madagascar as analysed by Bloch, the bisexual tomb of the ancestors replaces the house of the living as the source of blessing and fertility (Bloch 1971, 1986). But the tombs of Datu Museng and Maipa Deapti are the objects of veneration not just for their own descendants, but for an entire ethnic group. The merging of Austronesian with Islamic symbols of the unity and equality of all humans in the afterlife has transformed the ancestors of the descent group into the Saints of the *ummat*. It is this aspect of the Sinrili' that derives most clearly from Austronesian mythology rather than from Sufi allegory: the primordial Unity of Being is represented in an androgynous form, as a relationship between opposite-sex siblings who share a womb. This is radically different from the predominantly patriarchal symbolism of Middle Eastern monotheism, in which the symbolic focus is on the relationship between Father and Son (Abraham/Ibrahim/God and Isaac/Ismail/Jesus).

Conclusion

In the Sinrili' Datu Museng, a man of humble origin has a secret twinship with a royal princess. To marry his twin he must prove his high rank, and to prove his high rank, he must marry his twin. He obtains high rank by going outside the local social order altogether and acquiring universal knowledge in Mecca. This universal knowledge enables him to overcome even the incest taboo, although such unions are not meant for this world. The original unity and equality experienced by opposite-sex siblings in the womb is recoverable only after a radical separation in life, and is perfected only in the tomb.

The core metaphor for social solidarity and equality in this story is that of opposite-sex siblingship transformed into spouseship. While the unity, separation and reunification of twins received a Sufi gloss at the hands of the Makassar, at bottom the metaphor retained the same egalitarian meaning that it had in non-Islamic societies in the area. Siblingship and marriage are the key kin relations in these societies. They point in a lateral, egalitarian direction as opposed to the vertical, hierarchical direction of unilineal descent. The difference between societies like the Buid and societies like the Makassar is that for the latter real unity and equality exists only in the other world, in the before- and afterlife. This world is marked by a constant struggle to overcome division and hierarchy.

In the Sinrili' Datu Museng, we can see that esoteric religious knowledge acquired by wandering around the perimeter of the Indian Ocean functioned as a sort of wild card in an increasingly hierarchical social order. Men of unknown origin could travel outside the bounds of familiar social space and return to claim a new place at the top of society. The fluidity of their social identity could also allow them to serve as foci of resistance to European rule, as they brought to bear the global prestige of Islam against the global power of colonial armies.

Societies in which this sort of individual achievement was possible ultimately posed a much greater problem for colonial rulers than did societies like those of central and eastern Java whose social hierarchies became increasingly rigid from the seventeenth century on. The eruption of extra-social forces brings death and destruction on a terrifying scale. The entire social order is shaken as the Governor himself loses his life. But it is a social order that is corrupt from the top down, since it is headed by an impure infidel. The local social hierarchy has been decapitated by the Company, the unity of social, political and religious power which existed during the seventeenth century has been split in three. No longer can the supreme ruler in Ujung Pandang serve as the apex of the systems of hypergamy, vassalage and mystical purity in the manner of the first ruler to convert to Islam, Sultan Abdullah Awwal al-Islam, for infidels cannot even marry according to the Law, much less mediate between their subjects and Allah on a mystical plane. They can only exercise naked political power. By contrast, Nene' Rangan represents the forces of Nature, Datu Museng the quest for the Divine, Maipa Deapati the Divine itself.

Parallels to the Christian Philippines

The practice of visiting the tombs of Islamic saints, *ziarah*, is remarkably similar to the rituals performed around the dead Christ by peasants in the Christian Philippines during Holy Week. Cannell suggests that the image of Christ between his crucifixion on Good Friday and resurrection on Easter Sunday is the dominant symbol of Philippine Christianity because it constitutes a liminal period during which a channel is opened between the world of the living and the world of the dead. While blessings can flow unilaterally from dead ancestors to their descendants, interaction with the spirits of the dead always brings with it the danger that one will be pulled across the boundary. Only Christ can transcend the irreversible flow of life and move back and forth across the border. In this sense, the dead Christ is the ultimate shaman who has completely mastered the spirits of the other world. One can participate in his experience of death without fear of losing one's soul to the dead (Cannell 1998).

In Cannell's view, Christianity was readily adopted by the great mass of Filipinos in the seventeenth century because of the way it avoided an oppressive feature of pre-Hispanic relations with the spirit world. In this system, the spirits were modelled on the patrons of the social world. Ordinary people had to enter into one-sided relations with their patrons and ancestor spirits in which one was likely to fall ever deeper into debt. Where Rafael argues that it was the image of Paradise as a realm of perfect mutuality and equality that attracted pagan Filipinos to the new faith, Cannell argues that there is little evidence of interest in the afterlife among them (Rafael 1993). Instead, the Christian saints and above all Christ Crucified were introduced as figures of mystical power who transcended the local social structure and who would provide whatever worshippers needed to fulfil their side of a religious vow. Thus devotees need not fear death as a consequence of interacting with the spirit world if they did so through Christ, nor need they fear debt-bondage (Cannell 1998: 183–99).

The ultimate saintly figure in Islam is Muhammad. In the Sufi tradition, he is regarded as being the most perfect of men, and his essence, the Light or Truth of Muhammad, is regarded as being coeval with God's creation. Subsequent Saints are regarded as being manifestations of the same divine principle.

> The Perfect Man is the *Qutb* (axis) on which the spheres of existence revolve from first to last. He hath various guises and appears in diverse bodily tabernacles … His own original name is Mohammed … In every age he bears a name suitable to that age. I once met him in the form of my Shaikh, Sharafu'ddin Ismail al-Jabarti. (al-Jili quoted in Nicholson, 1921: 105)

Following Cannell's lead, we might suggest that for the mass of villagers in seventeenth-century Sulawesi, the main attraction of Islam was the avenue it opened up for a less threatening, more balanced relationship with the spirit world, one which provided an alternative to the oppressive debt relations villagers had to endure with their social superiors. In both the Philippines and

Indonesia, the seventeenth century saw the gradual humbling of local aristocracies as Spanish and Dutch military power was brought to bear on them. The ruling elites also came to see an alliance with the Saints and their earthly representatives as necessary to their continued legitimacy. The seventeenth century ended with a very different model of mystical and political power from the one with which it had begun.

The Symbolic Origin of Inequality

The basic point with which I started this paper is that societies like the Buid exist within a larger sociocultural region, in which they constitute an extreme example of social egalitarianism combined with religious imagery that represents hierarchy as a form of anti-social predation. Societies in this category valorise egalitarian relations not just among men, but between men and women and even between adults and children. Such egalitarian 'extremism' can only be understood as a cultural rejection of an opposite set of values: the debt-bondage and slave-raiding characteristic of coastal societies, especially in the early colonial period. The analysis of the Epic of Datu Museng showed that a similar rejection of these values can be found embedded in popular interpretations of religion in the lowlands as well.

Now, the extremely high value attached to egalitarian social relations among the Buid and many other small-scale shifting cultivators in Southeast Asia is also found in 'immediate-return' hunting and gathering societies scattered throughout Asia and Africa. Woodburn has long argued against the idea that such societies must be viewed as part-societies whose values are moulded primarily by their resistance to outside forces. Since immediate-return hunting and gathering is an internally coherent, environmentally adaptive and individually rewarding way of life, there is no need to appeal to influences like 'encapsulation' and 'oppression' to explain it.

> African hunter-gatherers ... are, for the most part, descendants of groups that have a long history of hunting and gathering ... the fact that so many of them are genetically or linguistically distinctive and different from their farmer neighbours certainly renders implausible the suggestion that in general they are impoverished drop-outs forced to hunt and gather. (Woodburn 1988: 61–62)

Indeed, as Woodburn describes it, this way of life is so stable and rewarding that the main theoretical task is to explain why it was ever abandoned in the past and how those who have been socialised into it can ever abandon it in the future (Woodburn, 1988: 63).

It is striking that virtually all of the peoples who lived exclusively by hunting and gathering in Island Southeast Asia during the twentieth century, such as the Batek of Malaysia and the Aeta of the Philippines, were 'Negritos', i.e. they appeared to be descendents of peoples who lived in the area before the arrival of Austronesian- or Austroasiatic-speaking agriculturalists. Thus the argument I have been advancing with regard to the co-evolution of egalitarian and hierarchical values among the Austronesian agriculturalists of

Island Southeast Asia does not apply to these hunting and gathering societies. Their way of life generates a form of radical egalitarianism that does not need to oppose itself to an external form of social hierarchy.

Woodburn does suggest, however, that even immediate-return hunting and gathering societies tend to generate an internal hierarchy in the religious domain. This may be the weak point in the system, one that allows delayed-return social relations to develop, and, ultimately, a delayed-return economy. Egalitarian societies stress not just equality and autonomy from specific others but also submission of the individual to the group. In hunting and gathering societies, this is universally expressed through the mandatory sharing of the meat of large game animals, but it is also often expressed through mandatory participation in certain collective rituals. They include the collective singing of the Batek, the *molimo* ritual of the Mbuti and above all the collective dancing of the !Kung. Woodburn's account of the latter could be applied word for word to Buid séances and sacrifices (Gibson 1988):

> Sharing in this context is not merely analogous to the secular sharing of meat. It is consecrated sharing produced in the context of the joint participation of the entire community, a potent dramatisation of the production of the egalitarian community that has manifest appeal both to the reason and to the emotions of the participants. Its potency derives from its oppositional character: the shared unity of the participants in their joint opposition to the undifferentiated spirits of the dead, the bringers of illness and death. (Woodburn, Volume 1)

Ritualised sharing, primarily of meat but also of other valued goods and activities, subordinates the individual to the group in the name of the common good. It is directed against the possibility of one individual or faction asserting itself at the expense of the community. Egalitarianism in these societies is oppositional, even in the absence of a threatening outside power. It is society asserting itself against the internal possibility of hierarchy.

But ritualised sharing also has the potential to subordinate one social category to another social category. The hierarchical implications of the mandatory submission of the individual to the group arise when some part of society comes to stand for the whole. In many societies the collective interest of the group is represented by initiated men, defined in opposition to women and uninitiated men. This is true even among the Buid, where every adult man is a practising spirit medium while only a few women acquire the ability to invoke a spirit familiar. It is also true among the Hadza, where senior men monopolise the cult of the sacred meat.

Why are Hadza men able to appropriate this role for themselves? I would argue that it is based on a division of labour between men and women in hunting and gathering societies that is almost universal, according to which only men hunt large game animals while women gather plants and small animals. The meat of large game animals is subject to the most elaborate rules of sharing and it comes to symbolise the submission of the individual to the group. By contrast, the plants and small animals gathered by women are only shared within the domestic group and come to symbolise factional loyalty. Even in the most egalitarian hunter-gatherer societies, the division of labour between male and female provides a basis for a symbolic association of men with communal solidarity and of women with factionalism.

The seeds of hierarchy thus lie in those aspects of social life in which the desires of the individual are subordinated to the needs of the group, combined with the ability of one part of the social whole to claim the right to interpret and represent those needs. This slippage is easiest to see where the role of representing the interests of the group is identified with a hereditary social estate with exclusive rights to political office, as it is among the Makassar. But the slippage exists even among the Hadza and the Buid, where senior men enjoy a privileged relationship to the rituals and sacred objects that symbolise the well-being of the group.

References

al-Attas, Syed Naguib 1986. *A Commentary on the Hujjat al-siddiq of Nur al-Din al-Raniri.* Kuala Lumpur: Ministry of Culture.

Bloch, M. 1971. *Placing the Dead.* London: Seminar Press.

—— 1986. *From Blessing to Violence.* Cambridge: Cambridge University Press.

Bowen, J. 1993. *Muslims Through Discourse.* Princeton: Princeton University Press.

van den Brink, H. 1943. *Dr. Benjamin Frederik Matthes.* Amsterdam: Nederlandsch Bijbelgenootschap.

Cannell, F. 1998. *Power and Intimacy in the Christian Philippines.* Cambridge: Cambridge University Press.

Carsten, J. 1997. *The Heat of the Hearth.* Oxford: Clarendon Press.

Conklin, H. 1964. 'Ethnogenealogical method'. In: W.H. Goodenough (ed.), *Explorations in Cultural Anthropology.* New York: McGraw-Hill.

Donselaar, W.M. 1855. 'Beknopte beschrijving van Bonthain en Boelecomba op Zuid Celebes'. *Bijdragen tot de Taal-, Land- en Volkenkunde,* 3: 163–87.

Dumont, L. 1970. *Homo Hierarchicus.* Chicago: Chicago University Press.

Freeman, D. 1970. *Report on the Iban.* London: Athlone Press.

Geertz, C. and H. Geertz. 1975. *Kinship in Bali.* Chicago: Chicago University Press.

Gibson, T. 1985. 'The Sharing of Substance Versus the Sharing of Activity Among the Buid of Mindoro'. *Man,* 20(3): 391–411.

—— 1986. *Sacrifice and Sharing In the Philippine Highlands.* London: Athlone Press.

—— 1988. 'Meat Sharing as Political Ritual: Forms of Transaction vs Modes of Subsistence'. In: T. Ingold, D. Riches and J. Woodburn (eds.), *Hunters and Gatherers Volume II: Property, Power and Ideology.* London: Berg Publishers.

—— 1990a. 'Raiding, trading and Tribal Autonomy in Island Southeast Asia'. In: J. Haas (ed.), *The Anthropology of War.* New York: Cambridge University Press.

—— 1990b. 'On Predatory States in Island Southeast Asia'. *Comparative Austronesian Project Working Paper No. 2.* Canberra: Research School of Pacific Studies, The Australian National University.

—— 1994. 'Childhood, Colonialism and Fieldwork Among the Buid of the Philippines and the Konjo of Indonesia'. In: Jeannine Koubi and Josiane Massard (eds), *Enfants et Sociétés d'Asie du Sud-Est.* Paris: L'Harmattan.

—— 1995. 'Having Your House and Eating It: Houses and Siblings in Ara, South Sulawesi'. In: Janet Carsten and Stephen Hugh-Jones (eds.), *About the House: Buildings, Groups, and Categories in Holistic Perspective.* Cambridge: Cambridge University Press.

—— 2000. 'Islam and the Spirit Cults in New Order Indonesia'. *Indonesia,* 69: 41–70.

—— forthcoming. 'The Legacy of Shaikh Yusuf in South Sulawesi'. To appear in *Traditions of Learning and Networks of Knowledge in the Indian Ocean.* Curzon Press.

Goudswaard, A. 1865. 'Siwa Dienst in Zuid Celebes'. *Mededeelingen van wege het Nederlandsche Zendelinggenootschap,* 9: 75–103, 289–314.

Hamonic, G. 1985. 'La fête du grand Maulid a Cikoang, regard sur une *tarekat* dite "shi'ite" en Pays Makassar'. *Archipel,* 29(1): 175–91.

Headley, S. 1987. 'The Idiom of Siblingship: One Definition of "House" in Southeast Asia'. In: C. Macdonald (ed.), *De la hutte au palais,* Paris: Éditions du CNRS.

Hodgson, M. 1974. *The Venture of Islam.* Chicago: University of Chicago Press.

Ligtvoet, A. 1987 (1875) 'Bijdragen tot de geschiedenis van het Sultanaat Sumbawa'. In: J. Noorduyn (ed.), *Bima en Sumbawa,* VKIT 129. Dordrecht: Foris. Publications.

Matthes, B.F. 1860. *Makassarsche Chrestomathie.* Amsterdam.

McKinley, R. 1981. 'Cain and Abel on the Malay Peninsula'. In: M. Marshall (ed.), *Siblingship in Oceania.* Ann Arbor: University of Michigan Press.

Nicholson, R.A. 1921. *Studies in Islamic Mysticism.* Cambridge: Cambridge University Press.

Noorduyn, J. 1987. *Bima en Sumbawa,* VKIT 129. Dordrecht: Foris Publications.

Parry, J. 1986. '*The Gift,* the Indian Gift and the "Indian Gift"', *Man,* 21(3): 453–73.

Pelras, C. 1996. *The Bugis.* Oxford: Blackwell Publishers.

Rafael, V. 1993. *Contracting Colonialism.* Durham: Duke University Press.

Rahman, F. 1979. *Islam.* Chicago: Chicago University Press.

Ras, J.J. 1973. 'The Pandji Romance and W.H. Rassers' Analysis of its Theme'. *Bijdragen tot de Taal-, Land- en Volkenkunde,* 129: 412–56.

Rassers, J. 1922. *De Pandji Roman.* Leiden.

Reid, A. 1993. *Southeast Asia in the Age of Commerce, Volume Two: The Age of Expansion.* New Haven: Yale University Press.

Rosaldo, M. 1980. *Knowledge and Passion.* Cambridge: Cambridge University Press.

Rosaldo, R. 1980. *Ilongot Headhunting, 1883-1974.* Stanford: Stanford University Press.

Rousseau, J. 1980. 'Iban Inequality'. *Bijdragen tot de Taal-, Land- en Volkenkunde,* 136: 52–63.

1990. *Central Borneo.* New York: Oxford University Press.

Schärer, H. 1963. *Ngaju Religion.* The Hague: Martinus Nijhoff.

Sutherland, H. 1983. 'Slavery and the Slave Trade in South Sulawesi, 1660s–1800s'. In: A. Reid (ed.), *Slavery, Bondage and Dependency in Southeast Asia.* St. Lucia: University of Queensland Press.

Warren, J. 1981. *The Sulu Zone, 1768–1898.* Singapore: Singapore University Press.

Woodburn, J. 1988. 'African Hunter-gatherer Social Organization'. In T. Ingold, D. Riches and J. Woodburn (eds), *Hunters and Gatherers, Volume I: History Evolution and Social Change.* Oxford: Berg Publishers.

—— 1998. 'Sharing is Not a Form of Exchange'. In: C.M. Hann (ed.), *Property Relations.* Cambridge: Cambridge University Press.

—— Volume I of this book. 'Egalitarian Societies Revisited'.

Notes on Contributors

Kirk Endicott received a Ph.D. from Harvard University and a D.Phil. from the University of Oxford, both in social anthropology. He taught at California State University at Northridge, the University of Malaya, Cornell University, the Australian National University, and Dartmouth College, where he is currently a Professor of Anthropology. Address: Department of Anthropology, Dartmouth College, 6047 Silsby Hall, Hanover, NH 03755-3547, U.S.A., email: kirk.endicott@dartmouth.edu

Thomas P. Gibson is an Associate Professor of Anthropology at the University of Rochester. He received his B.Sc. and Ph.D. from the London School of Economics. Before moving to Rochester, he taught at Manchester and Cambridge Universities. He has conducted fieldwork in the Philippines (1979–81, 1985) and Indonesia (1988, 1989), and library research in the Netherlands (1994). He is currently working on a series of monographs about ritual and Austronesian, Islamic and post-colonial forms of knowledge in Indonesia. Address: Department of Anthropology, University of Rochester, 439 Lattimore Hall, RC Box 20161, Rochester, New York 14627, U.S.A., email: tpgib@mail.rochester.edu

Mathias Guenther earned his Ph.D. from the University of Toronto and is Professor at Wilfrid Laurier University in Waterloo, Ontario. He also taught, as Visiting Professor, at the Institute for Ethnology and African Studies and at the Institute for Historical Ethnology at the Universities of Mainz and Frankfurt. His primary fieldwork site, since 1968, has been the western Kalahari of the Ghanzi District of Botswana, principally among the Nharo (Naro) farm Bushmen (or San). Address: Department of Anthropology, Wilfrid Laurier University, Waterloo, Ontario N2L 3C5, Canada, email: mguenther@sympatico.ca

Robert K. Hitchcock received his MA and Ph.D. in Anthropology from the University of New Mexico, Albuquerque, New Mexico, U.S.A. Currently, he is a Professor of Anthropology and Geography, the Coordinator of African Studies, and the Coordinator of Conflict and Conflict Resolution Studies at the University of Nebraska-Lincoln. He serves along with Megan Biesele as a co-director of the Kalahari Peoples Fund (KPF), which has been providing assistance to the San and other indigenous peoples of southern Africa since 1973. Address: Department of Anthropology and Geography, University of Nebraska-Lincoln, 121 Bessey Hall, Lincoln, NE 68588-0368, email: rhitchco@unlnotes.unl.edu

Ian Keen studied anthropology at University College London (1970–73), and then gained his Ph.D. at the Australian National University in 1978. He has conducted fieldwork among Aboriginal people in northeast Arnhem Land, the Alligator Rivers region, and Tennant Creek in the Northern Territory of Australia, and in Gippsland, Victoria. He is the author of *Knowledge and Secrecy in an Aboriginal Religion* (Oxford 1994) and *Aboriginal Economy and Society* (Oxford 2004), as well as many articles in edited books and scholarly journals. He also edited the collection *Being Black* (AIATSIS 1988). He lectured in anthropology at the University of Queensland and at the Australian National University where he is currently a Visiting Fellow. Address: Department of Archaeology and Anthropology, Australian National University, Canberra, ACT 0200, Australia, email: Ian.Keen@anu.edu.au

Justin Kenrick received a BA in Social Anthropology at the University of Cambridge and his Ph.D. in Social Anthropology at the University of Edinburgh. He works with the Forest Peoples Programme (www.forestpeoples.gn.apc.org) to support Central African Forest Peoples' rights to determine their own futures. He currently lectures in Social Anthropology at the University of Glasgow. Address: Department of Sociology, Anthropology and Applied Social Sciences, Adam Smith Building, Bute Gardens, Glasgow, G12 8RT, Scotland, email: j.Kenrick@socsci.gla.ac.uk

Axel Köhler took his MA in ethnology at the Free University in Berlin and his Ph.D. at the University of Manchester where he also taught. He was an honorary research fellow with the Department of Social Anthropology at the University of Manchester. Currently, he holds a post as a researcher in visual anthropology and as a lecturer in social sciences at the Centre for Mexican and Central American Studies of the University of the Sciences and Arts of Chiapas (CESMECA-UNICACH) in San Cristóbal de Las Casas, Chiapas, Mexico. Address: CESMECA-UNICACH, Calzada Tlaxcala # 76 (esquina con Diego Rivera), Barrio de Tlaxcala, San Cristóbal de Las Casas, C.P. 29230, San Cristóbal de Las Casas, Chiapas, México, email: axelkoehler@hotmail.com

Richard B. Lee received his Ph.D. from Berkeley and is a Professor of Anthropology at the University of Toronto. He has been conducting long-term field research with the San of Botswana since the 1960s and is co-founder of the Kalahari Peoples Fund (KPF). His works include *Man the hunter* (1968) and the *Cambridge Encyclopaedia of Hunters and Gatherers* (1999) as co-editor and *The !Kung San: men, women and work in a foraging society* (1979). Address: Department of Anthropology, University of Toronto, Toronto Ontario M5S 1A1, Canada, email: rblee@chass.utoronto.ca

Jerome Lewis took his BA and Ph.D. in anthropology at the London School of Economics and Political Science. He has been a researcher for the Forest Peoples Programme, GTZ (Gesellschaft für Technische Zusammenarbeit – Germany) and the Minority Rights Group. Currently, he is a teaching and research Fellow in the Department of Anthropology at the London School of Economics and Political Science. Address: Department of Anthropology, London School of Economics and Political Science, Houghton Street, London, WC2A 2AE, U.K., email: J.D.Lewis@lse.ac.uk

Jean Lydall received a Postgraduate Academic Diploma in Social Anthropology from the London School of Economics. She is a free-lance anthropologist and filmmaker who has produced many award winning ethnographic films on the Hamar. She has conducted repeated and extensive fieldwork in Hamar, southern Ethiopia and occasional teaches at the University of Mainz. Jean Lydall is currently in Ethiopia working as free-lance researcher at the South Omo Research Center. Address: c/o Institute of Ethiopian Studies, University of Addis Ababa, P.O.Box 1176, Addis Ababa, Ethiopia, email: sorc@telecom.net.et

Lye Tuck-Po received graduate degrees in anthropology from the University of Hawai'i at Manoa. She has undertaken a number of research, consultancy, and activist positions. Her academic positions included a postdoctoral fellowship at Kyoto University's Center for Southeast Asian Studies and a visiting international professorship at Randolph-Macon Woman's College in Virginia. She currently lives in Malaysia. She has edited *Orang Asli of Malaysia: A Comprehensive and Annotated Bibliography* (Kyoto, 2001) and, with Wil de Jong and Ken-ichi Abe, *The Political Ecology of Tropical Forests in Asia: Historical Perspectives* (Kyoto, 2002), and authored *Changing Pathways: Forest Degradation and the Batek of Pahang, Malaysia* (Lexington Books, 2004). Address: 106 Taman Bukit Bunga, 44000 Kuala Kubu Baru, Malaysia, email: tuckpo@tm.net.my

James F. Weiner earned his Ph.D. at Australian National University in 1984 and has carried out extensive fieldwork in Papua New Guinea and in Aboriginal Australia. He held teaching positions at the Australian National University and the University of Manchester and was Professor of Anthropology at the University of Adelaide. He is the author of *The Empty Place* (1991), *The Lost Drum* (1995) and most recently *Tree Leaf Talk* (2001). Currently, he is a full-time consultant anthropologist in the field of Aboriginal Native Title in Australia. Address: PO Box 82, Curtin, ACT 2605, Australia, email: james.weiner@anu.edu.au

Thomas Widlok took his M.Sc. and Ph.D. in anthropology at the London School of Economics where he has also taught. He has been a researcher with the Cognitive Anthropology Research Group in Nijmegen, the University of Cologne, the Center for African Area Studies (Kyoto University) and the Max Planck Institute for Social Anthropology in Halle. Currently, he is lecturer in anthropology at the University of Heidelberg and research staff at the Max Planck Institute for Psycholinguistics in Nijmegen: Address: Department of Anthropology, Institut für Ethnologie, Universität Heidelberg, Sandgasse 7, 69117 Heidelberg, Germany, email: Thomas.Widlok@urz.uni-heidelberg.de

Wolde Gossa Tadesse took his M.Sc. and Ph.D. in Anthropology from the London School of Economics. He is affiliated to the Max Planck Institute for Social Anthropology where he was a member of a research staff from 2000-2003. Currently he is with the Christensen Fund in California. Address: The Christensenfund, 145 Addison Avenue, Palo Alto, CA 94301, U.S.A., email: wolde@christensenfund.org

Index

www.ingramcontent.com/pod-product-compliance
Ingram Content Group UK Ltd.
Pitfield, Milton Keynes, MK11 3LW, UK
UKHW021837100926
8556IPUK00004B/387

9 781571 816177